THE CONTROL OF CORPORATE

FEEM Studies in Economics

Foundazione Eni Enrico Mattei (FEEM) is a non-profit, non-partisan research institution established to carry out research in economics with special reference to sustainable development. The volumes in this series are the main results of FEEM's research activities and conferences in economics. They are approved on the basis of the standard Oxford University Press refereeing procedure. The series is guided by the following Scientific Advisory Board:

The Control of Corporate Europe

Edited by

FABRIZIO BARCA
MARCO BECHT

OXFORD

UNIVERSITY PRESS

OXFORD

UNIVERSITY PRESS

Great Clarendon Street, Oxford OX2 6DP

Oxford University Press is a department of the University of Oxford.
It furthers the University's objective of excellence in research, scholarship,
and education by publishing worldwide in

Oxford New York

Auckland Bangkok Buenos Aires Cape Town Chennai
Dar es Salaam Delhi Hong Kong Istanbul Karachi Kolkata
Kuala Lumpur Madrid Melbourne Mexico City Mumbai Nairobi
São Paulo Shanghai Taipei Tokyo Toronto

Oxford is a registered trade mark of Oxford University Press
in the UK and in certain other countries

Published in the United States
by Oxford University Press Inc., New York

British Library Cataloguing in Publication Data

Data available

Library of Congress Cataloging in Publication Data

The control of corporate Europe / edited by Farizio Barca, Marco Becht.
p. cm.
Includes bibliographical references and index.
1. Corporate governance—European Union countries—Case studies. 2. Corporate
governance—United States. 3. Big business—European Union countries—Case studies.
4. Big business—United States. 5. Corporations—European Union countries—Finance—Case
studies. 6. Corporations—United States—Finance. 7. Stockholders—European Union
countries—Case studies. 8. Stockholders—United States. I. Barca, Fabrizio.
II. Becht, Marco.
HD2844 .C663 2001 338.7′4′094—dc21 2001036757

ISBN 0-19-924742-0 (hbk.)
ISBN 0-19-925753-1 (pbk.)

1 3 5 7 9 10 8 6 4 2

Typeset by Newgen Imaging Systems (P) Ltd., India
Printed in Great Britain
on acid-free paper by
T.J. International Ltd., Padstow, Cornwall

Preface

Over the last few years there has been a proliferation of international comparisons of financial and corporate systems. After decades during which journals and books have been dominated by analyses of financial institutions and markets in North America, there is mounting interest in the way in which financial and corporate systems work elsewhere. This interest has been stimulated by several factors. Firstly, the 1980s saw the removal of many barriers to the free flow of capital. Financial institutions and systems that had previously operated largely in isolation found themselves coming into direct contact and competition with each other. Secondly, the post-WW2 period was dominated by the spectacular growth of the Japanese and then other East Asian economies. In Europe, the German economy grew rapidly in relation to some of its neighbours. Many people regarded the financial systems of Japan and Germany as important contributors to the success of their economies. The recent success of the US economy has turned the tables and today the Anglo-American financial systems are the recommended models for the new global economy. Thirdly, from an academic perspective financial practice was failing to conform in several areas with the predictions of financial theory. Other factors, what economists term agency considerations, appeared more significant and international comparisons offered the opportunity of shedding more light on these considerations than domestic studies alone could provide.

It is against this background that the European Corporate Governance Network (ECGN) launched this study of corporate control in Europe. The ECGN was founded in 1996 as a vehicle for encouraging comparative empirical research on corporate governance in Europe. Lack of hard data has been a major impediment to such research, and the ECGN brought together local research teams familiar with the language and corporate culture of their own countries to investigate issues of common interest. The book is a collection of papers reporting how listed companies are controlled in different European countries. There is also a chapter on the USA that serves as a benchmark against which to compare the European studies. The data collection efforts of the country teams focused on variables for which there were common (and high) disclosure standards, in particular the Large Holdings Directive (88/627/EEC) in Europe and the '13D' standard under the Williams Act in the United States. Each country team was asked to provide an analysis of voting blocks that allowed comparisons of the size and distribution of voting power concentrations to be determined. Beyond that the teams were encouraged to focus on whatever aspects of corporate control were most relevant to their countries. The book therefore provides a framework for undertaking international comparisons of corporate control and a detailed assessment of voting control as it currently exists in Europe.

The European Corporate Governance Network gratefully acknowledges financial assistance from the Directorate General for Industry of the European Commission,

Fondazione Eni Enrico Mattei (FEEM) and the Politecnico di Milano. The country teams presented preliminary results from the study at two conferences at Fondazione Eni Enrico Mattei in Milan in March 1997 and November 1998. We are grateful to the FEEM for their assistance in organizing the conferences. Numerous individuals and institutions supported the work of the teams:

• Becht and Mayer are grateful for financial support from the Goldschmidt Chair for Corporate Governance at the Solvay Business School of the Université de Bruxelles while completing the work on the introduction of this book. They are also grateful to David Dando of Institutional Shareholder Services in London, Fred Philippi and Weil, Gotshal & Manges LLP in New York, Iñigo Zavala, and Unilever Plc/NV for data and information. They also thank participants at the Annual Meeting of the American Economics Association in New Orleans 2001, the European Conference of the Belgian Directors Institute (BDI), the Friday seminar at ECARES (Université Libre de Bruxelles), the Kiel Week Conference 2000, and seminars at Hebrew University in Jerusalem and the Oslo School of Management, Patrick Bolton, and Jim Shinn for comments on previous versions of the chapter.

• The Austrian team is grateful to Manfred Heider, Marco Pagano, and Robert Sumann for comments.

• The Belgian team thanks Mathias Dewatripont, Christoph van Elst, Marc Goergen, Rez Kabir, Piet Moerland, and Eddy Wymeersch for advice and comments. The Brussels Stock Exchange provided the control data that is central to the Belgian chapter and the team thanks Mr O. Lefebvre (its President), Mr L. Delboo, Mr D. Maertens, and Mr A. Renders for their help and support. The team is also very grateful to Bureau van Dijk (http://www.bvd.com) and Mr B. Van Ommeslaghe for providing access to Bureau van Dijk's company data. Mr D. Carnoy and particularly Mr J-C. Ruche have been most generous in answering numerous questions. Mr Fiers and Mr Van Watershoot of Banque Bruxelles Lambert provided copies of BBL's publications on ownership, and Banque Degroof supplied a copy of their Belgian Company Profiles. The team would also like to thank Mrs Lein, Mr Kirsch, and Mr Colinet of the Commission Bancaire et Financière, Mr Cocquyt of the Office de Contrôle des Assurances, and Mrs Anne Vincent of CRISP for their help and advice.

• The French team thanks M. Mourant from Paris–Bourse SBF who made available to them the CAC 40 notifications and D. Davidoff from Paris–Bourse SBF, M. Champarnaud from COB and V. Thollon Pommerol from INSEE (National Institute of Statistics and Economic Studies) for their advice in gathering information. Claude Truy from the Bank of France gave very valuable research assistance and perspicacity in putting together the information on financial institutions.

• The German team is grateful to Stefan Sperlich, Christian Wulff, participants at the 1997 and 1998 ECGN Conferences, the 1997 Bankenworkshop in Münster, and the finance workshops at Tilburg University, and the University of Amsterdam for comments. It thanks Holger Schäfer of the *Bundesaufsichtsamt für den Wertpapierhandel*, Frankfurt a. M. and the DAX companies for providing data and material. Bureau van Dijk (http://www.bvdep.com) supported the research by providing access to their

German CD-ROM collection. Böhmer is grateful for financial support from the *Deutsche Forschungsgemeinschaft* (DFG).

• The Italian team thanks M. Morvillo, M. Perassi, and G. Ronzani for providing information and useful suggestions, and I. Longhi and C. Ortenzi for assistance with editing.

• The Dutch team thanks participants of the 1997 and 1998 ECGN conferences and participants of the 1999 workshop of the Dutch Network Institutional Economics (Corporate Governance: Empirical Evidence from The Netherlands) at the University of Groningen.

• The Spanish team is grateful to Vicente Salas for his advice and comments. The team is also grateful to the CNMV for providing data and to the Spanish Ministry of Education for the financial support through the PB97-0185-C03 project.

• The Swedish team would like to thank Sven-Ivan Sundqvist for constructive comments and clarifications. Peter Högfeldt gratefully acknowledges financial support from the Foundation for Economics and Law and the Tom Hedelius and Jan Wallander Foundation.

• The UK team gratefully acknowledges comments and advice from Marco Becht, Julian Franks, Carles Gispert, Colin Mayer, Joe McCahery, Piet Moerland, and Currim Oozeer.

• For the US chapter Becht is grateful to Mark Roe and Roberta Romano for comments, David Dando of ISS, and Ginny Rosenbaum of IRRC for data on takeover protections, and to Bureau van Dijk Electronic Publishers for access to the Global Researcher Database.

More generally we are grateful to J. M. Fombellida at the European Commission who kindly provided the text of the proposal for the Large Holdings Directive (88/ 627/EEC) we reproduce in the Appendix and for valuable comments on the work of the Network as a whole from the Scientific Committee, whose names are listed below.

Finally we would like to thank Rebecca Bryant, Andrew Schuller, and their team at Oxford University Press for everything they did to help our multicultural manuscript reach the printing press, and John Callow, our copy-editor, for his rigour and patience.

Country teams: Jonas Agnblad (Sweden; Nordic Capital); Marco Becht (Belgium, Germany, USA; ULB Brussels); Erik Berglöf (Sweden; Stockholm School of Economics); Marcello Bianchi (Italy; CONSOB, Rome); Magda Bianco (Italy; Banca d'Italia, Research in Law and Economics Department); Laurence Bloch (France; INSEE Paris); Ekkehart Böhmer (Germany; New York Stock Exchange); Ariane Chapelle (Belgium; Banque Bruxelles Lambert and ULB, Brussels); Rafel Crespi-Cladera (Spain; Universitat Autònoma Barcelona); Abe de Jong (Netherlands; University of Tilburg); Luca Enriques (Italy; University of Bologna); Miguel A. García-Cestona (Spain; Universitat Autònoma Barcelona); Marc Goergen (UK; School of Management, UMIST); Klaus Gugler (Austria; University of Vienna); Peter

Högfeldt (Sweden; Stockholm School of Economics); Rezaul Kabir (Netherlands; University of Tilburg); Susanne Kalss (Austria; Wirtschaftsuniversität, Vienna); Elizabeth Kremp (France; Banque de France); Teye Marra (Netherlands; University of Tilburg); Luc Renneboog (Belgium; UK, University of Tilburg); Ailsa Röell (Netherlands; Princeton); Alex Stomper (Austria; University of Vienna); Helena Svancar (Sweden; Securitie Banken); Josef Zechner (Austria; University of Vienna).

Executive coordinator: Marco Becht (ECARES, ULB Brussels).

Steering committee: Fabrizio Barca (Ministero del Tesoro); Erik Berglöf (Stockholm School of Economics); Patrick Bolton (Princeton University); Francesco Brioschi (Politecnico di Milano); Marco Pagano (Universitá di Salerno); Colin Mayer (Oxford University); Ailsa Röell (Princeton University).

Scientific committee: Fabrizio Barca (Ministero del Tesoro); Theodor Baums (University of Frankfurt); Lucian Bebchuk (Harvard University); Erik Berglöf (Stockholm School of Economics); Sudipto Bhattacharya (London School of Economics); Patrick Bolton (Princeton University); Francesco Brioschi (Politecnico di Milano); Paul Davies (London School of Economics); Mathias Dewatripont (ECARES/ULB); Ron Gilson (Columbia Law School and Stanford Law School); Leo Goldschmidt (EASD); Oliver Hart (Harvard University); Martin Hellwig (University of Mannheim); Gerard Hertig (Swiss Institute of Technology); Bengt Holmström (MIT); Klaus Hopt (Max-Planck Hamburg); Colin Mayer (Oxford University); Marco Pagano (University of Salerno); Rafael Repullo (CEMFI); Mark Roe (Columbia Law School); Ailsa Röell (Princeton University); Roberta Romano (Yale University); Andrei Shleifer (Harvard University); Domenico Siniscalco (Fondazione Eni Enrico Mattei); Elu von Thadden (University of Lausanne); Jean Tirole (University of Toulouse) Eddy Wymeersch (University of Ghent).

Contents

List of Figures

List of Tables

Notes on Contributors

Jonas Agnblad holds an M.Sc. in Business Administration and Economics from the Stockholm School of Economics. His master's thesis ('Ownership and Control in Swedish Listed Companies' (1999, co-author Helena Svancar)) mapped and analysed the use of various corporate governance mechanisms in companies listed on the Stockholm Stock Exchange. Agnblad has a professional background in finance and is currently working for Nordic Capital, a leveraged buy-out fund based in Stockholm.

Fabrizio Barca is General Director for Development at the Italian Treasury, President of the OECD Territorial Policies Committee, and Director of a Research Programme on Corporate and Public Administration Governance at Sienna University. He has previously been at the Bank of Italy as Division Chief at the Research Department and Chief of the Department of Development Policies at the Italian Treasury. He graduated from Rome University and undertook an M.Phil. degree and research activity at the Universities of Cambridge (1978–80), MIT (1989–90), and Stanford (1994). He had appointments at the Universities of Bocconi, Sienna, Modena, and Rome, where he taught corporate finance and Italian economic history. His works include papers and books on the theory of the firm, evidence on SMEs, corporate governance, and the history of Italian capitalism.

Marco Becht born 1966, teaches at the Institute for European Studies, the Solvay Business School, and the Law Faculty of the Université Libre de Bruxelles. He graduated from the London School of Economics and Political Science and holds a Ph.D. in economics from the European University Institute in Florence. He is a Resident Fellow at ECARES and a Research Associate of CEPR. He was previously at the Centro de Estudios Monetarios y Financieros (CEMFI) in Madrid and the European Commission's Directorate for Industry (DG III). Becht is the executive coordinator of the European Corporate Governance Network (ECGN) and the scientific adviser of the Corporate Governance Committee of the European Association of Securities Dealers (EASD). Becht's research focuses on corporate governance and empirical corporate finance.

Erik Berglöf is Director of the Stockholm Institute of Transition Economics at the Stockholm School and a Research Fellow of CEPR. He was previously assistant professor at ECARE, Université Libre de Bruxelles, and has held visiting positions at Stanford University. He has written extensively on financial contracting and corporate governance. In particular, he has applied theoretical insights to the study of differences between financial systems, and specific ownership and control arrangements. He has also been involved in several capacity-building initiatives in transition countries, including as Director of the Centre for Economics and Financial Research (CEFIR) in Moscow. He has served as special adviser to the prime minister of Sweden and on several government commissions and EU-related panels. In addition, he has been a consultant to the World Bank and the IMF.

Marcello Bianchi is currently responsible for the Statistical Analysis unit at the Economic Studies Department of Consob (Stock Exchange and Public Companies Italian Authority) where he has worked since 1990. He was in charge of design and management of the ownership disclosure system for listed companies and listed groups, including the creation of the Consob Ownership Disclosure Database. Previously he was economist at Centro Europa Ricerche (CER) and at Montedison group. He graduated from the University of Rome in 1985. He has published articles on ownership structure of Italian listed companies and listed groups, coalitions and reciprocal shareholding, takeover regulation, and the role of institutional investors in corporate governance.

Magda Bianco is senior economist at the Research in Law and Economics Department of the Bank of Italy, where she has worked since 1989. Between 1992 and 1996 she was Professor of Industrial Organization at the Università degli Studi di Bergamo. Bianco holds a Ph.D. in economics from the London School of Economics and Political Science, and a master's degree in economics. Her research interests are in the field of corporate finance and corporate governance. She has published articles on Italian corporate governance, bank–firm relationships, financial structure, and development.

Laurence Bloch is currently technical adviser on the staff of the French Foreign Trade Minister. As 'Administrateur de l'INSEE (National Institute of Statistics and Economic Studies)' (civil servant), she has held several positions in the Ministry of Economy, Finance, and Industry, particularly in INSEE, in the fields of macroeconomics and forecasting, and structural studies on firms and employment. Bloch has conducted studies on corporate finance and investment, imperfections in the credit market, and has organized a seminar on French Corporate Governance in the Ministry of Economy, Finance and Industry (1996–7), attended by managers, lawyers, and economists. Bloch graduated from ENSAE (National School of Statistics and Economic Administration) and holds a Ph.D. (French equivalent) in Economics from the University of Paris-Nanterre and ENSAE. She has published empirical studies, firstly on consumption and household behaviour, then on corporate behaviour—Tobin's q and investment, bankruptcies, and imperfections in the credit market.

Ekkehart Böhmer is currently Senior Economist at the New York Stock Exchange. This study was completed while he held a Heisenberg Research Fellowship, sponsored by the German Science Foundation (DFG). He is also a visiting scholar at the University of Georgia in Athens, Georgia. He received his Ph.D. in Finance from the University of Georgia and was an assistant professor at Louisiana State University. He obtained his Habilitation at Humboldt University in Berlin and subsequently joined the US Securities and Exchange Commission as a financial economist. Böhmer's main research interest is in corporate finance with a particular emphasis on corporate governance and securities issuance.

Ariane Chapelle teaches finance at the Solvay Business School and at the Faculty of Economics at the Université Libre de Bruxelles. She is a research fellow of the Centre Emile Bernheim of Solvay Business School and manages a team in the credit risk management department of the Banque Bruxelles Lambert (ING group). She graduated from the Solvay Business School and holds a degree in Econometrics and a Ph.D. in economics from the Université Libre de Bruxelles. Her research interests are in corporate governance and corporate finance.

Rafel Crespí-Cladera is Associate Professor of Managerial Economics at the Universitat Autònoma of Barcelona. Currently he is teaching at the Universitat Illes Balears as a visiting professor. His research interests are in the field of corporate governance, mainly in empirical corporate finance, ownership structure and management. He graduated from the University of Barcelona and holds a Ph.D. from the Universitat Autònoma of Barcelona. He has also taught at the Universitat Pompeu Fabra and has been a visitor at the University of Tilburg at the Centre for Economic Research.

Abe de Jong is an Assistant Professor of Finance at the Erasmus University, Rotterdam. He has a Ph.D. in economics from the University of Tilburg (1999). Abe has been an Assistant Professor at the University of Tilburg and a visiting researcher at Florida State University. His research interests are in the area of empirical corporate finance and include capital structure choice, dividend policies, and corporate governance.

Luca Enriques S.J.D. (Bocconi University, Milan), LL.M. (Harvard Law School), J.D. (University of Bologna), joined the Faculty of Law of the University of Bologna after working for the Bank of Italy in Rome. In 1997 and 1998, he collaborated with the Italian Ministry of the Treasury in the drafting of the Consolidated Act on Financial Intermediation 1998. He has published several articles in Italian as well as international law reviews on topics relating to corporate governance, takeovers, institutional investors, and corporate groups.

Miguel A. García-Cestona is an Associate Professor of Managerial Economics at the Universitat Autònoma of Barcelona and serves also as a scientific adviser to the Centre d'Economia Industrial within the Fundació Empresa i Ciencia (UAB). His research interests are in the fields of the theory of the firm and comparative institutional analysis. Recent papers deal with the bank–industry relationship in Spain, the Japanese main bank system, and issues on corporate governance. He graduated from Universidad de Zaragoza and holds a Ph.D. from Stanford University at the Graduate School of Business.

Marc Goergen holds an M.Sc. in economics from the Free University of Brussels (ULB) and an MBA in European Business from Solvay Business School, Brussels. He completed his D.Phil. in economics at Keble College, Oxford before joining both the School of Accounting and Finance, University of Manchester and the School of Management, UMIST as a lecturer in 1997. He spent 1998 as a lecturer at the ISMA Centre at the University of Reading. In 1999, Goergen moved back to the School of Management at UMIST. His areas of research include initial public offerings, corporate governance, ownership disclosure, dividend policy, and corporate investment. His book, *Corporate Governance and Financial Performance*, was published in November 1998 by Edward Elgar. Goergen teaches corporate finance, investment finance and financial economics.

Klaus Gugler has been assistant professor in the Economics Department of the University of Vienna since September, 1995. He holds a Ph.D. in economics from the University of Vienna. His Ph.D. thesis is on investment spending and ownership structure, and his research areas are industrial organization and corporate governance.

Peter Högfeldt is associate professor of finance at the Stockholm School of Economics and has just returned from a sabbatical at the Graduate School of Business at the University of Chicago. After graduate studies at the London School of Economics and MIT (Department of Economics) he joined the SSE. He is a research associate of the Stockholm Institute of Transition Economics (SITE). He initiated and was one of the organizers of the 1995 Nobel Symposium on Law and Finance. His research interests are in the field of corporate finance, law and finance, Initial Public Offerings, and venture capital. He has worked for the Swedish government and Sveriges Riksbank (the Central Bank of Sweden).

Rezaul Kabir is an Associate Professor of Finance at the University of Tilburg and a Guest Professor of Empirical Corporate Finance at the University of Antwerp. His research interests are in the area of empirical corporate finance, corporate governance, and corporate restructuring.

Susanne Kalss is Professor of Private and Corporate Law at the Univerity of Klagenfurt and is head of a research project (START) at the University of Economics at Vienna dealing with different questions of corporate law after Centros from the historical and comparative point of view. Her main fields of research are corporate, economic, and securities law.

Elizabeth Kremp is currently Division Chief of Structural Studies at the Industrial Statistics and Surveys Department (SESSI, DiGITIP) in the Ministry of Economy, Finance and Industry, Paris. While working on this study, she was scientific adviser at the Companies Observatory of the Bank of France. She studied at ENSAE (National School of Statistics and Economic Administration) in Paris and obtained her Ph.D. in international economics at the University of Paris 1. She specialized in panel data studies while she was a research economist at the National Bureau of Economic Research (NBER). Kremp's empirical works include papers on productivity in French services, trade credit, impact of French firms' restructuring on profits, and more recently on ownership concentration and corporate performance.

Teye Marra is Assistant Professor at the Faculty of Management and Organization of the University of Groningen. Teye received his Ph.D. in economics from the University of Tilburg (2001). He was a lecturer in the Finance Department and a member of the CentER Accounting Research Group at the University of Tilburg. His research interests are in the area of empirical corporate finance and financial accounting.

Colin Mayer is Peter Moores Professor of Management Studies at the University of Oxford's Saïd Business School and Léo Goldschmidt Visiting Professor at the Solvay Business School in Brussels. He is the Director of the Oxford University Financial Research Centre and a Professorial Fellow of Wadham College, Oxford. He has previously been Chairman of the European Science Foundation Network in Financial Markets and Co-director of the Centre for Economic Policy Research's Network in Financial Markets. He is a Director of Oxford Economic Research Associates Ltd. (OXERA), a Delegate of the University Press, an Honorary Fellow of St Anne's College, Oxford and on the editorial board of numerous economics and finance journals.

Luc Renneboog is Associate Professor of Finance at the Department of Finance of the University of Tilburg and research fellow at the CentER for Economic Research (Tilburg). Previously, he held appointments at the Catholic University of Leuven and visiting appointments at Oxford University, London Business School, Venice University, and Centro Universitario de Estudios Financieros (Madrid). He graduated with degrees in management engineering and in philosophy from the Catholic University of Leuven, with an MBA from the University of Chicago and with a Ph.D. in Financial Economics from the London Business School. His research interests are corporate governance, dividend policy, financial distress, and the economics of art.

Ailsa Röell is Senior Research Economist at the Bendheim Center for Finance at Princeton University, and part-time Professor of Finance at the University of Tilburg. Röell has previously held appointments at the London School of Economics and at ECARES, Université Libre de Bruxelles. Röell graduated in economics from the University of Groningen and received her Ph.D. degree from Johns Hopkins University. She is a research fellow of CEPR and a board member of various professional journals. Her research fields include stock market microstructure, corporate finance, and corporate governance.

Alex Stomper is affiliated with the University of Vienna. After writing his dissertation at the University of Vienna, he has taught courses at the University of British Columbia and the University of Naples. At the moment, his research interests are in the area of banking, corporate finance, and industrial organization.

Helena Svancar holds an M.Sc. in business administration and economics from the Stockholm School of Economics. Her master's thesis ('Ownership and Control in Swedish Listed Companies' (1999, co-author Jonas Agnblad) mapped and analysed the use of various corporate governance mechanisms in companies listed on the Stockholm Stock Exchange. Svancar has a professional background in finance and is currently working in the corporate finance department for the Nordic investment bank Enskilda Securities (part of the SEB Group).

Josef Zechner is Professor of Finance at the Department for Business Studies of the University of Vienna (since 1993), a Research Fellow at the Centre for Economic

Policy Research (CEPR). He was the president of the European Finance Association in 1998, tenured Associate Professor of Finance at the University of British Columbia, 1990–3, and Assistant Professor of Finance at the University of British Columbia, 1985–90. His research interests include corporate finance and banking, in particular questions related to financial regulation, capital structure choice, corporate governance, initial public offerings, and risk management.

1

Introduction

M. BECHT AND C. MAYER

1. EXISTING STUDIES OF OWNERSHIP AND CONTROL

The classic study of the ownership and control of corporations is Berle and Means, 1932. On the basis of an analysis of US corporations, they concluded that 'the separation of ownership from control has become effective—a large body of security holders has been created who exercise virtually no control over the wealth which they or their predecessors in interest have contributed to the enterprise. The separation of ownership from control produces a condition where the interests of owner and of ultimate manager may, and often do, diverge, and where many of the checks which formerly operated to limit the use of power disappear' (Berle and Means 1932).[1]

Berle and Means' analysis stimulated a huge literature on the control problems created by the separation of ownership and control. Their arguments were amplified in the 1960s when 'managerial discretion' was either praised as a superior alternative to pure profit maximization, or cursed as the driver of an economic concentration that would choke the economy as a whole.[2] Manne (1965) argued that the market for corporate control, not management, governs the 'modern corporation' but Grossman and Hart (1980) cast doubt on the effectiveness of this mechanism. Pessimism culminated in Jensen's (1989) prediction of 'The Eclipse of the Public Corporation' and a move to private corporations with high levels of debt. Leveraged buyout partnerships and blockholders, in particular German and Japanese banks, were the favourite monitors. Recently the US public corporation, with apparently strong outside directors, shareholder activists, and strong legal protection of shareholders, is again the global favourite. But the latest evidence suggests that managers are as powerful as ever. Weak boards with ample formal power, insurmountable takeover barriers, and anti-blockholder regulations continue to prevent owners from exerting control.

To date, very little is known about the control of corporations outside the United States. In fact, such has been the influence of Berle and Means that the textbook description of dispersed ownership and separation of ownership and control has been presumed to be universally applicable. But over the last few years, evidence has emerged that has questioned this view.

Franks and Mayer (1995) described two types of ownership and control structures—what they termed the 'insider and outsider' systems. The outsider system corresponds to the Berle and Means description of the USA—ownership is dispersed amongst a large number of outside investors. Both the UK and USA have outsider systems. In the UK, a majority of equity is held by financial institutions, predominantly pension funds and life assurance companies. In the USA, individual shareholders are more widespread. But in neither country do institutions or individuals hold a large fraction of shares in a company. As a consequence, they exert little direct control over corporations and the separation of ownership and control described by Berle and Means is observed.

However, Franks and Mayer also noted a quite different system that existed in Continental Europe. There, few companies are listed on stock markets and those companies that are listed have a remarkably high level of concentration of ownership. Franks and Mayer observed that in more than 80% of the largest 170 companies listed on stock markets in France and Germany, there is a single shareholder owning more than 25% of shares. In more than 50% of companies, there is a single majority shareholder. The corresponding figures for the UK were 16% of the largest 170 listed companies had single shareholders owning more than 25% of shares and 6% had single majority shareholders. Concentration of ownership is staggeringly high on the Continent in comparison with either the UK or USA.

Franks and Mayer noted that the ownership of Continental European companies is primarily concentrated in the hands of two groups: families and other companies. Cross-shareholdings and complex webs of intercorporate shareholdings are commonplace in some countries. Companies frequently hold shares in each other in the form of pyramids by which company A holds shares of company B which holds shares of company C, etc. They also observed that bank ownership of corporate equity was generally quite modest, despite the attention that has been devoted to the role of bank shareholdings in cementing bank–firm relations. In some but by no means all Continental European countries, ownership by the state is appreciable. Barca et al. (1994) report similar results for Italy.

La Porta et al. (1997 and 1999) have recently extended Franks and Mayer's study to many more countries. They have found that the observation on insider systems which Franks and Mayer made about Continental European countries applies widely around the world. They conclude that the Berle and Means corporation is much less applicable than previously thought. Instead, the insider system appears to dominate.

Interesting though these studies are, they both have serious methodological problems. Firstly, the coverage of the studies is very limited. The Franks and Mayer analysis refers to the largest 170 firms in France, Germany, and the UK. The La Porta et al. (1999) study is restricted to the largest 20 firms in each of their 27 countries.[3] Franks and Mayer have a reasonably large number of large corporations but in a very small number of countries; La Porta et al. have a very small number of companies in a large number of countries.

Secondly, the analysis of control in both papers is rudimentary. In fact, though both papers refer to ownership, what they actually measure is voting control. Data on ownership are in general simply not available and all that can be measured is voting rights. More significantly, an analysis of control of corporations is complex. Even at the first level, individual voting blocks are often tied together in formal coalitions through formal and informal voting pacts or similar arrangements. Voting power is often more concentrated than statistics based on shareholder lists or simple direct stakes suggest. Furthermore, control can be in the form of pyramids in which the control that the owner at the top of the pyramid exerts can combine the voting power of the stakes at the bottom. In order to identify where control resides, it is necessary to trace it back up through the pyramid to the ultimate shareholders at the top of the pyramid. La Porta *et al.* (1999) attempt to do this but their data cannot capture the full complexity of control arrangements that exist in corporate Europe, as we describe below.

Over the last few years, the possibility of undertaking a much more precise analysis of the control of European corporations has emerged. This has arisen as a consequence of vastly improved disclosure standards in Europe. To facilitate the creation of a truly European equity market, the European Union has adopted the Large Holdings Directive (88/627/EEC). This Directive has created a unique opportunity to study corporate control. Access to these data has been improved by cross-listings and integration of capital markets. Companies with a foreign listing in the United States have to file a Form 20-F that includes a special section on the 'Control of the Registrant'. Voting blocks of 10% or larger that have been reported to the companies as a result of the European directive must be disclosed. In future, it will also be possible to perform this type of analysis in Eastern Europe since, before they can join, the accession countries of the European Union will have to transpose the European Union's Directives. As a result, better information on voting power concentration will become available for these countries as well. Internationally, the OECD Principles of Corporate Governance and related efforts by IOSCO are likely to make disclosure more effective and to provide further research opportunities.

Until a few years ago, international comparisons of financial systems focused on the financing of firms and, in particular, the role of banks in funding companies. Distinctions were drawn between supposedly bank-oriented financial systems, such as Germany and Japan, and the market-oriented systems of the UK and USA. But closer analysis revealed the fragility of these distinctions. Mayer (1988), Edwards and Fischer (1994), and Corbett and Jenkinson (1996) noted that the amount of lending coming from German banks has been modest over a long period of time. Edwards and Fischer (1994) argued that there is little support for the conventional wisdom that German banks are actively involved in monitoring and controlling corporations.

In the case of East Asia, in particular Japan, research focused on the relative performance of *keiretsu* and non-*keiretsu* companies (Aoki 1990; Prowse 1992; Kaplan and Minton 1994). Initially it appeared that the closer bank–firm relations in *keiretsu* groups are reflected in fewer credit constraints and the provision of more financing during periods when companies are in financial difficulty (Hoshi, Kashyap and Scharfstein 1991). However, even this view has been questioned over the last few years. Kang and Stulz (1997) reported that bank-dependent firms suffered significantly larger wealth losses and invested less than other firms during 1990 to 1993 when the Japanese stock market dropped appreciably. Weinstein and Yafeh (1998) recorded that close bank–firm ties increased the availability of capital to Japanese firms but did not lead to higher profitability or growth because of banks' market power.

The distinction between bank- and market-oriented financial systems is therefore fragile. In contrast, the differences in ownership and control of corporations noted above are pronounced. This raises two questions. Firstly what are their causes and, secondly, what are their consequences. We examine existing debates on these two issues in section 2 of this introduction. In section 3 we summarize the results of the European Corporate Governance Network study, and in section 4 we conclude the paper.

2. THE CAUSES AND CONSEQUENCES OF OWNERSHIP CONCENTRATIONS

Over the last few years much attention has been given to the influence of regulation and legal form on corporate ownership and control. Black (1990) and Roe (1994) pioneered the 'over-regulation' thesis that has been a dominant force in the debate. Roe (1994) documents that regulation prevents potentially important investors from holding blocks. Black (1990) argues that regulation makes it costly to hold blocks and causes shareholder passivity in the United States.

If the separation of ownership and control is induced by regulation and not efficient, why was the regulation introduced and why is it not repealed? Roe argues that the rise of the Berle and Means corporation in the United States was not simply a response to the forces of economic efficiency but a reflection of populist politics. Concerns about concentration of control in particular in the hands of such banks as J. P. Morgan led to a backlash in the imposition of regulation restricting the involvement of banks in corporate activities. Dispersed ownership therefore resulted from the introduction of regulatory impediments to concentrations in ownership prompted by a populist political agenda. Bebchuk and Roe (1999) argue that inefficient regulation can persist as a result of 'path-dependence'.

The over-regulation argument views the difference between the USA and other countries as reflecting impediments to the free choice of corporate structure in the USA. However, over the last few years an exactly contrary view has been presented. Far from US corporations being impeded by regulation from choosing appropriate structures, 'under-regulation' and, in particular, weak investor protection undermines the financing of firms in most countries of the world. According to La Porta et al. (1997), concentrations of ownership and complex control vehicles are a response to inadequate protection of investors. Faced with a risk of exploitation by self-interested managers, investors require powerful mechanisms for exercising control and they do so through holding large ownership stakes in companies and exerting voting power that is disproportionate to the amount that they invest in firms. This argument has been formalized by Bebchuk (1999), who presents a rent-seeking theory of the evolution of ownership and control and voting power leverage respectively. If blockholder control is induced by under-regulation and not efficient, why has no regulation been introduced? La Porta et al. (2000) invoke similar arguments to those of Roe (1994) and Bebchuk and Roe (1999): rent-seeking blockholders are powerful and have prevented stock exchanges and regulators from curbing their power.[4]

Easterbrook and Fischel (1991) adopt a third position. They argue that the corporate structures we observe have an economic purpose. The Berle and Means corporation and the closely held corporation are efficient, but in different contexts. If they were not, they would not have grown and survived. Easterbrook (1997) argues that the structure and needs of the financial system and the forces of the market create the necessary regulation, not the other way round.

Roe views the US corporation as being weighed down by regulatory restrictions imposed by an earlier political agenda; La Porta *et al.* argue that strong investor protection in common law countries and under-regulation elsewhere has allowed external financing to occur on a larger scale under common law. Easterbrook (1997) argues that the size of a country's stock market, as determined, for example, by its pension system, determines regulation. For Roe, the regulatory barriers to, for example, bank participation in corporate ownership should be broken down. For La Porta *et al.*, stronger investor protection is required in most countries of the world. For Easterbrook and Fischel, regulation adapts to the needs of the market.

In this paper, we show that regulation visibly affects the relationship between ownership and control. We consider how the control of dominant investors changes as outside ownership is brought in. Dual class shares, non-voting shares and pyramids allow dominant investors to exert disproportionate degrees of voting power as outside ownership comes in. This is termed 'a private control bias'. Rules forcing blockholders to interact with a company on 'arm's-length basis' or preventing or discouraging shareholders from exercising voting rights disperse voting power. This can either create a market or a management control bias. In the absence of anti-takeover devices dispersed voting power can be exercised through a hostile bid: Manne's (1965) market for corporate control. If the bidder holds a minority stake of sufficient size or has other incentives to launch a bid, minority investors can free ride on the control exerted by others and thereby derive control disproportionate to their investment. However, rules that discourage voting blocks can also lead to a 'management bias'. In most countries a variety of formal and informal devices shielding management from external control exist (poison pills, voting caps, weak and captured boards). Protecting minorities by curbing the voting power of the blockholder can severely tilt the balance of cash-flow rights and power in favour of management.

Figure 1.1 illustrates this. It shows that rules protecting dominant investors push the line linking ownership to control upwards to the left. Control therefore declines less than proportionately with reduction in ownership. On the other hand, rules preventing or discouraging shareholders from exercising voting rights push the ownership-control line down to the right. Control then declines more than proportionately with ownership.

There is a divergence of view about the consequences of ownership concentration. The most popular view of corporate governance is the agency one. Managers run firms according to their own interests and agenda when the company is widely held. As far as possible, incentives are used to align the interests of managers and shareholders but active monitoring and control of companies is also required. But as noted by Berle and Means, in the presence of dispersed ownership, investors have little incentive to

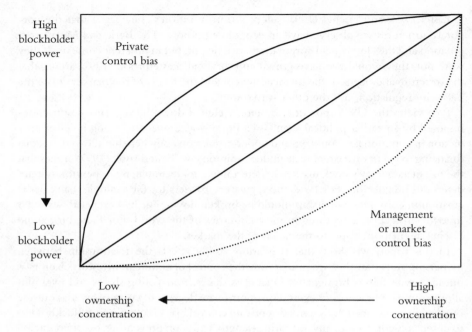

Figure 1.1. *Private control bias and management or market control bias.*

Note: Power increases proportionally with ownership under 'one-share-one-vote', in the absence of pre- and post-bid anti-takeover devices and under 'neutral' regulation. Rules and devices protecting dominant investors push the line linking ownership to control upwards to the left. Control therefore declines less than proportionally initially with reductions in ownership. On the other hand, strong minority protection pushes the ownership-control line down to the right. Control then declines more than proportionally with ownership. In the absence of anti-takeover devices such as staggered boards, this results in a market control bias or, more likely, in a management control bias. Strong minority protection regulation has similar effects to anti-takeover devices in imposing restrictions and limits on the power of blockholders.

engage actively in this and instead prefer to 'free ride' on the monitoring performed by others. Some ownership concentration is therefore required to ameliorate managerial agency problems (Berle 1958).

But while concentrations of ownership may reduce agency problems, they create a second conflict. The interests of holders of large blocks of shares may diverge from those of minority investors. Large shareholders are in a position to engage in activities that benefit them at the expense of minority investors. In Jensen and Meckling (1976) the owner-manager can freely choose the level of private benefit consumption because he/she retains all control rights while selling only cash-flow rights. The most obvious example of such 'private benefits' is shifting assets and corporate value through transfer pricing between companies in which large shareholders have an interest. In some countries there are explicit restrictions on these activities, requiring for example, that parent and subsidiary act on an arm's-length basis and use market testing to price transactions. In other countries, there are few restrictions.

While the 'over-regulation' literature sees weak owners confronted with strong managers in countries with dispersed ownership, the rent-seeking literature argues that strong owners in countries with concentrated ownership and/or control exploit weak minorities. This 'under-regulation' literature argues that the latter is the more serious problem confronting most countries and the emergence of ownership concentrations in the face of weak investor protection is a deficiency not an advantage of these systems.

Carlin and Mayer (2000*a* and *b*) and Mayer (2000) argue that there is no one dominant system. Different types of ownership and control are suited to different types of activities. They argue that concentrated ownership benefits activities that require long-term, committed investors. Dispersed ownership benefits short-term investments that require greater flexibility and less commitment. In particular, Mayer (2000) argues that there is a need to match periods for which control can be expected to be retained (what is termed the 'influence period') with the 'realization period' of projects (the time taken for projects to come to fruition). Too short an influence relative to a realization period leads to rejection of long-term investments. Too long an influence relative to a realization period leads to inefficient retention of control. Dominant owners are able to retain control over long periods whereas managers facing markets in corporate control with dispersed ownership are subject to short influence periods. The latter therefore promote efficient transfers in control for investments with short realization periods whereas the former encourage investments in activities with long realization periods.

3. FRAMEWORK OF ANALYSIS

In this section, we will characterize the different combinations of ownership and control that will be analysed in the following sections. We begin with a dynamic setting where a manager owns all the cash-flow and control rights of a private company. Control rights and cash-flow rights are sold along five 'stylized paths'. Next, we show how the paths map into ownership: voting power cross-sections and point out the perceived advantages/disadvantages of each. Finally, we show what conclusions can be drawn when empirical observations are limited to voting power cross-sections.

Goergen (1998) reports empirical evidence on the evolution of ownership and control of German and UK firms. He finds that control is usually not sold in initial public offerings (IPOs) in either country. For a sample of 55 comparable German and UK IPOs, he finds that the pre-IPO shareholders retained 76.4% of the voting rights in Germany and 62.8% in the United Kingdom immediately after the IPO. However, further sales of ownership and control occurred subsequently and after six years, the old shareholders retained 45% of the voting rights in Germany, but only 30% in the United Kingdom.[5]

In some cases, no voting rights are sold through the initial public offering at all. In Germany, 69.4% of IPOs between 1970 and 1995 involved the sale of ordinary voting shares ('one-share-one-vote'), 28.3% non-voting shares ('one-share-no-vote') and 2.3% both. Through other legal instruments, for example dual-class stock with multiple voting rights and non-voting shares, pre-IPO shareholders can retain control and sell the majority (and in some cases all) of the cash-flow rights.

Figure 1.2 classifies such evolutions of ownership and control into five stylized paths. Without private equity financing, in the private firm ownership and voting power are usually concentrated.[6] Different combinations of ownership and voting power result when cash-flow and control rights are sold on a stock market, and thereafter with further sales over the lifecycle of the company.

3.1. *Little equity is sold (path 1)*

In the initial public offering, enough equity is sold to meet the listing requirements, but little of the remainder is sold. Voting power and ownership are concentrated. Since majority or super-majority control is not contestable, private benefits are likely to accrue to the incumbent manager-blockholder. Due to its small shareholder base, the market for the company's stock is illiquid. This has been the preferred path in many continental European countries, especially in Belgium.

3.2. *Control is locked in; further equity is sold in blocks (path 2) or dispersed (path 4)*

The incumbent locks in control by preventing third parties from exercising and/or acquiring voting power and exerts control independent of the amount of cash-flow rights held. Path 2 leads to a combination of dispersed voting power and concentrated ownership, path 4 to dispersed ownership and voting power. In both cases, control is not contestable.

Historically, a limited amount of voting power irrespective of ownership was the norm, especially under common law. 'One-member-one-vote' was a progressive concept in times when not all men (and no women) were allowed to vote in political elections.[7] In early corporations in England, 'since the charter was issued by the crown, the corporation was considered a part of the government and each member of the corporation was entitled to one vote if given by him in person' (Axe 1942).

Dunlavy (1998) records that scaled or flat voting caps were the norm in the charters of nineteeth-century corporations in France, Germany, the United States, and the United Kingdom. Before the introduction of general incorporation, charters were granted individually, often imposing voting scales. For example, Dunlavy (1998: 25) reports that the well-known *Disconto-Gesellschaft* in Berlin 'allowed only shareholders of at least 1,000 Thaler (about $700) to vote in the general assembly and each had one vote only' (Hübner 1854: 2/98); the 1852 charter of the famous *Crédit Mobilier* restricted voting rights 'to the largest 200 shareholders' who received one vote for less than forty, and 'one vote for each forty shares up to a maximum of five votes (or ten votes, including proxies) . . . ' (Hübner 1854: 199). According to Dunlavy (1998: 18), the voting scale imposed by the Virginia law of 1836 regulating all manufacturing corporations allowed shareholders to cast 'one vote for each share up to 15, one vote

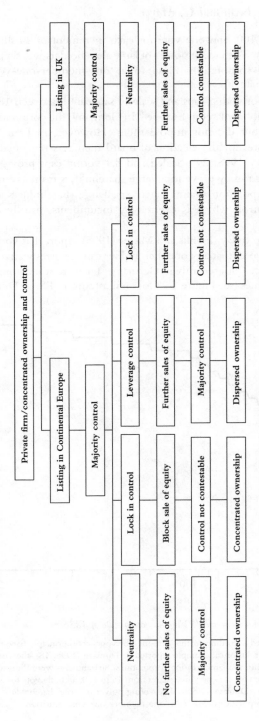

Figure 1.2. *Evolution of ownership and control.*

Note: Ownership and control are sold in five 'stylized paths'. Starting from a private firm where all cash-flow rights and control rights are held by the founder, the company is listed by selling the minimum amount of equity required (typically 25% of the cash-flow rights). Simultaneously, a capital structure is chosen. There are three choices: neutrality ('one-share–one-vote' and no pre- or post-bid anti-takeover defences), voting rights are leveraged over cash-flow rights or control is locked in through voting right and/or transfer restrictions (see Figure 1.1). Under 'neutrality', if there are no further sales of equity the founder has majority control and ownership (of cash-flow rights) is concentrated. When there are further sales of equity, control becomes contestable and ownership dispersed; the Berle–Means Corporation. When control is locked in, ownership can be sold in a block without affecting the ability of the founder to exert control. With further sales of equity, ownership becomes dispersed while control remains incontestable. When voting rights are leveraged over cash-flow rights, majority control can be combined with dispersed ownership. When we can observe ownership and voting power concentrations in a cross-section we can distinguish dispersed ownership without majority control from other combinations. However, we cannot determine whether control is contestable or not (in the UK control is almost always contestable, in the United States it is not). When we observe the concentration of voting power, we can identify majority control, but not how it is obtained.

M. Becht and C. Mayer

for every five shares from 15 to 100, and one vote for each increment of 20 shares above 100 shares' (Dunlavy 1998). The voting power of large shareholders was capped very severely, putting Virginia corporations close to a 'one-member-one-vote' situation (see Figure 1.3).

It appears that the imposition of voting caps and scales disappeared between 1840 and 1880 in the United States, but only later in Europe.[8] In Germany, the corporation law of 1884 allowed for caps, but did not impose them. However, in France a compulsory voting cap of 10 votes for the election of board members remained in force at least until 1898 (Dunlavy 1998: 29). Scaled and flat voting caps provide a certain degree of minority protection by preventing large shareholders from exerting control; they also shield the corporation against takeovers. Large shareholders and the market are deprived of control, which is exerted by incumbents, usually the management.

Neither path is still uncommon today. Franks and Mayer (1995) report that voting caps, which limit the maximum votes that any one shareholder can cast irrespective of their holdings, were commonplace until recently in Germany. They are still common among Spanish blue-chip companies (see Figure 1.23 for an illustration). Royal Dutch

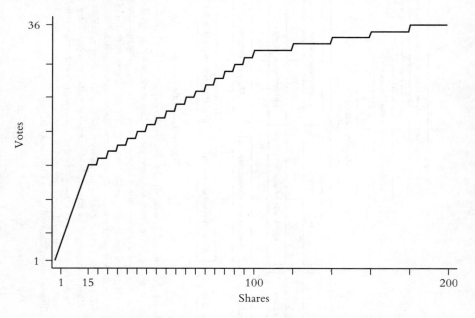

Figure 1.3. *'One-member-one-vote': Virginia voting scale of 1836.*

Note: Listed companies that are controlled according to the 'one-member-one-vote' principle have practically disappeared. Hence we draw on a historical example reported in Dunlavy (1998: 18), the voting scale imposed by the Virginia law regulating all manufacturing corporations. Shareholders were allowed to cast 'one vote for each share up to 15, one vote for every five shares from 15 to 100, and one vote for each increment of 20 shares above 100 shares' (Dunlavy, 1998). The voting power of large shareholders was capped very severely, putting Virginia corporations close to a 'one-member-one-vote' situation.

Shell, Europe's most valuable business group in the FT 500 list (28 Jan. 1999, www.ft.com/FT500) and no. 4 in the 1998 global ranking, has a voting right limit of 48,000 votes, 0.002% of all voting rights.

3.3. *Cash-flow rights are sold in excess of voting rights (path 3)*

Using dual-class stock, non-voting stock, non-voting ownership certificates, trust companies, and similar devices cash-flow rights can be sold almost independently of voting rights (see Appendix for a list of such devices and Figures 1.19, 1.21, 1.22, 1.24 for an illustration). Following this path, ownership is dispersed and voting power concentrated. At the turn of the century, corporations in the United States were controlled by blockholders. But many of these blockholders commanded voting rights in excess of their cash-flow rights using dual-class stock, pyramids, voting trusts, and similar devices. Hilferding (1910) observed that 'with the development of the joint-stock company there emerges a financial technique, the aim of which is to ensure control over the largest possible amount of capital with the smallest amount of one's own capital. This technique has reached its peak of perfection in the financing of the American railway system.' Today, dual-class stock is not uncommon in the United States. In Europe, path 3 has been popular in Sweden, the Netherlands and, to some degree, in Austria and Germany.

3.4. *Cash-flow rights and control are sold to the market (path 5)*

In the absence of statutory anti-takeover devices proportional sales of cash-flow and voting rights lead to a situation of dispersed voting power and ownership. Control is transferred to the market.

The corporate finance literature emphasizes the private benefits that accrue to managers when ownership and voting power are dispersed. Salomon Brothers (Lewis 1990) and RJR Nabisco in the 1980s are colourful examples of the consumption of private benefits by managers who are largely uncontrolled by their dispersed share-holders. This literature also recommends control change (hostile takeovers and debt as a disciplining device in LBOs) as the tools that put an end to such practices. In the case of RJR Nabisco, the arrival of 'Barbarians at the Gate' (Burrough and Helyar 1990) permanently grounded the corporate air force of its then president and chief executive officer, Ross Johnson.

3.5. *Implications*

The dynamic view depicted in Figure 1.2 illustrates that the issue of 'one-share-one-vote' is not central. In terms of control, the different paths are distinguished by the degree to which control can be contested (paths 1–4 versus path 5 in Figure 1.2). Control may not be contestable, even under 'one-share-one-vote'. This distinction is reflected in popular European books on corporate control. The German best-seller *Nieten in Nadelstreifen* ('Nitwits in Pinstripe Suits'; Ogger 1991) is about unassailable blockholders as much as about managers. Both classes are depicted as self-serving, nepotistic, unaccountable and, therefore, incompetent. In Italy, the popular complaint about the *salotto buono* is not the ways its members exert control, but the fact they shield each other from control challenges. The same is true in France.[9]

This view is consistent with Hellwig (2000). He argues that corporate governance in different countries is determined jointly by 'differences in social, political and legal traditions' and 'seemingly different institutional arrangements in different countries may serve similar functions, catering for similar interests' (p. 6). The common theme is 'career patterns, intrigues, and resource allocation in insider systems with mutual interdependence' (p. 1), where the incumbents are well protected against control challenges (paths 1–4).

The relationship between ownership and control is not only affected by the relation between cash flow and voting rights but also the relation between voting and control rights. The ability of voting blocks to exercise control may be limited by two main factors: protection of minority investors and protection of management.

The United Kingdom has extensive protection of minority investors that takes the form of rights of minorities to approve transactions between subsidiary and parent firms and equal price rules in takeovers. In the UK, once an investor has acquired 30% of the shares of a firm, it has to make an offer for all of the shares in the firm, at a price that is no less than the highest price paid for the accumulation of shares to that point. Minority investors therefore enjoy substantial benefits from takeovers in the presence of equal price rules. More importantly, the listing requirement of the London Stock Exchange require companies to ensure that their relationship with 30%+ block-holders is at 'arm's length'.

In practice, this 'arm's-length' requirement imposes very severe limitations on a blockholder's ability to monitor corporate management. The composition of the board must be such that all its significant decisions are taken independently of controlling (30%+) shareholders and the company must implement rules that allow it to deal with the conflicts of interest of directors appointed by the controlling shareholder (Section 3.13 of the London Stock Exchange Listing Requirements). In particular, the listings agreement can specify that the controlling shareholder cannot appoint more than 5 out of 12 directors, the removal of directors not appointed by the controlling shareholder is subject to a 2/3-majority board decision, and capital increases must not dilute the voting power of non-controlling shareholders (cited in Wymeersch 2000). While there is no doubt that these provisions protect minority shareholders, they also prevent large shareholders from monitoring the board and corporate management. Short of a fully fledged bid it is very difficult to bring more than 30% of voting power to bear on a plc listed on the London Stock Exchange. However, since very few UK-listed companies have adopted anti-takeover measures, takeover bids are a last resort for bringing these autonomous boards under shareholder control.

In the United States there are similar rules that prevent large shareholders from exercising their voting power. For example, Black (1990) reports that shareholders acquiring 10–20% of voting rights are considered to exert control. To protect minority shareholders large shareholders are held liable like directors. In combination with other minority protection provisions US boards, like UK boards, can be immune to monitoring by blockholders.

However, unlike in the UK the United States does not have a mandatory bid rule and tender offers must be negotiated with the board. As a result devices that enable boards to protect small shareholders from large shareholders become devices that are used to protect boards (and management) from takeover bids. One example is super-majority provisions that require 80% majorities to pass shareholder resolutions. The response of the board of Honeywell Inc. to a proposal by one Harold J. Mathis, Jr. to abolish its super-majority-voting requirement is exemplary of the ambiguous nature of such provisions:

These special voting provisions of the Company's Certificate of Incorporation and By-laws are intended to provide protection for all shareowners against self-interested actions by one or a few large shareowners. Similar provisions are included in the governing documents of many public corporations. Such provisions are intended to encourage a person making an unsolicited bid for the Company to negotiate with the Board of Directors to reach terms that are fair and provide the best results for all shareowners. Without such provisions, it may be possible for the holders of a majority of the shares represented at a meeting to take actions that would give them effective control of the Company without negotiating with the Board to achieve the best results for the other shareowners. (Item 5, Proxy Statement, Honeywell International Inc., filed 3/13/2000)

The independence of US boards from shareholder influence is further illustrated by their ability to ignore shareholder proposals. A striking recent example is Eastman Kodak. Figure 1.4 reports the control structure of the company. The 27 officers, directors and nominees of the Eastman Kodak jointly own less than 2% of the voting shares of the company and there are no 5%+ blockholders. The company has twelve directors who are equally divided into three classes and elected for staggered three-year terms. Hence it is impossible to replace more than one-third of directors in any one year. In addition, the company by-laws require a 80% super-majority for major decisions, including any changes to the by-laws. Shareholder proposed to declassify the board in 1997, 1998, 1999, and 2000 and won a majority of the votes attending. The board ignored the shareholder resolution on the grounds that in each of these years the votes cast in favour of the motion only represented 30–40% of the votes outstanding and that a super-majority of 80% of the shares outstanding was required (Eastman Kodak Inc., Proxy Statement, filed 3/13/2000). Even if a super-majority had been won, the board could have ignored the resolution. Proposals filed under the widely-used SEC Rule 14a–8 are only precatory in nature (Black 1998).

Like Eastman Kodak, most S&P500 put a variety of anti-takeover devices in place at the beginning of the 1990s. Danielson and Karpoff (1998) tabulate the number of anti-takeover devices in a sample of 513 (mostly S&P500 companies) traced by Institutional Shareholder Services between 1984 and 1989. In 1989 the median number of devices was 6.0, ranging from external control provisions (like poison pills and blank cheque preferred stock) through internal control provisions (like classified boards and supermajority amendments) to state anti-takeover laws (like freeze-out or control share acquisition laws). In addition in 441 of the 512 firms directors and officers

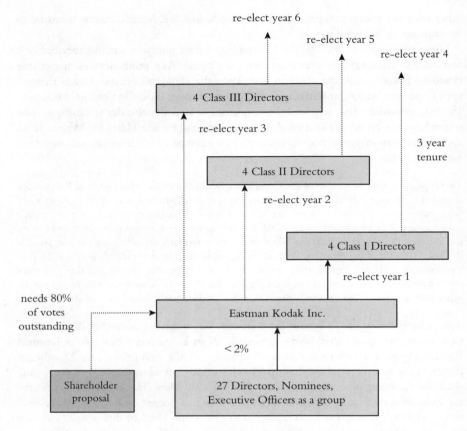

Figure 1.4. *Management control through staggered board and super-majority
amendment: Eastman Kodak Inc.*

Note: The control structure of Eastman Kodak Inc., is quite typical for S&P500 companies. The 27 officers,
directors and nominees of the Eastman Kodak jointly own less than 2% of the voting shares of the company
and there are no 5%+ blockholders. The company has twelve directors that are equally divided into three
classes and elected for staggered three-year terms. Hence it is impossible to replace more than one-third of
directors in any one year. In addition, the company by-laws require a 80% super-majority for major
decisions, including any changes to the by-laws (Eastman Kodak Inc., Proxy Statement, filed 3/13/2000).
Danielson and Karpoff (1998) record that 277 of the 512 companies in their sample had a classified board
structure in 1989 and 134 had passed a super-majority amendment.

enjoyed liability indemnity. Already blunted by the business judgement rule, the threat
of shareholder suits is further diminished by this type of insurance. As in the case of
Eastman Kodak, shareholder activists have been largely unable to repeal these provisions
(Black 1998).

On the Continent, there are far fewer restrictions on large shareholders. In some
countries shareholder voting power can be brought to bear almost fully on boards and

companies, for example in Belgium. A 30%+ of shareholders can call an extraordinary meeting and dismiss all directors with a simple majority vote. A 50%+ of shareholders has almost full command over boards. Staggered board provisions are fruitless because the voting power of shareholders is supreme. Conversely, due to their weakness, boards can provide very little protection to minority shareholders of Belgian companies.

However, in other countries of Continental Europe, significant protection is provided once shareholdings reach certain critical levels. Firstly, there are disclosure rules relating to the accumulation of shareholdings above critical levels of, for example, 3%, 5%, or 10%. Secondly, in Austria and Germany, shareholdings in excess of 25% can block certain key actions of a firm regarding, for example, the issuance of new equity. Thirdly, once shareholdings exceed 75% in Germany there is a requirement that transactions be undertaken at arm's length to avoid actions that discriminate against minorities. On the other hand, 75%+ of blockholders can change the company statutes (almost) at will.

The main purpose of this study was to collect data that allowed us to map ownership into control and determine the degree of private versus market or management control. The country teams also tried to determine how voting power is concentrated without concentrating ownership, how voting power translates into control and, hence, how control is separated from ownership. As we will show in the next section, European securities regulation does not provide for the disclosure of all the necessary data. The Large Holdings Directive (88/627/EEC) provides for the disclosure of 10%+ ultimate voting blocks, not for the disclosure of cash-flow rights (ownership). The same is true of Regulation 13D in the United States. Hence, the systematic comparative analysis presented in this chapter focuses on voting power. However, it is possible to go further in some countries and some of the individual country chapters present results on the separation of cash-flow from voting rights as well.

4. METHODOLOGY

Traditionally, European corporations and their shareholders value privacy. In Austria, Belgium, Denmark, France, Germany, Luxembourg, the Netherlands, Portugal, and Spain most listed companies issue bearer shares. By definition, ownership and voting power are hard to trace. However, this can also be difficult in countries with registered shares (Finland, Greece, Ireland, Italy, Sweden, and the United Kingdom). Company law and securities regulations do not always force companies to provide access to share registers; alternatively, shares might be held in nominee accounts ('street names'). Even when the names of the beneficial owners are known, the share register provides no information on voting pacts and other arrangements that tie individual stakes into blocks of votes cast by the same person or entity.

The comparative analysis in this book relies on a new disclosure standard that partially overcomes these problems. It applies throughout the European Union and provides for the disclosure of 10%+ (often 5%+) voting blocks.

In 1988, the European Commission passed the Large Holdings Directive (88/627/ EEC) requiring member states to introduce laws forcing disclosure of shareholdings of companies listed on member state exchanges. These laws were gradually enacted during the 1990s and it is only recently that a comprehensive picture has begun to emerge. The Directive requires blockholders to disclose holdings when voting rights cross certain thresholds of, for example 10% or 20% of total votes. It therefore relates to control rather than ownership of firms.[10]

In the United States, the Securities and Exchange Act of 1934 provides for the disclosure of 'beneficial ownership'. According to SEC Rule 13d-3, 'a beneficial owner of a security includes any person who, directly or indirectly, through any contract, arrangement, understanding, relationship, or otherwise has or shares: (1) voting power which includes the power to vote, or to direct the voting of, such security; and/or (2) investment power which includes the power to dispose, or to direct the disposition of, such security.' Beyond 5%, all changes of 1% or more have to be notified. In addition, all changes in the composition of the voting block or in intentions of the blockholder have to be notified. Hence, 'beneficial ownership' is not ownership, at least not in the strict sense of the word.[11]

In the European Union, the Large Holdings Directive (88/627/EEC) provides for the disclosure of voting power.[12] It sets minimum standards for all companies that are registered in a member state and listed on an official stock market. Article 4(1) states that when 'the proportion of voting rights held [by a person or entity], exceeds or falls below one of the thresholds of 10%, 20%, 1/3, 50%, and 2/3, he shall notify the company and at the same time the competent authority'. Member states are free to set lower thresholds and narrower intervals. In 1997, the lower bounds ranged from 2% in Italy, 3% in the United Kingdom, 5% in most other countries, to 10% in, for example, Portugal and Finland.

In addition to any voting rights a person or entity might own and vote directly, Article 4 defines eight factors that can lead to 'attribution' of votes. The list reflects the variety of legal devices that can be used to detach votes from shares, or to hide the identity of the true owners, in the Union as a whole:

1. Votes attached to shares held by a nominee.
2. Votes held by someone the notifying party controls, for example a subsidiary in a business group.[13]
3. Voting pacts that oblige the owners of the shares 'to adopt, by concerted exercise of the voting rights they hold, a lasting common policy towards the management of the company in question'.
4. A *written agreement* for the temporary transfer of voting rights to the notifying party.
5. Votes that could be exercised by an agent who holds them as collateral, but only if the owner does not exercise the votes.
6. 'Voting rights attaching to shares of which that person or entity has the life interest' (in the German transposition: *Nießbrauch*).
7. Formal agreements that allow the notifying party to acquire voting rights (by any of the means listed above); when such votes are acquired the company must be notified, even when no threshold has been crossed.

8. Voting rights deposited with the voting agent for safekeeping when the owner did not give specific voting instructions.

We call the sum of voting power acquired through a direct stake plus the voting power acquired through any one of these devices a *voting block*. Since those who have ultimate command over voting power notify the voting rights we also refer to these as *ultimate voting blocks*. Two examples might help to clarify this definition and what does and does not get disclosed on the basis of the Directive.

Figure 1.5 illustrates the definition of an ultimate voting block. Company C2 is a listed company. It has five direct shareholders: foundation F1 holds a direct stake of 31%, holding company H1 10%, holding H2 9%, insurance company I1 6% and investment fund I2 2%. The holding companies are controlled by company C1 and this company has delegated all voting power it commands at C2 to the foundation via a

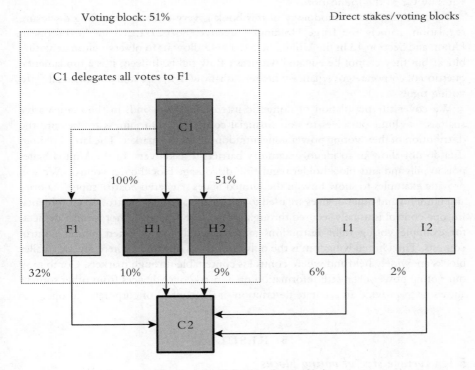

Figure 1.5. *Definition of voting block.*

Note: Company C2 is a listed company. It has five direct shareholders: Foundation F1 holds a direct stake of 31%, holding company H1 10%, holding H2 9%, insurance company I1 6%, and investment fund I2 2%. The holding companies are controlled by company C1 and this company has delegated all voting power it commands at C2 to the foundation via a written agreement. With a 5% notification threshold under the Large Holdings Directive, the votes controlled by C1 (10% from H1 and 9% from H2) are assigned to F1 and F1 must notify a 51% voting block. The direct stakes of F1, H1, H2, and I1 are also notified. We report the distribution of the voting blocks: 51% (F1) and 6% (I1).

written agreement. With a 5% notification threshold under the Large Holdings Directive, the votes controlled by C1 (10% from H1 and 9% from H2) are assigned to F1 and F1 must notify a 51% voting block. The direct stakes of F1, H1, H2, and I1 are also notified. We report the distribution of the voting blocks: 51% (F1) and 6% (I1). We do not report the distribution of direct stakes, because the composition of the voting block is not necessarily disclosed.

Traditional studies of corporate control, for example Franks and Mayer (1995), would have reported the distribution of direct stakes and sought to trace chains of direct stakes (C1 to H1 to C2, and C2 to H2 to C2). Since the disclosure threshold in Germany prior to the Large Holdings Directive was 25% they would have been limited to identifying the foundation's 32% stake. More recent applications of the tracing method, for example La Porta *et al.* (1999) would have traced the 10% chain (C1 to H1 to C2) because H1 is a listed company, but failed to detect the delegation of votes by C2 to the foundation.

To conclude, the methodology of this book is very close to prevailing disclosure regulation, namely the Large Holdings Directive (88/627/EEC) in the European Union and Section 13 in the United States. These allow us to observe ultimate voting blocks but they cannot be equated with cash–flow rights. Indeed, it is a fundamental question of corporate governance whether cash–flow rights are sold proportionately to voting rights.

We cover the population of domestic listed companies and, in the comparative analysis, we limit ourselves to non-financial companies. Our aim is to measure the distribution of their voting power concentration across the market. The large holdings data do not allow us to identify statutory barriers to takeovers. In the United States poison pills and anti-blockholder regulation discourage blockholder control. We will provide examples to show how in the United States staggered boards, super-majority amendments and other devices are used to secure management control. In Continental Europe control is usually secured through blocks, but where it is not, similar devices, for example voting right restrictions and staggered boards, often inhibit control contests. The United Kingdom is the only country in our study where several smaller blocks are widely held and where control is contestable through markets. Combining our voting power data with information on anti-takeover devices from other sources allows us to provide an accurate description of the control of corporate Europe.

5. RESULTS

5.1. *Average size of voting blocks*

Table 1.1 reports the proportion of votes controlled by the largest voting block in eight countries. In 50% of non-financial listed companies in Austria, Belgium, Germany, and Italy, a single blockholder (an individual investor or group of investors) controls more than 50% of voting rights. In 50% of Dutch, Spanish, and Swedish companies, more than 43.5%, 34.5%, and 34.9% respectively of votes are controlled by a single blockholder. In contrast, the median blockholder in the UK controls only 9.9% of

Table 1.1. *Size of ultimate voting blocks by rank*

Country	No. of companies	Largest voting block: Median	2nd Largest voting block: Median	3rd Largest voting block: Median
Austria[1]	50	52.0	2.5	0.0*
Belgium[2]	140	56.0	6.3	4.7
Germany[3]	372	57.0	0*	0*
Spain[4]	193	34.5	8.9	1.8
France[5]	CAC40	20.0	5.9	3.4
Italy[6]	214	54.5	5.0	2.7
Netherlands[7]	137	43.5	7.7	0*
Sweden[8]	304	34.9	8.7	4.8
UK[9]	207	9.9	6.6	5.2
USA[10]				
NYSE	1309	5.4	0*	0*
NASDAQ	2831	8.6	0*	0*

*No 5%+ voting block.

Note: The table reports the size of the largest, 2nd largest and 3rd largest median voting block for non-financial companies listed on an official market. For France only the main stock price index (CAC 40) is covered.

Sources: This volume: [1]Gugler, Kalss, Stomper, and Zechner, Figure 2.1, data for 1996; [2]Computed by Becht, data for 1995; [3]Becht and Böhmer, Figure 5.2, data for 1996; [4]Crespí-Cladera and García-Cestona; [5]Bloch and Kremp; [6]Bianchi, Bianco, Enriques, Table 6.6, data for 1996; [7]de Jong, Kabir, Marra, and Röell, Table 7.5, data for 1996; [8]Agnblad, Berglöf, Högfeldt, and Svancar, Table 9.3A, data for 1998; [9]Goergen and Renneboog, data for 1992, excludes blocks held by directors; [10]Becht, data for 1996, includes blocks held by directors and officers.

votes and in the United States the median size of blockholding of companies quoted on both NASDAQ and NYSE is just above the disclosure level of 5% (8.6% and 5.4%).

The picture looks very different when one goes down to the second and third largest blocks (Table 1.1). The median size of the second largest voting block is 2.5% in Austria, 10.2% in Belgium, 5.9% in France, 7.6% in Italy, and 8.7% in Sweden. In Germany it is below the disclosure level. The median size of the third largest voting block is 4.7% in Belgium, 3.4% in France, 3.0% in Italy, and 4.8% in Sweden. In both Austria and Germany it is below the disclosure level. The size of voting blocks therefore decreases rapidly beyond the largest shareholder. Voting power is concentrated on the Continent not only because of the existence of large blockholders but also because of the absence of other voting blocks.

In the UK, the median size of the second largest block is 7.3%, and of the third largest block is 5.2%. The size of the largest block is therefore appreciably smaller in the UK than on the Continent but the size of blocks does not decline very rapidly thereafter. Indeed, the third largest block and beyond is larger in the UK than any other country in this study. Even beyond the tenth largest blockholding, the mean voting block in the UK is greater than 3%, whereas it is below disclosure levels in virtually all the Continental European countries in this study. On the Continent, the largest blockholder exerts dominant voting control in relation to other blockholders.

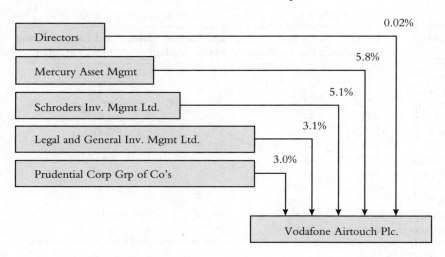

Figure 1.6. *Potential coalition control: Vodafone Airtouch Plc.*

Note: The control structure of Vodafone Airtouch Plc. is typical for UK listed companies (data from the Hemscott Company Guide 1999). A number of institutional investors hold 3–10% blocks and jointly can exercise a significant degree of voting power, frequently even more significant than in this example.

In the UK, no individual blockholder in general exerts dominant control; instead it can only come from coalitions of investors. Vodafone Plc. illustrates this point (Figure 1.6). A number of institutional investors hold 3–10% blocks and jointly can exercise a significant degree of voting power. The situation is the same in the United States but the potential coalition to exert effective control must be even larger than in the UK.

Voting power is much more concentrated on the Continent than in the UK or the USA. Coalitions between shareholders are required in the UK and USA to exercise control. This points to a private control bias on the Continent and a management or market control bias in the UK and USA. The next section will provide support for this from an analysis of distributions of voting control in different countries.

5.2. *Distributions of voting control*

Figures 1.7–1.16 show the cumulative distributions of largest voting blocks (from smallest to largest) in listed companies in seven European countries and for NYSE and NASDAQ companies in the USA. The figures report the fraction of companies in a country with largest blocks less than the values reported on the vertical axis. A cumulative distribution close to the 45° line reflects a uniform density of firms by voting blocks. A distribution above the 45° line reflects a preponderance of large voting block companies and a distribution below the 45° line indicates a large amount of dispersed voting control.

In Germany, the cumulative distribution is above the 45° line; in Austria, Belgium, and Italy, the distributions are close to the 45° line. In the Netherlands and Spain they

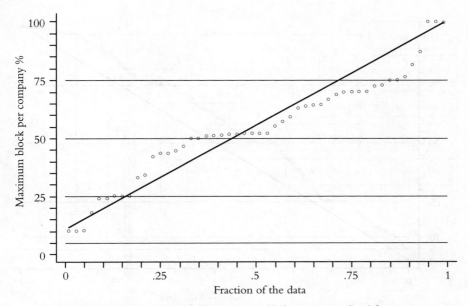

Figure 1.7. *Percentile plot of largest voting blocks in Austrian listed firms.*

Source: Gugler, Kalss, Stomper, and Zechner, this volume.

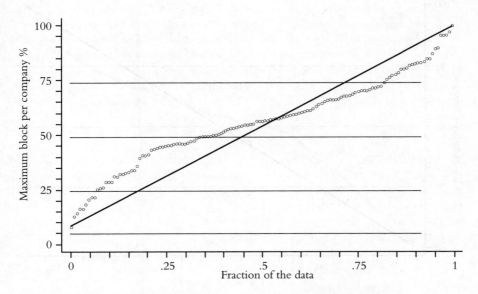

Figure 1.8. *Percentile plot of largest voting blocks in Belgian listed firms.*

Source: Becht, Chapelle, and Renneboog, this volume.

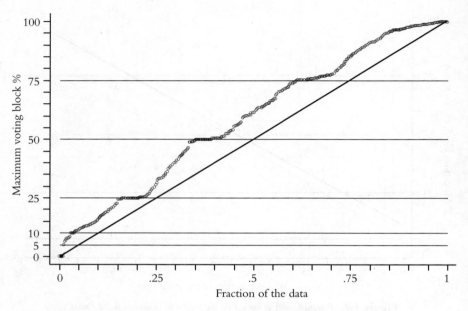

Figure 1.9. *Percentile plot of largest voting blocks in German listed firms.*

Source: Becht and Böhmer, this volume.

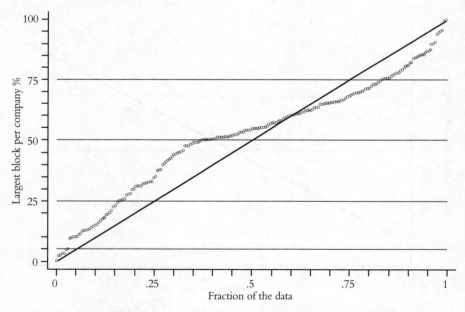

Figure 1.10. *Percentile plot of largest voting blocks in Italian listed firms.*

Source: Bianchi, Bianco, and Enriques, this volume.

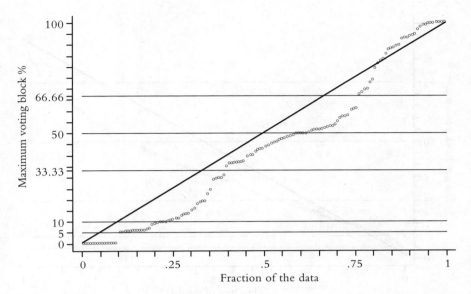

Figure 1.11. *Percentile plot of largest voting block in Netherlands listed firms.*

Source: de Jong, Kabir, Marra, and Röell, this volume.

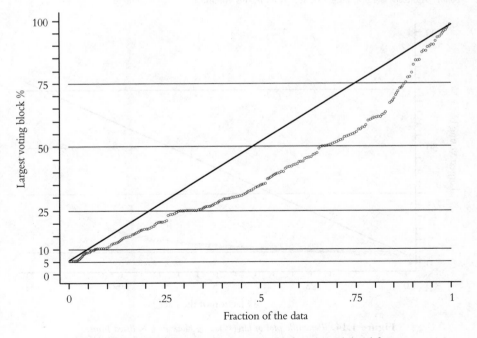

Figure 1.12. *Percentile plot of largest voting block in Spanish listed firms.*

Source: Crespí-Cladera and García-Cestona, this volume.

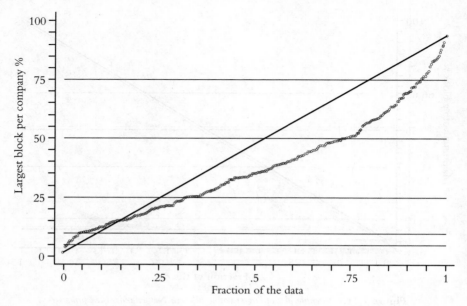

Figure 1.13. *Percentile plot of largest voting block in Swedish listed firms.*

Source: Agnblad, Berglöf, Högfeldt, and Svancar, this volume.

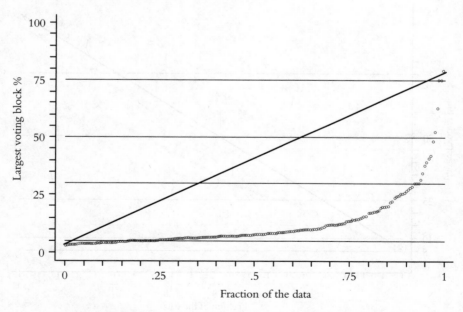

Figure 1.14. *Percentile plot of largest voting block in UK listed firms.*

Note: Annual reports for a sample of 250 randomly selected firms.

Source: Goergen and Renneboog, this volume.

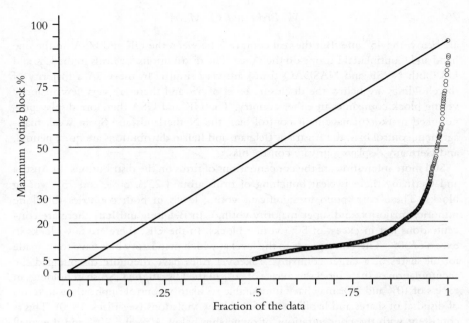

Figure 1.15. *Percentile plot of largest voting block for US companies listed on the NYSE.*

Source: Becht, this volume.

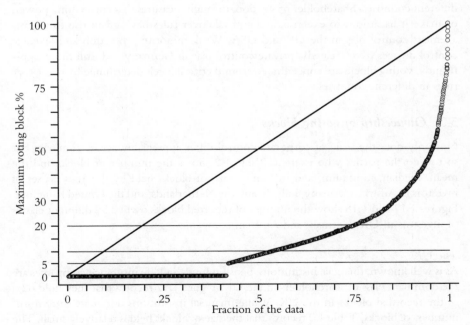

Figure 1.16. *Percentile plot of largest voting block for US companies listed on NASDAQ.*

Source: Becht, this volume.

are below the 45° line. But the real contrast is between the UK and USA on the one hand and Continental Europe on the other. The distributions for firms in the UK and US (both NYSE and NASDAQ firms) are very similar. In the USA a majority of shareholdings are below the disclosure level of 5% and there are very few majority voting block companies in either country. The UK and USA therefore display pronounced market/management control bias; the Netherlands and Spain weak management control bias; the Austrian, Belgian, and Italian distributions are quite neutral, and Germany displays a private control bias.

Still more interesting are the concentrations of firms on the distributions. In Austria and Germany there is clear bunching of firms around 25%, 50%, and 75% voting blocks. These correspond to significant voting levels in both countries (blocking minority, majority, and super-majority voting). In Belgium and Italy there are concentrations just in excess of 50% voting blocks. In the UK, there are few blocks in excess of 30%. This corresponds to the level at which mandatory bids have to be made for all shares of a target company. Takeover rules have therefore discouraged the accumulation of share blocks in excess of 30% in the UK. In the USA shareholdings in excess of 10% and 20% may have undesirable regulatory control implications in terms of disposal of shares and liabilities for federal law violations (see Black 1990). This is consistent with the concentrations of ownership below 10% and 20% and the small number of shareholdings in excess of 20% of companies on the NYSE.

The plots suggest that regulation has a significant influence on control patterns in different countries. Shareholder protection, through measures that curb voting power, or make it hazardous to exercise, and anti-takeover rules have given rise to a management control bias in the UK and USA. Weak minority protection and leverage control devices have created a private control bias in Germany and, still more significantly, voting blocks are concentrated around critical levels determined by regulatory rules in different countries.

5.3. *Ownership of voting blocks*

Not only does the scale of corporate control differ appreciably across countries but so too do the parties who exert it. Table 1.2 shows the number of blocks and the mean, median, minimum, and maximum size of blocks held by different classes of investors in Austria, Germany, Italy, Spain, the Netherlands, and the United Kingdom. Figures 1.17 and 1.18 show the number of reported blocks owned by different classes of investors in UK, German, and Austrian companies.

The UK
As is well known, financial institutions, pension funds and life insurance companies are the dominant class of shareholders in the UK. Figure 1.17 records that they hold 62% of the recorded blocks in the UK. While financial institutions dominate in terms of numbers of blocks, Table 1.2 records that the size of blocks held is relatively small. The median size of blocks held by insurance companies is 4.0% and by investment and pension funds is 7.0%.

Table 1.2. *Voting blocks by blockholder type*

Range	Austria[1]					Germany[2]					Spain[3]				
	No.	Min.	Mean	Med.	Max.	No.	Min.	Mean	Med.	Max.	No.	Min.	Mean	Med.	Max.
Government	9	24.0	53.1	51.0	81.6	18	8.2	45.3	40.7	99.0	37	5.7	46.8	49.0	95.2
Banks	11	6.4	42.0	41.9	100	77	5.1	23.8	15.0	99.0	48	5.0	21.2	13.6	91.5
Insurance						34	5.0	11.9	20.1	96.7	56	5.0	20.8	14.6	91.5
Families/Individ.	45	5.0	26.0	12.3	100	205	5.0	26.9	18.2	100	163	5.0	16.0	9.5	87.5
Domestic Firms	10	6.6	39.4	51.5	64.3	180	5.0	61.6	70.6	100	203	5.0	24.1	16.7	98.0
Foreign Firms	26	5.7	31.6	18.7	87.0						125	5.0	20.7	9.1	97.2
Assoc./pools						21	5.9	45.2	49.1	100					
Holding						53	6.9	52.9	50.3	100					
Investment Firm						36	5.5	25.1	40.0	99.0					
Bank rel.inv.firm						5	10.2	18.1	11.0	41.4					
Foundation						16	8.0	50.1	51.6	98.1					
Other						3	13.0	18.9	20.2	23.6					
All Blocks	101	5.0	33.1	22.7	100	648					632	5.0	20.7	12.3	98.0

Table 1.2. (Continued)

Range	Italy[4]					The Netherlands[5]					United Kingdom[6]				
	No.	Min.	Mean	Med.	Max.	No.	Min.	Mean	Med.	Max.	No.	Min.	Mean	Med.	Max.
Government	34	0	6.8	0	97.4	48	0.0	4.4	0.0	39.8	6		6.7		
Banks	156	0	9.5	0	95.6	34	0.0	8.3	0.0	93.0	71		5.1		
Insurance	13	0	1.1	0	93.9	36	0.0	8.9	0.0	97.1	226		4.0		
Families/Individ.	234	0	20.1	0	95.4						61		5.2		
Domestic Firms	160	0	20.3	2.0	100	22	0.0	1.4	0.0	27.0	102		10.6		
Foreign Firms	116	0	9.1	0	99.9										
Invest./Pen. Fund	57	0	0.8	0	8.9	6	0.0	0.4	0.0	19.0	474		7.0		
Exec. Directors											117		4.5		
Non-Exec. Direc.											184		5.0		
Real Estate											1		0.1		
Other Financ. Inst.	18	0	1.1	0	66.9	61	0.0	11.1	0.0	85.6					
State						4	0.0	1.1	0.0	50.0					
Admin. Office						54	0.0	26.9	0.0	100					
Total	788	0	68.4	71.5	100						1,242				

Sources: This volume: [1]Gugler, Kalss, Stomper, and Zechner, Table 2.7, data for 1996; [2]Becht and Böhmer, Table 5.5, data for 1996; [3]Crespí-Cladera and García-Cestona; [4]Bianchi, Bianco, Enriques, data for 1996; [5]de Jong, Kabir, Marra, and Röell, Table 7.7, data for 1996; [6]Goergen and Renneboog, data for 1992.

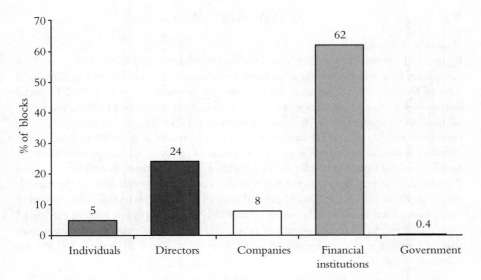

Figure 1.17. *Percentage of voting blocks associated with different types of investors in the UK.*

Note: Financial institutions, pension funds, and life insurance companies are the dominant class of shareholders in the UK. They hold 62% of the recorded blocks in the UK. Directors hold 24% of the blocks, companies 8%, and individuals 5%. For the raw counts, see Table 1.2.

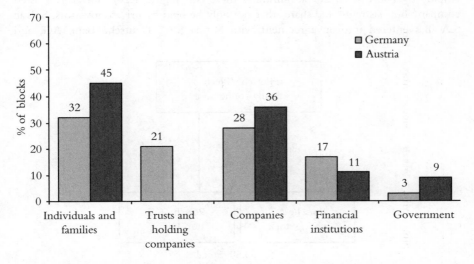

Figure 1.18. *Percentage of voting blocks associated with different types of investors in Germany and Austria.*

Note: In Germany and Austria, families and individuals and other companies dominate the blockholdings. In Germany, individuals and families hold 32% of blocks, other companies 28%, trusts and holding companies 21%, financial institutions 17%, and government 3%. In Austria, individuals and families hold 45% of blocks, companies 36%, financial institutions 11%, and government 9%. For the raw counts, see Table 1.2.

Austria and Germany

Figure 1.18 shows that, in Germany and Austria, families and individuals and other companies have the largest blockholdings. In Germany, individuals and families hold 32% of blocks, other companies 28%, trusts and holding companies 21%, financial institutions 17%, and government 3%. In Austria, individuals and families hold 45% of blocks, companies 36%, financial institutions 11%, and government 9%. The median size of block held by families is 26.9% in Germany and 26.0% in Austria. An example of family control in Germany is Porsche AG (Figure 1.19). Approximately 50 members of the Porsche/Piech family, who have signed a written voting pact, control Porsche AG. Jointly they control 100% of the voting rights with 10% of the capital. Although there is in general no requirement to disclose the ownership of non-voting stock under German law, it is estimated that the family also owns 10% of the issued non-voting stock. The median size of blocks held by companies is much larger than that of families in Germany (61.6%) and somewhat larger in Austria (39.4% for domestic firms).

Belgium

Foreign ownership is an important feature of Belgian corporate control, in particular from France and Luxembourg. Control is sometimes exerted via pyramid structures and, as in other Continental European countries, a range of anti-takeover devices are employed. The case of Solvac illustrates these (see Figure 1.20). Solvac is a listed company but has registered shares that can only be held by private investors. Solvac S.A. has entered into an agreement with Sofina S.A., Deutsche Bank AG, and

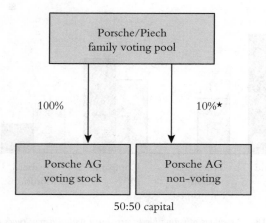

Figure 1.19. *Private control bias through non-voting stock: Porsche AG.*

Note: Porsche AG is controlled by approximately 50 members of the Porsche/Piech family who have signed a written voting pact. Jointly they control 100% of the voting rights with 50% of the capital. Although there is no requirement to disclose the ownership of non-voting stock under German law (except in special cases) it is estimated that the family also owns 10% of the issued non-voting stock.

Source: Hoppensted Aktienführer 1999.

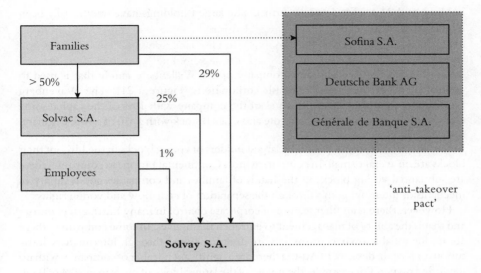

Figure 1.20. *Majority control and concentrated ownership: Solvay S.A.*

Note: Solvay S.A. has three known shareholder groups: the Boel, Solvay, and Janssen families (29%), Solvac S.A. (25%), and the company's employees (1%). Solvac S.A. is a holding company that has been formed to control Solvay S.A. Although Solvac is listed, it has issued registered shares that can only be held by private investors. Solvac's stock is illiquid and on 31 December 1998 it was estimated to trade, compared to the company's intrinsic value, at a discount of 28.6% (Banque Degroof 1999). Solvac introduces a small degree of pyramiding into this control structure. Through Solvac S.A., the families exert majority control. To protect the company further, for example against family disputes, Solvay has entered an anti-takeover pact with 'friends' (Sofina S.A., Deutsche Bank AG, and Générale de Banque S.A.). The Boel, Solvay, and Janssen families control Sofina S.A. (Banque Degroof 1999).

Générale de Banque S.A. to ward off any hostile takeover bids for Solvay S.A. Sofina S.A. is controlled by the Boel, Solvay, and Janssen families.

Italy
Table 1.2 records a dominant role for families and domestic firms in Italy. Pyramidal holdings are widespread and are primarily associated with holdings by families, coalitions of corporate shareholders, and the state. Financial institutions, including banks, have only played a limited role in the voting control of Italian companies.

The Netherlands
In the Netherlands, there are a substantial number of large blocks held by administration offices that are often controlled by the boards of the companies they control.

Spain
In Spain, families and firms are again the largest holders of share blocks. The average size of the blocks is similar to that of Italian companies (a median of 16.0% for family

holdings and 24.1% for domestic firms). The largest holdings have traditionally been associated with the state.

Sweden
Investor AB is the listed holding company of the Wallenberg family that is used to control many of the largest Swedish corporations (Figure 1.21). The Wallenberg Foundation controls 41% of the votes of the company with 19% of the capital using Class A stock with one-share-one-vote and Class B stock with 1/10 of a vote per share.

In sum, financial institutions are the largest holders of voting blocks in the UK but their blocks are on average small. In contrast, in most Continental European companies there are substantial voting blocks in the hands of families and companies and a variety of mechanisms intensifying this through the separation of cash-flow and voting rights.

However, there is another feature of corporate control in many European countries and that is the ability of management to entrench themselves. In some companies, there are no identifiable owners or owners are disenfranchised through intermediary institutions or lock-in devices. In Austria there are a significant number of companies with no identified owner. For example, the holder of the largest block of more than 40% of Bank Austria is an ownerless association, *Anteilsverwaltung Zentralsparkasse* (AVZ).

In the Netherlands, the largest blocks of shares are held by 'administrative offices'. These issue depository shares that give certificate holders the right to attend and speak at shareholders' meetings and to call for extraordinary meetings. But they have no votes; voting rights attached to shares can only be exercised by administrative offices. Often the boards appoint themselves (the so-called 'structural regime' that is compulsory for

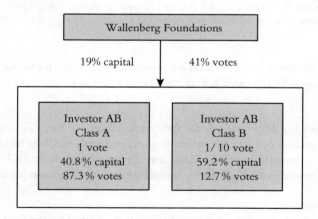

Figure 1.21. *Private control bias through dual-class stock: Investor AB.*

Note: Investor AB is the listed holding company of the Wallenberg family that is used to control many of the largest Swedish corporations (see Chapter 9). The Wallenberg Foundation controls 41% of the votes of the company with 19% of the capital using Class A stock with one-share-one-vote and Class B stock with 1/10 of a vote per share.

Source: *Annual Report 1999*, situation 31/12/1999.

Figure 1.22. *Private control bias through a trust office: ING Groep NV.*

Note: The Netherlands provides an instrument for achieving a complete separation between ownership of cash-flow rights and voting power, the Administratie Kantoor (or trust office). ING Groep NV has placed all its voting stock into such a trust office which, in turn, issues certificates that are traded on the stock exchange. The certificates represent all the cash-flow rights of the underlying shares but none of the voting rights. The trust office could be controlled by a family, but in the case of ING it is controlled by the (self-appointing) board of ING.

Source: Becht 1999.

companies with certain characteristics). ING Groep NV (Figure 1.22) has placed all its voting stock into such a trust office which, in turn, issues certificates that are traded on the stock exchange. The certificates represent all the cash-flow rights of the underlying shares but none of the voting rights. The trust office could be controlled by a family, but in the case of ING it is controlled by the (self-appointing) board of ING.

In Spain and France, voting right restrictions provide formidable protection from shareholder influence and control contests. Banco Bilbao Vizcaya Argentaria S.A. (Figure 1.23) illustrates how Spanish blue-chips employ voting right restrictions with staggered boards. A voting cap of 10% is combined with a two-year shareholder requirement; a potential director must have been a shareholder for two years before election to the board. A staggered board clause stipulates that a director can only become president or vice-president after serving on the board for three years. The president has substantial procedural power and is supported by a standing sub-committee (*Comision Delegada Permanente*), the members of which must have been on the board for at least three years and include the president and the vice-president. Taken together, this arrangement limits the potential power of outsiders and gives the incumbents procedural powers to prevent undesired changes.

An alternative protection device recorded in the Netherlands is to issue preferred shares to friendly investors. These shareholders have the right to make a binding nomination for the appointment of management. 'Potential capital' is a further device for preventing transfers of control. They are like poison pills except that issued capital goes to friendly investors, for example foundations, in the event of a hostile bid.

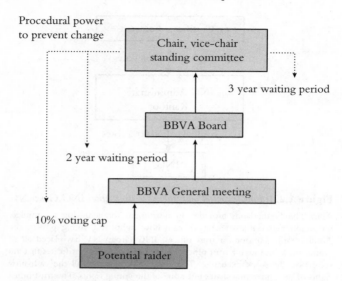

Figure 1.23. *Management control bias through voting-rights restriction and staggered board: BBVA.*

Note: Banco Bilbao Vizcaya Argentaria S.A. (BBVA; FTSE Global 500 rank no. 196, 24 April 2000) shows how Spanish blue-chips can combine voting right restrictions with staggered boards. The voting cap of 10% (Article 31 of company statutes in April 2000) is combined with a two-year shareholder requirement; a potential director must have been a shareholder for two years before election to the board (Article 35). The staggered board clause stipulates that a director can only become president or vice-president after serving 3 years on the board (Article 38). The president has substantial procedural power (Article 39) and is supported by a standing subcommittee (*Comision Delegada Permanente*). The members of this committee must have been on the board for at least three years, they must include the president and the vice-president and they nominate the executives with 2/3 of the votes of the board (Article 49). Taken together, the arrangement limits the potential power of outsiders and gives the incumbents ample procedural power to prevent undesired change.

Unilever illustrates this (Figure 1.24). Unilever comprises Unilever NV—the Dutch part—and Unilever Plc.—the UK part. They trade as a single entity. This is achieved through two holding companies NV Elma and United Holdings Limited which are held in turn by the Unilever companies and have cross-shareholdings in each other. They in turn hold special shares and deferred stock in Unilever NV and Plc. respectively. The significance of these special shares and deferred stock is that only they can nominate persons for elections as members of the Boards of Directors of NV and Plc. In other words, elections to the board of Unilever are by two companies fully owned by Unilever. This is said to be required to 'ensure unity of management of the Unilever Group' (Unilever's 20F declaration p. 33).

There are far fewer takeover defences available to companies in the UK, but Table 1.2 reports that there are a large number of share blocks held by both executive and non-executive directors. In the presence of highly dispersed shareholdings these share blocks may provide management with a significant degree of protection.

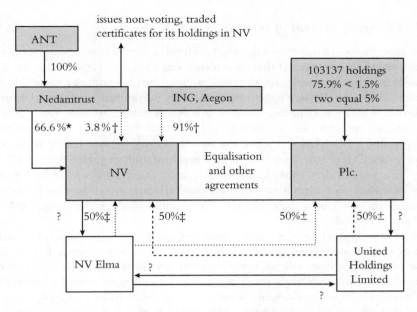

Figure 1.24. *Management control bias through legal devices: Unilever Plc./NV*

Note: Unilever Plc/NV has a complicated control structure. NV has locked control into Plc., and vice versa. In addition, NV leverages voting power through a trust company and uses preference shares to fend off unsolicited bids for control. *Cross-lock in*: NV has the sole right to nominate directors for election at Plc., and vice-versa. This is achieved through a cross-holding structure involving two holding companies, N.V. Elma and United Holdings Limited that hold 50% of special shares and deferred shares in NV and Plc. Since N.V. Elma is a subsidiary of NV and United Holdings Ltd of Plc., Elma cannot vote its special shares of NV and United Holdings cannot vote its deferred shares in Plc. (Unilever Form 20–F 1998, p. 33). Hence, the other shareholders of NV and Plc. can refuse to elect the directors Plc. and NV nominate, but they cannot nominate other directors for election. In addition, 'each of Unilever's ten directors is a full-time executive and is a director of both NV and Plc.' (*Unilever Annual Review 1998*, English version in guilders). *Voting power leverage*: NV has issued 3 classes of shares; special shares (‡), ordinary shares (★), and three types of cumulative preference shares (7%, 6%, 4%; †), representing 0.3%, 70.5% and 29.2% of par-value respectively. Nedamtrust holds 66.6% of the ordinary shares and 3.8% of the cumulative preference shares. For its 66.6% stake in the ordinary shares it has issued non-voting certificates that are traded on the stock market. Nedamtrust itself is owned and controlled by ANT. *Veto power of preference shareholders*: ING and Aegon hold approx. 91% of the cumulative preference shares. In the unlikely event that a bidder would acquire the ordinary shares of Plc. or NV, the bidder would be unable to break up the 'equalization and other agreements' that bind Plc. and NV without the consent of 2/3 of the preference shareholders.

There is therefore an alternative to the above conclusions of private control bias on the Continent and management control bias in the UK and USA. There is a high degree of management entrenchment in all countries, either through lock-in vehicles on the Continent or through anti-takeover mechanisms in the UK and USA. Market control or control by a blockholder who has the best interest of all shareholders in mind are rare.

5.4. *Changing patterns of control*

This paper provides a snapshot of the voting control of European companies at the end of the twentieth century. But there is evidence that these patterns are changing. The Agnelli group, for example, has disposed of companies operating in chemicals and cement. Banks are playing a larger role, particularly in companies in financial distress. Takeover legislation requiring mandatory bids when shareholdings reach 30% is encouraging concentrations of shareownership around this level, as has already been documented for the UK. In Spain, the significance of the state has declined with privatizations. Some state control has been maintained through golden shares but these have not been widely applied. In Sweden, cross-shareholdings have largely disappeared. Dual-class shares have been eliminated in many firms. There has been more intervention by minority shareholders in, for example, blocking the merger between Volvo and Renault.

With the dismantling of mechanisms for separating cash flow from voting rights comes a move away from private control biases and neutral control. It is unclear how far these processes will go. It is even more unclear whether they will give rise to market control with freely operating markets in corporate control or simply tilt Continental Europe to a management control bias with US-style managerial entrenchment through anti-takeover devices. The evidence of a free market in corporate control emerging in Continental Europe is limited to date. There is much antipathy towards markets in corporate control both on social grounds and for the short-termist reasons discussed above in relation to 'influence' and investment 'realization' periods. If control leverage devices are extinguished and voting control as well as cash-flow rights become more widely dispersed, we may well see the emergence of more managerial lock-in mechanisms to take their place. It may, for example, be no coincidence that voting caps are reported to be on the rise in France.[14]

6. CONCLUSIONS

Section 2 described three conflicting views of the influence of regulation on ownership and control of corporations. According to Roe (1994), dispersed ownership and control in the USA result from a populist agenda of imposing regulatory impediments on concentration of control in the hands of a small number of investors. According to La Porta *et al.* (1999), the dominance of large shareholder blocks in most countries of the world is a reflection of inadequate investor protection. According to Easterbrook and Fischel (1991) regulation reflects the needs of managers and investors. Roe's thesis implies that corporate governance deficiencies result from over-regulation, that of La Porta *et al.* (1999) implies that improved corporate governance will come from more regulation, while Easterbrook and Fischel suggest that Europe and the United States have the regulation and corporate governance systems that are best suited to their activities.

What emerges from this paper is a remarkable contrast with the traditional, Anglo-American view of the corporation. Concentration of voting control is strikingly higher in Continental European companies than in their UK or US counterparts. Control is concentrated not only because of the presence of large investors or core investor groups, but also because of the absence of significant holdings by others. In contrast, in the UK and USA, not only are there few large shareholders but also the second, third, and smaller shareholdings are not appreciably smaller than the largest. This gives rise to the possibility of effective control through coalitions but not by individual shareholders. However, since a typical block in the UK is twice as large as in the United States (10% versus 5%), the potential for coalition control is larger in the UK than in the United States.

Still more striking than differences in average sizes of shareblocks is the complete distribution of the largest shareholdings. In most Continental European countries, there is a fairly uniform distribution of the largest voting blocks. In contrast, in the UK and USA there is a strong 'market/management bias' towards dispersed control. However, it would be wrong merely to contrast Continental European with Anglo-American control. There is a marked variation within Europe, ranging from a 'private control bias' in Germany to a modest management-control bias of the Anglo-American variety in the Netherlands and Spain. Indeed, the largest Spanish companies already combine complete protection of management from takeovers with a very broad shareholder base, just like many of their US counterparts. Still more interesting is the concentration of voting blocks around certain critical levels—blocking minority and super-majority holdings in Austria and Germany and majority control in several other countries. Regulation has affected the entire pattern and distribution of corporate control in all countries. As a general proposition, we believe that control is concentrated in forms in which regulation confers particular advantages: shareblocks are concentrated at levels at which there are significant control benefits.

We suggested in section 2 that this may be important in terms of the relation between the control and activities of firms. In principle, market control efficiently reallocates control to those who derive the greatest benefit from exerting it. However, it also limits the period for which anyone can expect to be able to retain control ('influence periods'). Market control therefore efficiently reallocates control of projects with short 'realization periods' but may discourage the implementation of projects with long realization periods. According to this view, the relevance of corporate control for real activities is a reflection of the relation of influence to realization periods. Different types of corporate control and therefore regulatory arrangements are suited to different forms of corporate activities: industries whose investments have short realization periods thrive in systems with market control whereas those with long realization periods benefit from management control.

One of the troublesome, or puzzling, implications of our analysis is the fragility of market control. Even in countries where voting power and ownership are dispersed, management control is often not contestable. Devices such as poison pills, anti-takeover charter provisions, options for issuing voting stock to friendly parties, and voting caps can be used to limit the control that external investors can exert. Voting power dispersion overestimates the importance of external control in countries, such as the UK and USA, which may have a management- not a market-control bias. The primary distinction is not then between market and private control but between management and private control. Do projects with short realization periods not find enough financing or is market control rare because such projects are rare?

Even in countries with dominant shareholders, we have observed a variety of mechanisms that management can employ to protect itself from external investor interference. If, as a consequence, corporations are run by managers who are able to shield themselves from external influence by investors then control by owners will be largely irrelevant. The Berle and Means view of strong managers/weak owners may therefore be applicable even in the presence of dominant blockholders and the formal distinction between patterns of corporate control may be of little relevance in the face of a class of largely unaccountable management. Whether this alternative description is correct is yet to be established but regardless of whether it is, this paper serves as a reminder of the multifarious nature of capitalism within, let alone outside, Europe.

Appendix. Comparison with other comparative methods

The method applied in this paper relies on the availability of voting control data that is disclosed in accordance with the Williams Act in the United States (Schedule 13D), the Large Holdings Directive (88/627/EEC) or comparable securities regulation standards. Although such standards are becoming more widespread, they are not applied universally, not even in the OECD. For example, Bøhren and Ødegaard (2000) report that in Norway only direct stakes are disclosed, not the ultimate voting blocks we rely on in this book.

In the absence of voting block disclosure one has to resort to the traditional direct stake methods applied by Berle and Means (1932), the TNEC (1940), and Larner (1966). The same is true for the identification of ultimate 'owners' (blockholders). They must be traced starting from the listed company through chains of direct stakes, often confined to chains of listed companies. A recent comparative study of this type is La Porta et al. (1999). In this appendix we illustrate the difference between the methods.

La Porta et al. (1999) examine whether firms have substantial owners. They use the *Worldscope* database to identify the 20 largest and 20 medium-sized companies in each country they cover and classify them into discrete 'ownership' categories, tracing 'ultimate ownership' through 10% (20%) control chains of listed companies. They define a corporation as having a controlling shareholder (ultimate owner) if the shareholder's direct and indirect voting rights in the firm exceed 20%. In addition, they record deviations of voting from cash-flow rights by determining the minimum percentage of capital that a shareholder requires to control 20% of the voting rights. Claessens et al. (2000) apply the same methodology to much wider cross-sections of Asian countries.

The key difference between La Porta et al. (1999) and this study is that La Porta et al. do not attempt to measure voting power concentration, 'because a theoretically appropriate measure requires a model of the interaction between large shareholders, which we do not have' (p. 476). They do not therefore attempt to establish concentration of power. We use the Large Holdings Directive to record reported voting blocks. We illustrate the differences between our approach and that of La Porta et al. (1999) using some of the examples provided in their paper which are covered in this book as well.

The simplest cases are companies that have a flat control structure. The first such case La Porta et al. (1999: 481) consider is Microsoft. In Sept. 1996, the year they analyse, Microsoft had three principal shareholders: Bill Gates (23.7%), Paul Allen (9%), and Steven Ballmer (5%). According to the Microsoft Proxy Statement (Form 14A) filed on 27 Sept. 1996, these individuals declared that the disclosed beneficial ownership 'represents sole voting and investment power' (the sole power to vote or dispose of shares that they would not necessarily have to own). This means that, formally, Messrs Gates, Allen, and Ballmer declare that they do not have a firm commitment to vote these shares in an agreed way. Mr and Mrs Gates might be thought to have such an agreement. However, Mr Gates (in a footnote to the relevant table) disclaims beneficial ownership of the 27,280 shares owned by his wife (meaning that Mr Gates declares that Mrs Gates is free to vote her shares against her husband and/or to dispose of them at her own will). Indeed, the 22 Directors and Officers of Microsoft as a group (joint voting and investment power of 38.7%) disclose their stakes individually, i.e. declare that they have no formal agreement to vote or dispose of their shares jointly.

La Porta *et al.* (1999: 481) classify Microsoft as a family-owned firm that is not controlled through a pyramid, does not have cross-ownership and where it takes 20% of the cash-flow rights to obtain 20% of the voting rights. Becht (1999), in this book, notes that Microsoft has three 5%+ *voting blocks*, that the blockholders are called Gates, Allen, and Ballmer, that the largest block is 23.7%, the second largest block 9%, the third largest block 5% and that there are no other 5%+ blocks. The question whether Bill Gates, or Mr Gates, Allen, and Ballmer, individually or jointly, have control of Microsoft is not addressed.

To illustrate further methodological differences for companies with flat control structures, consider the case of SAP AG, the German software company.[15] Like Microsoft, SAP has a relatively flat control structure, i.e. there is hardly any pyramiding and no cross-ownership. According to Hoppenstedt (1997), the German data source of La Porta *et al.* (1999), in 1996 SAP AG had seven 'principal shareholders': Hasso Plattner (21.06%), the Tschira Family (7.45%), the Klaus Tschira Foundation (11.56%), the Dietmar Kopp Family (10.29%), the Dietmar Kopp Foundation GmbH (15.31%), the Eugenia Trust, St. Helier, Jersey (5.8%), and the Hector Family (4.43%). La Porta *et al.* (1999) would attribute control to Hasso Plattner, both on their 10% and 20% criterion, and classify the company as family-controlled. Furthermore, since SAP has only issued DM304,930,750 of its DM506,163,400 capital as voting stock, they would conclude that only 12.1% of capital is required to acquire 20% of the voting rights (i.e. their variable v = 20% would be set equal to 12.1%).

We take a different approach, in line with the way in which these data are notified. In the case of SAP, the founders have signed a voting pact (*Konsortialvertrag*). Like La Porta *et al.* (1999), we do not have a 'model of the interaction between large shareholders'. But we do know that the founders of SAP AG cast their votes together because they have to notify them jointly. We note that the SAP voting pool commands a voting block of 62.5% and compute concentration statistics over these blocks.

Electrabel, the Belgian electricity holding, is 'possibly the most complex example' provided by La Porta *et al.* (1999). There are two 10% control chains, one leading to Suez Cie (via Powerfin, Tractebel, Genfina, and Générale de Belgique), the other to the Frére-Desmarais discussed in the Belgian chapter of this book (via Powerfin, Tractebel, Electrafina, GBL, Pargesa, and other companies not reported in La Porta *et al.*). Suez is classified as the ultimate owner because it controls 27.5% + 8.02% of the votes in Tractebel, while Frère-Desmarais only control 19.97% (La Porta *et al.* 1999: 490).

Using our methodology, Electrabel has one 47.8% voting block that results from a voting pact (BBL 1996: 30). These (ultimate) voting blocks and the identity of the blockholders are analysed in this chapter. The Belgian country chapter goes further. The voting block is decomposed into three smaller blocks: Cofibel (2.28%), Fortis AG Group (2.28%), and Suez (44.42%). These intermediate blocks are decomposed, again, into smaller direct stakes. The Fortis AG block consists of 7 direct stakes, the Suez group block consists of 17 direct stakes.

We do not assign 'control' as a discrete variable but report the blockholder's identity and absolute voting power. The SEC's suspects that undertakings with a 10%+ beneficial owner (voting block) are controlled and is almost sure that 20%+ beneficial owners exert control (Black 1990). La Porta *et al.* (1999) follow this American convention in their comparative study and consider a shareholder with a direct stake of 10% (20%) to exert control. We report the distribution of blocks and enable the reader to infer the proportion of 'widely held' companies at the cutoff point that is most appropriate or interesting in the context of the total distribution of blocks or the corporate governance system under study.

Our methodology has another advantage when compared to La Porta *et al.* (1999). In the European Union and in the United States it is not possible to trace complete group structures, especially when non-listed or offshore companies are involved. However, under the Large Holdings Directive and Section 13 in the United States, those in command of voting blocks have to reveal their identity and reveal the total number of votes they can cast. All votes they can cast at will have to be notified, even when the blockholder does not own them (directly or indirectly). Hence, from the control perspective, it is not necessary (or possible) to trace the ownership chain between the company and the blockholders. Furthermore, tracing control chains in hierarchical groups through ownership links overlooks the other legal devices block-holders can use to acquire voting power without ownership.

Our methodology has the disadvantage that we cannot compute the ultimate cash-flow rights of the blockholders, which are not disclosed under the Large Holdings Directive or Section 13 in the United States. *Moodys International*, the data La Porta *et al.* (1999) draw on for their 'Cap = 20% control leverage' variable, cannot do so either, not even in the case of completely 'flat' control structures. However, this is not what *Moodys* computed. They report the per-centage of cash-flow rights that are, theoretically, required to purchase 20% of the control rights (if they were for sale). For example, SAP AG has issued almost 50% of its par value as non-voting stock. We do not know how many of the non-voting shares are owned by the members of the SAP voting pool. Hence, we cannot compute the cash-flow rights associated with their 62.5% voting block (and direct voting stakes). However, since the capital structure is disclosed *Moodys* could calculate that it would only take 12.1% of the cash-flow rights to purchase 20% of the control rights of SAP AG.

In European hierarchical groups, in general, we can neither measure actual nor theoretical cash-flow rights to voting-rights ratios. La Porta *et al.* (1999: 478) avoid this problem by con-sidering a company to be controlled through a pyramid if at least one company in the 10% (20%) control chain is a listed company. Since 10%+ direct voting power stakes of listed companies are disclosed, it is possible to compute the cash-flow to voting-rights ratio. However, these are usually more complex holdings than pyramids in which deviations of one share from one vote are much harder to determine, even on a theoretical basis.

NOTES

1. Of course, this idea was not new and already well articulated before, and the empirical evidence they gathered of limited quality; see Zeitlin (1974), Stigler and Friedland (1983), and Leech (1987).
2. See Mason (1959) for a representative selection of these different views.

3. It is unclear whether the La Porta *et al.* (1999) study refers to the largest 20 companies in each of their countries or the largest 20 companies in *Worldscope*, which is their main data source. Since *Worldscope* coverage is far from comprehensive, the 20 companies do not necessarily correspond with the largest 20 in any one country.

4. In the political theory of Roe (1991) US managers influence regulation to obtain or protect rents.

5. Goergen (1998), table 5.2.

6. See Kaplan and Stromberg (2000) for a detailed analysis of the evolution of ownership, debt and control in the portfolio companies of US venture capitalists, pre- and post-IPO.

7. Hence, the 'one-man-one-vote' arrangement is also referred to as 'corporate suffrage' (Dunlavy 1998: 11).

8. Dunlavy (1998: 7) cites several commentators from *Imperial* Germany who, at the beginning of the century, were appalled by the concentration of economic power in the United States, and who asserted that German corporate control was more 'democratic' than corporate control in the United States; for example Liefmann (1918: 173, 197).

9. The emphasis on the 'one-share-one-vote' might stem from the policy debate surrounding the SEC's unsuccessful attempt to impose the concept on US domestic issuers by adopting its 1988 Rule 19c-4 'Governing Certain Listing or Authorization Determinations by National Securities Exchanges and Associations'. Section (a) provided that 'The rules of each exchange shall provide as follows : No rule, stated policy, practice, or interpretation of this exchange shall permit the listing, or the continuance of the listing, of any common stock or other equity security of a domestic issuer, if the issuer of such security issues any class of security, or takes other corporate action, with the effect of nullifying, restricting or disparately reducing the per share voting rights of holders on an outstanding class or classes of common stock of such issuer registered pursuant to Section 12 of the Act.'

At the instigation of the Business Roundtable, a Federal Court struck down the Rule in 1990. It asserted that the SEC did not have the mandate to pass a rule on 'one-share-one-vote', even though the rule only affected listing requirements; instead, it was regarded as the domain of state corporate law (*The Business Roundtable* v. *SEC*, 905 F.2d 406 (D.C. Cir. 1990).

In Europe, the draft Fifth Directive of the European Union also tried to impose 'one-share-one-vote', but this time through company law. Article 33 (1) provided that 'The shareholders right to vote shall be proportionate to the fraction of the subscribed capital which the shares represent'. However, Article 33 (2) allowed for 'restriction or exclusion of the right to vote in respect to shares which carry special pecuniary advantages', but only up to 50% of the subscribed capital. Also, the full voting rights had to be granted if the pecuniary advantages were not realized. See, 'Amended proposal for a Fifth Council Directive based on Article 54 of the EEC Treaty concerning the structure of public limited companies and the powers and obligations of their organs, as amended by the Second and Third Amendment, OJ (1991) C7, p. 5 and OJ (1991) C321 p. 9'. The Directive was never adopted and has been shelved.

Currently, the pressure on companies to comply with 'one-share-one-vote' is growing again. The OECD's Principles of Corporate Governance shied away from a call for 'one common share, one vote' but the International Corporate Governance Network's (ICGN) Principles did not. ICGN, under the influence of institutional investors and the proxy voting industry, 'affirms that divergence from a 'one-share-one-vote' standard ... is undesirable' (ICGN 1999: 7).

10. Prior to the transposition of the Directive and this research, very little was known about the concentration of voting power in Europe. Researchers had to rely on national disclosure provisions and it was not always clear whether voting–rights or cash–flow rights were observed and reported. At the beginning of this research, the most comprehensive comparative blockholding statistics available were those of Brodin and Lie (1995). Their study was conducted on behalf of the Federation of European Stock Exchanges (FESE) but their results were uneven and, as in many other studies, there was considerable confusion between the ownership of cash–flow and voting rights. Berglöf (1997) sought to compile a comparative table with European ownership statistics and voting power statistics. He was unable to do this and instead had to rely on figures in the working paper version of La Porta *et al.* (1998) and in his previous paper, Berglöf (1988). Berglöf's (1988) study relies on older studies for France, the United States, Japan, the United Kingdom, Sweden, and Germany. The OECD was unable to do much better when it drafted the background for a conference on 'The Influence of Corporate Governance and Financial Structure on Economic Performance' that was held in Paris in February 1995. Moerland (1995) cites Charkham (1994: 105) who reports ownership statistics taken from flow of funds accounts. Barca *et al.* (1994) tried to find descriptive blockholding statistics that they could compare with their detailed Italian results. They used the figures cited in Berglöf (1988) and others. Franks and Mayer (1995) compiled their own ownership figures for listed companies in Germany, France, and the UK.
11. Disclosure by 5%+ blockholders is made on Form 13D. For the United States, this reports 5%+ blocks that were disclosed through the SEC's Schedule 14A, the proxy statement.
12. The Directive is also referred to as the 'Transparency Directive' or 'Anti-Raider Directive'.
13. The Directive's Article 8 provides its own definition of control. An undertaking is 'controlled' when a shareholder (or group of shareholders) commands more than 50% of the voting power or has the ability to appoint a majority of the board members.
14. *Financial Times*, 27 Apr. 2000, '*French Groups Curb Voter Rights*', by Samer Iskandar and Simon Targett.
15. This example is not reported in La Porta *et al.* (1999), but they use Hoppenstedt as their principal source of German data.

REFERENCES

Aoki, M. (1990), 'Toward an Economic Model of the Japanese Firm', *Journal of Economic Literature*, 28/1: 1–27.

Axe, L. H. (1942), 'Corporate Proxies', *Michigan Law Review*, 41: 38–65.

Barca, F., M. Bianchi, F. Brioschi, L. Buzzacchi, P. Casavola, L. Filippa, and M. Paganini (1994), *I Modelli di Controllo e La Concentrazione Proprietaria Messi a Confronto Empiricamente*, ii. *Assetti, Proprietàe Controllo Nelle Imprese Italiane Medio-Grandi*, Bologna: Il Mulino.

BBL (1996), 'Actionnariat des Sociétés Belges Cotées à Bruxelles', *Equity Research* (June), Brussels: Banque Bruxelles Lambert.

Bebchuk, L. (1999), 'A Rent-Protection Theory of Corporate Ownership and Control', Cambridge, Mass: NBER Working Paper 7203.

—— and M. Roe (1999), 'A Theory of Path Dependence in Corporate Ownership and Governance', *Stanford Law Review*, 52/1: 127–70.

Becht, M. (1999), 'European Corporate Governance: Trading-Off Liquidity Against Control', *European Economic Review*, 43: 1071–83.

Berglöf, E. (1988), 'Capital Structure as a Mechanism of Corporate Control: A Comparison of Financial Systems', in M. Aoki, G. Bo, and O. Williamson (eds.), *The Firm as a Nexus of Treaties*, London: European Sage.

—— (1997), 'Reforming Corporate Governance: Redirecting the European Agenda', *Economic Policy* (April): 93–123.

Berle, A. A. (1958), ' "Control" in Corporate Law', *Columbia Law Review*, 58: 1212–25.

—— and G. C. Means (1932), *The Modern Corporation and Private Property*. New Brunswick and London: Transaction Publishers (1991 repr., New York: MacMillan Company).

Black, B. S. (1990), 'Shareholder Passivity Reexamined', *Michigan Law Review*, 89: 520.

—— (1998), Shareholder Activism, in P. Newman (ed.), *The New Palgrave Dictionary of Economics and the Law* (3 vols.), New York: Stockton Press; London: Macmillan Reference.

Bøhren, Ø. and A. Ødegaard (2000), 'The Ownership Structure of Norwegian Firms: Characteristics of an Outlier', Norwegian School of Management, Oslo, mimeo.

Brodin, A. P. and A. E. Lie (1995), *Share Ownership Structure in Europe*, Oslo: Federation of European Stock Exchanges and Oslo Stock Exchange.

Burrough, B. and J. Helyar (1990), *Barbarians At the Gate: The Fall of RJR Nabisco*, New York: Harper & Row.

Carlin, W. and C. Mayer (2000*a*), 'Finance, Investment and Growth', mimeo, University of Oxford.

—— —— (2000*b*), 'How Do Financial Systems Affect Economic Performance?', in X. Vives (ed.), *Corporate Governance: Theoretical and Empirical Perspectives*, Cambridge: Cambridge University Press.

Charkham, J. (1994), *Keeping Good Company: A Study of Corporate Governance in Five Countries*, Oxford: Clarendon Press.

Claessens, Stijn, Simeon Djankov, and Larry-H. P. Lang (2000), 'The Separation of Ownership and Control in East Asian Corporations', *Journal of Financial Economics*, 58/1–2: 81–112.

Corbett, J. and T. Jenkinson (1996), 'The Financing of Industry, 1970–1989: An International Comparison', *Journal of the Japanese and International Economies* 10/1: 71–96.

Danielson, M. G. and J. M. Karpoff (1998), 'On the Use of Takeover Provisions', *Journal of Corporate Finance: Contracting, Governance and Organization*, 4/4: 347–71.

Dunlavy, C. A. (1998), 'Corporate Governance in Late 19th-Century Europe and the US: The Case of Shareholder Voting Rights', in K. J. Hopt *et al.* (eds.), *Comparative Corporate Governance: The State of the Art and Emerging Research*, Oxford: Clarendon Press.

Easterbrook, F. H. (1997), 'International Corporate Differences: Market or Law?', *Journal of Applied Corporate Finance*, 9/4: 23–9.

—— and D. R. Fischel (1991), *The Economic Structure of Corporate Law*, Cambridge, Mass.: Harvard University Press.

Edwards, J. and K. Fischer (1994), *Banks, Finance and Investment in Germany*, Cambridge: Cambridge University Press.

Franks, J. and C. Mayer (1995), 'Ownership and Control', in H. Siebert (ed.), *Trends in Business Organization: Do Participation and Cooperation Increase Competitiveness?*, Tübingen: Mohr (Siebeck).

Goergen, M. (1998), *Corporate Governance and Financial Performance: A Study of German and UK Initial Offerings*, Cheltenham: Edward Elgar.

Grossman, S. and O. Hart (1980), 'Takeover Bids, the Free-Rider Problem and the Theory of the Corporation', *Bell Journal of Economics*, 11/1: 42–64.

Hellwig, M. (2000), 'On the Economics and Politics of Corporate Finance and Control', in X. Vives (ed.), *Corporate Governance*.

Hilferding, R. (1910), *Finance Capital: A Study of the Latest Phase of Capitalist Development*, London: Routledge & Kegan Paul. (1981 rep., ed. T. B. Bottomore).

Hoppenstedt (1997, 1999), *Hoppenstedt Aktienführer*, Darmstadt: Hoppenstedt Verlag.

Hoshi, T., A. Kashyap, and D. Scharfstein (1991), 'Corporate Structure, Liquidity, and Investment: Evidence from Japanese Industrial Groups', *Quarterly Journal of Economics*, 106/1: 33–60.

Hübner, O. (1854), *Die Banken*, Leipzig: Heinrich Hübner.

International Corporate Governanec Network (ICGN) (1999), 'Statement on Global Corporate Governance Principles' (www.icgn.org).

Jensen, M. C. (1989), 'The Eclipse of the Public Corporation', *Harvard Business Review*, 67: 61–74.

—— and W. H. Meckling (1976), 'Theory of the Firm: Managerial Behavior, Agency Costs and Ownership Structure', *Journal of Financial Economics*, 3/4: 305–60.

Kang, J.-K. and R. Stulz (1997), 'Is Bank-Centred Corporate Governance Worth It? A Cross-Sectional Analysis of the Performance of Japanese Firms During the Asset Price Deflation', mimeo.

Kaplan, S. N. and B. A. Minton (1994), 'Appointments of Outsiders to Japanese Boards: Determinants and Implications for Managers', *Journal of Financial Economics*, 36/2: 225–58.

—— and P. Stromberg (2000), 'Financial Contracting Theory Meets the Real World: An Empirical Analysis of Venture Capital Contracts', Cambridge, Mass.: National Bureau of Economic Research, Working paper.

La Porta, R., F. Lopez de Silanes, and A. Shleifer (1999), 'Corporate Ownership Around the World', *Journal of Finance*, 54/2: 471–517.

—— —— —— and R. W. Vishny (1997), 'Legal Determinants of External Finance', *Journal of Finance*, 52: 1131–50.

—— —— —— —— (2000), 'Investor Protection and Corporate Governance', *Journal of Financial Economics*, 58: 3–27.

Larner, R. J. (1966), 'Ownership and Control in the 200 Largest Non-Financial Corporations', 1929–1963, *American Economic Review*, 16/4: 781–2.

Leech, D. (1987), 'Corporate Ownership and Control: A New Look at the Evidence of Berle and Means', *Oxford Economic Papers*, 39/3: 534–51.

Lewis, M. (1990), *Liar's Poker: Rising Through the Wreckage on Wall Street*, New York: Penguin Books.

Liefmann, R. (1918), *Kartelle und Trusts und die Weiterbildung der volkswirtschaftlichen Organisation*, 3rd edn., Stuttgart: Verlag von Ernst Heinrich Moritz.

Manne, H. (1965), 'Mergers and the Market for Corporate Control', *Journal of Political Economy*: 110–20.

Mason, E. S. (ed.) (1959), *The Corporation in Modern Society*, Cambridge Mass.: Harvard University Press.

Mayer, C. (1988), 'New Issues in Corporate Finance', *European Economic Review*, 32/5: 1167–83.

—— (2000), 'Ownership Matters', Brussels, Inaugural Lecture.

Moerland, P. W. (1995), 'Corporate Ownership and Control Structures: An International Comparison', *Review of Industrial Organization*, 10: 443–64.

OECD Ad-hoc Task Force on Corporate Governance (1999), *OECD Principles of Corporate Governance*, Paris: OECD.

Ogger, G. (1991), *Nieten in Nadelstreifen*, Munich: Droehmer Knaur.

Prowse, S. (1992), 'The Structure of Corporate Ownership in Japan', *Journal of Finance*, 47/3: 1121–40.

Roe, M. (1991), 'A Political Theory of American Corporate Finance', *Columbia Law Review*, 91/10.

—— (1994), *Strong Managers, Weak Owners: The Political Roots of American Corporate Finance*, Princeton: Princeton University Press.

Temporary National Economic Committee (TNEC) (1940), *The Distribution of Ownership in the 200 Largest Nonfinancial Corporations* (Prepared under the auspices of the Securities and Exchange Commission, Monograph no. 29), Washington: Government Printing Office.

Stigler G. J. and C. Friedland (1983), The Literature of Economics : The Case of Berle and Means, *Journal of Law and Economics*, 26/2 (June), 237–68.

Weinstein, D. E. and Y. Yafeh (1998), 'On the Costs of a Bank-Centered Financial System: Evidence from the Changing Main Bank Relations in Japan', *Journal of Finance*, 53/2: 635–72.

Wymeersch, E. (2000), 'Do We Need a Law on Groups of Companies?', Paper presented at the Conference on Company Law and Capital Markets, Sienna, 30–31 Mar. 2000.

Zeitlin, M. (1974), 'Corporate Ownership and Control: The Large Corporation and the Capitalist Class', *American Journal of Sociology*, 79/5: 1073–119.

2

The Separation of Ownership and Control in Austria

KLAUS GUGLER, SUSANNE KALSS, ALEX STOMPER,
AND JOSEF ZECHNER

1. INTRODUCTION

Until now the structure of Austrian corporate governance has remained largely unexplored. This is due partly to the complex structure of the system and partly to the lack of readily available data. This is thus a first step towards the systematic analysis of corporate governance in Austria.

For a sample of listed non-financial corporations, we compare the structure of ownership to the voting-power structure and analyse the separation of ownership and control. Our data on voting blocks stem from public disclosures under the Austrian Stock Exchange Act corresponding to the transparency directive, EU 88/627.

On the European scene, Austria appears to be the country with the highest concentration of ownership. The average stake of the largest shareholder in our sample of 62 listed firms is greater than 50%! Corresponding to ownership, we find a high concentration of voting power. In two-thirds of the cases, the largest blockholder exerts majority control. Where there is majority control, there are usually no other substantial voting blocks. Where no single blockholder can exert majority control, however, there are typically several significant minority blocks. In short, the analysis of Austrian corporate governance must be concerned with conflicts of interest between majority and minority owners additionally to the problem of monitoring the management in companies with dispersed ownership. Minority voting blocks exist only if the holders of such blocks can accumulate enough voting power to restrict other blockholders' ability to expropriate them.

The sharper the separation of ownership and control, the greater the potential for such conflicts of interest. For the firms in our sample, we find that the separation of ownership and control reflects the nature of the largest blockholder. The ratio of the largest shareholder's voting rights to cash-flow rights averages 41% higher when the blockholder is a family than when it is a foreign firm. This reflects the fact that family ownership typically takes the form of pyramiding while the holdings of foreign firms and banks are usually direct. Nevertheless, the ratio of voting rights to cash-flow rights is 58% higher, on average, when the largest blockholder is a bank. In contrast to families, banks use 'separation devices' other than pyramiding, such as non-voting stock and voting pacts.

We analyse how different 'separation devices' affect the ratio of voting rights to cash-flow rights held by the largest blockholder. When a firm is controlled via a pyramid, then an extra 'layer' increases this ratio by about 20%. The issuance of non-voting stock raises it by as much as 37%.

The chapter is structured as follows. Section 2 sets the stage for our empirical analysis and describes the data. Sections 3, 4, and 5 analyse, respectively, the ownership structure, the voting structure and the separation of ownership and control of the firms in our sample. Section 6 concludes.

2. THE SEPARATION OF OWNERSHIP AND CONTROL: SETTING THE STAGE

2.1. *Separation devices*

According to the Austrian Stock Corporation Act, every shareholder is entitled to attend the general meeting irrespective of the type of shares he/she holds. In general, each share of common stock has one vote. Strictly forbidden are multiple voting rights. However, the articles of incorporation may set a maximum number of votes per stockholder. Other ways of deviating from 'one-share-one-vote' are as follows:

- *Non-voting stock*: It is possible to issue non-voting preference shares up to half the overall nominal value of ordinary shares (i.e. one-third of total equity). Holders of preference shares are entitled to annual (preferential) dividend payments. If these annual dividends are not paid for two successive years, the preference shares take on voting rights until the claims of their holders are met.
- *Proxies*: In practice, many minority shareholders do not attend the general meeting but are represented by depository banks. To exercise their depository votes, these banks need a specific written authorization by the shareholder. The authorization can be revoked at any time and expires automatically after 15 months.
- *Voting pacts*: Voting pacts are a common instrument used by shareholders to establish a common voting policy at the general meeting. There are no special legal provisions on these pacts. In general, if a shareholder reneges on a voting pact this infringement does not affect the validity of the resolution passed.
- *'Ownerless' legal forms*: In the Austrian banking sector, there exist 'ownerless' legal forms, in the sense that there are legal entities without clearly defined residual owners. As a consequence, control is not in the hands of any owner, in other words there is complete separation of ownership and control. Detailed information on these legal forms is given in the appendix. The following example illustrates why they can be regarded as a 'separation device'.

The holder of the largest block of more than 40% of the voting rights of Bank Austria, the country's largest bank, is an ownerless association, Anteilsverwaltung Zentralsparkasse (AVZ). Bank Austria in turn holds more than 98% of the equity in the number two bank, Creditanstalt.

Together the two banks have sizeable equity stakes in many non-financial corporations. In the case of Lenzing AG 50.1% of the votes are controlled by Bank Austria, hence, by AVZ. The remaining 49.9% are dispersed. However, since AVZ is an ownerless legal form, there is complete separation between ultimate ownership and control.

This example is quite typical; a large portion of the Austrian banking sector, in fact, is effectively ownerless, and banks tend to hold significant equity stakes in other Austrian firms.

2.2. *The data*

The analysis of ownership structures (i.e. cash-flow rights) is based on data provided by the *Wirtschafts-Trend-Zeitschriftenverlagsgesellschaft m.b.H* for the year 1996. In assembling this data set, the *Wirtschafts-Trend-Zeitschriftenverlag* used information collected by a credit-rating agency, the *Österreichischer Kreditschutzverband von 1870*, as well as information supplied by the corporations themselves. The data set is publicly available on the trend TOP 500 CD-ROM and includes information on ownership structures, pyramids, and key accounting data. In addition, the Vienna Stock Exchange provided us with historical data for 1996 summarizing information on ultimate voting blocks that was publicly disclosed pursuant to the transparency directive.

2.3. *The transparency directive*

Austria implemented the transparency directive in 1990. Section 91 of the Stock Exchange Act specifies notification thresholds of 5%, 10%, 25%, 50%, 75%, and 90% of the total voting rights of the company. Two of these thresholds, 5% and 90%, are not called for in the directive, but are important because certain minority rights and majority rights are linked to them. Besides direct holdings, disclosure requirements also apply to some forms of indirect control over voting rights.[1]

Concerning the contents of a notification, the disclosure requirement comprises neither the exact portion of voting rights controlled nor the 'channel' of control. Instead, blockholders must only disclose which notification threshold has been crossed and in which direction. In practice, however, additional information is often disclosed voluntarily.

Concerning the mechanics of a notification, the Act on the Supervision of Investment Services states that the crossing of a notification threshold must be announced by the blockholder to the *Bundeswertpapier-Aufsicht* as well as the corporation in question within 7 days. Under Section 93 of the Stock Exchange Act corporations must inform the general public by announcement in an official newspaper within an additional 9 days. If a corporation learns that its control structure has been materially altered (by comparison with what is publicly known) without proper prior notification, it must inform the general public immediately.

Although the law does not specify drastic sanctions for non-compliance with the provisions of the Stock Exchange Act, control changes appear to be regularly disclosed in practice. Based on these disclosures, the Vienna Stock Exchange provides snapshots of the current voting structure of listed corporations. However, these snapshots only state which notification threshold has been crossed in the course of a control change. The Exchange maintains a confidential data base on the exact size of the voting blocks. Our empirical findings are based on this information. Our sample covers about 80% of the listed non-financial corporations in Austria.

3. OWNERSHIP STRUCTURE

Table 2.1 reports our findings. Ownership concentration in our sample of 62 listed firms turns out to be very high indeed. On average, the largest shareholder holds 52.4% of the corporation's equity. The average second largest stake is 10.6%, but in fact only 33 firms have even two large shareholders; for these firms, the median size of the second largest stake is 19.9%. This indicates that the holders of these stakes should have an incentive to monitor. The size of the second largest stakes indicates the potential for substantial conflict of interest between the holder of such a minority stake and the majority owner. Since such conflicts of interest could be resolved by a buyout, the dispersion of ownership may reflect either the absence of conflicts or the limited ability of majority owners to buy out minority holders. For example, a family may well want to retain control over a firm while wealth constraints prevent it from buying out other shareholders. But a family can structure its holdings as a pyramid in order to reduce the cost of control. In this case, a separation between ownership and control results.

In general, different types of owners may structure their holdings differently. Table 2.2 breaks down direct ownership by firm size and types of owner, categorizing the latter as banks, domestic firms, foreign firms, the state, families, and dispersed (public) ownership. To explore the consequences of pyramiding, we add to each owner's direct equity holdings any stake held indirectly via another domestic firm. Table 2.3 reports our findings. Relative to direct ownership, families nearly triple their ownership to 27.2% of equity when indirect ownership via pyramiding is also

Table 2.1. *62 listed firms: Average direct ownership by firm size class and ownership stakes*

Size class (by sales)		Average equity stakes (% of total equity)			
Size class (%)	No. of firms	1st stake	2nd stake	3rd stake	Rest
Largest					
90–100	7	48.9	7.0	0.7	43.4
75–90	9	48.0	9.2	2.7	40.1
50–75	15	59.6	15.5	3.1	21.8
25–50	15	48.6	9.4	2.5	39.5
10–25	9	50.5	11.8	5.9	31.8
0–10	7	56.8	6.9	1.4	34.9
All firms	62	52.4	10.6	2.9	34.1

Source: Trend Verlag.

Table 2.2. *62 listed firms: Average direct ownership by firm size and owner category*

Size class (by sales)		Owner category					
Size class (%)	No. of firms	Banks	Domestic firms	Foreign firms	State	Family	Public
Largest							
90–100	7	1.4	36.0	4.1	7.3	7.7	43.5
75–90	9	19.0	15.1	6.5	11.4	11.1	36.9
50–75	15	16.7	31.1	24.9	3.5	2.3	21.5
25–50	15	2.7	24.8	21.8	0.0	11.2	39.5
10–25	9	15.3	23.4	19.8	0.0	10.8	30.7
0–10	7	13.8	24.3	13.8	0.0	13.2	34.9
All firms	62	11.4	25.9	17.1	3.3	8.9	33.4

Source: Trend Verlag.

counted. The large difference between ultimate and direct state ownership reflects the fact that most state-owned firms are controlled through a 100% state-owned holding company. In contrast, the holdings of banks and foreign firms are usually direct. The cash-flow stakes of foreign firms actually decrease when pyramiding is taken into account, since some foreign firms have domestic ultimate owners.

Different types of owners dominate in different size-classes. Probit regressions show that the larger the firm, the more likely the largest ultimate owner is to be the state or a bank, whereas families dominate among smaller firms. We do not find any relationship between the occurrence of foreign firms as largest ultimate owners and firm size.

4. VOTING POWER

In this section, we use data provided by the Vienna Stock Exchange to explore the distribution of voting-power in listed corporations in 1996. This data set cumulates information on changes in the control structure of Austrian listed firms that has to be published under Section 91 of the Stock Exchange Act. Unfortunately, the data set does not contain information on all listed companies. Out of our sample of 62 non-financial firms, data on the exact size of voting blocks is available for 52. We also exclude two corporations where no voting block in excess of 5% was disclosed publicly because our ownership data raise doubts whether any such blockholders actually exist. For the remaining firms, we have information on the identity of the holders of the voting blocks and on the portion of voting rights they controlled.

Figure 2.1 illustrates our findings regarding the distribution of ultimate voting rights. Table 2.4 reports some concentration measures. The concentration of voting power is very high. Firm size does not seem to have any effect on the concentration of voting power—as is illustrated by Table 2.5.

Figures 2.2 and 2.3 show a histogram and a percentile plot, respectively, of the size of the largest ultimate voting block. In a large number of firms the largest ultimate

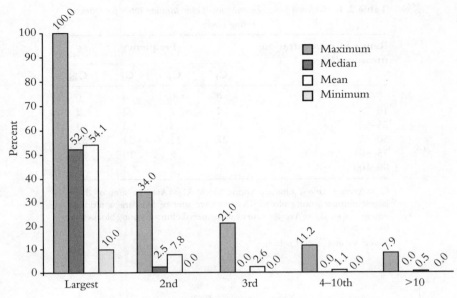

Figure 2.1. *Ultimate voting blocks by rank of blocks in 50 listed firms.*

Table 2.3. *62 listed firms: Average ultimate ownership by firm size and owner category*

Size class (by sales)		Owner category					
Size class (%)	No. of firms	Banks	Domestic firms	Foreign firms	State	Family	Public
Largest							
90–100	7	1.4	0.0	4.1	33.8	7.7	53.0
75–90	9	21.4	0.0	6.5	11.4	21.5	39.2
50–75	15	21.4	0.0	15.2	8.9	24.0	30.5
25–50	15	2.7	0.0	21.1	0.0	38.3	37.9
10–25	9	18.6	0.0	19.8	0.0	30.9	30.7
0–10	7	13.8	0.0	19.4	0.0	31.9	34.9
All firms	62	13.3	0.0	15.3	7.6	27.2	36.6

Source: Trend Verlag.

voting block exceeds 60% meaning that its holder can presumably override any attempt by minorities to impede resolutions at the general meeting. An accumulation of voting blocks can also be observed in the 10% and 25% region. Stakes of this size imply enhanced shareholder rights, such as the right to vote a merger that requires at least 25% of the votes.

In two-thirds of the cases, the largest blockholder exerts majority control. Table 2.6 shows that where there is majority control, there are usually no other large blocks.

Table 2.4. *50 listed firms: Frequencies of concentration ratios for ultimate voting blocks*

Range of concentration measure (%)	Frequency			
	C_1	C_3	C_5	C_{all}
0–10	0	0	0	0
10–25	7	2	2	2
25–50	9	5	3	3
50–75	27	32	32	32
75–90	4	8	10	10
90–100	3	3	3	3

C_1 = Average largest ultimate voting block. C_3 = Average sum of three largest ultimate voting blocks. C_5 = Average sum of five largest ultimate voting blocks. C_{all} = Average sum of all registered ultimate voting blocks (i.e. blocks > 5%).

Source: Vienna Stock Exchange.

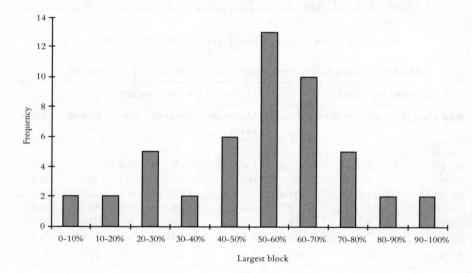

Figure 2.2. *Histogram of largest ultimate voting block.*

But where no shareholder exerts majority control, there are typically several significant minority blocks.

These findings indicate that any analysis of Austrian corporate governance must focus on conflicts between majority and minority owners. Minority voting blocks exist only when their holders can accumulate enough voting power to restrict the majority owner's ability to expropriate them.

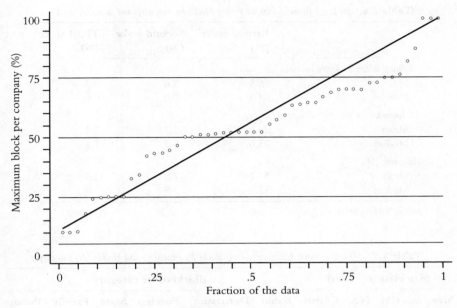

Figure 2.3. *Percentile plot of largest ultimate voting block.*

Source: Vienna Stock Exchange.

Table 2.5. *50 listed firms: Concentration measures for ultimate voting blocks by firm size*

Size class (by sales) (%)	No. of firms	C_1	C_3	C_5	C_{all}
Largest					
90–100	5	37.2	53.8	53.8	53.8
75–90	8	57.8	66.4	67.5	67.5
50–75	12	67.8	71.6	71.6	71.6
25–50	12	53.5	64.5	67.3	67.9
10–25	8	44.9	56.5	59.6	60.2
0–10	5	48.1	60.0	62.0	62.0
All firms	50	54.1	63.7	65.3	65.5

C_1 = Average largest ultimate voting block. C_3 = Average sum of three largest ultimate voting blocks. $C5$ = Average sum of five largest ultimate voting blocks. C_{all} = Average sum of all registered ultimate voting blocks (i.e. blocks > 5%).

Source: Vienna Stock Exchange.

Table 2.7 breaks down our data on voting blocks by type of blockholder and firm size. The Vienna Stock Exchange provides information about listed firms' voting blocks in other listed firms. We report this information in a separate column, 'Domestic listed firms'. In order to avoid double counting, the voting blocks of blockholders in the other categories are reported net of any voting rights they may control in a listed firm via another listed firm. Nevertheless, we refer to these voting

Table 2.6. *50 listed firms: Ultimate voting blocks by majority and minority control*

	Largest stake (%)	Second stake (%)	Third stake (%)
34 firms under majority control			
Mean	66.5	3.6	0.3
Median	64.3	0.0	0.0
16 firms under minority control			
Mean	28.6	15.7	7.4
Median	25.0	15.0	7.1
All firms (50)			
Mean	54.1	7.8	2.6
Median	52.0	2.5	0.0

Source: Vienna Stock Exchange.

Table 2.7. *50 listed firms: Ultimate voting blocks by firm size and blockholder category*

Size class (by sales)		Blockholder category					
Size class (%)	No. of firms	Banks	Domestic listed firms	Foreign firms	State	Family	Public
Largest							
90–100	5	1.4	10.1	8.6	33.7	0.0	46.2
75–90	8	10.8	13.6	3.8	22.0	17.4	32.5
50–75	12	19.1	0.7	18.9	11.1	21.7	28.4
25–50	12	0.5	4.3	26.9	0.0	36.3	32.1
10–25	8	0.0	14.5	24.9	0.0	20.9	39.8
0–10	5	26.7	11.8	0.0	0.0	23.6	38.0
All firms	50	9.3	7.9	16.4	9.6	22.4	34.5

Source: Vienna Stock Exchange.

blocks as 'ultimate' voting blocks since they include any voting rights that are controlled indirectly by a blockholder via one of the 'channels' specified in Section 91 of the Stock Exchange Act.

The state, along with its cash-flow rights in the largest firms, also holds significant voting blocks. Families tend rather to hold significant voting blocks in the smaller size-classes.

Table 2.8 shows that there are also differences between the size of voting blocks held by different types of blockholders. The voting blocks of families are typically much smaller than those of other categories. Unlike institutional investors in the Anglo-Saxon countries, Austrian banks hold voting blocks to exert corporate control. The size of their blocks is usually sufficient to give them majority control—and all the more so considering absenteeism and proxy voting.

5. THE SEPARATION OF OWNERSHIP AND CONTROL

As we mentioned earlier, there are several reasons why the distribution of voting power in a corporation may diverge from its ownership structure: pyramiding, the existence of non-voting stock, and so on. To explore the separation of ownership and control in Austria's listed non-financial companies, we compute the ratio of the ultimate voting rights to the ultimate cash-flow rights (VRCFR) of the holders of the largest ultimate voting blocks in each firm. We exclude firms where we cannot identify the ultimate holder of the largest voting block. After exclusion of firms with such an opaque control structure, there remains a sample of 41 listed firms.

Figure 2.4 shows how the separation of ownership and control varies with firm size. Surprisingly, the ratio of ultimate voting rights to ultimate cash-flow rights of the largest blockholder is highest in the smallest firms. This reflects the prevalence of family ownership and the resort to pyramiding in order to retain control at comparably low cost. Consistently, Figure 2.5 shows that the separation of ownership and control is especially marked in the case of firms where a family holds the largest voting block.

In order to disentangle the effects of firm size and the type of the holder of the largest voting block in a corporation, we run an OLS regression. We regress the logarithm of the ratio of ultimate voting rights to ultimate cash-flow rights (LVRCFR) on dummy variables corresponding to the different types of the largest blockholders (BANK, STATE, FAMILY) as well as firm size (SALES). By omitting the dummy variable indicating foreign firm control, we choose firms controlled by foreign firms as our reference point. Table 2.9 reports the results.

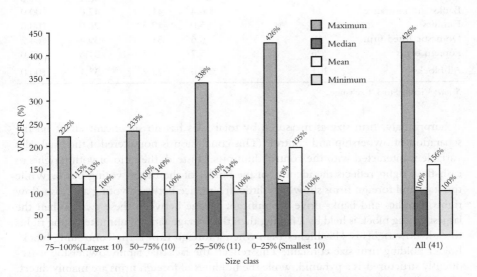

Figure 2.4. *The separation of ownership and control: Ratio of voting rights to cash-flow rights of largest blockholder (VRCFR) by size class.*

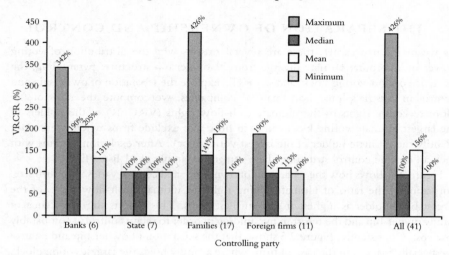

Figure 2.5. *The sepration of ownership and control: Ratio of voting rights to cash-flow rights of largest blockholder (VRCFR) by type of owners.*

Table 2.8. *50 listed firms: Ultimate voting blocks by blockholder category*

Blockholder category	No. of blocks held	Voting blocks (% of votes)			
		Min.	Median	Mean	Max.
Government	9	24.0	51.0	53.1	81.6
Banks and insurance	11	6.4	41.9	42.0	100.0
Families	45	5.0	12.3	26.0	100.0
Domestic listed firm	10	6.6	51.5	39.4	64.3
Foreign firms	26	5.7	18.7	31.6	87.0
All blocks	101	5.0	22.7	33.1	100.0

Source: Vienna Stock Exchange.

Surprisingly, firm size as measured by total sales has no significant effect on the separation of ownership and control. (This conclusion is not altered if the total sales variable is interacted with the control dummies.) Instead, the ratio of voting rights to cash-flow rights reflects the identity of the holder of the largest voting block. While the state and foreign firms show very little divergence between voting and cash-flow rights, families and banks drive a significant wedge between these two. When the largest voting block is held by a family, then the average ratio of ultimate voting rights to cash-flow rights is 41% higher than when a foreign firm is the controlling block-holder holding firm size constant. This reflects the fact that family ownership is frequently structured as a pyramid, while the holdings of foreign firms are mainly direct. When the largest blockholder is a bank, the ratio averages 58% higher than in the control group firms controlled by foreign firms. Since the holdings of both foreign

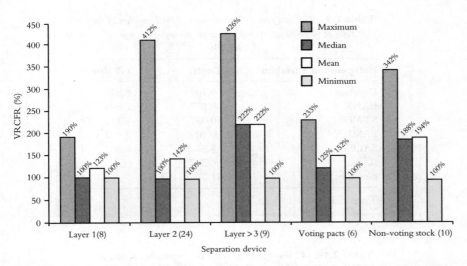

Figure 2.6. *The separation of ownership and control: Ratio of voting rights to cash-flow rights of largest blockholder (VRCFR) by separation device.*

firms and banks are mainly direct, this very substantial difference must be due to other separation devices than pyramiding. In fact, in bank-controlled firms there is often non-voting stock.

Figure 2.6 compares the effects of different separation devices such as pyramiding, non-voting stock, and voting-pacts. We distinguish between different layers in a pyramid at which a firm may be located, 'Layer 1' corresponding to the top of the pyramid. Obviously, the further the firm is from the top, the greater the potential for separation of ownership and control. The average ratio of ultimate-voting rights to ultimate cash-flow rights of the largest blockholder therefore rises when control is exercised via an additional layer. The ratio averages 1.23 for firms that are located at the top of the pyramid and 2.22 for those firms below the third layer (Figure 2.6). Apart from pyramiding, the issuance of non-voting stock causes a large divergence from the principle of 'one-share-one-vote'.

In order to quantify the effects of different separation devices, we run an OLS regression in which the dependent variable is the logarithm of the ratio of voting rights to cash-flow rights (LVRCFR) (see Table 2.10). The independent variables 'PACT' and 'NONVOT' are dummies equal to one when there is a voting pact and when there is non-voting stock, respectively. 'LAYER' gives the number of hierarchical layers 'above' the firm in the pyramid including the top layer. Unfortunately, the small size of the sample does not allow us to use interaction variables that might capture differences in the separation of ownership and control when different types of blockholders use the same separation device to retain control.

One additional layer between the firm and the largest blockholder at the top of the pyramid increases the ratio of ultimate voting rights to ultimate cash-flow rights on average by about 20% (significant at the 5% level). The existence of non-voting stock

Table 2.9. *41 listed firms: Determinants of the logarithm of the ratio of ultimate voting rights to ultimate cash-flow rights (LVRCFR)*

Independent variables	Coeff.	t-Value
Constant	0.107	0.878
BANK	0.577	2.843[***]
STATE	−0.037	−0.153
FAMILY	0.409	2.695[**]
SALES	$4.51 \ 10^{-6}$	−0.402
R^2-bar	0.237	
No. Obs.	41	

[***]significant at the 1% level.
[**]significant at the 5% level.

Table 2.10. *41 listed firms: The effect of separation devices on the logarithm of the ratio of ultimate voting rights to ultimate cash-flow rights (LVRCFR)*

Independent variables	Coeff.	t-Value
Constant	−0.118	−0.656
PACT	−0.037	−0.215
NONVOT	0.371	2.615[**]
LAYER	0.200	2.673[**]
SALES	$-1 \ 10^{-5}$	−1.185
R^2-bar	0.266	
No. Obs.	41	

[**]significant at the 5% level.

increases it by an average of 37% (significant at the 5% level). Voting pacts and firm size have no significant effect on the VRCFR ratio.

6. CONCLUSIONS

This chapter analyses ownership and control for a sample of Austrian listed non-financial corporations. By European standards, Austria seems to be the country with the highest concentration of ownership and voting power. State ownership and control dominates among large firms, while families prevail as majority owners of small firms. Banks and foreign investors play a significant role as owners and holders of voting blocks in all size-classes.

Our findings about voting power concentration and the structure of voting blocks indicate that, apart from the classical manager–shareholder conflict, the conflict between large and small shareholders is of importance. Minority voting blocks exist only when the holders of such blocks can build up enough voting power to restrict other blockholders' ability to expropriate them.

Most likely, the potential for conflicts of interest between blockholders increases with the separation of ownership from control. We find that the type of the largest blockholder determines the extent of such separation. The ratio of the ultimate voting rights to the ultimate cash-flow rights of the largest blockholder is especially high when this blockholder is either a family or a bank.

We also quantify the effect of different 'separation devices' that enable an owner to retain control over a disproportionately large voting block. Both pyramiding and the issuance of non-voting stock result in the significant separation of ownership and control.

Our findings represent a first step towards a systematic analysis of Austrian corporate governance. An appropriate further step would be to explore the effect of the separation of ownership and control on corporate performance. Such an analysis should yield valuable insights into possible inefficiencies in the governance of Austrian corporations.

Appendix

A. *Legal forms*

Like that of most countries, Austrian corporate law distinguishes between legal forms involving personal liability of the entrepreneur and those in which a corporate entity serves as a 'shelter' to avoid shareholders' personal liability for the obligations of the company (see e.g. Simon 1995; Kastner *et al.* 1990). Basically, Austrian law recognizes sole proprietorships and personal trading companies on the one hand and corporations on the other. The following legal forms exist in Austria:

- *Non-corporate legal forms:* Sole proprietorship (*Einzelkaufmann*); civil law partnerships (*Gesellschaft bürgerlichen Rechts* or *GesbR*); general partnerships (*Offene Handelsgesellschaft* or *OHG*); limited partnerships (*Kommanditgesellschaft* or *KG*); small registered partnerships (*Offene Erwerbsgesellschaft* or *OEG*); small registered limited partnerships (*Kommandit-Erwerbsgesellschaft* or *KEG*); silent partnerships (*Stille Gesellschaft*); European economic interest grouping (*Europäische Wirtschaftliche Interessenvereinigung* or *EWIV*).
- *Corporate legal forms:* Companies with limited liabilty (*Gesellschaft mit beschränkter Haftung* or *GmbH*); stock corporations (*Aktiengesellschaft* or *AG*); commercial cooperatives (*Erwerbs- und Wirtschaftsgenossenschaften*); mutual insurance associations (*Versicherungsvereine auf Gegenseitigkeit* or *VVaGs*).
- *Other legal entities:* Savings banks (Sparkassen); private foundations (Privatstiftung).

B. *Basic population statistics*

We use census data as of 1991 provided by the Austrian Statistical Office in order to compute basic statistics regarding the Austrian corporate landscape. Table A2.1 gives a breakdown of active companies by legal form. Most numerous are sole proprietorships (EU). In 1991, there were 166,420, or 73.8% of all companies in Austria (225,367). In terms of employees, the most

K. Gugler, S. Kalss, A. Stomper, J. Zechner

Table A2.1. *Total number of active companies by legal form in 1991*

Legal form	Companies		Employees	
	Number	**% of total**	**Number**	**% of total**
Stock corporation (AG)	733	0.33	282,578	11.79
Company with limited liability (GmbH)	37,491	16.64	868,904	36.25
Limited partnership with a company with limited liability (GmbH & CoKG)	5,649	2.51	168,855	7.04
Limited partnership (KG)	4,358	1.93	96,440	0.40
General partnership (OHG)	2,212	0.98	44,805	1.87
Small registered limited partnership (KEG)	64	0.03	193	0.01
Small registered partnership (OEG)	137	0.06	492	0.02
Civil law partnership (GesbR)	4,779	2.12	29,366	1.23
Sole proprietorship (EU)	166,420	73.84	641,417	26.76
Commercial cooperative (Gen)	1,552	0.69	61,569	2.57
Other legal forms	1,972	0.88	202,238	8.44
Total	225,367	100.0	2,396,857	100.0

Source: ÖSTAT (Austrian Statistical Office).

important legal form is the limited liability company (GmbH); in 1991, there were 37,491, employing 868,904 people or 36.3% of the private sector work force (excluding civil servants). The largest companies are organized as stock corporations (AGs); just 733 (0.33%) employ nearly 12% of the employees.

Tables A2.2 and A2.3 provide information on the total number and percentages, respectively, of companies broken down by sector of activity and legal form. The sector of activity is defined by the Austrian Statistical Office according to the ÖNACE classification scheme. Slight inconsistencies between Table A2.1 and Tables A2.2 and A2.3 concerning the total number of companies arise due to ÖSTAT estimation procedures. Most Austrian companies operate in the retail sector (more than 68,000 or 30.1%), followed by tourism (17.9%), and manufacturing (nearly 30,000 or 13.2%). More than one-third of limited liability companies are in the retail sector. Stock corporations (AG) operate disproportionately often in the manufacturing sector (23.4% of AGs) followed by credit and insurance (20.7%), real estate (17.5%), and the retail sector (17.2%). Interestingly, there is a cluster of Commercial Cooperatives (Gen) in the credit sector (nearly 60%), the Raiffeisen cooperatives.

We compute the standardized residuals of frequency in Table A2.3 relative to fitted values when legal form and sector are independent categorical variables. The Pearson Chi-squared test with 40 degrees of freedom rejects the null hypothesis of independence of legal form and sector at a p-value below 0.01.

Tables A2.4 and A2.5 display the distribution of the number and percentages of companies by size-class measured in headcount and legal forms. Obviously, the distribution of the number of sole proprietorships is skewed towards the smaller size categories. The largest group consist only of the owner-entrepreneur, with no employees. Companies with limited liability (GmbH) are prevalent in the size-classes from 20 to 999 employees; more than 95% of them employ fewer than 100 people. The legal form of the stock corporation (AG) is most prevalent in the largest size-class.

Table A2.2. *Number of companies by sector and legal form (1991)*

Sector	GmbH	EU	AG	Other	GmbH & CoKG	Gen	OHG	GesbR	KG	OEG	KEG	Total
Agriculture and forestry	10	117	0	2	3	22	2	2	0	1	1	160
Fishery	0	1	0	0	0	0	0	1	0	0	0	2
Mining	92	188	5	0	36	0	6	9	18	0	0	354
Manufacturing	5,915	20,253	171	68	1,397	179	448	558	950	10	6	29,955
Utilities	60	102	29	97	8	32	3	9	17	0	0	357
Construction	4,005	10,173	21	32	817	4	157	190	323	5	2	15,729
Retail and wholesale trade	13,388	47,936	126	82	1,996	269	1,015	1,125	2,052	29	15	68,033
Tourism	4,508	33,168	18	356	390	12	295	1,027	511	26	22	40,333
Transport and communications	2,122	6,722	77	141	423	16	68	94	113	3	0	9,779
Banking and insurance	292	1,057	151	148	25	923	7	26	8	2	0	2,639
Real estate and consulting	5,728	19,374	128	174	370	86	128	1,147	272	42	13	27,462
Education	56	784	0	117	2	3	1	47	0	1	1	1,012
Health care, veterinary services, and social services	110	13,444	0	270	18	1	5	154	3	6	0	14,011
Other services	1,203	13,104	5	485	163	5	77	392	90	12	4	15,540
Total	37,489	166,423	731	1,972	5,648	1,552	2,212	4,781	4,357	137	64	225,366

Source: ÖSTAT (Austrian Statistical Office).

Table A2.3. *Percentages of companies by sector and legal form (1991)*

Sector	GmbH	EU	AG	Other	GmbH & CoKG	Gen	OHG	GesbR	KG	OEG	KEG	Total
Agriculture and forestry	0.03	0.07	0.00	0.10	0.05	1.42	0.09	0.04	0.00	0.73	1.56	0.07
Fishery	0.00	0.00	0.00	0.00	0.00	0.00	0.00	0.02	0.00	0.00	0.00	0.00
Mining	0.25	0.11	0.68	0.00	0.64	0.00	0.27	0.19	0.41	0.00	0.00	0.16
Manufacturing	15.78	12.17	23.39	3.45	24.73	11.53	20.25	11.67	21.80	7.30	9.38	13.29
Utilities	0.16	0.06	3.97	4.92	0.14	2.06	0.14	0.19	0.39	0.00	0.00	0.16
Construction	10.68	6.11	2.87	1.62	14.47	0.26	7.10	3.97	7.41	3.65	3.13	6.98
Retail and wholesale trade	35.71	28.80	17.24	4.16	35.34	17.33	45.89	23.53	47.10	21.17	23.44	30.19
Tourism	12.02	19.93	2.46	18.05	6.91	0.77	13.34	21.48	11.73	18.98	34.38	17.90
Transport and communications	5.66	4.04	10.53	7.15	7.49	1.03	3.07	1.97	2.59	2.19	0.00	4.34
Banking and insurance	0.78	0.64	20.66	7.51	0.44	59.47	0.32	0.54	0.18	1.46	0.00	1.17
Real estate and consulting	15.28	11.64	17.51	8.82	6.55	5.54	5.79	23.99	6.24	30.66	20.31	12.19
Education	0.15	0.47	0.00	5.93	0.04	0.19	0.05	0.98	0.00	0.73	1.56	0.45
Health care, veterinary services, and social services	0.29	8.08	0.00	13.69	0.32	0.06	0.23	3.22	0.07	4.38	0.00	6.22
Other services	3.21	7.87	0.68	24.59	2.89	0.32	3.48	8.20	2.07	8.76	6.25	6.90
Total	16.63	73.85	0.32	0.88	2.51	0.69	0.98	2.12	1.93	0.06	0.03	100.00

Source: ÖSTAT (Austrian Statistical Office).

Table A2.4. *Number of companies by employee size class and legal form (1991)*

No. of employees	GmbH	EU	AG	Other	GmbH & CoKG	Gen	OHG	GesbR	KG	OEG	KEG	Total
0	391	64,870	14	484	311	6	274	1,598	368	74	27	68,049
1	4,772	31,703	50	346	252	91	197	643	308	20	13	38,087
2–4	11,840	42,193	68	462	789	184	501	1,191	875	31	18	57,277
5–9	7,972	18,117	63	204	1,056	307	523	769	1,020	5	5	29,021
10–19	5,538	6,992	65	180	1,299	349	348	419	855	7	1	15,198
20–49	3,953	2,140	73	138	1,196	359	234	139	589	0	0	8,232
50–99	1,508	299	73	68	433	153	73	14	199	0	0	2,621
100–199	843	82	67	48	196	73	38	7	82	0	0	1,354
200–499	487	26	97	20	100	22	16	1	43	0	0	769
500–999	122	1	84	8	15	6	5	0	14	0	0	241
1000+	63	0	78	14	1	2	3	0	4	0	0	161
Total	37,489	166,423	732	1,972	5,648	1,552	2,212	4,781	4,357	137	64	221,010

Source: ÖSTAT (Austrian Statistical Office).

Table A2.5. *Percentages of companies by employee size classes and legal form (1991)*

No. of employees	GmbH	EU	AG	Other	GmbH & CoKG	Gen	OHG	GesbR	KG	OEG	KEG	Total
0	1.04	38.98	1.91	24.54	5.51	0.39	12.39	33.42	8.45	54.01	42.19	30.79
1	12.73	19.05	6.83	17.55	4.46	5.86	8.91	13.45	7.07	14.60	20.31	17.23
2–4	31.58	25.35	9.29	23.43	13.97	11.86	22.65	24.91	20.08	22.63	28.13	25.92
5–9	21.26	10.89	8.61	10.34	18.70	19.78	23.64	16.08	23.41	3.65	7.81	13.13
10–19	14.77	4.20	8.88	9.13	23.00	22.49	15.73	8.76	19.62	5.11	1.56	6.88
20–49	10.54	1.29	9.97	7.00	21.18	23.13	10.58	2.91	13.52	0.00	0.00	3.72
50–99	4.02	0.18	9.97	3.45	7.67	9.86	3.30	0.29	4.57	0.00	0.00	1.19
100–199	2.25	0.05	9.15	2.43	3.47	4.70	1.72	0.15	1.88	0.00	0.00	0.61
200–499	1.30	0.02	13.25	1.01	1.77	1.42	0.72	0.02	0.99	0.00	0.00	0.35
500–999	0.33	0.00	11.48	0.41	0.27	0.39	0.23	0.00	0.32	0.00	0.00	0.11
1000+	0.17	0.00	10.66	0.71	0.02	0.13	0.14	0.00	0.09	0.00	0.00	0.07

Source: ÖSTAT (Austrian Statistical Office).

C. *The company with limited liability, the stock corporation, and the commercial cooperative*

Table A2.6 compares limited liability companies with stock corporations.

Organizationally, the supreme organ of both a stock corporation and a company with limited liability is the general meeting. The most striking difference between the two lies in the position of the managing directors: whereas in the stock corporation they are quite independent, in a company with limited liability they have to obey instructions of the shareholders. While the managing director of a stock corporation can be removed from office early only with substantial cause by the supervisory board, in a company with limited liability he can be revoked at any time by the shareholders. For any given ownership concentration, this implies that direct monitoring is much easier in these companies than in stock corporations.

These differences are reflected in the provisions concerning the establishment of a supervisory board to monitor the management board. A supervisory board is mandatory for stock corporations. By contrast, in a simple limited liability company a supervisory board is only required when the company is quite large (share capital of more than 1 million schillings and more than 50 shareholders or more than 300 employees). If a limited liability company controls a group with more than 300 employees or runs an investment fund, it also must have a mandatory supervisory board. Similar provisions determine whether a company with limited liability has to appoint auditors.

To summarize, the stock corporation is characterized by a mutually dependent system of checks and balances comprising the management board, the supervisory board, and the general meeting of shareholders. While the supervisory board of a stock corporation is the principal link between the general meeting and the management board, the owners of a simple limited liability company are in much closer contact with the management.

Table A2.7 compares the legal forms of the commercial cooperative and the stock corporation. The main difference lies in their different purposes: whereas corporations aim for profit, the purpose of the cooperative consists in the promotion of its members.

Both stock corporations and commercial cooperatives have to appoint supervisory boards. However, whereas the board of a stock corporation is elected by the general meeting, a commercial cooperative is not obliged to call regular general meetings of its members. The possibility of holding a meeting of representatives instead of members implies the possibility of excluding members from the direct control of the board. In any case, the ability of the members of a commercial cooperative to control the management is limited by the voting structure: each member casts only one vote, regardless of the number of membership stakes held. Moreover, the transfer of membership stakes between members may be subject to approval by the management. As a consequence, commercial cooperatives generally have a uniform distribution of voting rights among members.

D. *Legal forms without a clearly defined residual owner*

Whereas all the above mentioned legal forms have owners, there are also legal entities lacking a clearly defined residual owner. Whenever these 'ownerless' legal entities hold a controlling stake in a stock corporation, the resulting hybrid legal form is potentially characterized by an especially sharp divergence between ownership and control. As we can see below, such hybrid legal forms make up a large part of the Austrian financial sector. Hence, the separation of ownership and control is of great practical importance all the more so in view of the substantial equity holdings of financial institutions in large Austrian non-financial companies documented in the empirical part of this survey.

Table A2.6. *Company with limited liability vs. stock corporation*

Legal form	Min. capital (ATS)	Mandatory reserves	Supervisory board, auditors	Transfer of shares	Owners listed in company register
Company with limited liability	500,000 (Euro 35,000)	For large firms: 5% of annual profits; up to a maximum of 10% of share capital	Voluntary for small firms; mandatory for large firms	Notarial deed	Yes
Stock corporation	1,000,000 (Euro 70,000)	5% of annual profits; up to a maximum of 10% of share capital.	Mandatory	Free (or as specified in by-laws)	No

Table A2.7. *Commercial cooperative vs.* stock corporation

Legal form	Purpose	General meeting	Voting	Transfer of shares
Commercial cooperative	Promotion of members	May be replaced by meeting of representatives	One vote per member (if not stated otherwise in the by-laws)	If provided for by by-laws: subject to approval by management
Stock corporation	Shareholder profit maximization	Mandatory	One vote per share of common stock	Free (if not otherwise provided, for in by-laws)

D.1. *The private foundation*

A potentially drastic separation of ownership and control may prevail under the legal form of a private foundation. The private foundation was established in Austria in 1993. Such a foundation must execute and fulfil the purpose specified by the founder. This purpose may be private or public, charitable or not. It should be stressed, however, that a foundation may not trade or run a business itself but may only hold shares and other assets. The private foundation has two mandatory organs, the managing board and the auditors. The board must consist of at least three members. The managing board is the most important body as it manages and represents the foundation. The beneficiaries or other persons with an economic interest in the sound operation of the foundation have no right either to be members of the managing board or to nominate its members. If a supervisory board exists, only half of its members may be beneficiaries or have an economic interest in the operation of the foundation.

D.2. *The savings-bank*

Savings banks are founded either by municipalities (*Gemeindesparkasse*) or by savings-bank associations (*Vereinssparkasse*). Savings banks have no owner but they have a special relationship with their municipality or the savings-bank association in that these founders guarantee for the savings-bank. While upon foundation, the founders have to provide sufficient capital, this capital subsequently belongs to the savings-bank and is not paid back to the founder. Savings banks have two organs: the board of directors (*Vorstand*) and the savings-bank council (*Sparkassenrat*) which can be compared to the supervisory board. Since savings-banks do not have owners, they cannot raise capital by issuing shares. In order to mitigate this problem, a special hybrid legal form was created, the so-called savings-bank stock corporation (*Sparkassen-Aktiengesellschaft*). A savings-bank stock corporation is a savings-bank that owns equity in a stock corporation. The legal construction therefore comprises institutions at three levels: the municipality or savings-bank association (i), which controls the saving bank (ii), which holds equity of the savings-bank stock corporation (iii).

An example of such a hybrid legal form is the largest Austrian bank, Bank Austria, which recently acquired control over *Creditanstalt* (Stock Corporation). Bank Austria itself was formed by a merger involving a savings-bank founded by the municipality of Vienna, so that the city of Vienna guarantees Bank Austria's liabilities in case of default. However, triggered by the recent acquisition of *Creditanstalt* by Bank Austria, a bill has been drafted to amend the rules about the relationship with the state and, in particular, the guarantee relationship between savings-banks and municipalities.

D.3. *The mutual insurance association*

In Austria only stock corporations and mutual insurance associations are allowed to conduct insurance business, upon permission by the competent authority. A mutual insurance association is an economic association that provides insurance to its members. A member of an insurance association at the same time contracts insurance with this association. However, mutual insurance associations can offer insurance to non-members as well. Large mutual insurance associations have to maintain three organs: the board of directors, the supervisory board, and a supreme organ that may be either the meeting of members or the meeting of representatives. Like commercial cooperatives, they can exclude the members from control whenever the articles of association specify that a meeting of representatives replaces the meeting of members. Like savings-banks, they cannot issue shares. To give them access to the capital market, a special type of restructuring for insurance associations was allowed in 1991. According to Section 61a of the Insurance Supervision Act, mutual insurance associations are now permitted to transfer their business partly or wholly to a stock corporation founded solely for this purpose. In this case, only the mutual insurance association itself receives stock, but no stock is distributed to the members of the association.

Mutual insurance associations also hold significant stakes in other Austrian companies. As an example, a mutual insurance association, Wiener Städtische Versicherung, holds a 9% stake of the equity of Bank Austria. Like the savings-bank council of Bank Austria, this mutual insurance association is presided over by the Mayor of Vienna.

E. *The prevalence of 'ownerless' legal forms in the banking industry*

Figure A2.1 shows the relative importance of the various legal forms in the credit sector in Austria as measured by total assets in 1995. This figure depicts the situation before Bank Austria

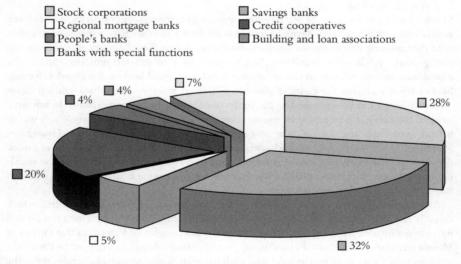

Figure A2.1. *The credit sector in Austria (shares of sector's total assets, 1995).*
Source: ÖNB.

(Savings Bank) acquired control over *Creditanstalt.* The most important legal forms are savings-bank (*Sparkassensektor*) with a 'market share' of 32%, and credit cooperatives (mainly the *Raiffeisensektor,* 20% of total assets). Problems associated with the separation of ownership and control should be expected here because ownership structures are typically not well defined. Since *Creditanstalt* was the largest bank organized as a stock corporation, 32% is a lower bound of the 'ownerless' segment of the credit sector. Complementary to market shares, in a study of the ownership structure in Austria, Beer *et al.* (1991) found that the state ultimately owned 24%, savings-banks 17.4%, and commercial cooperatives 13.5% of the equity in the credit sector.

The Development of Austrian Stock Corporations Act and Capital Markets Law since 1998

- In 1998, a new section was added to the *SparkassenG* (Savings Bank Act) to allow for the transformation of savings-banks into private foundations. The purpose of this modification of the act is to reduce political influence in the governance of savings-banks and to render Austrian savings-banks more comparable to similar foreign banks.
- In 1999, the Austrian Takeover Act 1998 (BGBl I 1998/127) came into force. Since then, the rules of the act apply to all listed stock corporations with registered offices in Austria. Compared with the latest proposal for a European Take-Over Directive, the Takeover Act is not limited to transfers of control blocks. Instead, it also applies to voluntary public bids by bidders not aiming to acquire a control block. The act pursues two different main objectives, (i) fair and equal treatment of shareholders, and (ii) the protection of minority shareholders. So far, there have been eleven public bids (public offers and mandatory bids) and several times the Takeover Commission was asked to interpret the Act's rules. The most notable case is the recent transaction between '*Bank Austria AG*' and the German '*Hypotheken-Vereinsbank-AG*': this transactions poses questions concerning the possibility of 'contracting around' the Takeover Act.
- Similar to the Second Capital-Directive (Second Council Directive 77/91/EEC of 13 December 1976) and a German law, *Gesetz zur Kontrolle und Transparenz im Unternehmensbereich* (DBGBl I 1998/24), the *Aktienrückerwerbsgesetz* (BGBl I 1999/187) enables listed stock corporations (registered in Austria) to repurchase their shares for any purpose other than trading (see section 65, subsection 1, item 9 of the Stock Corporation Act). However, these share repurchases are limited to 10% of equity capital and require prior authorization by the general meeting.
- The recent *Kapitalmarktoffensiv-Gesetz* aims at improving the condition of Austrian capital markets with a special focus on options markets. For similar reasons, there have come into force reforms of some tax laws as well as of labour legislation.
- The *Aktienoptionengesetz* establishes a framework to grant stock options to executives, directors, and employees. In addition, it stipulates new disclosure obligations for corporations that repurchase shares and states explicitly that shareholders must be treated equally.

NOTES

1. Section 92 of the Stock Exchange Act lists situations in which indirect control of voting rights is deemed equivalent to direct control. The most important are (i) voting rights held

by other persons or entities in their own name but on behalf of the person or entity in question; (ii) those held by an undertaking controlled by the person or entity in question; (iii) those held by a third party with whom the person or entity in question has concluded a long-term written agreement obliging the former to adopt a certain voting policy; (iv) those held by a third party that has a written agreement with the person or entity in question temporarily transferring control to the latter; (v) those attached to shares deposited with a person or entity that can be exercised even in the absence of specific instructions from the holders.

REFERENCES

Becht, M. (1997), 'Strong Blockholders, Weak Owners and the Need for European Mandatory Disclosure', Executive report, Université Libre de Bruxelles, in *The Separation of Ownership and Control: A Survey of 7 European Countries*. Preliminary report to the European Commission, vol. 1, Brussels: European Corporate governance Network.

Beer, E., B. Ederer, W. Goldmann, R. Lang, M. Passweg, and R. N. Reitzner (1991), *Wem gehört Österreichs Wirtschaft wirklich? Studie der Kammer für Arbeiter und Angestellte für Wien*, Vienna: Orac Verlag.

Franks, J. and C. Mayer (1996), 'Ownership, Control and the Performance of German Corporations', LBS Working paper.

Kastner, W. *et al.* (1990), *Gesellschaftsrecht*, 5th edn., Vienna: Manz Verlag.

La Porta, R., F. Lopez-de-Silanes, A. Shleifer, and R. W. Vishny (1996), 'Law and Finance'. NBER Working paper no. 5661.

Reich-Rohrwig (1992), 'Verbreitung und Gesellschafterstruktur der GmbH in Österreich, in Festschrift für Walther Kastner.

Simon, N. (1995). 'Introduction to Austrian Company Law', in Gröhs and Pollak, *Austrian Law & International Business: Company Law and Accounting in Austria*.

3

Shareholding Cascades: The Separation of Ownership and Control in Belgium

MARCO BECHT, ARIANE CHAPELLE, AND LUC RENNEBOOG

1. INTRODUCTION

Different degrees of ownership concentration reflect the trade-off between, on the one hand, the diversification advantage of investing in many assets and, on the other hand, the (private) benefits of controlling a firm. As Franks and Mayer (1995) point out, it is puzzling that the resolution of this trade-off has taken such a variety of forms in different countries. They classify the ownership structures into two categories: insider and outsider systems. The equity markets of this first system are characterized by few listed companies, an illiquid capital market where ownership and control is infrequently traded, and complex systems of intercorporate holdings. Consequently, these structures are appropriately described as *insider* or enterprise-oriented systems as it is the corporate sector or families and individuals who hold controlling interests and outsider investors, while able to participate in equity returns through the stock market, are not able to exert much control. Continental Europe and Japan fit into this broad classification. In contrast, the Anglo-American system is a market-oriented or *outsider* system and is characterized by a large number of listed companies, a liquid capital market where ownership and control rights are frequently traded, and few intercorporate holdings.[1] There are few large, controlling shareholdings and these are rarely associated with the corporate sector itself. Diversified shareholdings are useful from the point of view of risk reduction but discourage active participation of investors.

The main characteristics of the Belgian corporate ownership and equity market can be summarized as follows: (i) few—merely 140—Belgian companies are listed on the Brussels stock exchange; (ii) there is a high degree of ownership concentration with an average largest direct shareholding of 45%; (iii) holding companies and families, and to a lesser extent industrial companies, are the main investor categories whose share stakes are concentrated into powerful control blocks through business group structures and voting pacts; (iv) control is levered by pyramidal and complex ownership structures; and (v) there is a market for share stakes. Properties (i) to (iv) imply that Belgium can be portrayed as a prototype of the 'insider system'. However, typical for Belgium is the importance of cascades of holding companies which are used to lever control.[2] Consequently, an ultimate investor can control a target company while holding relatively few cash-flow rights.

2. THE SEPARATION OF OWNERSHIP AND CONTROL IN BELGIUM: THE LEGAL ASPECTS

2.1. *Corporate landscape: the prevalence of the limited partnership (SPRL) and the stock corporation (SA)*

Belgium numbers approximately 220,000 firms, most of which are small with half of them counting less than five employees or less than BEF10 million of total assets. Two legal forms dominate: the *Société Privée à Responsabilité Limitée* or the *Besloten Vennootschap met Beperkte Aansprakelijkheid* (SPRL or BVBA, a limited liability partnership) and the *Société Anonyme* or *Naamloze Vennootschap* (SA or NV, a stock corporation). There are about 90,000 companies of each type.[3] Tables 3.1, 3.2., and 3.3 present an overview of the legal corporate forms, their capital requirements, number of companies, equity transfer procedures, and accounting information disclosure rules.

SPRLs are the most numerous among small firms (99% of SPRLs are firms with less than BEF100 million of total assets). Their ownership certificates are nominative and the transferability of the certificates is subject to restrictions, for example the agreement of the other partners. Most large firms are SAs (84% of firms over 100 million of total assets are SAs). Their distinguishing feature is the possibility of issuing bearer shares with no restriction on their transferability.

There are currently approximately 140 Belgian registered firms that are listed on the official market of the Brussels Stock Exchange. They are of various sizes and belong to all sectors of the economy. Holding companies account for 23% of the market capitalization, while electricity and gas companies represent 20% of the capitalization on the Brussels Stock Exchange. Other sectors with a high market capitalization are banks and financial services companies (14%), chemical companies (9%), and insurance companies (8%). Market capitalization is highly concentrated among a few large firms: the Top 10 account for 50% of the total market capitalization, while the Top 50 represent 95% of the market capitalization. Turnover is low for smaller listed firms: the BEL20 market index, which includes 20 firms, accounts for 83% of the total market turnover.

2.2. *Ownership disclosure legislation*

The notification rules
Up to 1989, little was known about the ownership structure of companies listed on the Belgian stock exchanges, given the general use of bearer shares and the lack of ownership disclosure obligation. The takeover battle in 1988 between the French Compagnie Financière de Suez and the de Benedetti group for the largest Belgian

Table 3.1. *Company types: Liability, partners and managers*

Names	Limited liability	Minimum capital (BEF)	Smallest no. of owners	Smallest no. of managers	No. of firms in Belgium
Private firms					
Société en Nom Collectif (SNC)	No	No	2	1	0
Société en Commandite Simple – Commenditaire Vennootschap (SCS)	No for the active managers (commandités) and yes for passive managers (commanditaires)	No	2	1	0
Mixed firms					
Société Privée à responsabilité Limitée – Vennootschap met Beperkte Aansprakelijkheid (SPRL/BVBA)	Yes	750,000	2	1	91,000
Société Privée à responsabilité Limitée Unique (SPRLU)	Yes	750,000	1 (Single-owner firm)	1	13,300
Société Coopérative – Cooperatieve Vennootschap (SC/CV)	Yes, if specified in the statutes	750,000	3	1	16,600
Public firms					
Société en Commandite par Actions – Commanditaire Vennootschap met Aandelen (SCA)	Yes	2,500,000	2	3 (the managers are partners designated by the statutes of the firm)	250
Société Anonyme/Naamloze Vennootschap (SA/NV)	Yes	2,500,000	2	3 (2 is possible if there are only shareholders)	92,000

Table 3.2. *Company law: Foundation, transfers, transparency*

Names	Deposit of statutes and of list of owners at foundation	Transfer procedures	Manager's ownership	Buy-out of own shares	Publicity of the list of the partners
Private firms					
Société en Nom Collectif (SNC)	Yes	Submitted to the agreement of all other partners. Notified in the firm's register	No limit	Not allowed	No
Société en Commandite Simple – Commanditaire Vennootschap (SCS)	Yes	Submitted to the agreement of all other partners. Notified in the firm's register	No limit for active partners	Not allowed	No
Mixed firms					
Société Privée à responsabilité Limitée – Vennootschap met Beperkte Aansprakelijkheid (SPRL/BVBA)	Yes	Restricted to agreed partners or submitted to the agreement of half of the partners having three-quarters of the capital. Notified in the firm's register	No limit	No limit. Must be bought with reported profit. Voting rights are suspended as long as owned by the firm	No

Société Privée à responsabilité Limitée Unique (SPRLU)	Yes	Submitted to the agreement of the single partner. Transform the firm into a SPRL or another SPRLU. Notified in the firm's register	100%	—	—
Société Coopérative – Cooperatieve Vennootschap (SC/CV)	Yes	No transfer allowed	No limit	Not allowed	No
Public firms					
Société en Commandite par Actions – Commanditaire Vennootschap met Aandelen (SCA)	Yes	No restriction to transfer. Notification in the register if shares are nominative	No limit for active partners	Same rules as for SA	No
Société Anonyme/ Naamloze Vennootschap (SA/NV)	Yes	No restriction to transfer. Notification in the register if shares are nominative	Ruled by the statutes	Same rule as for SRPL. Distribution to employees allowed	No

Table 3.3. *Accounting rules: Form, contents and control of annual accounts*

Names	Obligation to make and deposit annual accounts[a]	Information on ownership in annual accounts	Information on shareholdings in annual accounts	External control of annual accounts	Consolidated accounts
Private firms					
Société en Nom Collectif (SNC)	Yes	No	No	No	No
Société en Commandite Simple – Commanditaire Vennootschap (SCS)	Yes	No	No	No	No
Mixed firms					
Société Privée à responsabilité Limitée – Vennootschap met Beperkte Aansprakelijkheid (SPRL/BVBA)	Yes	No	No	Yes. Rules for SA apply	No
Société Privée à responsabilité Limitée Unique (SPRLU)	Yes	Yes, by definition	No	Yes	—
Société Coopérative – Cooperatieve Vennootschap (SC/CV)	Yes	No	No	Yes. Rules for SA and SPRL apply	No
Public firms					
Société Anonyme/Naamloze Vennootschap (SA/NV)	Yes	Yes, for shareholders owning more than 10% of the votes	Yes, from 10% of one category of shares in a firm	Yes. Auditors must be officially agreed (réviseurs) if the firm exceeds a certain size	Yes if the firm is large enough or controls one or more other firms
Société en Commandite par Actions (SCA)	Yes	As above	As above	As above	As above

[a] Form of annual accounts: depends on size of firm whether full or abridged.

holding company, Generale Maatschappij van België (Société Générale de Belgique), highlighted the problems due to informational uncertainty regarding shareholdings and voting rights. The EU Transparency Directive[4] provided the framework in which new legislation concerning corporate control and ownership could be initiated. An Ownership Disclosure Law[5] was introduced in 1989 and amendments to the company law with regard to takeovers were made in 1991.

The Ownership Disclosure Law requires all investors, both individuals and companies, to reveal their share stakes in those companies governed by Belgian law, all or part of whose securities conferring voting rights are officially listed on a stock exchange located in a Member State of the European Union. In spite of the legislation's title, the legislation is about the declarations of important holdings of voting rights and not about holdings of capital. Notification is obligatory if a shareholding equals or exceeds a threshold of 5%[7] of voting rights. Furthermore, shareholders have to declare any increases and decreases in ownership and their new ownership position if their stake exceeds a multiple of 5% of the voting rights or falls below such a threshold.[8] For instance, a company that has revealed that it owns a stake of 11% will have to notify the Banking Commission[9] again once this ownership stake reaches 15% or more, or decreases below the 10%-threshold.

Real and potential voting rights
The notification percentages refer to real and potential voting rights. As a result, ownership of securities convertible into shares (convertible bonds, warrants, etc.) is treated similarly in terms of disclosure as vote-bearing shares in the company.[10] So, when investors make voting-rights declarations, they include: (i) the percentage of the actual total voting rights they own, proportional to all the actual voting rights outstanding; (ii) the potential voting rights, as a percentage of the aggregate of all potential voting rights; and (iii) the percentage of cumulative actual and potential voting rights in the company based on the aggregate number of the voting rights associated with all outstanding shares and convertible instruments.[11]

Indirect ownership, investor groups, and voting pacts
The transparency legislation does not only apply to natural and legal persons owning voting rights directly, but also to those investors who control voting rights indirectly via a pyramid structure of intermediate companies.[12] Investors are obliged to reveal whether they are affiliated to an investor group of companies or whether they act 'in concert'[13] with other investors. Throughout the chapter we distinguish among direct shareholdings, group blocks and voting blocks. Group blocks are the sum of the direct shareholdings controlled by the same ultimate investor (an individual, a family, an industrial company). Voting blocks consist of direct shareholdings or group blocks of which the (ultimate) investors have made voting agreements. If the real or potential voting rights of the individual investor, the group block or the voting block exceed or fall below the notification thresholds, the cumulative and individual direct and indirect ownership positions, and changes in voting rights should be disclosed. The Commission for Banking and Finance suggests that the ultimate controlling shareholder of

a business or investor group assume notification responsibility for voting rights of its own direct and indirect holdings and for those share stakes held by investors this 'reference shareholder' is affiliated to or acts in concert with.[14] In the case of voting pacts, the same rules as for business groups apply.

In addition, once the stake of an investor (or of the investors belonging to the same investor group) reaches 20% of the voting rights of the company or falls below this threshold, the strategic intent with regard to the target has to be declared to the Banking Commission and the target.[15]

Notification process

The investor who purchases or sells shares (the voting rights) or potential voting rights has to disclose his control position and the changes-herein to the target company and to the Commission for Banking and Finance in Brussels at the latest on the second working day after the transaction, if a notification threshold has been transgressed. Standardized sheets guarantee homogeneity in the declarations. Apart from the number and percentage of real and potential voting rights, a notification sheet reveals the identity of the investor, the investor's business group (if appropriate), voting pacts, policy statements (20% rule), and the date referring to the change in voting rights.

The target company who has been notified about changes in ownership by substantial investors, has a maximum of one working day after disclosure to pass on this information to the Documentation and Statistics Department of the Brussels Stock Exchange (Maertens 1994). This department updates its on-line ownership database DBPart, makes this information available *ad valvas* on the trading floor (*parquet*)[16] and prepares the information for publication in the *Cote de la Bourse*,[17] a Stock Exchange publication that is inserted in the two Belgian financial newspapers, *De Financieel Economische Tijd* and *L'Echo*. The same notification timing applies to disclosure of investors' policies (20% ownership rule). Moreover, the target company will have to publish this voting-rights information in its annual report.

An investor's failure to disclose a substantial shareholding may lead to an interdiction to the investor in question to participate to the annual meeting, to a cancellation of the annual meeting which has been called for, to a suspension of the exercise of all or part of the rights pertaining to the securities for a certain period and even to liability to penalties.[18] The voting rights of recently acquired major shareholdings (5% and more) can only be exercised 45 days after notification.[19]

Ownership disclosure of non-listed companies

The EC Directive and the subsequent national legislation only refer to transparency of listed companies. Still, Belgian law also requires every corporate shareholder of a non-listed *Société Anonyme* (NV) registered in Belgium, to notify this company as soon as this shareholder holds more than 10% of the total votes of one category of shares. When the notification decreases to less than 10%, a similar notification has to take place. However, in practice, this rule is not strictly respected (Becht 1997). There is still an indirect way of gathering partial information on shareholdings in non-listed public firms. All SAs (NVs), both listed and non-listed, are obliged to publish in their annual reports, the content of their shareholding portfolios in other firms, be they Belgian or foreign.

The shares of private firms (like the SPRL or BVBA) are always nominative and the owners are registered in a register of partners. To the public, the ownership structure is not accessible; only the partners, fiscal authorities, and third parties having an interest in the firm, like debtors or creditors, can consult the register.

2.3. *Voting rights dilution and restrictions, and the rights of the minority shareholders*

In principle, the general assembly takes decisions based on a simple majority of the voting rights. Since 1991, the balance of corporate power has shifted to the controlling shareholders who have been given legal instruments to entrench their position in the company and to protect themselves against undesired takeovers. Anti-takeover instruments, like share repurchase schemes or issuance of warrants, can be installed by the board of directors at any moment in time if the shareholders have given authorization to the board. Such an authorization remains valid for a maximum of 5 years but can be reinstated for a similar period (Wymeersch 1994a).[20] Such measures have further reduced the likelihood of hostile takeovers in Belgium.[21]

However, to provide more protection to small shareholders a super-majority of 75% of the voting rights voted at the general assembly is needed with regard to decisions about changes in the acts of incorporation, increases of the equity capital, limitations or changes in the preferential rights of existing shareholders to purchase shares in new equity issues, changes in the rights of different classes of shareholders,[22] repurchases of shares, and changes in the legal form of the corporation (Lievens 1994).

Since 1991, minority shareholders or a group of minority shareholders owning at least 1% of the equity capital or shares with a value of not less than BEF50 million, can appoint one or more experts who can scrutinize the company's accounting and its internal operations.[23] The appointment of experts is conditional on indications that the interests of the company have been violated. Shareholders owning at least 1% of the votes can initiate a minority claim against the directors for the benefit of the company, if it can be proven that the directors have managed or supervised the company poorly and if the minority shareholders have voted against the directors' discharge[24] at the annual meeting. For instance, a minority claim would be justified when directors ensured that the company paid out benefits to large shareholders they represent to the detriment of the company.[25]

Another important change, since the law of 1991, is the abolition of automatic voting rights restrictions.[26] This abolition was motivated by the fact that the restrictions could be easily evaded by redistributing the shares to family members, friends, and subsidiaries. Still, as in Germany, individual companies can apply voting-rights restrictions by including such clauses in the acts of incorporation. While automatic voting restrictions are abolished, voting agreements among shareholders for (renewable) periods of 5 years are allowed since 1991 if these agreements do not limit the responsibilities of the directors or are used to create different classes of voting rights.

2.4. *Limitations on cross-shareholdings*

Belgian law restricts cross-shareholdings between two firms to a maximum of 10% of the voting capital. This rule applies for two independent firms when one of the two firms has its headquarters in Belgium. It applies also between a mother firm and its subsidiaries: the subsidiaries taken together may not hold more than 10% of the mother's voting capital. Furthermore firms are obliged to liquidate the cross-shareholdings acquired in violation (or ignorance) of the law. Shares have to be liquidated within one year and the votes attached to the shares are suspended before the alienation.

2.5. *Ownership cascades and pyramids as main separation devices*

A substantial number of share stakes are held by other companies which in turn are held by other shareholders. Such cascade or pyramidal ownership structures have been typical in the Belgian corporate landscape, but are beginning to disappear. For example, the pyramid structure used by the French Suez group to control the Belgian electricity utility Electrabel is disappearing. Suez has started to delist its Belgian utility interests and to convert them into ordinary, closely held subsidiaries.

However, some important pyramidal structures still exist, most notably the Belgo-Canadian Frère-Desmarais group (see Appendix). A series of holding companies and legal instruments is used to control a vast industrial empire with relatively small cash-flow stakes. The structure has a double vertex. On the European side Baron Albert Frère presides over a control chain that involves a family holding, two non-listed Belgian holdings, a listed Belgian holding and a Dutch holding company. On the Canadian side, Paul Desmarais Sen. controls three companies that control the Power Corporation of Canada and the Power Financial Corporation, two listed companies. Through a series of Canadian, Dutch, Belgian, and Swiss holding companies the partners control a number of important Belgian and French companies.

Previous examples clarified that the true owners of the Belgian sample companies are mostly not the direct shareholders (at ownership level 1), but that control is exercised by an ultimate shareholder on a higher ownership tier in the pyramid. It is important to identify these ultimate voting blockholders so that the percentages of voting rights held by direct or first-level shareholders controlled by the same ultimate investor can be aggregated into investor groups. Such an investor group is named after and classified according to the identity and shareholder class of the ultimate shareholder.[27] Fortunately, the Large Holdings Directive forces such blockholders to declare their voting power, no matter how 'distant' they are from the listed company where they cast the votes.

3. DATA COLLECTION

Ownership data were collected for the period 1989, the adoption of the transparency legislation, until 1995. In 1989 and 1995, respectively, 186 and 140 companies were listed.[28] 40% of the Belgian listed companies are holding companies with multi-industry investments, 13% are in the financial sector (banking, insurance and real estate), and 47% are industrial and commercial companies.

Data on the ownership structure over the period 1989–95 were collected from the Documentation and Statistics Department of the Brussels Stock Exchange, which maintains a daily updated database BDPart (Bourse Data Participations) of the shareholding structure of Belgian listed companies. BDPart provides data on the first level of shareholding (direct ownership) in all Belgian listed companies, such as the names of the investors, the number of shares declared, number of shares issued and the percentage of ownership. Apart from voting rights linked to the shareholdings, BDPart also displays potential voting rights linked to securities that will represent voting rights when converted or exercised. Previous ownership positions in the BDPart database are overwritten once new ownership information becomes available. To capture a company's ownership position at the end of its fiscal year since 1989 and changes in shareholdings during each year, about 5,000 hardcopy Notifications of Ownership Change from 1989 till 1994 were consulted. Apart from details on voting rights, the investors' status (independent, affiliated, or acting in concert with other investors) was compiled from the Notifications in order to construct the shareholdings of business groups and voting pacts. With this information about major direct shareholdings and indirect control, the multi-layered ownership structure was reconstructed for each company over the period 1989–94. The shareholding data from BDPart and the Notifications of Ownership Change over the period 1989–94 were verified with ownership data of the database of the National Bank which is based on annual reports.[29] For indirect ownership data of 1995, a more elaborate methodology has been used. We used the CD-Rom 'Bel-first', produced by Bureau Van Dijk with tapes supplied by the Central Bank, to gather all shareholdings that Belgian firms are required to report to the Central bank if such a shareholding exceeds 10% of the voting capital of the target firm. By collecting all the large investments of Belgian companies, we reconstructed the ownership pyramid of Belgian companies. The year-books of *Trends 20,000*, which comprise industry-sector classification and financial data for most listed and non-listed Belgian companies, were used to classify all Belgian investors into the following categories: (i) holding companies, (ii) banks, (iii) institutional investors, (iv) insurance companies, (v) industrial companies, (vi) families and individual investors, (vii) federal or regional governments, and (viii) real estate investors. Foreign companies owning a large share stake in Belgian companies were classified with information from *Kompass*.

As disclosure is only obligatory for shareholdings exceeding 5% (or 3% if the company so chooses) our ownership data are truncated. Still, we were able to collect many shareholdings of less than 5% because, when an investor with a small shareholding belongs to an investor group or is involved in a voting pact, his share stake will be disclosed as well. Furthermore, the potential voting rights, referring to warrants and convertibles are to be disclosed such that, along with these potential voting rights, small stakes or real voting rights are also disclosed. For 5 companies, the stock exchange did not receive any ownership notifications. These companies were not included in our 1995 database.[30]

4. DIRECT SHAREHOLDINGS, GROUP BLOCKS, AND VOTING BLOCKS

The Belgian transparency legislation requires investors not to disclose cash-flow rights, but deals with voting rights. Still, the discrepancy between direct share stakes and voting rights is rather small as the principle of 'one-share-one-vote' is usually upheld within one ownership tier. Direct share stakes are shareholdings on the first owner-ship tier and belong to a single shareholder. Some of these direct share stakes belong to group blocks as they are controlled by an ultimate shareholder who may use a pyramid of intermediate companies to control several direct shareholdings. Finally, there are also voting coalitions between shareholders or group blocks, which we call voting blocks. Of the 140 companies listed on the Brussels Stock Exchange, for 135 com-panies there was at least one ownership notification in 1995. Overall, there are 269 notified voting blocks, 431 group blocks, and 551 direct shareholdings. Table 3.4 shows that the average listed firm has 5 direct shareholders, 3 group blocks, and 2 voting blocks; 80% of the voting blocks count 2 to 5 shareholders. In three-quarters of the cases a group block corresponds to a voting block.

4.1. *Direct shareholdings*

Figure 3.1 shows the direct voting power of the largest and subsequent share stakes of the 135 listed companies in 1995. All shareholders are considered in isolation (without considering the fact whether they take part in a voting block). The largest shareholder holds on average 45% of the votes (see also Table 3.5) while the second largest owns 12.8%. This confirms that Belgian direct ownership is highly concen-trated. In order to get majority control of 50%, the largest shareholder ought to form a coalition with the second or third largest shareholders. Still, in practice, atomistic shareholders do not usually exercise their voting rights on the annual meetings such that the largest average shareholder might have absolute de facto control.

The histogram of the largest direct share stakes of Figure 3.2 exhibits peaks at the 25% and the 50% thresholds, indicating the importance of blocking minorities and majority control respectively. There are relatively few direct voting blocks in the range 35–50%. In Belgium, the mandatory bid rule requires shareholders who accu-mulate a shareholding which leads to a change in control at a price higher than the market to make a tender offer for the other outstanding shares. In practice, it is the court that can decide whether a control change has taken place or not. If a stake of about one-third of the voting rights is acquired, in most cases this is regarded as a control change. Therefore, either companies deliberately remain underneath the 33.3% threshold or acquire more than 50% of the voting rights. The mandatory bid threshold might also explain why there are relatively many share stakes of more than 66.66% of the voting rights.

On average, the sum of the direct share stakes held by large shareholders (who own at least 5% of the outstanding shares) amounts to more than 65% in 1994 (Table 3.6).

Table 3.4. *Frequency distribution of direct shareholdings, group blocks, and voting blocks, 1995*

No.	Direct stakes			Group blocks			Voting blocks		
	Frequency	Percentage	Cum. %	Frequency	Percentage	Cum. %	Frequency	Percentage	Cum. %
1	25	18.5	18.5	38	28.2	28.2	60	44.4	44.4
2	19	14.1	32.6	35	25.9	54.1	43	31.9	76.3
3	23	17.0	49.6	17	12.6	66.7	19	14.1	90.4
4	11	8.2	57.8	12	8.9	75.6	7	5.2	95.6
5	13	9.6	67.4	10	7.4	83.0	2	1.5	97.0
6	7	5.2	72.6	10	7.4	90.4	1	0.7	97.8
7	6	4.4	77.0	3	2.2	92.6	2	1.5	99.3
8	5	3.7	80.7	2	1.5	94.1	1	0.7	100.0
9	5	3.7	84.4	2	1.5	95.6	—	—	—
10	6	4.4	88.9	3	2.2	97.8	—	—	—
11	3	2.2	91.1	1	0.7	98.5	—	—	—
12	4	3.0	94.1	—	—	—	—	—	—
Number of firms	135			135			135		
Number of shareholdings	551			431			269		

Notes: Group blocks are the sum of those direct shareholdings controlled by the same ultimate investor. Voting blocks consist of a combination of group blocks when ultimate investors controlling those group blocks have formed a voting pact regarding the conditions under which voting rights are exercised or regarding priority rights in case of selling the group block.

Sources: Own calculations based on DBPart, individual notifications, and annual reports.

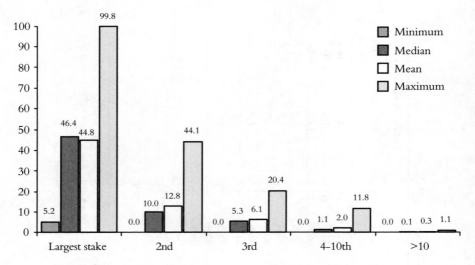

Figure 3.1. *Direct stakes by rank of stake for all listed companies in 1995.*

Note: For each of the 135 notified companies the stakes were ranked. For blocks of equal size (ties) the average rank was assigned. This was never the case for the largest stake. For each category the minimum, median, mean, and maximum were computed for all stakes in the category.

Table 3.5. *Size concentration of large direct shareholdings and of voting blocks (percentages)*

Measure	Mean	Std. dev.	Min.	Max.
Panel A: Direct shareholdings				
C_1: Largest shareholding	44.75	20.88	5.22	99.76
C_3: Sum of largest 3 stakes	59.28	20.1	15.25	99.97
C_5: Sum of largest 5 stakes	62.25	19.42	15.76	99.97
C_{20}: Sum of largest 20 stakes	63.75	19.2	15.76	99.97
C_{all}: Sum of all stakes	63.83	19.18	15.76	99.97
Panel B: Ultimate voting blocks				
C_1: Largest ultimate voting block	55.77	19.8	8.45	99.76
C_3: Sum of largest 3 voting blocks	62.6	19.03	15.76	99.97
C_5: Sum of largest 5 voting blocks	63.19	19.08	15.76	99.97
C_{20}: Sum of largest 20 voting blocks	63.37	19.07	15.76	99.97
C_{all}: Sum of all voting blocks	63.37	19.07	15.76	99.97

Notes: This table shows the average of the largest direct shareholdings and the sum of the 3, 5, 20 and all direct shareholdings (panel A). Panel B shows similar measures, but based on ultimate voting blocks in 1995.

Sources: Own calculations based on DBPart, individual notifications, and annual reports.

Cumulative direct ownership is higher, almost 70% in the financial sector, and around 65% for both holding companies and the industrial and commercial companies. It is clear that the concentrated ownership structure does not facilitate hostile takeovers if the acquirer does not initially have a large toehold. Panel A of Table 3.5

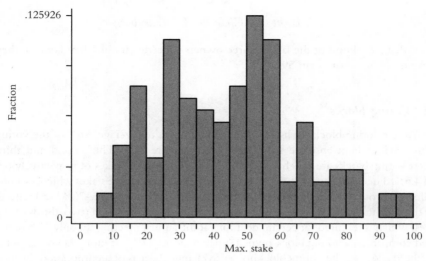

Figure 3.2. *Histogram of the largest direct stakes in 1995.*

Note: Histogram with the maximum direct stake for 135 notified companies. The five companies with no notified stake are not included.

Table 3.6. *Ownership concentration in all Belgian companies listed on the Brussels Stock Exchange (percentages)*

	Accumulated shareholdings held by:					
	All investors	Holding companies	Families companies	Industrial	Belgian investors	Foreign investors
Panel A : All sample companies (155 firms)						
Direct shareholdings	65.4	32.7	3.9	14.6	49.4	16.0
Ultimate voting blocks	65.4	26.7	15.6	10.8	39.6	24.4
Panel B: Holding companies (64 firms)						
Direct shareholdings	63.9	36.7	5.2	13.1	46.9	17.1
Ultimate voting blocks	63.9	34.4	14.1	8.3	36.1	28.0
Panel C: Financial sector (banks, insurance, and real estate) (19 firms)						
Direct shareholdings	70.0	26.5	1.2	5.5	55.0	15.0
Ultimate voting blocks	70.0	26.2	5.3	5.4	38.4	23.6
Panel D: Industrial and commercial companies (72 firms)						
Direct shareholdings	65.5	30.8	3.5	18.3	50.2	15.3
Ultimate voting blocks	65.5	20.0	19.7	14.5	43.0	21.4

Notes: This table aggregates the shareholdings of 5% or more held by the main shareholder categories. The shareholder classes (holding companies, industrial and commercial companies, and families) consist of both Belgian and foreign investors. 'Ultimate voting blocks' means that those direct shareholdings controlled by the same ultimate shareholder or belong to a voting coalition are summed.

Sources: Own calculations based on information from the BDPart database of the Brussels Stock Exchange, ownership notifications of the documentation centre of the Brussels Stock Exchange, and annual reports.

shows that a coalition of the largest three owners is needed for absolute control; they own on average more than 59%.[31]

4.2. Voting blocks[32]

The largest voting blocks in listed companies control, on average, 56% of the voting rights, giving them absolute majority control (Figure 3.3). The second and third largest voting blocks are much smaller with combined share stakes of respectively 6.6 and 4.5%. The histogram (Figure 3.4) with the largest direct share stakes which are controlled by a voting block shows peaks at the 50–60% level and the 65–70% level reflecting the absolute majority threshold and the qualified majority level (two-thirds of the votes) which is required for certain decisions at the annual meeting. In only 17% of the listed companies, a voting block owns a super-majority (75% or more), a voting rights threshold allowing the voting blockholder to change the acts of incorporation, including voting rights (see also Figure 3.5).[33] Table 3.7 details the most important blockholders by name and Table 3.8 by type. For example, the Generale Maatschappij/Société Générale controlled by the French holding Suez-Lyonaise des Eaux, is present as a voting blockholder in 16 listed companies and controls an average voting rights package of over 50% (Table 3.7).

The evolution of ownership in concentrated companies with a shareholding of at least 25%[34] since 1989 is given in Table 3.9. Ownership concentration of the largest direct shareholding has increased slightly over a 6-year period since the transparency

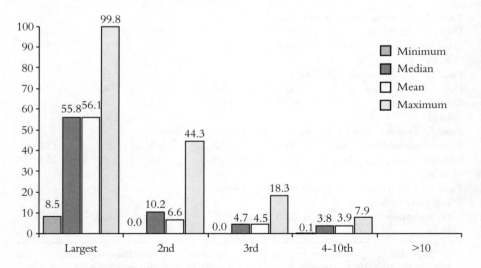

Figure 3.3. *Voting blocks by rank of block for all listed companies in 1995.*

Note: For each of the 135 notified companies the blocks were ranked. For blocks of equal size, average rank was assigned. This was never the case for the largest stake. For each category the minimum, median, mean, and maximum were computed for all stakes in the category.

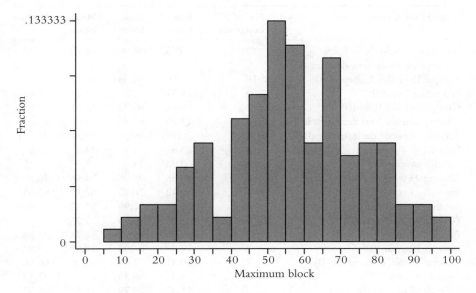

Figure 3.4. *Histogram of the largest voting block in 1995.*

Note: Histogram with the maximum voting block for 135 notified companies. The five companies with no notified stake are not included. The are no maximum voting blocks smaller than 5%.

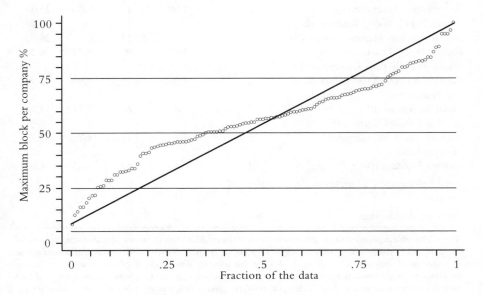

Figure 3.5. *Percentile plot of largest voting blocks.*

Note: Percentile plot of the largest voting blocks for all sample companies, excluding five companies without notified holdings.

Table 3.7. *Number and size of voting blocks per blockholder (percentages)*

Voting blockholder name	No. of companies	Min. block	Max. block	Mean block	Median
Société Générale de Belgique – Compagie Financière de Suez (Fr)	12	0.03	94.96	40.15	45.42
Banque Paribas – Cobepa (Fr)	10	3.06	81.35	45.44	39.36
Soges Star Fund (B)	10	1.51	5	3.96	4.43
Groupe familial Boel (B)	7	9.89	69.79	41.81	45.05
Groupe familial Van der Mersch (B)	6	13.99	82.56	52.97	67.1
Société Générale de Belgique (B-Fr)	4	50.19	69.98	59.31	58.53
Sofina (B)	4	3.8	71.4	24.7	11.8
Famille Saverys (B)	4	0.02	24	6.07	0.12
Almanij Holding Group (B)	3	40.35	94.98	70.46	76.05
Mr. Guy Paquot (B)	3	50.42	70.43	62.17	65.65
Groupe familial Janssen (B)	3	32.13	71.98	57.32	67.86
Groupe AG – Fortis (B)	3	1.76	10.73	5.26	3.3
Banque Degroof (B)	3	2.94	7	4.74	4.28
Lonrho Belgium (B)	2	77.9	81.83	79.87	79.87
Groupe Bruxelles Lambert (B)	2	60.31	73.62	66.96	66.96
Groupe Danone (Fr)	2	5.3	89.33	47.32	47.32
Région Wallonne (B)	2	13.27	79.79	46.53	46.53
Banques Paribas (Fr)	2	7.68	75.23	41.46	41.46
Heideberg Zement Groupe (G)	2	33.52	44.41	38.97	38.97
Artois – Piedboeuf – Interbrew Groupe (B)	2	34.83	35.28	35.06	35.06
Gewestelijke Investerings- maatschappij voor Vlanderen (B)	2	9.99	47.14	28.56	28.56
Ackermans Van Haaren Groupe (B)	2	3.39	50.51	26.95	26.95
Royale Belge/Union des Assurances de Paris Groupe (B/Fr)	2	3.49	14.99	9.24	9.24
Groupe des Assurances Generale de France (Fr)	2	7.24	8.75	7.99	7.99
Mutuelle Solvay (B)	2	2.87	12.6	7.74	7.74
Groupe Familial Verbert (B)	2	5	5	5	5
Mercury Asset Management Group (UK)	2	4.64	4.76	4.7	4.7
Cobepa Holding (B-Fr)	2	0.65	7.41	4.03	4.03
Total holders with 2 blocks or more	102				
Total all blockholders	269				

Notes: The table reports summary statistics over these shareholder classes. Among blockholders, the case of the SUEZ/Generale Maatschappij van België (Générale de Belgique (GMB/SGB) group, with a portfolio of 73 stakes in 16 different listed firms (12 + 4), is the most striking example of the presence of French shareholders on the Brussels Stock Exchange. Paribas is another significant example. Soges is a special case since it is an investment fund. Soges belongs to the GBL group but it acts independently for its investments. This type of shareholder holds relatively small stakes (no more than 5%) and it is not an active shareholder. Besides holding companies, Belgian family groups are important: Boël, Janssen, Van der Mersch own large family holdings which often hold controlling blocks in several listed firms.

Sources: Own calculations based on information from the BDPart database of the Brussels Stock Exchange, ownership notifications of the documentation centre of the Brussels Stock Exchange, and annual reports.

Table 3.8. *Ownership concentration by type of ultimate blockholder (percentages)*

Blockholder type	No. of blockholders of this type	Mean	Min.	Max.	Median
Belgian state	1	50	50	50	50
Individuals (Belgian)	51	27.66	0.02	82.33	13.99
Individuals (Foreign)	2	39.48	7.85	71.1	39.48
Individuals (French)	1	84.15	84.15	84.15	84.15
Belgian listed firm	25	32.69	0.19	81.83	32.07
Belgian listed firm – foreign French firm	1	62.82	62.82	62.82	62.82
Belgian non-listed firm	49	25.06	0.14	96.58	9.25
Belgian non-listed firm – foreign firm	1	69.71	69.71	69.71	69.71
Belgian non-Listed firm – foreign French firm	3	58.31	53.88	61.5	59.54
Foreign firm	4	24.14	3.24	60.76	16.28
Foreign German firm	1	33.52	33.52	33.52	33.52
Foreign French firm	22	32.44	0.03	88.77	30.35
Foreign French firm – Belgian listed firm	1	45.86	45.86	45.86	45.86
Foreign French firm – Belgian non-listed firm	1	65.34	65.34	65.34	65.34
Foreign Italian firm	1	0.58	0.58	0.58	0.58
Foreign Japanese firm	2	37.24	6.94	67.53	37.24
Foreign firm of Luxembourg	13	29.02	3.12	59.87	20.32
Foreign Dutch firm	3	39.44	3.91	57.43	56.97
Foreign Swiss firm	3	4.74	3.11	5.9	5.22
Foreign British firm	3	5.6	4.76	6.99	5.06
Foreign American firm	4	37.77	3.05	84.17	31.93
Flemish government	1	99.76	99.76	99.76	99.76
Walloon government	1	13.27	13.27	13.27	13.27
State of Zaire	1	11.88	11.88	11.88	11.88

Note: Each of the 195 blockholders was classified. The table reports summary statistics by class of owner.

legislation. Considering only those companies with a largest shareholding of more than 25%, the average largest direct shareholding has increased from 55% to about 58%. Ultimate levered control is defined as the product of the intermediate shareholdings between the sample company and the ultimate controlling shareholder.[35] The average levered shareholding's increase from 38% to almost 42% is largely due to a shortening of the ownership pyramids. All in all, from 1989 to 1994, there have been no substantial changes in the aggregate concentration of ownership in Belgian listed companies. Renneboog (2001) shows that there is an active market in controlling share stakes in Belgium, but given the value of control as reflected in the control premium, share blocks do not tend to get dispersed.

Table 3.9. *Largest direct and ultimate levered shareholdings, and the control leverage factor*

		1989	1990	1991	1992	1993	1994
Sample size		160	156	156	156	152	146
Ultimate ownership	Mean (%)	2.2	2.2	2.1	2.1	2.1	2
level	Std. dev. (%)	1.364	1.29	1.188	1.159	1.002	0.956
Direct largest	Mean (%)	55.1	56.4	57.2	57.8	57.9	58.3
shareholding	Std. dev. (%)	19.737	19.509	19.923	20.632	20.321	19.635
Ultimate levered	Mean (%)	38	38.5	40.3	41.7	41.5	42.2
shareholding	Std. dev. (%)	22.524	22.906	23.988	24.6	24.563	23.852
Control leverage factor,	Mean (%)	3.6	3.6	3	2.9	2.8	2.7
(direct/ultimate	Std. dev. (%)	8.391	8.65	6.756	6.71	6.556	6.86
shareholding)							

Notes: This table presents the ultimate ownership level, defined as the highest level of ownership in an uninterrupted control chain (direct shareholdings are level 1). Ultimate control is control based on (i) a majority control (minimal 50% of the voting rights) on every ownership tier of the ownership pyramid, or (ii) shareholdings of at least 25% on every tier in the absence of other shareholders holding stakes of 25% or more. A chain of fully owned subsidiaries are considered as one single shareholder. The direct largest shareholding is the average direct largest share stake of at least 25%. The ultimate levered shareholding is calculated by multiplying the share stakes of subsequent ownership tiers. The control leverage factor is the ratio of the direct shareholding divided by the ultimate levered shareholding. For instance, company A, whose shares are widely held, owns 40% of company B which, in turn, owns 40% of company C. The ultimate shareholder level is 2, the direct largest shareholding (of B in C) is 40%, the ultimate shareholding is 16% (40% × 40%), and the leverage factor is 2.5 (40/16). There was no direct shareholding of at least 25% in 17 sample companies, which were not included in this table. Standard deviation in parentheses.

Sources: Own calculations based on data from the BDPart database and ownership notifications.

4.3. *Categories of shareholders*

Table 3.6 also exhibits the cumulative ownership of the three most important investor classes: holding companies, families and individual investors, and industrial and commercial companies.[36] From panel A can be concluded that holding companies are the largest direct investors; they hold on average 33% of the shares and account for half of the substantial ownership stakes in Belgian companies. Domestic and foreign holding companies have invested more in the Belgian holding companies than in the industrial and in the financial sector. Direct investment by industrial and services companies totals almost 15% (panel A) and is focused on other Belgian listed industrial and commercial companies (panel D). Families' direct investment is of less importance with an average stake of about 4%. The table shows not only ownership at the direct level but also the average stake held by voting blocks, where the voting blocks (labelled 'ultimate' in the table) are classified into shareholder categories based on the identity of the ultimate controlling shareholder.

Holding companies
The analysis on the basis of voting blocks reveals that, although holding companies remain the most important shareholder class in Belgian listed companies, their average

cumulative shareholding on an ultimate control basis decreases to 26.7% from an average direct shareholding of 32.7 (panel A, Table 3.6). The differences are explained by the fact that family-controlled holding companies are now classified according to the identity of the ultimate investors, namely, families and individuals. Belgian holding companies are substantial investors in all sectors: in other Belgian holding companies (panel B), in the financial sector (panel C), and in industrial and commercial companies (panel D). The importance of the Belgian holding companies and the lack of large share stakes held by banks should be understood in its historic framework: banking and investment business had to be separated by law in 1934. This resulted in the creation of large financial holding companies which became the major shareholders in the financial institutions and diversified their investments over a wide gamut of industrial and commercial sectors. Pyramidal ownership structures allowed holding companies to exercise levered control with relatively small share stakes (an example is provided in the Appendix).[37]

Industrial and commercial companies

The average shareholding held by industrial and commercial companies decreases from a direct shareholding of 14.6% to a shareholding of 10.8% as some companies are controlled by either holdings or families and individuals. Industrial and commercial companies seem more inclined to hold substantial stakes in other industrial firms (panel D).

Family shareholders

Belgian families own a voting-rights majority in 15% of the industrial and commercial companies and hold 26% of the shareholdings of at least 25%. Individual and family investors frequently do not hold shares directly in Belgian listed and non-listed companies, but use intermediate companies as their average concentrated ownership amounts to almost 16%, while direct stakes held by individual and family investors average only 4% (panel A). Family shareholdings are most distinctly present in the ownership structure of industrial and commercial companies (panel D) with an average substantial shareholding of nearly 20%.

Financial institutions

As of 1934, 'credit institutions' were prohibited from taking share participations in industrial companies. Only since the 1993 Credit Institutions Act[38] which implemented the Second Banking Directive of the European Union, are credit institutions (banks, savings banks, and other financial institutions) entitled to hold shares in industrial corporations and holding companies. Currently, credit institutions are allowed to hold up to 60% of their equity in shares of non-financial companies, with a maximum of 15% of their equity capital invested in a single company. There is no limitation with regard to the percentage of the outstanding shares of an individual company a credit institution is allowed to own.

In practice, banks still do not invest much in shares of non-financial companies to avoid conflicts of interest:

- According to Belgian law, banks are held liable towards creditors of bankrupt companies, if the banks granted credit to these companies at times when a reasonably prudent banker should not have granted nor maintained the credit. A substantial shareholding in a financially distressed company by a bank might influence that bank's decision with regard to ceasing additional credit.
- Since most banks are controlled by a holding company which might be a substantial shareholder in a company, it is doubtful whether banks would be able to make independent decisions with regard to a shareholding in that company or granted loans.
- Most investment and pension funds are managed by a bank which ensures the distribution of the investment fund's certificates (shares). Legally, investment and pension funds' management should use the voting rights associated with the shares of a company they have invested in, independent of the managing bank.

The government
In principle, the federal state does not invest in listed Belgian companies. But it owns 50% of the shares of the National Bank, of which the shares are listed in the Brussels Stock Exchange, and 50% of the 'public credit institutions'. The role of the public credit institutions has been broadened to that of a bank and these banks have been privatized. The 'public investment companies', owned by the regional governments hold blocks in shares of a few listed companies. Those investments were made either to save ailing companies or to provide small risky companies with growth capital so as to stimulate and support entrepreneurial and industrial expansion. In general, in contrast to France, federal and regional governments have not considered their shareholdings in companies as a long-term financial investment. Only in 2% of the listed companies, the state still holds a share stake via the regional investment companies.

Employee shareholdership
Since 1991, mechanisms of beneficial acquisition of shares by employees have been introduced. In general, employee ownership in most companies remains low. For instance, employees of Petrofina own 5.4% of the shares; in de Bank Brussels Lambert, employees hold 7%; in Creyf's Interim 0.9%; in Desimpel Kortemark 0.5%; in Royale Belge, 0.69% (Wymeersch 1994a).

Institutional investors
Belgian institutional investors (insurance companies, pension funds, credit institutions, investment funds, and investment companies) usually hold small share stakes (of under 5%), but own in aggregate about 18% of the shares in Belgian listed companies.[39] For instance, the average shareholding of all Bevek/Sicav investment funds[40] in the 60 most traded Belgian companies, amounted to 4% in 1995 and the

average shareholding of pension funds measures about 1.5%.[41] Insurance companies are legally allowed to invest up to 25% of their reserves in shares listed on the Belgian stock exchanges, but owned only about 12% of the Belgian shares over the period 1986–91. Most institutional investors reinforce the present majority's power by systematically voting in favour of management or, more commonly, by not taking part in the general assembly.

4.4. *Foreign shareholder classes*

The relative importance of domestic and foreign investors is examined in the last two columns of Table 3.6. More than 75% of the direct large shareholdings (or an average of 49.4% of the voting rights) are held by Belgian investors, while foreign investors' direct investments account for an average of 16%. This proportion is similar for holding companies (panel B) and the industrial firms (panel D), but for the financial sector, domestic investments are higher with an average of 55% (panel C). When we consider voting blocks, columns 5 and 6 show that foreign investors often use Belgian intermediary companies to control Belgian listed companies. Domestic ownership in a Belgian company amounts to nearly 40%; slightly lower (36%) in holding companies, and somewhat higher (43%) in industrial and service companies. Foreign investors hold about 38% of the substantial shareholdings (or an average of 24.3% of the total number of shares) in Belgian listed companies.

Of the foreign investors, it is primarily the holding companies that hold large share stakes and control with a majority stake 15% of all the Belgian listed companies.[42] Foreign holding companies invest predominantly in Belgian holding companies, one-quarter of which they control with a majority of the voting rights. This way foreign holding companies also indirectly invest in unlisted Belgian companies with shares held in the investment portfolios of Belgian holding companies. Foreign industrial companies prefer Belgian industrial companies as long-term investments, while foreign banks and insurance companies are substantial shareholders in the Belgian financial and insurance sector. Foreign institutional investors do not rely heavily on the Belgian stock market.

Although shareholders from a wide variety of countries[43] are present in the ownership structure of Belgian listed companies, the main investors are from the neighbouring European countries. Dutch investors own an average direct share stake of 3.8% and invest predominantly in Belgian industrial and commercial companies. German direct average ownership is low. German industrial companies mainly invested in the concrete industry via, for example, Heidelberger Zement. Investors from Luxembourg own, on average, directly 4.1% of Belgian companies, and have invested mainly in industrial and commercial companies. But, companies from Luxembourg are almost never the ultimate investor and are used as intermediary investment vehicles by, for instance, French companies. North American and UK shareholders hold large stakes in only 3 companies. Only one large shareholding of a Belgian listed company is Japanese: Ashaki acquired a majority stake in the glass manufacturer Glaverbel. The average French direct average shareholding is higher and close to 4.3%. The single most important foreign ultimate investors are French; their accumulated substantial shareholdings amount on average to almost 13%. They invest mainly in the Belgian holding companies of which they own an average stake of 19% and in the financial sector in which they hold an average of 14% of the voting rights. Via controlling participations in Belgian large holding companies, French investors control a substantial part—estimated at 30%—of all the listed and unlisted industrial companies in Belgium. In fact, it is the French holding companies, rather than French family investors or industrial companies that have acquired a substantial stake in the Belgian listed companies. French insurance companies own significant shareholdings in the Belgian banks and insurance companies.

5. CONCLUSIONS

This chapter has documented how the ownership disclosure requirements have been translated in national law and that ownership is strongly concentrated in Belgium with the largest shareholder owning an average direct stake of 45%. The direct shareholdings are large, but actual ownership concentration is even higher by the formation of group blocks: some ultimate investors control via intermediate (holding) companies. Furthermore, voting blocks are formed by voting coalitions between ultimate investors such that the average largest voting block amounts to 56%.

Institutional investors seldom hold more than 5% of the voting rights, but overall account for about one-fifth of the shares. The presence of large foreign shareholders in Belgian listed companies is important; holdings from Luxembourg are often found as intermediate companies in the cascade structure, but are rarely ultimate controlling shareholders. In contrast, French holding companies like the Groupe Suez-Lyonaise des Eaux and the Paribas holding Cobepa control a substantial part of the listed (and non-listed) Belgian companies.

This chapter has also reported recent changes in legislation which have made existing shareholders even more powerful in warding off takeover threats. Even so, Belgian shareholders do not pay a high price for control as ownership cascades violate the 'one-share-one-vote' rule. The cash-flow rights, which reflect the actual equity stake, owned by an ultimate shareholder are often substantially lower than his control rights.

Appendix. The Frère-Desmarais pyramid

Overall structure

The Frère-Desmarais pyramid has a double vertex. On the European side Baron Albert Frère presides over a control chain that involves a family holding, two non-listed Belgian holdings, a listed Belgian holding, and a Dutch holding company. On the Canadian side, Paul Desmarais

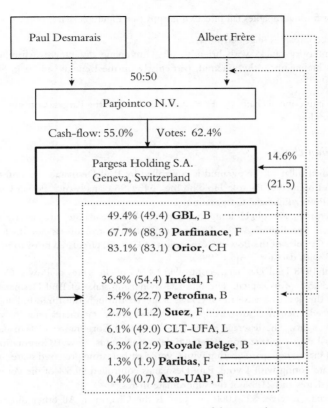

Figure A3.1. *Overall structure of the pyramid.*

Note: The data refer to 31 December 1997. Listed companies are framed with emphasis or printed bold-face. Indirect links are represented by dashed lines, direct links by solid lines. Voting rights are between brackets, while cash-flow rights are not.

Sources: Annual Report Pargesa Holding 1997 and annual reports of portfolio companies.

Sen. controls companies that control the Power Corporation of Canada and the Power Financial Corporation, two listed companies.

The non-listed holdings are used to bring in the capital of 'friends' through share blocks. The listed companies are used to collect funds from capital markets. There are several instances when legal devices (such as dual-class shares with multiple voting rights) are used to lever-age voting power relative to cash-flow rights, even at the level of the individual pyramid companies.

The two control chains meet in a Dutch holding company (Parjointco N.V.), in which each partner holds 50% of the capital and voting rights. Parjointco controls the Swiss Pargesa Holding S.A. that is listed on the Swiss stock exchange. Pargesa is the point of entry to the group's portfolio. Portfolio companies fall into two groups (see Figure A3.1):

- Controlled companies (e.g. Petrofina)
- Friendly minority blocks with 'friends', often involving distant cross-shareholdings with companies higher up in the pyramid, particularly on the Benelux side (e.g. Suez, Paribas, AXA-UAP)

The Desmarais control chain, the Frère control chain and the Pargesa portfolio can be cut in three sub-cascades.

The Canadian chain

The Canadian pillar of the pyramid is controlled by Paul Desmarais. It consists of 5 companies: Gelco Enterprises, Pansolo Holding Inc., 3439496 Canada Inc., Power Corporation of Canada, and Power Financial Corporation.

Gelco Enterprises, Pansolo Holding Inc., and 3439496 Canada Inc., are directly controlled by Paul Desmarais (see Figure A3.2). The exact ownership structure is not disclosed (source: Management Circular of the Power Corporation of Canada, circulated prior to the meeting of 15 May 1998 with data for 7 April 1998).

On 7 April 1998 Paul Desmarais controlled 64.9% of the votes of Power Corporation of Canada and 30.5% of its capital. The ultimate ownership stake of Paul Desmarais cannot be computed at this level because the leverage achieved through the three holding companies cannot be traced. 'Beneficial ownership' in Canadian proxy statements refers to voting rights, not cash-flow rights. The leverage at the level of Power Corporation of Canada is achieved through a dual class capitalization and multiple voting rights. Power Corporation has issued three types of shares: non-participating with 0 votes, participating preferred shares with 10 votes and subordinate voting with 1 vote. Paul Desmarais controlled 99.5% of the votes attached to the preferred shares and 21.8% of the subordinate shares.

Paul Desmarais receives $250,000 per year as the Chairman. All other directors received $15,000 (the chairman of the audit and compensation committee received an additional $10,000 and all directors receive a bonus of $1,000 for each meeting they attend). Desmarais has been the Chairman of the Executive Committee of the company since 1968. André Desmarais and Paul Desmarais Jr. are the two co-chief executives. They received a salary of $700,000 plus $1,000,000 in bonus respectively in 1998 (source: Management Circular of the Power Corporation of Canada, circulated prior to the meeting of 15 May 1998 with data for 7 April 1998).

On 31 December 1997 the Subordinate Voting Shares were listed on the Montreal exchange, The Toronto stock exchange, and the Vancouver stock exchange. The Participating Preferred Shares are listed on the Montreal exchange. (source: Annual Report 1997).

Power Financial Corporation collects additional funds from the markets. The company controls several financial services companies in the United Kingdom and holds a 50% stake in the joint investment vehicle of Paul Desmarais Sen. and Albert Frère: the Dutch holding company Parjointco. The 50% stake in Parjointco N.V. is held via Power Financial Corporation B.V. a wholly owned subsidiary of Power Financial Corporation registered in Rotterdam in the Netherlands.

The Benelux pillar

The Frère Group consists of a chained series of holding companies. It is headed by the Frère-Bourgeois Group which is said to include a Dutch holding company registered in Rotterdam

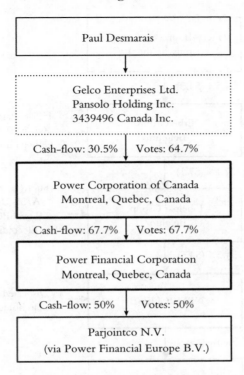

Figure A3.2. *The Canadian control chain.*

Note: Listed companies are printed in bold type. Control is exerted via a series of holding companies. Unknown amounts of external capital are collected via three holding companies. Substantial amounts of external capital are collected via two listed companies. The ultimate cash-flow stake of Paul Desmarais in Parjointco is smaller than 10.35%. Listed companies are framed with emphasis or printed bold-face.

and a Dutch trust company. The capital is owned to 100% by Baron Albert Frère and his family (see Figure A3.3).

The first holding company (Erbe Group) provides a link with the French Paribas banking group. Pargesa, the Swiss investment holding company controlled by Parjointco, holds a 1.9% stake in Paribas, which provides for some double gearing.

The second holding company brings in capital from AXA-UAP, the Suez Group (via its Belgian holding company, Generale Maatschappij van België/Societé General de Belgique), and Electrafina, a Parjointco/Pargesa controlled company. Pargesa holds a 0.7% stake in AXA. Parjointco/Pargesa/GBL and AXA jointly control the Royal Belge. Hence, there is a considerable degree of double gearing at the second level of the control chain.

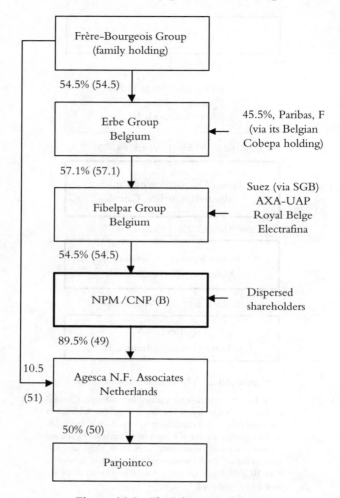

Figure A3.3. *The Belgian control chain.*

Note: Voting rights are between brackets, while cash-flow rights are not.

Source: Unless indicated otherwise, all information is taken from the Annual Report 1997 of Compagnie Nationale à Portefeuille (CNP).

The third level of the chain collects funds from shareholders through the Brussels market. The Nationale Portefeulle Maatschappij (NPM) or Compagnie Nationale à Portefeuille (CNP) is the main investment vehicle of Baron Frère. It is at this level that we learn most about the European activities of the Frère-Desmarais group.

The fourth level is a Dutch holding company that is controlled by the family holding (51% of the votes) but majority-owned by the listed company (89.5% of the cash-flow rights).

Finally, the Dutch holding company owns 50% of the Parjointco holding, the joint investment vehicle of the Frère-Desmarais group. At this level the Frère-Bourgeois cash-flow stake in Parjointco is, not taking into account the double gearing, $0.55 \times 0.57 \times 0.54 \times 0.9 = 0.15 + 0.105 = 25.5\%$.

The Pargesa and NPM/CNP portfolios

The portfolio of the group is not held directly by the Dutch Parjointco holding, but by the Swiss Pargesa holding (see Figures A3.4 and A3.5). Pargesa is listed on the Swiss Stock

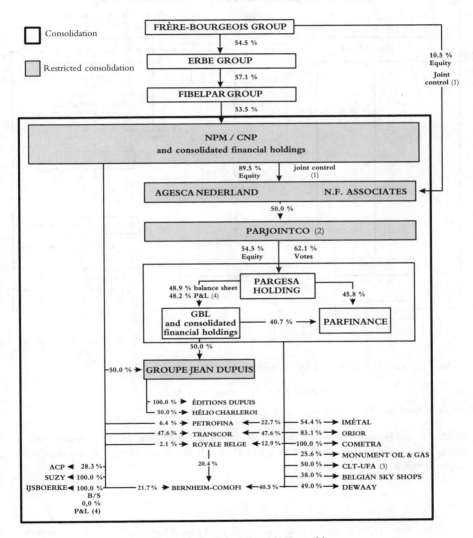

Figure A3.4. *The NPM/CNP portfolio.*

Source: NPM/CNP, Annual Report, 74.

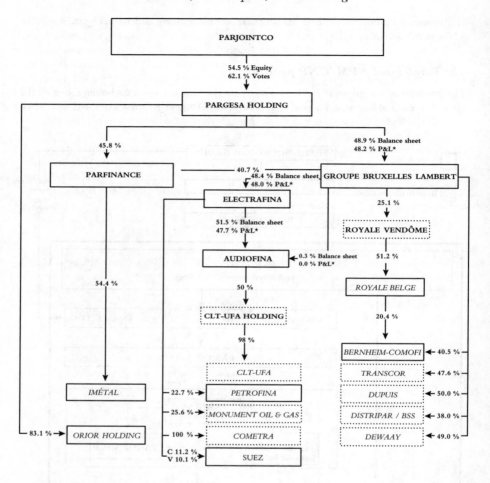

*shares acquired at the end of the year did not contribute to the 1997 profit

Figure A3.5. *The Parjointco portfolio.*

Source: NPM/CNP, Annual Report.

Exchange and brings in additional funds from the market and, again, from the French Paribas group. The voting power of Parjointco and Paribas is leveraged through a dual-class share capitalization.

NOTES

1. Wymeersch (1994*b*) makes a distinction similar to Franks Mayer (1992) between company-oriented and enterprise-oriented systems. A company-oriented system is characterized by the existence of a large number of listed companies. Most of their shares are effectively

traded on the markets. The monitoring function is essentially undertaken by the securities market and active market trading is an essential prerequisite for efficient monitoring. Privileged tools of intervention are the appointment of non-executive directors who are chosen for their technical abilities and the designation of special board committees. Ultimately, takeovers drive out inefficient management. The USA and the UK fall clearly under the definition of company-oriented corporate control systems. An enterprise-oriented system has a low number of listed companies, control is held by major shareholders so that a limited number of shares are effectively on the market. Monitoring does not take place via the market, but is regulated by group law.

2. In this sense, the Italian equity market is similar to the Belgian: few companies are quoted, concentration of ownership is high, pyramidal ownership structures with holding companies as intermediate investment vehicles are common (Bianchi and Casavola 1995). But, whereas the Italian state controls a large number of industrial groups and holding companies, Belgian state ownership is rare.

3. All listed companies are SAs or NVs with exception of 5 real estate Bevek/Sicav (firms): Cofinimmo, Cibix, Wereldhave, Befimmo, Warehouse Estates Belgium.

4. Council Directive of 12 December 1988 (88/627/EEC).

5. Law of 2 March 1989, 'Loi sur la transparence des participations importantes dans les sociétés privées', also called *Transparantiewetgeving* (transparency legislation) and Royal Decrees of 10 May 1989 and of 8 November 1989. The legislation was published on 24 May 1989 in the Belgian Official Journal (*Belgisch Staatsblad, Moniteur Belge*) and most of the relevant rules became effective on 3 June 1989.

6. Law of 18 July 1991.

7. Individual companies can reduce this threshold in the articles of incorporation to 3% (but not to less). Notification of changes in stakes by the shareholders will have to be made if the following thresholds are passed : 3%, 5%, 10%, 15%, and further multiples of 5% (Law of 2 March 1989, Section 5). Currently, about 20 companies have adopted the 3% threshold.

8. Until 31 December 1990, individuals and families ('natural persons') and companies ('legal persons') could send their notification to the Banking Commission and request confidentiality.

9. The Commission for Banking and Finance, usually abbreviated to the Banking Commission, is the Belgian equivalent of the SEC in the USA. In a strict legal sense, the authority of the Banking Commission in the area of ownership disclosure supervision and M&A activity is limited, but the Commission has considerable influence on market participants on the basis of its 'moral authority'.

10. Law of 2 March 1989, Section 1, paragraph 3. Note that this law was initially interpreted as referring to all potential voting rights regardless whether these voting rights were linked to existing securities (as in the case with common stock options) or securities that would be newly created (as in the case with warrants or convertible debt). Options on common stock would in this case entail double counting of voting rights. In the case of warrants or convertibles, there is no such double counting, as the voting rights will be created at the exercise time when a new share comes into being. Analysis of the notification sheets reveals that the confusion has gradually disappeared and that the disclosure has focused more on potential voting rights related to new securities (warrants and convertibles).

11. Banking Commission 1989: 4–6.

12. 'Note on the application of the Law of 2 March 1989.'

13. The definition of 'affiliated investors' is given in Article 5 of the Royal Decree of 10 May 1989 and is based on the Royal Decree of 8 October 1976 on the company's annual accounts and consolidation of accounts. 'Acting in concert' is defined in Article 7 of the Royal Decree of 10 May 1989. Companies acting in concert have agreements with regard to the possession, the acquisition, and the selling of securities.

14. Banking Commission 1989 p: 8–9.

15. Most 'strategy' statements, however, have a low informational content. For instance, on 14 March 1994, Generale Maatschappij van België (Société Générale de Belgique), the reference shareholder for Union Minière and Naviga, notified that these three shareholders had liquidated their combined shareholdings of 62% in Asturienne because 'the share stake is not considered as strategic'.

16. If a target faxes a ownership notification to the stock exchange in the morning, this information is disclosed to the floor at 11.00 a.m. at the earliest via the bulletin board (*ad valvas*) and via the on-line BDPart database. Important news is quickly dispersed via this channel via Tijd Electronic Services or Reuters.

17. The information in the *Cote de la Bourse* is the full responsibility of the stock exchange. The *Cote de la Bourse* in its current form appeared as of 1 January 1992. Before this date, the stock exchange disclosed information via de *Wisselkoerslijst* which was sent to about 1000 subscribers, mostly brokerage houses, banks, institutional investors, and news agencies.

18. Penalties are enumerated in Section 204 of the Coordinated Laws on Commercial Companies. Under the law of 2 March 1989, Sections 7–11, in May 1995, minority shareholders of PB Finance, a listed real estate company, sued the Dutch holding Euver in order to annul Euver's voting rights or to limit them to 5% because Euver had not disclosed the size of its shareholding (of 67%) to the Commission of Banking and Finance and there were suspicions of fraud.

19. Ownership Disclosure Law of 2 March 1989, Article 6.

20. The percentage of ownership of the major shareholders is often an underestimation of the real corporate power these shareholders can exercise. The board, nominated by the major shareholders, could interpret a takeover threat as 'grave and imminent danger' which would allow them to repurchase shares. Furthermore, the board can allow share warrants to be exercised or sold to friendly shareholders for a maximum of 10% of equity capital in order to dilute shareholdings of a potential raider. This authority, for a maximum but renewable period of 5 years, has to be granted specifically to the board by the annual general meeting. Autocontrol mechanisms can also be installed whereby the company's shares are held by a subsidiary. However, a subsidiary's stake in the mother company is restricted to 10%.

21. The mandatory bid rule which has existed since 1965 on a self-regulatory basis has been incorporated into the amendments of the Law of 1991. The rule requires the acquirer of shares, in as far as control has changed at a price higher than the market price, to bid for all remaining shares and the bid price should be set at a premium above the highest market price over the last 12 months. This way, equal treatment of shareholders is ensured since all shareholders are offered the benefit of the control premium. Furthermore, the propensity to trade large blocks, resulting in companies taken over against their will, is diminished.

22. There are additional conditions for changes in the rights of different classes of shareholders. The board of directors needs to document the reasons for the changes extensively and has to send that report to all shareholders before the annual meeting. On the annual meeting, the

proposal is only valid if 50% of the total outstanding voting rights are present and 75% of each category of shareholders votes in favour (Company Law, Article 71).

23. Law of 18 June 1991, Article 191. This law reduced the threshold from 20% to 1%.

24. At the annual general meeting, the directors are 'discharged' from liabilities that may arise in the future if shareholders present at the annual meeting judge, with information from the external auditors and data in the annual report, that the directors fulfilled their tasks adequately during the fiscal year.

25. Note that the minority claim (Company Law Articles 66 bis, paragraph 2, Article 132 bis, and Article 158 bis) is for the benefit of the company and not for the benefit of the minority shareholders directly, although the minority shareholders, like all shareholders, might benefit. Consequently, this procedure to appoint experts cannot be used following conflicts between shareholders, but only if the company's economic position and its long-term survival is endangered. Case law is rare, but the appointment of experts was justified in these cases: the stocks were overvalued, a company was badly managed and had negative earnings (Lievens 1994). In addition to lowering the threshold level for the minority claim, the rules of conflicts of interest have been tightened : personal liability cannot be excluded if directors take undue advantage of their position to the detriment of the company (Wymeersch 1994a). An individual liability claim can only be initiated if the shareholder can prove that he has experienced personal damage.

26. Before 1991, no shareholder could participate in the voting at the annual meeting for more than 20% of the voting rights associated with the total shares outstanding or for more than 40% of the voting rights associated with shares represented at the annual meeting. The restriction limiting the exercise of voting rights most had priority.

27. In section 4, we use the following definition: control exerted by an ultimate shareholder on a sequence of intermediate companies and, ultimately, on the sample company exists if (i) there is a series of uninterrupted majority shareholdings on every ownership tier throughout the pyramid, or (ii) if there is a large shareholding of at least 25% on every ownership level in the absence of other shareholders with stakes of blocking minority size or larger. This criterion is used in the tables to calculate group blocks and identify the ultimate shareholder.

28. The main reason for the reduction of listed companies is the de-listing of firms in coal mining and steel production either involved in a long liquidation process or existing as corporate shells.

29. The database of the National Bank also comprises data on large shareholdings as reported in the annual reports. However, the data on the Notifications of Ownership Changes are more detailed, often present organization charts of pyramidal ownership structures, and give all the ownership changes that took place during the fiscal year rather than the ownership structure at the end of the fiscal year.

30. These five companies are: Delhaize Le Lion, HSPL, Koramic Building Products, SCF, and Solvac. In some companies, like Delhaize and Solvac, a family owns a substantial share stake, but this shareholding is held by several members of the family who each hold less than 5% and consequently are not obliged to officially disclose their holding.

31. The detailed frequency distribution is reported in Becht and Chapelle (1997).

32. Given that group blocks mostly coincide with voting blocks, we focus in this section on voting blocks.

33. The percentile plot of Figure 3.5 details the histogram data.

34. There was no shareholding of at least 25% of 17 sample companies (or 9% of the sample in 1989).

35. To determine the ultimate controlling shareholder, we continued moving up in the shareholders' pyramid when the intermediate share stakes were (i) at least 50%, or (ii) at least 25% in the absence of other shareholders with a stake of more than 25% (in this last case the shareholder with more than 25% is likely to possess majority control of the voting rights exercised in the annual meeting). If company A (a widely held company) owns 50% in company B which owns 50% in company C, the ultimate levered control of company A in C is 25% (50% * 50%).

36. The columns with data on holding companies, families, and industrial companies do not add up to the numbers in the all investors column since the total cumulative concentrated ownership of this column is the sum of 8 investor categories. Institutional investors, banks, etc. do not hold substantial stakes in the sample companies and are not shown in this table.

37. Since 1967 (See Article 1 of Royal Decree no. 64 of 10 November 1967), there is a registration requirement for Belgian holding companies with a portfolio value of over BEF0.5 billion (£10 million). Company Law does not distinguish between different holding categories and in this paper the NACE classification of the National Bank and of the Bank Brussel Lambert is used. However, the group of holding companies is still rather hetero-geneous and includes holdings which are purely financial (e.g. Sofina), a combination of financial and industrial (Generale Maatschappij van België/Société Générale de Belgique), or more like a conglomerate (Tractebel).

38. Law of 2 March 1993. The Royal Decree of 8 May 1990 had already allowed the credit institutions to purchase shares up to 5% of their own funds since 1990.

39. Most share stakes held by institutional investors are under 5% and as such are not included in the analysis. Data about investment funds should be interpreted with caution since some investment funds investing in Belgian shares are domiciled in Luxembourg but managed by subsidiaries of Belgian banks. The Luxembourg authorities do not differentiate according to nationality of the managers of the fund. Regarding institutional investor shareholdings, Van der Elst (1998) reports an aggregate percentage of 17.7% of the votes in listed companies, while Wymeersch (1994b) reports 22% for a sample of listed and non-listed firms.

40. *Beleggingsfonds met veranderlijk kapitaal* (Bevek)/*Société d'Investissement à Capital Variable* (Sicav) (mutual fund with variable capital).

41. Until the end of 1990, the investors in investment funds could not be represented by the investment fund on annual general meetings of companies in which the investment fund held shares. In practice, this legal prohibition made it impossible that the voting rights of shares held by investment funds were exercised. The legislation intended to avoid that investment funds would become instruments of financial groups which could strengthen their control on quoted companies. However, the result of this legislation was not neutral since the position of controlling shareholders was even strengthened. The Law of 4 December 1990, Article 112, abolished this prohibition and stated that the acts of incor-poration can determine in which cases the investment fund is to exercise the voting rights.

42. Ownership tables with the relative importance of each of the foreign shareholder classes (holding companies, banks, institutional investors, insurance companies, industrial com-panies, families, and the government) are available upon request.

43. Shareholders of almost all the member states of the European Union, Switzerland, USA, Canada, Japan, Panama, Congo, Rwanda, Liberia, and the Cayman Islands hold stakes of at least 5% in Belgian listed companies.

REFERENCES

Becht, Marco (1997), 'Strong Blockholders, Weak Owners and the Need for European Mandatory Disclosure', Executive report, in *The Separation of Ownership and Control: A Survey of 7 European Countries*, Preliminary report to the European Commission, vol. 1, Brussels: European Corporate Governance Network.

—— and Ariane Chapelle (1997), 'Ownership and Control in Belgium', in *The Separation of Ownership and Control: A Survey of 7 European Countries*, Vol. 2.

Bianchi, M. and P. Casavola, (1995), 'Piercing the Corporate Veil: Truth and Appearance in Italian Listed Pyramidal Groups', Working paper Banca D'Italia, presented at Corporate Governance and Property Rights Workshop in Milan 16–17 June.

Franks, J. and C. Mayer (1992), 'Corporate Control: A Synthesis of the International Evidence', Working paper, London Business School.

—— —— (1995), 'Ownership and Control', in H. Siebert (ed.), *Trends in Business Organization: Do Participation and Cooperation Increase Competitiveness?* Tüebingen: J.C.B. Mohr, 171–95.

Lievens, J. (1994), 'De rechten van de minderheidsaandeelhouder', *Centrum voor fiscale wetenschappen in bedrijfbeleid EHSAL* (Fiscale Hogeschool seminaries), seminar on 9 June.

Maertens, M. (1994), *Loi sur la transparence du marché: Circulation de l'information*, Brussels: Brussels Stock Exchange.

Renneboog, L. (1997), 'Shareholding Concentration and Pyramidal Ownership Structure in Belgium', in M. Balling, E. Hennessy, and R. O'Brien, (eds.) (1998), *Corporate Governance, Financial Markets and Global Convergence*, Boston: Kluwer Academic.

—— (2001), 'Ownership, Managerial Control and the Governance of Poorly Performing Companies Listed on the Brussels Stock Exchanges', *Journal of Banking and Finance*, 24: 1959–95.

Van de Elst, C. (1998), 'Aandeelhouderschap en aandeelhoudersstructuren in de Belgische beurgenoteerde vennootschappen en in een Europees perspectief', in Instituut voor Bestuurders (ed.), *Corporate Governance: Het Belgische Perspectief*, Antwerp: Intersentia, p, 124.

Wymeersch, E. (1994a), Aspects of Corporate Governance, *Journal of Corporate Governance*, 2: 138–49.

—— (1994b), 'Elements of Comparative Corporate Governance in Western Europe', M. Isaksson and R. Skog (eds.), *Aspect of Corporate Governance*, Stockholm: Juristforlaget, 83–116.

4

Ownership and Voting Power in France

LAURENCE BLOCH AND ELIZABETH KREMP

1. INTRODUCTION

This chapter provides an overview of French ownership structure and voting power, both in terms of institutional and legal framework and of quantitative analysis.[1] It tries to answer the questions: are French firms widely held or do they have significant owners (in terms of voting or cash-flow rights)? Who are these significant owners: other companies, families, state, foreigners...? To which extent do ownership structure and voting power differ?

In theory, voting power may differ from direct ownership for three main reasons. One reason is the existence of multiple classes of shares (shares with no voting right or shares with multiple voting rights). Another reason is the existence of pyramids in the ownership structure of the firm. The third reason can appear through cross-share holdings.

These three explanations can be put forward in France. Multiple classes of shares do exist. Allowed since the French business law of July 1966, they can encourage faithful share holdings and limit the influence of large foreign shareholders. Pyramid structures *do* exist in France but have not been systematically and precisely measured. However, a recent study shows that the number of groups have exploded in France, from 1,300 in 1980 to 6,700 in 1995 (Vergeau and Chabanas 1997).

Now, as explained by Baudru and Kechidi (1998) and Morin (1996), cross-share holdings in large groups are a characteristic of the French model, called 'financial core', and have been extended in 1986, with the first wave of privatizations. Nevertheless, at present foundations of this model seem to be weakened. Comparing the size of cross-share holdings and foreigners' ownership for 10 privatized firms, shows that this organization has not been able to really prevent the increasing of foreign presence in French capitalization.

In terms of corporate governance, agency problems may arise in a company when there is a separation of ownership and management. This situation often occurs when there is a separation of direct ownership and voting power: controlling shareholders who directly influence corporate decisions may not act in the interest of minority shareholders and may lead to expropriation of minority shareholders. Theoretically

Grossman and Hart (1988) and Harris and Raviv (1988) showed that the rule 'one-share-one-vote' maximizes the cost of control for a managing team which would lower the public value of the company. They suggested that the rule 'one-share-one-vote' is optimal in many cases not so much because it gives shareholders the right incentives to take decisions but rather because it forces someone who wants to obtain the company's control to acquire a share of the company's dividend stream commensurate with this control.

The European Large Holdings Directive of December 1988, which imposes notifications as soon as an owner acquires a significant stake of a firm's capital or ceases to have one, has been transposed in the French law of August 1989 regarding safety and transparency of financial markets. Thus, this 1989 law amends the French Business Law of July 1966, which already included disclosure rules.

The empirical analysis is held on two datasets. One collects data on voting power (direct and indirect voting rights) in the CAC 40, the top 40 firms ranked by market capitalization of common equity at the end of 1995. The second one collects information on direct ownership, available in August 1996, in a very large sample of 283,322 firms, including 674 listed firms and in particular the CAC 40 firms. The first part of this chapter describes the legal framework (section 1.1), the construction of the datasets (section 1.2), and the methodology (section 1.3). Section 2 looks at the degree of concentration and the distribution by blockholder of voting power on the CAC 40 firms. Section 3 focuses on direct ownership instead of voting rights, but on a much larger sample, comparisons of capital structure and concentration between the large sample, listed firms, and CAC 40 firms are therefore possible. Main conclusions are drawn in section 4.

1.1. *Legal framework: the transposition of the European Large Holdings Directive into the French law of August 1989*

According to the French law no. 89–531 of 2 August 1989, any natural person or legal entity acting by himself or in concert, who comes to own directly or indirectly, more than 5%, 10%, 20%, 1/3, 50%, or 2/3 of the capital of a company (listed on the official list, or on the second market, or belonging to the over-the-counter market, with its head office on French territory), or comes to cross these thresholds, must notify the company itself within fifteen days and the 'competent authorities' within five active stock market days. An example of a notification published by the SBF is given in Appendix 1. The 'competent authority' was the SBF (*Société des Bourses Françaises*), and became the French Financial Markets Council (CMF, *Conseil des Marchés Financiers*) in 1996, when CMF was created persuant to the Financial Activities Modernization Act of 2 July 1996, which transposes into French law the article 4 of the European Directive on investment services of 10 May 1993.

The French law no. 89 modifies the article 356-1: creation of a new threshold of 2/3, restriction of the application to listed target companies only,[2] and introduction of the principle that concerted action must be taken into account in appreciating the level of direct and indirect ownership.

Moreover, this new law introduces three new articles in the French Business Law. The new article 356-1-1 substitutes the account in shares by one in voting rights. When the number of voting rights does not correspond to the number of shares, or when the number of shares is equivalent to the number of voting rights but their distribution does not coincide, the percentages of thresholds to notify are calculated in terms of voting rights. This device takes into account the existence in France of multiple classes of shares (see Appendix 2).

The new article 356-1-2 defines voting rights (directly and indirectly) to be taken into account for the calculation of the stake and defines the control (transposition of the articles 7 and 8 of the European Directive). The assimilated shares or voting rights of the concerned shareholder to be taken into account are:

- Shares or voting rights owned by other persons on behalf of the concerned shareholder;
- Shares or voting rights owned by companies which are controlled by the concerned shareholder, with the control defined as in article 355-1 (see below);
- Shares or voting rights owned by a third party with whom the concerned shareholder takes concerted action (see the new article 356-1-3);
- Shares or voting rights that the concerned shareholder (or the other persons previously mentioned above) can purchase by his own initiative according to an agreement.

The new article 356-1-3 of the Business Law defines persons taking concerted action. These persons have entered into an (written, verbal, tacit) agreement with the aim of purchasing or selling voting rights or exerting their voting rights in the view of a common policy towards the company. Such an agreement is presumed to exist:

- Between a company, the chairman and the executives;
- Between a company and the other companies which it controls (vertical agreement);
- Between companies controlled by the same persons (horizontal agreement).

Persons taking concerted action are jointly under the obligations of the law. The article 355-1 describes several cases of control: legal control and control in facts, presumption of control, and indirect control.

A person or a legal entity controls a firm:

- When he owns directly or indirectly a fraction of capital giving him the majority (more than 50%) of the voting rights in the annual meetings of a firm (legal control);
- When he owns the majority of the voting rights because of an agreement with other partners or shareholders (legal control);
- When he determines, by the voting rights he owns, the decisions in annual meetings of a firm (de facto control).

The control is *presumed* when a person or a legal entity owns, directly or indirectly, a fraction of the voting rights greater than 40% and no other partner or shareholder owns directly or indirectly a fraction greater than his.

Whether it is *legal* control or de facto control, this control can be direct or indirect. The indirect control exerts indirectly from one firm to another through one or several firms. So, a firm A holds directly no share in the firm C but controls it indirectly because of the shares it owns in the firm B, which owns by itself shares in C.

Examples:

(i) In terms of voting rights, A owns respectively 60% of B and C. B and C each own 30% of D. Hence, the 30% owned respectively by B and C are owned indirectly by A. Therefore, A owns indirectly 60% of D and controls it.

(ii) A owns respectively 30% of B and C. B owns 60% of D, and C owns 40% of D. In this case, A has no direct or indirect stake in D.

On the basis of articles 356-1 and 356-2, public companies (*sociétés par actions*) should inform their shareholders of their ownership distribution. More precisely, the annual report must mention (art. 356-3):

- The identity of natural persons or legal entities owning more than 5%, 10%, 20%, 1/3, 50%, 2/3 of the capital or of the voting rights;
- The modifications which occurred during the fiscal year, in particular those being the subject of notifications;
- The names of controlled companies and the share of capital of the company they own.

This obligation concerns public companies. The listed companies can fill up this obligation: they have this information because of the notifications. But, on contrary, non-listed companies do know their direct shareholders (because of the nominative shares) but often don't know their indirect shareholders, and so usually don't fill up this obligation.

Now a company can impose in its articles a lower minimum threshold, down to 0.5%. In this case when a natural person or a legal company crosses this threshold, it must notify the company but does not have to notify the competent authority.

1.2. *Data*

This chapter is based on two datasets on ownership and voting power:

(a) The first dataset collects voting rights by blockholder (directly, indirectly, and in concert) for the top 40 firms ranked by market capitalization of common equity at the end of 1995. This dataset has been constructed from the information available in the annual reports (see 1.1). When this information was not available or incomplete, it has been completed with the notifications themselves published by the SBF (see Appendix 1).

These publications are not standardized and are sometimes fairly raw. Some hypotheses have been made to classify the blockholders into six different categories: individuals, state, banks and insurance companies, employees, non-financial firms, foreign) notably when concerted action exists. In particular, in privatized firms, shareholders belonging to a stable shareholder structure—which has been used in 1987 with the first wave of privatizations 'to ensure that a controlling block of the voting rights are put in the hands of a relatively small group of other companies'[3]—has been considered as taking concerted action and therefore as a unique blockholder.

(b) The primary source used to build the second dataset is the information collected by the French Central Bank, called *Fiben* (*Fichier Bancaire des ENtreprises*) supplemented by *Bafi* (*BAse Financière*) in order to make up for data concerning financial firms.

The database *Fiben* deals with information of different kinds (descriptive qualitative data but also accounting data) on 2,320,000 firms, 1,280,000 managers, 150,000 annual balance sheet data, 495,000 judicial incidents, and 18,000 decisions of judicial bans. This dataset is not public but is used by the Central Bank for its own purposes and is sold to the banks.

The descriptive information on firms and managers is updated by the bulletins of legal notices (*Journaux d'annonces légales*), commercial courts (*Greffes des Tribunaux de Commerce*), contacts with credit institutions, or information given by firms. Since April 1991, the different branches of the Bank of France have introduced data about the capital distribution of firms belonging to their districts. No information is available on voting rights. Sources are reports of meetings, legal notice reports (*Journaux d'annonces légales*), firms' tax balance sheets. Information from other datasets is not used.

The database called *Bafi* (*BAse Financière*) is available at the Banking Supervision Authority (*Commission Bancaire*) and concerns especially financial firms. As *Fiben*, this database is not available to the general public.

The dataset put together for this study covers the information available in August 1996 for 283,322 firms. The list of listed companies has been collected from the official publication of the SBF-*Bourse de Paris*, called *La Cote Officielle* (Official List).

For each firm, identified by its number *SIREN*, its industry classification, its size, and its owners (firms, banks, individuals, 'float' . . .) are recorded (see Table 4.1 for the shareholders' classification.[4] Then, the capital's percentage for which the owner is unknown has been computed by difference, and called 'unknown' thereafter. 112,644 firms have some capital for which the owner is unknown. This unknown percentage can have very different meanings, and there is not information available to choose among them ('float', institutional investors, non-residents, but also small shareholders that can be firms, banks, mutual funds, or insurance companies). In some cases, 'float' is clearly identified. In others, it is not and this unknown capital may be held by small unidentified shareholders. Therefore no assumption can be made without further information.

1.3. *Methodology*

To analyse these datasets, either in terms of voting power or in terms of capital structure, the same methodology is used. The central point concerns the inclusion or not of the zero stakes in the computation of concentration and distribution by blockholders.[5] Another issue is the possible aggregation of investors by categories. We explain the three ways of defining a blockholder's share. While this point looks very technical, these different definitions answer very different questions.

Table 4.1. *Classification of the shareholders in the Bank of France dataset*

	NAF code	French label
Banks	65	Intermédiation financière (dont OPCVM*: 652E)
	671	Administration de marchés financiers, gestion de portefeuille, autres auxiliaires financiers
Insurance	66	Assurance
	672	Auxiliaires d' assurances
Holdings	714	Administration d' entreprises
Firms		All other firms (i.e. not banks, insurance and holdings) identified by a *SIREN*
Foreign		All firms (financial and non-financial) identified by a foreign *SIREN* (starting with a digit 2)
Float		Public (ensemble des petits porteurs)
State		Etat
Employees		Salariés
Individuals		Famille, personnes, indivision, succession, divers
Unknown		Computed by difference between the percentage of capital held by all above listed criteria and 100

The firm i belongs to the I population and its capital can be held by different classes of investors j. I_j is the number of *firms* that have at least one investor from the j *category* in their capital. I_{jl} is the number of *investors* (owners) in the j category of investors because each firm can have several investors in the same j category. Several investors l belonging to the same j category can hold stakes in the same i firm. The percentage is noted $PCTj_l^i$. For each firm i, one can aggregate all the percentages of the different investors l from the same category j, as if there was only one investor per firm in that category.

$$PCTj^i = \sum_l PCTj_l^i.$$

The mean of the percentage of capital held by an investor can be computed using one of the three denominators defined above: the total number of firms (I), the number of firms that have an investor from the category j (I_j), the number of investors in a j category (I_{jl}).

Three different means: three different questions

(1) *On average, what is the percentage of capital held by a category of investors?* The sum of these different means over all the categories of investors equals 100.

$$Mean\_all_j = \frac{\sum_{i \in I} PCTj^i}{I}$$

(2) *What is the average percentage of capital held by a category of investors, when that category of investors is a firm's stakeholder?* In that case, the denominator is not the total number of firms (I), but the total number of firms which have that category of investors as owners. One has to aggregate for a firm, all the different investors from the same category, as if there was only one investor per firm in that category.

$$Mean\_cat_j = \frac{\sum_{i \in I_j} PCTj^i}{I_j} = \frac{\sum_{i \in I_j} \sum_l PCTj_l^i}{I_j}$$

(3) *What is the average percentage of capital held by an investor of a category?* In that case, the denominator is the total number of investors in a category.

$$Mean\_inv_j = \frac{\sum_{i \in I_j} PCTj_l^i}{I_{j_l}}$$

Example
There are 283,322 firms in the dataset. Among them, 1,324 have at least one insurance firm (j) as an owner. On average, insurance firms hold 0.3% of the capital of all firms (first mean). Insurance firms are identified 1,749 times as investors. If an insurance company holds stake, it holds on average 41.7% of firms (second mean). But, on average the amount held by insurance companies when they held stakes is 54.2% (third mean).

2. VOTING POWER AND THE CAC 40 FIRMS

2.1. *Concentration and distribution of voting power*

The sum of all the known or identified voting blocks (C_{all}) amounts to around 40% (37.4% in median and 42.1% in average). The largest voting blockholder holds about 20–30% (20.0% in median and 29.4% in average). He has not the absolute control himself (more than 50% of the voting rights), but has the majority of the known voting blocks (control in facts), given a total of known voting blocks around 40%.

The second largest blockholder lags rather far behind the first one, with median and average stakes around 6%. Even if the computation of the share of the second blockholder is restricted to firms with identified second owners (three-quarters of the sample) median and mean are still rather low, below 9%. So the second largest blockholder holds around 15% of the known voting blocks.[6]

Further ranks do not attain 5% of the total voting rights on median and average.

The histogram of the maximum voting block indicates one clear peak at 10–20%: one third of the CAC 40 firms have a first voting blockholder between 10% and 20%. As already stated, this peak corresponds to the control of the known voting blocks. In only a quarter of the CAC 40 firms the largest blockholder owns a stake superior or equal to 50%. In around 40% of the CAC 40 firms the largest blockholder holds a stake in excess of 33.3%, which is the mandatory bid threshold.

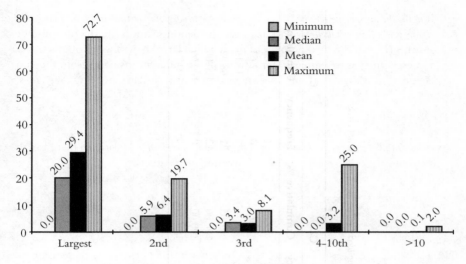

Figure 4.1. *Voting blocks by rank for CAC 40 companies.*

Note: Zero stakes are not excluded.

Sources: Annual reports.

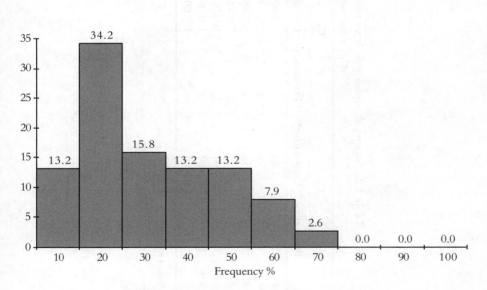

Figure 4.2. *Histogram of largest voting block in the CAC 40 companies.*

Sources: Annual reports.

Table 4.2. *Frequency distribution of the largest voting block (C_1), the 3 voting blocks (C_3), the 5 first voting blocks (C_5), and all the known voting blocks (C_{all})*

Range	C_1		C_3		C_5		C_{all}	
	Frequency	Cumulative%	Frequency	Cumulative %	Frequency	Cumulative %	Frequency	Cumulative %
0–4.999	1	2.63	1	2.63	1	2.63	1	2.63
5–9.999	4	13.16	0	2.63	0	2.63	0	2.63
10–24.999	18	60.52	8	23.68	4	13.16	4	13.16
25–49.999	6	76.31	18	71.05	22	71.05	21	68.42
50–74.999	9	100.00	11	100.00	11	100.00	12	100.00
75–89.999	0	100.00	0	100.00	0	100.00	0	100.00
>90	0	100.00	0	100.00	0	100.00	0	100.00

Source: Annual reports.

In about half of the CAC 40 firms the three first voting blocks (C_3), the five first voting blocks (C_5), and all the known voting blocks (C_{all}) hold between 25% and 50% of the voting rights. The distribution of the five first voting blocks (C_5) is very close to the distribution of all known voting blocks (C_{all}), showing that for most firms, there are no more than five voting blocks identified.

2.2. *Distribution of voting power by blockholder*

The largest voting block category is banks and insurance companies with an average of 13.4% of the total voting rights. Firms are the second most important category with an aggregate stake of 11.5%. Individuals are the third category with an average stake of 7.2%.

But, when an investor of this category is present as a blockholder, individuals with an average of 30% hold the largest blocks. Then comes the State with an average of 18.3%, which has nearly in mean the control of the known voting blocks; it reflects the fact that privatization is not yet finished. After this, at the same level, come firms, foreign, and banks and insurance companies.

Table 4.3. *Voting blocks by blockholder type (percentage of capital held by a category of investors)*

	Individuals	State	Banks/insurance	Employees	Firms	Foreign
Min.	0	0	0	0	0	0
Median	0	0	4.8	0	3.5	0
Mean	7.2	4.8	13.4	1.2	11.5	4.1
Max.	69.5	72.7	64.7	8.5	56.5	65.8

Note: See section 1.3 for the methodology. Statistics here correspond to the first concept (median_all and mean_all).

Source: Annual reports.

Table 4.4. *Voting blocks by blockholder type (percentage of capital held by an investor of a category when he is present as blockholder)*

	Individuals	State	Banks/insurance	Employees	Firms	Foreign
Number of blockholders of this type	9	10	55	17	34	15
Min.	3.6	0.8	0.4	0.2	0.7	0.7
Median	29.0	8.2	5.7	2.2	5.3	5.8
Mean	30.2	18.3	9.3	2.9	12.3	10.2
Max.	69.5	72.7	64.7	8.5	56.5	65.8

Note: See section 1.3 for the methodology. Statistics here correspond to the third concept (median_inv and mean_inv).

Source: Annual reports.

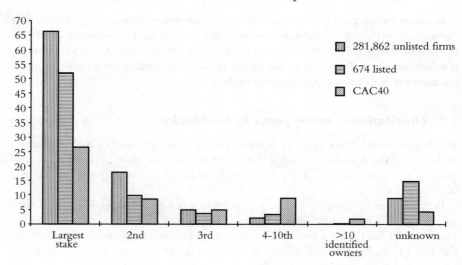

Figure 4.3. *Average ownership by ownership stake in percentages.*

Note: Zero stakes are not excluded.

Sources: Observatoire des entreprises, Banque de France.

3. COMPARISON OF DIRECT OWNERSHIP ON A LARGE SAMPLE, LISTED FIRMS, AND THE CAC 40

3.1. *Concentration of direct ownership*

Figure 4.3 compares the average ownership by ownership stake for all firms, listed firms, and firms belonging to the CAC 40 index. It gives the average ownership of the three first direct owners and the average ownership of the next 4 to 10 direct owners.

3.1.1. *Non-listed firms: the degree of concentration increases with size and is very high especially for large firms*

On average, the first identified owner of a non-listed company holds 66% of the capital. This is a very high number, which confirms this idea that the concentration of ownership is very important in France. This degree of concentration increases with the size of a firm: 63% for a firm with less than 20 employees, 88% for firms with 500 to 2,000 employees, or firms with more than 2,000 employees. This suggests that large non-listed firms are controlled by one owner.

One can argue that by looking at direct ownership instead of computing integrated ownership, the degree of concentration is biased. The problem is to determine in which direction is the bias. Because of double counting, this concentration could be overestimated. But in case of groups with several loops and large amounts of cross-share holdings, the degree of concentration can also be underestimated. The ultimate shareholder (i.e. the owner that does not have any shareholder) may end with a higher percentage in the integrated ownership matrix (i.e. taking into account all the loops among the different direct and indirect shareholders) than in the direct ownership matrix.

In any case, bringing together the information on concentration of ownership and on distribution of ownership suggests two different conclusions for non-listed firms:[7]

- Firstly, for non-listed firms with under 500 employees, the high level of concentration is not due to a bias of direct ownership versus integrated ownership, because individuals hold on average over 50% of non-listed firms. When they are identified as owners, they possess almost 80% of the capital, and each individual holds on average 36%. This result holds for all categories of firms with below 500 employees.
- Secondly, for large non-listed firms (500 to 2,000 employees, and over 2,000 employees), individuals hold comparatively a much smaller share (5–6%) whereas holdings possess on average between 40% and 45%. When identified as owners, they have around 90% of the capital of large non-listed firms. Therefore, when looking only at information on direct ownership, the concentration level is more difficult to figure out for those large non-listed firms.

Figure 4.3 shows that 6 out of 10 non-listed firms have a second identified owner, holding on average 18% of the capital, and when it exists, this owner has 30% of the capital. For large non-listed firms with over 500 employees, only 3 out of 10 firms have a second identified owner, with around 20% of the capital.

40% of non-listed firms have some unknown capital, representing on average 9% of their capital.

3.1.2. *Listed firms: the degree of concentration of direct ownership is lower than for non-listed firms but still very important*

The degree of concentration is a little lower for listed firms, but still over half of the capital: 52%. For the 40 firms belonging to the CAC 40, the share of the largest identified stake is around 27%, which is of the same order of magnitude as the degree of concentration computed with voting rights and presented earlier.

Seven out of ten listed firms have a second identified owner. When there is a second owner, this owner holds 10% of the capital. A little over half of the listed firms have three identified owners. These results do not differ significantly when they are computed by size.

We tried to construct the integrated ownership matrix for listed firms. The interpretation is not easy, because one has to avoid defining an ultimate ownership firm only because no information is available on its owners. To compute the integrated matrix for 680 listed firms in the French case, the first approximation is a matrix of around 2,000 firms. A first result suggests that the first owner of the 680 listed firms holds 56%. Concentrating on listed firms that have at least one identified firm as an owner (612 listed firms), this percentage declines to 49%. Using the integrated matrix, the first ultimate ownership has 32% of the capital.

65% of listed firms have a percentage of unknown capital, representing on average 17% of their capital.

3.2. *Distribution of direct ownership by investor*

Figures 4.4 and 4.5 show the average ownership by category of investors respectively for all non-listed firms and for listed firms. For each category, two means are reported (see definition section 1.3). Two comments have to be underlined. First, the great divergence between the levels of these two means, especially for non-listed firms, and the very high level of the second type of means, computed when a category of investors is present as an owner, confirms the high level of concentration. Second, the comparison of the two types of means for non-listed and listed firms emphasizes the much greater heterogeneity among firms in the capital structure of the former compared to the latter.

Our data confirms the results pointed out by OECD in its recent study on France, defining France as the country with Italy where financial institutions have the smallest share of firms' capital.

3.2.1. *Non-listed firms: individuals hold half of the capital and are identified as owners in 65% of the cases*

Individuals have by far the most important share: 65% of French companies have individuals as owners of their capital and on average these individuals hold half of the capital. These numbers cover very different situations, because they have effectively almost 80% of the capital when they are identified as owners and each individual holds on average 36% of the capital.

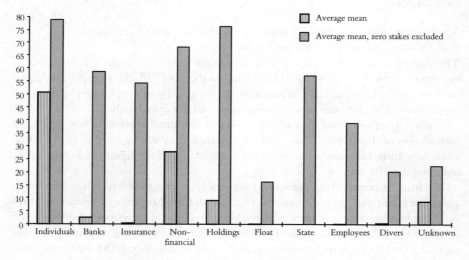

Figure 4.4. *Average ownership of non-listed firms by category of investors in percentages.*

Note: See paragraph on methodology for definitions of different means.

Sources: Observatoire des entreprises, Banque de France.

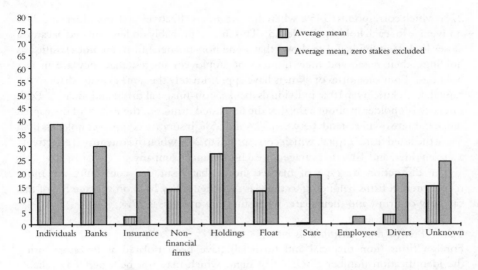

Figure 4.5. *Average ownership of listed firms by category of investors in percentages.*

Note: See paragraph on methodology for definitions of different means.

Sources: Observatoire des entreprises, Banque de France.

Non-financial firms are the second category of owners, with 28% of the capital. They have been separated from holdings, which own on average 9% of the capital.

When identified as owners,[8] financial institutions (banks and insurance companies) hold on average 3% of the capital of French firms. Banks and insurance companies are not very often identified as owners (respectively 4.5% and 0.5% of the cases), holding on average 2.7% and 0.3% of the capital. But, when they are owners, they own approximately the same share, i.e. around 60% of the capital.

3.2.2. *Size is decisive to characterize non-listed firms*
As already underlined when commenting on direct and indirect ownership of non-listed firms, the numbers are quite different for large non-listed firms (firms with over 500 employees). On average, individuals hold only 5% to 6% of the capital of non-listed firms, non financial and financial firms hold 85% to 90%, and only 3% of the capital is unknown. Even among these large non-listed firms, considerable differences exist. If on average, individuals hold only 5% to 6% of the capital, when they are present, they still hold half of the capital. On the contrary, holdings have on average 40% to 45% of the capital, but when they are owners, they have 90% of the capital.

3.2.3. *Listed firms: a more even distribution*
The type of ownership of listed firms appears to be more equally distributed. The first category of identified owners corresponds to holdings. Their share is over

27%, which corresponds to 45% when the category is effectively a shareholder, and 29% on average for each holding (Table 4.5). This share is probably underestimated because a closer look at individual data shows that some non-financial firms are not classified as holdings, their name and their number of employees suggest that they are in fact holdings.[9] Four categories of owners have approximately the same average share of the capital, i.e. a little over 10%: individuals, banks, non-financial firms, and 'float'.[10] Each category is a holder in about a third of the 680 listed firms. So, their share of the capital when they are owners stands between 30% and 35%. Insurance companies hold less than 3% of the listed firms' capital, which corresponds to 20% when the category is effectively a shareholder, and 10% on average for each insurance company.

The distinction by type of market shows that insurance companies are more represented in firms belonging to the Cash Market. They hold on average 5% of this category of firms, and their share, when they are owners, is 27%.

3.2.4. *Foreign firms identified as owners*
Foreign firms (non-financial and financial) have been isolated as investors, using the identification number *SIREN* first digit, which may not be a perfectly reliable method. Nevertheless, the opposition between non-listed and listed firms seems interesting. For non-listed firms, foreign firms hold on average less than 3% of the capital. When they are identified as owners (3% of the cases), they hold almost 80% of the capital, which is the same percentage as when individuals are identified as owners, and much higher when non-financial firms are (66%). For listed firms, the foreign-firm ownership is much more spread out. Foreign firms also owned on average 3% of the capital of the listed firms, but they are owners of 12% of the listed firms, and own 30% of those firms. These numbers suggest that foreign firms are the main owners (with the majority) of non-listed firms when they are identified as owners, but only one of the many shareholders when they are identified as owners of a listed firm.

These data do not allow answering the question of non-resident ownership, because non-residents can hold stakes through firms, 'float', banks, mutual funds, or unknown capital. Several studies focus on this question (Chocron and Marchand 1998; Chocron 1998; Maréchal 1998). Although they lead to different levels of estimates, due to different statistical methods and field coverage, they all agree in the increasing share holding by non-residents in French firms, especially for listed firms. For example Maréchal (1998), using a survey covering the main 40 listed firms (CAC 40), finds that non-residents hold on average 25% of these firms, most of them holding more than 10% of the capital, and nine of them (over 40) more than 40%.

3.2.5. *Distribution of firms using the type and size of the first owner*
In the next two figures, we look at the share held by the first holder, being either a firm (including holding and banks-insurance company), an individual, or float. We distinguish three levels: more than 50% of the capital, between 25% and 50%, and between 10% and 25%.

73% of firms are controlled (in the meaning of direct ownership of more than 50% of the capital) by only one shareholder: 37% of firms being controlled by another

Table 4.5. *Summary statistics by blockholder type (all firms and listed firms)*

	Individuals	Banks	Insurance	Non-financial firms	Holdings	Float	State	Employees	Divers	Unknown
All firms										
Mean_all	50.9	2.5	0.3	27.8	9.2	0.1	0.0	0.1	0.3	8.8
Mean_cat	78.9	58.7	54.2	68.2	76.2	16.1	57.1	38.8	20.1	22.2
Mean_inv	36.5	49.5	41.7	56.4	72.0	16.1	57.1			
Listed firms										
Mean_all	11.8	12.2	3.2	13.7	27.0	12.9	0.6	0.3	3.8	14.7
Mean_cat	38.3	30.1	20.1	33.6	44.5	29.5	19.2	3.2	18.9	24.2
Mean_inv	22.6	15.8	10.7	23.0	29.2	29.5	19.2			

Note: See 1.3 for the methodology.

Source: Observatoire des entreprises, Banque de France.

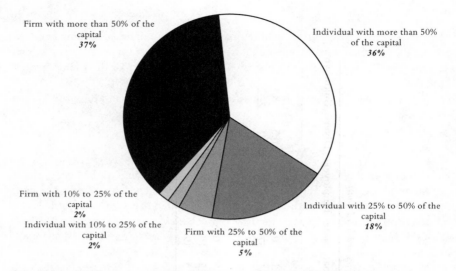

Figure 4.6. *Distribution of 282,322 firms using the type and the size of the first owner in percentages.*

Sources: Observatoire des entreprises, Banque de France.

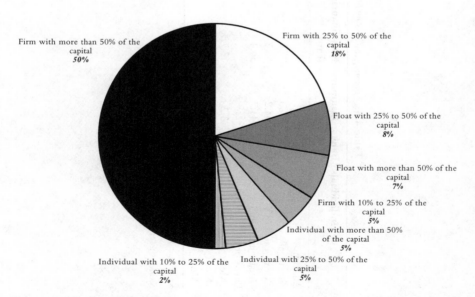

Figure 4.7. *Distribution of 680 listed firms using the type and the size of the first owner in percentages*

Sources: Observatoire des entreprises, Banque de France.

firm (financial or non-financial), and 35% by an individual. The third category, in the case of 18% firms, concerns firms whose first owner is an individual holding between 25% to 50% of capital. Finally, when the first identified direct owner is a firm (which is the case for 124,000 firms), this first owner has the majority of the capital in 80% of the cases.

Half of listed firms are controlled by a firm; 18% of them have another firm holding between 25% and 50% of the capital as a first owner.

4. MAIN CONCLUSIONS

Concentration of direct ownership and voting power is very high in France, both for non-listed and listed firms, and even for the CAC 40 firms. The largest direct owner of non-listed firms owns 66% of the capital. The degree of concentration is a little lower for listed firms but still very large: the share of the largest identified stake is 52%, over half of the capital. The largest direct owner or the largest voting blockholder of the CAC 40 firms holds around 20–30% and has the control in facts of the company. The comparison for CAC 40 firms of concentration through direct ownership or through voting rights gives fairly similar results.

The second direct owner lags far behind the first one: 18% in non-listed firms, 10% in listed firms, and between 5% and 10% in CAC 40 firms.

For non-listed firms, individuals hold half of the capital, non-financial and financial firms hold 40%, and for 9% of the capital, the owner is unknown. When banks, insurance, or holdings are owners, they have most often majority.

For listed firms, ownership is more evenly spread out, holdings being the most important category, followed by individuals, non-financial firms, 'float', and banks.

For the CAC 40 firms, banks and insurance companies are the main category of voting blockholders, followed by non-financial firms and individuals.

Families seem to play an important role in ownership and voting power, both in unlisted firms and in the CAC 40 firms. Around 40% of unlisted firms have, as first shareholder, individuals owning directly more than 50% of the capital. For the CAC 40 firms, individuals are not the largest blockholder, but when they effectively are present as blockholders, they hold around 30% of the voting rights and have the control in facts.

These results confirm and complete La Porta *et al.* (1998) main conclusions on the top 20 firms at the end of 1995, that firms with controlling shareholders rarely have other large shareholders, and that family control is rather common.

5. RECENT DEVELOPMENTS IN CORPORATE CONTROL IN FRANCE

Following the introduction of the Euro and the globalization of asset management, several important events occurred in 2000 concerning Paris market and regulations.

First, Paris market regulations are now featured on Paris web site, providing insight on official texts as well as details on market and clearing procedures (www.bourse-de-paris.fr).

Secondly, Paris adopted full cash-market trading. Paris Bourse SBF decided that all trading on the *Premier Marché* will be performed using the same cash-settlement procedures as the *Second Marché*, the *Nouveau Marché*, and the *Marché Libre*, thereby putting an end to the monthly settlement. Nevertheless, available simultaneously on the *Premier*, *Second*, and *Nouveau Marchés*, a deferred settlement service (*Service à Règlement Différé*, or SRD), allows shareholders to benefit from leverage and other special features of the monthly settlement market.

Thirdly and most important, The creation of Euronext, on 22 September 2000, led to the inception of the largest integrated exchange in Euroland. This new European exchange was born out of a full merger between the stock exchanges of Paris, Amsterdam, and Brussels and represents some 1,900 listed companies with a total market capitalization of approximately Euro2,700 billion. It offers a fully integrated trading, netting, clearing, and settlement solution on a pan-European basis. Nevertheless, regarding issuers, the choice has been to keep the regulatory environment they are familiar with, while being able to access additional liquidity through other countries' savings. Each company will have to issue quarterly reports in English using international accounting standards.

Finally, concerning the law regulations, at the end of 2000, two bills are under consideration: one is about the legal and institutional framework and the other one is a reform bill dealing with the financial market regulation authorities.

In terms of corporate law, the bill launched in March 2000 is called 'the New Economic Regulations' (NRE). After several amendments, this bill should be definitely adopted during the first semester 2001 and includes important measures on the transparency of the corporate governance. Four principles concerning corporations underlie this bill:

- Encouragement of the separation of the Chairman and CEO functions, while limiting the number of mandates that may be held concurrently in different boards of governors;
- Reinforcement of the transparency of firms' ownership by first allowing the identification of all shareholders, specially foreign ones who until now are exercising their rights through specific legal structures (trusts and nominees) and secondly by requiring more transparency regarding managers' compensation;
- Reinforcement of the minority shareholders' power in reducing the threshold of 10% to 5% in the exercise of their essential rights;
- Introduction of the use of new technologies, for example, by allowing electronic votes.

The reform bill announced in July 2000 and examined by the Council of State (*Conseil d'Etat*) in December 2000, concerns the regulation authorities of financial markets. It proposes the merging of the two existing prudential institutions, the COB (*Commission des Opérations de Bourse*) and the CMF (*Conseil des Marchés Financiers*). This new institution will be called AMF *(Autorité des Marchés Financiers)* and will be an administrative authority, independent and endowed with legal entity. This setting up should improve the efficiency of the system and would be more comparable to other countries' systems.

Appendix 1. **Decisions and notifications published by the SBF** (*Société des Bourses Françaises*) **no. 95–293 ACCOR (official list)**

Crossing of threshold

In accordance with article 356-1 of the modified law of 24 July 1966, the '*Caisse des Dépôts et Consignations*' (CDC), a state-controlled savings bank, notified the SBF on 20 January 1995 and by additional information on 25 January 1995 that following the acquisition by its subsidiary, the *Société CDC Participations*, of 1,146,684 double voting rights of the ACCOR company, it crossed upward the threshold of 10% of the total voting rights of this company on 17 December 1994 and that it now held, directly and indirectly, 3,276,574 voting rights of this company, representing 10.34% of the 31,669,795 existing voting rights.

These 3,276,574 votes (the voting block) stem from two stakes. One, 425,240 votes (1.34%) are cast through *Caisse des Dépôts et Consignations* (CDC); two, 2,851,334 votes (9.0%) are cast through *Société CDC Participations*. Since the CDC Participations is controlled by the Caisse, these stakes are added to the voting block (10.34%) that is notified by the Caisse.

Appendix 2. **Multiple classes of shares in France**

French companies can issue ownership certificates without voting rights. It is provided by the law without modifications of statutes:

- *Actions à dividende prioritaire* (ADP) (law no. 78–74 July 1978). They give right to dividend streams without any voting right. This type of shares can be created when an increase of capital or a conversion of shares occur. ADP cannot represent more than 25% of the capital.
- There is a possibility to separate two types of rights: certificates of investment, *certificats d'investissement* (CDV) (right to dividend streams); certificates of voting right, *certificats de droit de vote* (CI). These two types of certificates are issued simultaneously when an increase of capital or a splitting of existing shares occur. CDV are distributed among voting shareholders in proportion to their voting rights. The CDV are not transferable, but the CI are. The CI cannot represent more than 25% of the capital.

Differentiation of ownership certificates can also result from a modification of statutes:

- Shares with double voting rights. Only faithful shareholders (minimum two years of holding) can benefit from this type of shares. For listed companies, the maximum period of holding is 4 years.
- Preferred shares. This type of shares gives right to preferential financial advantages: increased dividend streams, cumulative dividend streams.
- Limitation of voting rights. The statutes can limit the influence of large shareholders (a maximum voting rights per shareholder can be imposed).

NOTES

1. Using the same dataset, the existence of a link between ownership concentration and performance is studied in Kremp and Sevestre (2000).

2. The obligation of notification concerns only the crossings of thresholds in listed companies. Previously, these clauses applied to major stakes held in all public companies, listed and unlisted. This restriction of the enforcement field of the transparency devices is based on the fact that since the 1982 Financial Law all the shares in unlisted companies have been nominative and thus shareholders of these companies are known.
3. Fanto (1995), cited in E. Jeffers (1998).
4. When not mentioned, foreign firms are classified with French firms in 'non-financial firms', 'Banks', 'Insurance', and 'Holdings'. For some comments, foreign firms (non-financial and financial) have been isolated, using the identification number *SIREN* first digit, which may not be a perfectly reliable method.
5. In the case of the data on voting rights in the CAC 40 firms, zero stakes include real zero stakes but also stakes under the minimum threshold.
6. 6% of 40% of known voting blocks.
7. The detailed information by size is not reported here, but is available in Bloch and Kremp (1997) (http://www.ecgn.ulb.ac).
8. Some financial institutions may be classified as holdings and/or financial companies may in fact hold some of the unknown capital.
9. But, in another way, the importance of holdings may imply an underestimate of banks and insurance companies, some of them being classified as holdings. It will be useful to try to classify holdings in terms of sector of activity (industry, services, and banks insurance . . .).
10. The fact that there is a large amount of capital for which the owner is not identified has to be underlined again. This represents on average 15% of the capital of all listed firms, and 24% of the capital of listed firms that have an unknown owner. For listed companies, it seems not unrealistic to interpret this unknown capital as mainly 'float'.

REFERENCES

Baldone S., F. Brioschi and S. Paleari (1996), 'Ownership Measures Among Firms Connected by Cross-Share holdings and a Further Analogy with Input–Output Theory', Working paper, Politecnico di Milano, June.
Baudru D. and M. Kéchédi (1998), 'Les Investisseurs institutionnels étrangers : vers la fin du capitalisme à la française', *Revue d'Economie Financière*, 96–105.
Bloch L. and E. Kremp (1997), 'Ownership and Control in France', Working paper for European Corporate Governance Network, October (http://www.ecgn.org).
Chocron M. (1998), 'La Détention des actions françaises cotées et de titres d'OPCVM actions en France de décembre 1996 à Septembre 1997', miméo presented at the Group on the Financing of the Firm held by the National Credit and Security Council.
—— and L. Marchand (1998), 'La Clientèle des principaux établissements dépositaires de titres en France au troisième trimestre 1997', *Bulletin de la Banque de France*, 49, (Jan.), 175–9.
European Corporate Governance Network (1996), 'Separation of Ownership and Control: A European Union Perspective'. Purpose and Scope of the Project, 1996/1997 Work Programme and Provisional Guidelines for the Institutional Statistical Survey, Brussels: ECGN.
Grossman S. and O. Hart (1988), 'One Share-One Vote and The Market For Corporate Control', *Journal of Financial Economics*, 20: 175–202.
Harris M. and A. Raviv (1988), 'Corporate Governance: Voting Rights and Majority Rules', *Journal of Financial Economics*, 20: 203–35.

Herald Tribune (1996), *French Company Handbook 1996, Detailed Profiles of France's Leading Companies, Including the Complete SBF120 Index*, Herald Tribune and SBF Paris Bourse: Paris.

Kremp E. (1996), 'The Impact of Restructuring on French Manufacturing Firms'Operating Performances During the Eighties', *Nota di Lavoro*, 2/96, Special issue on Corporate Governance and Property Rights, Fondazione Eni Enrico Mattei, Milano.

—— and P. Sevestre (2000), 'Ownership Concentration and Corporate Performance: Some New Evidence for France', in Lance Nail (ed.), *Issues in International Corporate Control and Governance*, North Holland: Elsevier Science, 15, 133–146.

Lamy (1996), *Sociétés commerciales*, Lamy: Paris.

La Porta R., F. Lopez-de-Silanes, A. Shleifer (1998), 'Corporate Ownership Around the World', NBER Working paper no. 6625, June.

L'Hélias S. (1997), *Le Retour de l'actionnaire : Pratiques du corporate governance en France, Aux Etats-Unis et en Grande-Bretagne*, Paris: Gualino Editeur.

Maréchal A. (1998), 'Les Critères d'investissement des grands gestionnaires de fonds internationaux dans les entreprises françaises', *Bulletin de la COB*, 322 (March).

Morin F. (1996), 'Privatisation et dévolution des pouvoirs, le modèle francais du gouvernement d'entreprise', *Revue Economique*, 6: 1253–68.

OECD (1996), *France, 1996–1997*, ch. 4 'The Corporate Governance of French Companies', Paris: OECD.

Vergeau E. and N. Chabanas (1997), 'Le Nombre de groupes d'entreprises a explosé en 15 ans', *Insee Première*, 53, (Nov.).

5

Ownership and Voting Power in Germany

MARCO BECHT AND EKKEHART BÖHMER

1. INTRODUCTION

Germany has always had a prominent place in the international corporate governance debate. The country is among the largest and richest industrial economies, and many German companies are world leaders in their fields. Moreover, German institutions often differ significantly from those found in other Continental European countries and even more markedly from those of the Anglo-Saxon countries.

There are several comprehensive accounts of the German corporate governance system. Charkham (1994) and Schmidt et al. (1997) provide institutional overviews. Edwards and Fischer (1996) concentrate on universal banking in Germany but pay a good deal of attention to corporate governance issues. Franks and Mayer (2001) analyse the role of ownership and control in disciplining management.

This chapter makes a number of contributions that go beyond these studies. First, we provide detailed summary statistics of voting power that became available for the first time in 1996, thanks to the transposition of the EU Large Holdings Directive (88/627/EEC). Hence the statistics are comparable to those obtained for other countries. We also examine the limitations of the new voting power data. Second, we give a detailed analysis of the separation of ownership and voting power in DAX companies, the 30 largest and most liquid German stocks. Throughout, we make detailed references to company law provisions and securities market regulations (an overview is contained in the Appendix).

The chapter is structured as follows. Section 2 offers a careful empirical analysis of the legal devices that are used to separate ownership and voting power, limited to DAX companies for reasons of data availability. Voting power concentration is combined with other devices to give German blue-chip governance its unique characteristics. In section 3 we analyse voting power for all German non-financial companies listed on an official market, finding that voting power concentrations for non-DAX companies are very high. Owing to data availability constraints, we cannot yet analyse the composition of the voting blocks or how voting power correlates with ownership or cash–flow rights. Section 4 concludes.

2. OWNERSHIP AND VOTING POWER

The companies covered in this section's analysis are the 30 DAX companies.[1] A careful analysis of the separation of voting power and ownership requires the inspection of corporate by-laws, voting lists from shareholder meetings, voting block, and ownership data. The main contribution of this section lies in the careful inspection of the by-laws.[2]

Table 5.1 shows the 20 DAX companies (out of 32, including Continental and Metallgesellschaft, which dropped out of the index in 1996) that have issued only voting bearer shares and thus conform to the 'one-share-one-vote' principle. The remaining firms on the index are listed in Table 5.2. We later show that the mean voting block for the companies that have issued non-voting shares or registered shares is significantly higher than for the 21 firms that comply with 'one-share-one-vote'.

The 'one-share-one-vote' group comprises four sub-groups, according to block size: Deutsche Telekom AG is in a class by itself, with a voting block of 74% controlled by the Federal Government; twelve companies have top blocks of between 28% and 50% (Adidas, Continental, Metallgesellschaft, Linde, Hoechst, Daimler-Benz, Degussa, Preussag, Dresdner Bank, Viag, Lufthansa, Karstadt); in six firms blockholders control from 5 to 20% (Bayer, Deutsche Bank, Schering, Veba, BASF, Thyssen). Two DAX companies have no known blockholders: Commerzbank and Mannesmann. This latter group was joined by Lufthansa in October 1997 when the Federal government sold its voting block (after converting the bearer shares into registered shares with transfer restrictions).

2.1. *Proxy voting by banks*

The last three columns in Tables 5.1 and 5.2 list the percentage of votes present at the 1992 general meeting of shareholders (1985 in parentheses) and the percentage of these attending votes cast by the 'Big 3' banks (Commerzbank, Deutsche Bank and Dresdner Bank) and by all banks.

We observe that bank proxy votes add voting power to existing voting blocks. In fact, by subtracting the votes reported as belonging to voting blocks of 5% or more from the votes cast by banks, we preclude the possibility that some blockholders might have their shares voted by banks.[3] There is only one case in which the number of votes cast by banks is lower than the votes that can be cast by the blockholders (32.2% versus 45.8%). This is not surprising, since the largest block (28.25%) in this company (VIAG) is held by the regional government of Bavaria, which may not want to depend on the banks for voting power. In all other cases, voting power is increased by between 10.1 percentage points (Degussa) and 47 percentage points (Commerzbank).

2.2. *Voting caps*

To protect themselves from hostile takeovers and, perhaps, to reduce their dependence on the proxy voting power of the banks, four companies in the 'one-share-one-vote' group diluted voting power through a voting cap. Among the firms with blocks

Table 5.1. *Separation instruments for DAX companies with bearer voting shares only*

Name	Largest ultimate voting block	Other blocks	Voting cap	% votes attending annual general meeting, 1992 (1985)[1]	% of these votes cast by 'Big 3'	% of these votes cast by All banks
Adidas-Salomon AG	S.O.G.E.D.I.M. SA, 39.8%	None	No	n.a. (n.a.)	n.a. (n.a.)	n.a. (n.a.)
BASF AG	Allianz AG, 12.36%[2]	None	2.62%[3]	50.4 (55.4)	40.4 (51.7)	94.7 (96.6)
Bayer AG[4]	Allianz AG, 5.007%	None	No	50.21 (53.18)	41.7 (54.5)	91.3 (95.8)
Commerzbank AG[5]	None over 5%	None	No	48.2 (50.5)	48.3 (60.81)	97.6 (96.8)
Continental AG[6]	Nord LB, 16.9%	3 blocks[7]	No	n.a. (35.3)	n.a. (38.8)	n.a. (95.6)
Daimler-Benz AG	Deutsche Bank, 24.4%	12.96% Kuwait Inv.	No	n.a. (81.0)	n.a. (61.7)	n.a. (69.3)
Degussa AG	Holding, 39.07%[8]	None	No	73.3 (70.9)	33.86 (41.8)	67.1 (73.3)
Deutsche Bank AG[9]	Allianz, 5.03%	None	No	46.8 (55.1)	49.2 (60.4)	94.7 (97.2)
Deutsche Telekom AG[10]	Fed. Republ., 74.9%	None	No	n.a. (n.a.)	n.a. (n.a.)	n.a. (n.a.)
Dresdner Bank AG[11]	Allianz 21.97%	2 Holdings just over 10%	No	74.6 (56.8)	53.7 (64.0)	98.2 (60.7)
Hoechst AG	Kuwait, 24.5%	FGC Holding, 10.2%[12]	No	71.4 (57.7)	69.5 (63.5)	98.3 (98.5)
Karstadt AG	Hertie Foundation, 29.4%	Two 10%+ blocks[13]	No	n.a. (77.6)	n.a. (78.9)	n.a. (87.3)
Linde AG	Allianz AG, 13.09%	Three 10%+ blocks[14]	10%	60.0 (53.0)	57.9 (60.0)	99.1 (90.4)
Lufthansa AG	Federal Rep., 36.4%	None	No	n.a. (n.a.)	n.a. (n.a.)	n.a. (n.a.)

Company						
Mannesmann AG	None	None	5%	37.2 (50.6)	38.8 (50.5)	98.1 (95.4)
Metallgesellschaft AG[15]	Kuwait, 20.2%	3 blocks[16]	No	n.a. (90.6)	n.a. (65.6)	n.a. (76.0)
Preussag	Westlb (via a holding), 29.1%	Holding, 10.4%[17]	No	n.a. (69.6)	n.a.(19.3)	n.a. (99.7)
Schering AG	Allianz AG, 10.6%	None	3.51%[18]	37.4 (46.6)	40.7 (51.5)	94.5 (99.1)
Thyssen AG	Thyssen Holding, 10.0001%	F. Thyssen Foundation, 8.58%	No	67.7 (68.5)	19.1 (32.6)	45.4 (53.1)
Veba AG	Allianz AG, 11.46%	None	No	53.4 (50.2)	42 (47.9)	90.9 (98.2)
Viag AG	State of Bavaria, 32.63%	None	No	69.7 (n.a.)	13.4 (n.a.)	(n.a.)

[1]Data from Baums and Fraune (1995); data in parentheses (for 1985 meeting) are from Gottschalk (1988). [2]10.6% of the Allianz block is held by an Allianz-controlled holding company; in 1992 it was proposed to abolish the voting cap, but only 3.17% voted in favour (Baums and Fraune 1995). [3]The voting cap is expressed in terms of face value (DM80 billion); the percentage is with respect to the total face value in 1996. [4]The source of 4.995% of Allianz' block votes is not disclosed. [5]In 1992 Commerzbank AG voted 34.58% of the attending votes at its own meeting. [6]Continental dropped out of the index on 20 September 1996 and was replaced by Münchner Rück; the Gottschalk (1988) data are for 1987. [7]Deutsche Bank 10.25%, Dresdner Bank 10.6%, Allianz 5.03%. [8]The holding company is owned by Henkel 46%, Dresdner Bank (27%), and Munich Re (27%) (Hoppenstedt KSD 1997). [9]In 1992 Deutsche Bank voted 32.07% (1987: 47.17%) of the votes cast at its own meeting. [10]Voting power data for 1997. [11]Dresdner Bank voted 44.19% (47.08%) at its own 1992 meeting, probably including Allianz votes. An opaque pyramid structure disguises significant Allianz influence. [12]The holding is Allianz-controlled. [13]Commerzbank 10.3%, Deutsche Bank 10%+20 votes. [14]Alico Holding 11.03%, Commerzbank 10.2%, and Dresdner Bank 10.01%. [15]Metallgesellschaft dropped out of the index on 18 November 1996 and was replaced by Deutsche Telekom. [16]Dresdner Bank 14.2%, Deutsche Bank 13.1% Daimler Benz 7.33%, Allianz 4.014%. [17]Westdeutsche Landesbank, Norddeutsche Landesbank, and Dresdner Bank own 33.33% of each. [18]The voting cap is expressed in terms of face value (DM12 million); the percentage is for total face value in 1996.

Table 5.2. *Separation instruments for DAX companies with bearer voting shares and/or other shares*

Name	Largest ultimate voting block	Other blocks	Voting cap	Different share types	% votes attending annual general meeting, 1992 (1985)[1]	% of these votes cast by	
						'Big 3'	All banks
Allianz AG[2]	Munich Re, 26%	4 blocks[3]	No	Registered voting with transfer restrictions	n.a. (66.2)	n.a. (23.4)	n.a. (60.1)
Münch. Rück AG	Allianz, 25%	4 blocks[4]	No	Registered voting with transfer restrictions and bearer voting shares (1.8%)	n.a. (n.a.)	n.a. (n.a.)	n.a. (n.a.)
Bay. Vereinsbank AG	Viag, 7.2%[5]	5.21% Deut. Bank	No	Registered, non-voting, voting, not traded, small fraction of total equity	56 (62.4)	22.5 (17.72)	84.7 (68.7)
RWE AG[6]	RW Holding, 12.1%	City of Essen (8.2%), Allianz (8.1%)	No	Registered voting (2%), bearer voting (92%), and non-voting (6%)	n.a. (n.a.)	n.a. (n.a.)	n.a. (n.a.)
Siemens AG	Siemens Holding, 14.03%[7]	None	No	Registered with multiple voting rights (×6), bearer voting shares (98.4%)	52.7 (60.6)	34.6 (32.5)	95.5 (79.8)
Bay. Motoren Werke AG	3 Quandt heirs, 17.9%, 17%, 13.2%	Holding, 10.02%	No	Voting, non-voting (1.17%)	n.a. (n.a.)	n.a. (n.a.)	n.a. (n.a.)

Company	Largest block	Second block	Voting cap	Share types			
Henkel KGAA[8]	Family block, 100%[8]	None		Voting (51%), non-voting (49%)		n.a. (n.a.)	n.a. (n.a.)
Man AG	Holding, 36.07%[9]	None	Until June 1996 No	Voting (72%), non-voting (28%)		48.2 (52.9)	18.9 (30.2)
Metro AG[10]	Metro Holding AG Switzerland, 67.16%	SHV Holdings NV, 8.9789%	No	Voting, non-voting		n.a. (n.a.)	n.a. (n.a.)
Sap AG	3 founders, 62.5%[11]	None	No	Voting (60.2%), non-voting (39.8%)		n.a. (n.a.)	n.a. (n.a.)
Volkswagen AG[12]	State of Niedersachsen, 20%	None	20%	Voting (81.2%), non-voting (18.8%)	38.3 (50.1)	44.1 (19.5)	15.1 (8.0)

[1]Data from Baums and Fraune (1995); figures in parentheses (for 1985 meeting) are from Gottschalk (1988). [2]Registered shares with transfer restrictions are included in the DAX index; Depotstimmrechte of Allianz-related banks: Dresdner Bank 11.14%, Bayrische Vereinsbank 10.7%, and Bayrische Hypobank 9.5%. [3]Bayrische Vereinsbank 10% + 1,500 votes, Deutsche Bank 10% + 1,500 votes, Dresdner Bank 10%, Bayrische Hypotheken und Wechselbank 5.001%. [4]Bayrische Vereinsbank (9.9%), Deutsche Bank (9.9%), Dresdner Bank (9.9%), DIA Holding (6.2%). [5]Since 1996, control has become more 'Bavarian.' In 1998: Viag 10.83%, Allianz 9.2%, Munich Re 5.4%. [6]Registered shares with transfer restrictions have multiple voting rights (×20). [7]Siemens Holding controlled by Siemens family; 6.94% of votes for all decisions; 14.03% for certain decisions. [8]Special legal form; unlimited liability partners have no votes (By-laws, Art. 22). The non-voting stock is included in the DAX index. The voting cap of 10% on voting shares was eliminated in 1996. All shareholders voted on this issue and a 10% conversion of non-voting to voting stock. Voting/non-voting proportions changed to 59% and 41% respectively. Attendance: 53.26%. [9]Attending non-voting stock included Deutsche Bank (42.68%) and Dresdner Bank (21.66%). [10]Regina Verwaltungsgesellschaft mbH disguises Allianz influence. The voting block includes 61 family members and two foundations. The voting pact was split on 19/09/96 and now has 48 members (50.3%). [11]Data for 1997; the company was first traded in 1996. [12]The founders have placed part of their shares in trusts and have signed a voting pact. For SAP AG only the non-voting stock is included in the index. The voting power of the founders is higher than the block statistics suggest because not all votes are in the contract and, hence, do not need to be notified. [13]By-laws bar proxy voting power by banks, but allow it with written voting instructions. Volkswagen is governed by a special law and not affected by the KonTraG.

smaller than 18.9%, these were Schering, BASF, and Mannesmann. Linde AG (where the sum of blocks is 33.3%) also has a cap.[4]

2.3. *Transfer restrictions*

Allianz AG and Munich Re comply with the 'one-share-one-vote' rule, but they have issued registered shares that are subject to transfer restrictions. All share transfers are subject to authorization by the management board.[5] In addition, these two companies have a 25% cross-shareholding that allows them to block by-law changes, so no outsider can remove the transfer restrictions. This represents a formidable take-over barrier.

Allianz AG and Munich Re are among the most important blockholders of listed companies in Germany, both in number of blocks held and in market value. This arrangement is accordingly of fundamental importance to the governance of many German blue-chip companies. Through their influence at Dresdner Bank AG and the Bavarian regional banks, the two companies also have significant access to the proxy voting mechanism.

Three other companies, RWE AG, Siemens AG and Bayrische Vereinsbank have issued shares with transfer restrictions, but only for a small part of their par value.

2.4. *Multiple voting rights*

RWE AG and Siemens have issued restricted shares with multiple voting rights (×20 and ×6). In the case of RWE AG, these give added voting power to the municipalities that used to depend on its electricity; in the case of Siemens AG, to the Siemens family.[6]

2.5. *Non-voting shares*

Eight DAX companies use the device of non-voting shares. Henkel KGAA, a mixed limited/unlimited liability company, is an extreme case. At the beginning of 1996, 49% of its outstanding equity consisted of non-voting stock, while 100% of the voting shares were held by the Henkel family. SAP AG had issued 39.8% of its equity as non-voting shares, while the founders and their families held more than 62% of the votes. In both cases the voting blocks are formed through formal voting agreements and foundations.

2.6. *Volkswagen AG*

Volkswagen AG has a special mechanism in place. The Region of Lower Saxony holds a 20% voting block, the company has a voting cap, and the by-laws prevent banks from exercising power via proxy voting. Banks must have explicit instructions to vote at Volkswagen meetings. Thus, the Region and the Volkswagen Board of Directors officially deny banks their proxy voting power. Nevertheless, this provision is largely cosmetic and Baums and Fraune (1995) report that banks voted 44% of the shares at the 1992 meeting.

2.7. *Lufthansa AG*

For Lufthansa AG too, special provisions apply since the October 1997 privatization. Privatized European airlines have a problem; they must comply with Council Regulation 2407/92/EEC on the 'licensing of air carriers'. To obtain an operating licence for a Member State 'the undertaking shall be owned and continue to be owned directly or through majority ownership by Member States and/or nationals of Member States. It shall at all times be effectively controlled by such States or such nationals' (Article 4-2). The German government and Lufthansa have opted for a twist on the Allianz-Munich Re solution. Before the 37.45% voting block of the Federal government was sold, Lufthansa's voting bearer shares were converted to registered shares with transfer restrictions. In addition, a special law was passed that allows German airlines to issue shares selectively (Article 4) or force shareholders to dispose of their shares (Article 5).

2.8. *Pyramidal groups*

DAX companies are often at the top of large pyramidal groups. However, even when holding companies control significant stakes, as in Degussa or Hoechst, it is not clear whether they serve the purpose of collecting outside capital from dispersed (or otherwise 'voteless') shareholders, or from creditors; in the former case, this would leverage voting power with respect to cash-flow rights.

The holding companies (*Vorschaltgesellschaften*) seem to act in lieu of voting contracts or other forms of formal coalition. They permit coalitions to be formed with greater legal certainty, flexibility, and ease. Several holding companies can be combined to form broader coalitions still.[7]

2.9. *Summary*

To conclude, German blockholders can rely on banks or use a number of other instruments to consolidate voting power among DAX companies. Both outside and founder blocks exist. Munich Re and Allianz are controlled by a board that has been self-perpetuating since its foundation. For Deutsche Bank we observe one 5.03% Allianz block, but like the other large banks, it is controlled through proxy votes cast by itself and other banks. Henkel and BMW are controlled by the descendants of the founders; SAP AG and METRO AG by the founders themselves. DEGUSSA AG was monitored by Henkel and Munich Re and Allianz; today it is controlled by Veba AG; BASF, BAYER, VEBA, Dresdner Bank and Hoechst, by Allianz. Whether Allianz board representation makes these blocks 'outsider' or 'insider' blocks is difficult to decide.

However, as we show in the next section, DAX companies are not representative. The median voting block for them is 11%, compared with 52.1% for the German market as a whole (374 non-financial companies). One explanation might be the stock market liquidity requirement of the DAX. Becht (1999) shows that ownership blocks absorb liquidity and argues that DAX companies and their blockholders are faced with a trade-off :

1. Ownership and voting power is dispersed. The stock will be liquid but the company might be vulnerable to hostile takeover.
2. Bank proxies or other means are used to concentrate voting power without concentrating ownership. This ensures some market liquidity and impedes hostile takeovers.

We have shown that DAX companies have taken the second course, employing a variety of legal devices.

3. VOTING POWER

In this section we analyse the disclosure and distribution of voting power for all officially listed German companies. The data are drawn from the *Bundesaufsichtsamt für den Wertpapierhandel* (BAWe 1996). The first official cross-sectional 'snapshot' of the distribution of voting blocks was taken on 30 September 1996; since then regular updates have been published on the BAWe's web site (www.bawe.de).

As is pointed out by Schneider (1995), only voting rights control, as opposed to cash-flow rights, is reported. Dormant voting rights such as those associated with preference shares (*Vorzugsaktien*), proxy votes exercised by banks, and votes exercised by investment funds need not be reported. Moreover, the concentration of voting control will be understated because not all cross-ownership links are publicly known. For example, family pools are only considered as an entity if there is a formal and explicit voting pact. Thus, the figures below provide only a lower bound on both stake size and the concentration of control.[8] Given the substantial concentration that is documented even so, however, this bias only strengthens the results.

3.1. *Data*

At the end of 1996, 436 firms were listed in the official market segments in Germany. The BAWe (1996) publication gives the cumulative result of all notifications pursuant to §§ 21, 22, and 41 WpHG since 1 January 1995. As only 402 firms were reported, 33 companies (or 7.6% of listed firms) had not received any notifications or had failed to report them. To obtain a fuller data set, we investigate the missing firms: Deutsche Telekom went public in October 1996, so was not traded in September; 17 firms were added to later versions of the BAWe report, even though in several cases their filings had come before September 1996. For an additional 11 firms, we find ownership information in *Hoppenstedt's Konzernstruktur-Datenbank* (KSD).[9] For six firms (Bremer Vulkan, Georg, Arn., Marschollek Lautenschl. und Partner AG, Terrex Handels-AG, Traub AG, and Würzburger Hofbräu AG) we were unable to get any reliable information, so we exclude them from the analysis. The final sample thus consists of 430 firms (the original 402 from BAWe (1996), 17 from BAWe (1998), and 11 from

KSD). For all firms we cross-checked KSD and BAWe data to eliminate errors and to confirm reported figures. We also discarded all stakes below 5% that are included in BAWe (1996) but not attributed to some other controlling party. These notifications are not required by law and are most likely erroneous.

3.2. *Contents of the control notifications*

The following sample notification by RWE AG is of particular interest, because it illustrates three important aspects of the German notification process.

RWE AG was notified by Allianz Aktiengesellschaft Holding about the latter's voting block as of 1 January 1995. The notification was made at the time of Allianz AG Holding's first annual meeting (in October 1995) under the provisions of § 41 of the law. As this was not a notification pursuant to § 21, RWE AG had one month (§ 41 III WpHG) and nine days (§ 25 I WpHG) to publish the notification. The notification was published in the *Börsenzeitung* no. 240 on 14 December 1995. Allianz Aktiengesellschaft Holding notified as the parent of a business group that publishes consolidated annual accounts (§ 24 WpHG). However, if it reported on behalf of a subsidiary, the name of the subsidiary would have to be mentioned. Hence, we infer that Allianz AG Holding is making the notification on its own behalf or on behalf of affiliated companies that individually fall below the notification threshold.

The notification breaks the 'attributed' shareholding down into:

- No. 2: Shares owned by a company or companies controlled by Allianz AG Holding (7.661%).
- No. 7: Shares deposited with Allianz AG Holding but whose owner has not left precise instructions for voting (0.015%).

The remaining 0.44% of RWE AG voting shares are a residual; we infer that they are directly owned by Allianz AG Holding.

The BAWe has taken the data from the notifications and tabulated them. The breakdown of the 'attribution reason' is not published. Instead, the BAWe publishes the aggregate of direct and attributed shares, representing the total percentage of shares controlled by the notifying company. It also reports the fraction of total votes that are controlled indirectly and hence attributed to the shareholder. We concentrate on such voting blocks (8.117% in the RWE example).

3.3. *Descriptive statistics*

In the following, we statistics for ultimate voting blocks (the sum of direct and attributed stakes), both by company and by blockholder. We also calculate a measure of concentration C_n, defined as the sum of the top n stakes or blocks.

3.3.1. *Summary statistics for individual companies*

All results in this section are based on aggregation across 372 industrial companies that reported to the BAWe by 1996. For more convenient comparison with the other

---

RWE Aktiengesellschaft

Essen

Announcement according to §§ 41 (3), 25 (1) Wertpapierhandelsgesetz

Allianz Aktiengesellschaft Holding, Berlin and Munich, has notified us that, in accordance

with § 41 (2) and § 24 of the Wertpapierhandelsgesetz, its share of our voting capital as of

1 January 1995 was 8.117%.

In the share of voting capital, the attributable voting rights of § 22 (1)
Wertpapierhandelsgesetz were

      No. 2   7.661%   and

      No. 7   0.015%

Essen, 12 December 1995

                                      RWE

                         Aktiengesellschaft

                         The Management

Figure 5.1. *Announcement of Allianz AG blockholding in RWE AG.*

Source: Translation of a notification published in the *Börsenzeitung*, no. 240, 14 Dec. 1995.

chapters we have excluded banks and insurance companies.[10] Blockholders control 648 voting blocks in the industrial companies, or 1.74 per company. Figure 5.2 shows block size grouped by rank. The top block, averaged across companies, is 57.0% of all voting rights, with a median of 49.6%. The second largest block averages just 2.9%. In short, most companies are dominated by a single voting block.

Figure 5.3 is a percentile plot of the top voting blocks. An interesting observation is their clustering at the 25%, 50%, and 75% levels. These 'steps', also illustrated in the corresponding histogram in Figure 5.4, correspond to the veto minority (which can be block statute changes), the simple majority, and a common qualified majority. Since the qualified majority can be set higher than 75% in the company by-laws, even voting blocks of less than 25% could represent a veto minority. These figures suggest that block sizes are carefully chosen and that control is an important consideration.

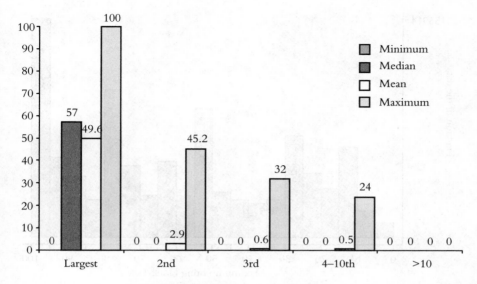

Figure 5.2. *Ultimate voting blocks by rank.*

Note: The histogram reports the minimum, median, mean, and maximum over voting blocks in listed non-financial companies by rank. When there are no 5% or larger ultimate voting blocks a zero was assigned. The blocks per company were sorted by size and a serial number was assigned. Ties were not taken into account, i.e. when there were two blocks of 20% the first became the largest and the second the second largest.

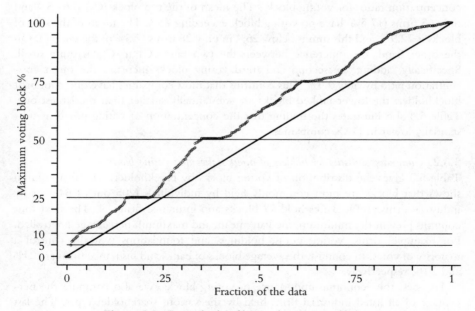

Figure 5.3. *Percentile plot of largest ultimate voting blocks.*

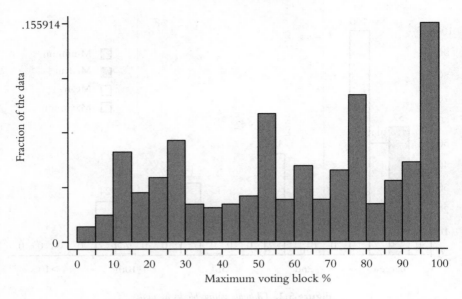

Figure 5.4. *Histogram of largest ultimate voting blocks.*

Tables 5.3 and 5.4 give the frequency distribution and summary statistics of concentration ratios for voting blocks. The mean of the top block (C_1) is 61.5% and only 65 firms (17.5%) have no voting block exceeding 25%. The mean of the sum of blocks is 72.9%, and this sum is below 25% in only 28 firms (7.5% of the sample). On the other hand, the difference between the two ratios C_1 to C_{all} is quite small. Specifically, adding the second and third voting blocks increases the mean concentration ratio by only 9.9%. This confirms that most companies have one dominant blockholder: the lower-ranked blocks are substantially smaller than the largest one. Table 5.4 also illustrates the finding that the concentration of voting power is substantially lower in DAX companies.

3.3.2. *Summary statistics for holders of direct stakes and voting blocks*

Table 5.5 gives the distribution of voting blocks by blockholder. The first column shows that blocks are most commonly held by individuals (205 out of 648) or by industrial firms (180). Banks hold 77 blocks and insurance firms 34. The next four columns present the minimum, median, mean, and maximum percentage controlled. For example, firms, voting pools, holdings, and foundations typically control a majority of votes. In contrast, the average blocks of banks and insurance firms are 24% and 20%, respectively.

To assess the economic importance of voting blocks, we also compute the percentage of all listed industrial firms held by the various shareholder types. The last two columns give the percentage of voting rights and the percentage of market

Table 5.3. Concentration ratios for ultimate voting blocks

Range	C_1			C_3			C_5			C_{all}		
	Frequency	%	Cumulated	Frequency	%	Cumulated	Frequency	%	Cumulated	Frequency	%	Cumulated
[10–5%]	4.0	1.1	1.1	4.0	1.1	1.1	4.0	1.1	1.1	4.0	1.1	1.1
[5–10%]	7.0	1.9	3.0	6.0	1.6	2.7	6.0	1.6	2.7	6.0	1.6	2.7
[10–25%]	54.0	14.5	17.5	18.0	4.8	7.5	18.0	4.8	7.5	18.0	4.8	7.5
[25–50%]	68.0	18.3	35.8	60.0	16.1	23.7	53.0	14.3	21.8	52.0	14.0	21.5
[50–75%]	95.0	25.5	61.3	89.0	23.9	47.6	82.0	22.0	43.8	81.0	21.8	43.3
[75–90%]	65.0	17.5	78.8	93.0	25.0	72.6	103.0	27.7	71.5	105.0	28.2	71.5
[90–95%]	21.0	5.7	84.4	27.0	7.3	79.8	28.0	7.5	79.0	27.0	7.3	78.8
[95–100%]	58.0	15.6	100.0	75.0	20.2	100.0	78.0	21.0	100.0	79.0	21.2	100.0
	372.0	100.0		372.0	100.0	100.0	372.0		372.0	100.0		

Sources: BAWe (1996, 1998), Hoppenstedt Verlag, KSD (1997).

Table 5.4. *Voting power concentration for index and non-index companies*

Ratio	Sample	Number	Minimum	Median	Mean	Maximum
C_1	all	372	0	65.8	61.5	100.0
C_3	all	372	0	76.5	71.4	100.0
C_5	all	372	0	78.2	72.7	100.0
C_{all}	all	372	0	78.8	72.9	100.0
C_1	DAX only	30	0	22.3	24.3	74.9
C_3	DAX only	30	0	35.4	32.2	74.9
C_5	DAX only	30	0	35.4	33.6	74.9
C_{all}	DAX only	30	0	35.4	33.6	74.9

value controlled. Blockholders control 70% of votes but only 46% of market value. This implies that the larger firms typically have a higher fraction of shares widely held. The largest holdings of voting rights are those of industrial firms (30%), followed by individuals (15%), and the two types of holding companies (11%). Banks (5%) and insurance firms (2%) report a low degree of control (not considering proxy votes). In terms of market value the pattern is very similar. The only exception is the government holding, which has a high market value owing to its majority stake in Deutsche Telekom.

An important caveat is that the figures may substantially understate the resources under control of the blockholders, especially when banks and insurance companies are involved. First, 50% of the voting rights essentially confer full control, so that in the worst case the last column of Table 5.5 shows only half the resources controlled. Since proxy votes often give banks majority control even when they own only a small block or none, this bias is likely to be most severe for banks. Second, the five top blockholders (Allianz, Münchner Rück, Deutsche Bank, Dresdner Bank, and Bayrische Vereinsbank) *jointly* control a majority of voting rights in one another. Since *joint* majority control does not trigger the mandatory reporting of blocks, the BAWe data generically understate the concentration of control. On the one hand, these five firms control one another; on the other, the voting blocks held in these firms and those held by them are not aggregated and may not all be reported. For example, a 1% stake held by each of the five need not be reported, even though this would produce a *joint* 5% block. Unfortunately, it is very difficult to construct a complete picture of all such arrangements in Germany from the BAWe data.

CONCLUSIONS

Voting power in German companies is highly concentrated. DAX companies are generally either majority-controlled by a large blockholder, or by banks via proxy votes. More than 50% of all listed companies are controlled by a single majority block, and only 17.4% are without a blockholder with at least a veto minority (25%). Even these figures

Table 5.5. *Size of ultimate voting blocks by blockholder type*

Blockholder type	Number of blocks held	Minimum voting block	Median voting block	Mean voting block	Maximum voting block	% of all 374 industrial firms	% of the market value of 372 industrial firms[1]
Foreign government[2]	3	13.0	20.2	18.9	23.6	0.2	1.1
Bank	77	5.1	15.0	23.8	99.0	4.9	3.6
Industrial firm	180	5.0	70.6	61.6	100.0	29.6	12.7
Association, voting pool, co-ops[3]	21	5.9	49.1	45.2	100.0	2.5	1.8
Government	18	8.2	40.7	45.3	99.0	2.2	10.5
Holding company[4]	53	6.9	50.3	52.9	100.0	7.5	4.2
Investment firm[5]	36	5.5	25.1	40.0	99.0	3.9	2.0
Bank-related investment firm	5	10.2	11.0	18.1	41.4	0.2	0.5
Individual[6]	205	5.0	18.2	26.9	100.0	14.8	5.9
Foundation	16	8.0	50.1	51.6	98.1	2.2	1.1
Insurance company	34	5.0	11.9	20.1	96.7	1.8	2.7
Total	648	5.0			100.00	69.8	46.0

[1] For two firms the market value was not available. Market value is based on all equity shares and year-end prices for 1996.

[2] Foreign companies are included in the category 'industrial firm'.

[3] These legal devices were put in the same category because they contractually bind a small number of individuals who wish to share control; also includes partnerships and similar unlimited liability companies.

[4] *Verwaltungsgesellschaften* and Holding companies.

[5] *Beteiligungsgesellschaften.*

[6] Includes *Kommanditgesellschaften* that are named after an individual.

Sources: BAWe (1996, 1998), Hoppenstedt Verlag, KSD (1997). Own blockholder classification.

underestimate the real concentration of voting power because of significant proxy voting by banks, which is inversely correlated with block size, and cross-ownership.

The dominant blockholders, in number of stakes and value, are Allianz AG and Deutsche Bank AG. There is evidence on control links between the dominant blockholders. To understand their governance and strategy remains a key to understanding the corporate control of listed companies in Germany.

Appendix[11]

1. *Introduction*

Here we focus on the legal and institutional background.[12] We emphasize *Aktiengesellschaften* as the only legal form that can be listed. However, other legal forms also play an important role, because they often belong to groups together with AGs. Listed companies may own and control non-listed companies and vice versa. Groups combining listed and non-listed companies pose the biggest challenge for disclosure and transparency, because they involve firms subject to strict disclosure rules and others with lax ones. Overall transparency is difficult to ensure in these cases.

1.1. *Company types*

German commercial laws define several ways to organize firms with limited or unlimited liability for owners. Table A5.1 lists the basic characteristics of the main forms. The main legal divide is between the forms that provide limited liability and the others, which do not. All limited-liability firms are heavily regulated, while the others have considerable freedom in drafting by-laws and designing contractual relations between owners and other stakeholders. We try to measure the extent of this freedom by a subjective assessment of the degree of imperativeness of the legal rules (last column). It should be noted that some 'low imperativeness' forms are of substantial importance in Germany, most notably *Vereine* (unions) and *Stiftungen* (foundations). The former are sometimes large enterprises (for example, the largest German automobile association (ADAC) is organized as a union, and so are all soccer clubs).[13] Foundations often appear as dominant stakeholders or sole owners of the largest companies. Other forms, like the GbR or the *stille Gesellschaft*, play only minor roles.

1.2. *Ownership versus control of Aktiengesellschaften*

German law allows various devices that detach control rights from cash-flow rights. Table A5.2 summarizes the main practices and their implications for transparency. First, shares may have limited but not multiple voting rights. As we have seen, the AktG explicitly allows non-voting shares up to the number of common shares outstanding.[14] Non-voting shares are a powerful mechanism potentially able to double the relative voting power of ordinary shares, but they are used mostly by smaller, family-owned companies. Also, non-voting shares can be converted into voting shares by those controlling the majority of voting and non-voting shares. Since the ownership of non-voting shares is not usually disclosed, they may be an important pool of hidden power.

Multiple voting rights per share were generally illegal in 1996, but they could be authorized by regional authorities.[15] Company statutes may further impose voting caps that limit the

Table A5.1. *Important legal forms of private companies*

	Limited liability	Minimum capital (thousand DM)	Smallest number of founders	Smallest number of managers	Degree of imperativeness of legal rules
Aktiengesellschaft (AG)	Yes	100[1]	1[2]	1[3]	High
Gesellschaft mit beschränkter Haftung (GmbH)	Yes	50[4]	1[5]	1[6]	High
Kommanditgesellschaft auf Aktien (KGaA)	General partners: No Shareholders: Yes[7]	100[8]	5[9]	1[10]	High
Kommanditgesellschaft (KG)	General partners: No Limited partners: Yes[11]	—	2[12]	1	Medium
GmbH (or AG) & Co. KG[13]	Yes	50	1	1	Medium
Offene Handelsgesellschaft (OHG)	No	0	1	1	Medium
Eingetragene Genossenschaft (e. G.)	Usually[14]	0	7[15]	2[16]	Medium
Gesellschaft bürgerlichen Rechts (GbR)	No	—	1	1	Low
Stille Gesellschaft[17]	Yes[18]	—	—	—	Low
Eingetragener Verein (e. V.)	Yes	0	7[19]	1[20]	Low
Stiftung[21]	Not applicable	—	—	—	Low
Banks, any legal form except sole proprietorship	Depends on legal form	Euro 5 million[22]	Depends on legal form	2[23]	Very high

[1] § 7 AktG. [2] § 2 AktG. [3] § 76 I AktG. [4] At least 0.5 per owner; § 5 I GmbHG. [5] § 1 GmbHG. [6] § 6 I GmbHG. [7] § 278 I AktG. General partners are referred to as *Komplementäre*, shareholders as *Kommanditaktionäre*. [8] § 7 AktG. [9] § 280 AktG. [10] § 76 I AktG. [11] § 161 I HGB. General partners are referred to as *Komplementäre*, limited partners as *Kommanditisten*. [12] At least one general partner and at least one limited partner, § 161 I HGB. [13] This is a hybrid form where the general partner of a KG is a (limited-liability) GmbH. While the GmbH & Co KG is the most widely used hybrid form, the (unlimited-liability) general partner may also be an AG, and the enclosing form may also be an OHG. If a GmbH or an AG are involved, all regulations affecting these forms still apply. [14] The e. G. is generally a limited-liability company (§ 2 GenG). Company by-laws may deviate from this rule (§ 6 (3) GenG); in case of bankruptcy, members may be obligated to pay, in addition to their initial investment, a limited or an unlimited amount to creditors. [15] § 4 GenG. [16] § 24 II GenG. [17] This is not a stand-alone organization, but rather a way to participate in any other organizational form. [18] § 232 II HGB. [19] § 56 BGB. [20] § 261 BGB. [21] More precisely, this refers to 'rechtsfähige Stiftungen bürgerlichen Rechts' that operate a business. [22] § 33 I KWG, net of securities that have a cumulative preferential dividend. [23] § 33 IV KWG.

Table A5.2. *Legal devices to leverage control in listed AGs*

Device	Current relevance	Limitations	Implications for transparency
Non-voting shares	All AGs can issue two classes of stock	Nominal value of non-voting shares must not exceed that of voting shares	None: distribution of voting rights across classes of stock published in annual report
Multiple-vote shares	Only relevant in a few formerly state-owned firms, being phased out in 1998[1]	Illegal unless specifically approved by regional government	None: shareholders with multiple voting rights per share are published in annual report
Voting caps	May be imposed by company by-laws, but being phased out in 1998[2]	In practice easy to circumvent	Reduces transparency: to circumvent caps, shareholdings must be disguised by depositing them with friendly parties
Proxy voting	Possible in all AGs. Widely used by banks, especially in listed companies with a significant % of dispersed shareholdings	Voting instructions must be sought; but usually none are provided	Reduces transparency significantly. It is not possible to determine who owns the shares and who controls the votes (the owner or the person voting the shares)
Large share blocks	Widely used, weak minority protection allows blockholders to pursue interests that may not match that of other shareholders	Certain (legal) transfers from minority shareholders require 75% of votes at meeting	None given the WpHG: voting blocks must be disclosed

Pyramids	Used by listed companies but rarely used to control listed companies	None except potentially higher administrative costs	Reduces transparency: intermediate levels may legally hide true ownership structure
Cross-shareholdings	Few large but many small cross-shareholdings that are not disclosed.	Need at least three companies to circumvent voting limitation; limited to 25%	(see comment above on pyramids)
Contractual control arrangement	Widely used	Requires 75% vote at meeting	None: must be published in annual report
Personal interlocks	Widely used	Needs supporting voting block at meeting (blockholder, bank)	Reduces transparency: affiliation of supervisory board members is often not obvious; often creditors without shareholdings are represented, who do not benefit from providing transparency to (potential) shareholders

[1] The KonTraG, effective from 1 May 1998, explicitly outlaws multiple voting rights. Existing multiple voting rights are to be phased out over a five-year period.
[2] The KonTraG, effective from 1 May 1998, explicitly outlaws voting caps. Existing caps are to be phased out over a two-year period.

percentage of votes by individual shareholders.[16] Voting caps are often said to reduce the power of large shareholders, but informal voting pacts can be used to overcome the caps. Voting caps adversely effect a transparency: once it is revealed, substantial voting power cannot be exercised. Again, the company by-laws establishing the voting cap can be hard to obtain (see the discussion on access to company registers).

Large blocks per se do not leverage voting power relative to cash-flow rights, but the poor safeguards for minority shareholders effectively allow sizeable transfers to blockholders once a coalition controls 75% of the votes. Specifically, a 75% majority may legally make an obligatory tender bid to minority shareholders below the market price.[17] In this sense a 75% coalition effectively controls 100% of the voting rights. Given the power of blockholders over corporate disclosure policy, the impact on transparency simply hinges on the latter's attitude.[18]

Probably the most important devices for leveraging control are cross-shareholdings, contractual arrangements, and pyramids. Cross-holdings effectively imply potentially illegal holdings of own shares and increase the voting power of any blockholder. In addition, they foster inefficient 'voting cartels', in which the management teams vote in favour of each other at their respective shareholders' meetings. Contractual arrangements delegating control are widely used by German groups. Pyramids with outside equity on various levels may concentrate highly leveraged control at the top. In so far as intermediate group levels may not have to report ownership or stakes held, pyramids substantially reduce transparency.

Finally, supervisory-board composition may have substantial influence on control leverage. First, some shareholders may be overrepresented. This is true especially for banks and other financial institutions. To the extent that banks with board members also hold debt, their incentive for transparency with other shareholders may be limited indeed. Second, interlocking directorates between companies have the same effect as cross holdings.

1.3. Special Reporting Requirements for listed AGs
German law sets forth several requirements for listed securities. The following describes the rules for listing equity shares on each market segment.

1.3.1. Amtlicher Handel (official market).
The issuer, together with a credit institution that has a seat on a German exchange, can apply for listing.[19] Credit institutions do not need another institution to accompany the applications. It is mandatory to publish a prospectus[20] and an interim financial report during the fiscal year.[21] For an initial listing, the expected market value of the listed shares must generally exceed DM2.5 million, and at least 25% of the issue must be widely held, but the exchange may admit smaller issues or a lower percentage if it anticipates a sufficiently deep market.[22] It is further required that the issuer have existed for at least three years, unless the issue is expected to be in the interest of the issuer and the public.[23]

The prospectus must contain detailed information on the securities to be listed; the contents are comparable to SEC form S-1. In addition to basic information on the issuer and price, size, and cost of the issue, it must contain all potential restrictions on transfers and the procedure for future issues of the same security.[24] The issuer must also publish the nature and result of any tender offers or exchange offers for the security during the year prior to listing.[25] With respect to control, the prospectus must list all shareholders with 5% or more of equity or votes, all the shares held by management and board, and any other natural or legal persons that have a controlling influence.[26] Interim financial reports must provide basic information on the issuer, at least sales and profits in line with the requirements for regular annual reports.[27]

1.3.2. Geregelter Markt (regulated market). The issuer, together with a credit institution that has a seat on a German exchange, can apply for listing.[28] Credit institutions need not be accompanied by another institution. The issuer must publish a financial report at the time of the listing (not a more detailed prospectus[29]), but no additional reports during the fiscal year. For an initial public offering, however, the issuer must publish a prospectus[30] giving basic information on issue and issuer but less comprehensive than that required for official listings. The prospectus does contain the items listed in the previous sections, except for shares held by management and board.[31]

1.3.3. Other market segments. Listing requirements for all other market segments (*Freiverkehr* and *Neuer Markt*) are set by the exchanges and not governed by law. The only legal requirement is a prospectus (as described in section 1.3.2.) in the case of initial public offerings.[32]

2. Transposition of the EU Transparency Directive

2.1. Background

In Germany, the Transparency Directive (88/627/EEC) was transposed as part of a securities trading law (*Wertpapierhandelsgesetz*, WpHG, BGBL 30. 7. 1994, I S. 1749ff.) that contains a series of measures designed to strengthen the financial markets.[33] The sections based on the EU Transparency Directive became effective on 1 January 1995. The WpHG also provides the legal basis for creating a securities trading commission (*Bundesaufsichtsamt für den Wertpapierhandel*, BAWe). The BAWe formally sets regulations and penalties for insider trading, prompt publication of price-relevant information (*ad-hoc Publizität*), and the rules for operating securities houses.

2.2. The mechanics of the notification process

The mechanics of the notification process are simple and closely follow the Transparency Directive. The main features are the following: filings are made and published on paper, the shareholder notifies the company and the company notifies (and pays for notifying) the market, and notifications can take up to 16 days to reach the market.

2.3. Who has to report voting stakes?

§ 21 WpHG (notifications of direct shareholdings), § 22 (notifications of shares 'attributed' to a shareholder because he or she controls the way the shares are voted), and § 41 (first time notification since the law came into force) are the legal 'triggers' for the notification process.

§ 21 states that someone crossing 5%, 10%, 25%, 50%, or 75% (through purchase, sale, or other means) of the votes of a German company listed on an official EU market must notify according to the mechanisms set out in section 2.2 above The requirement does not depend on the share of voting capital but the fraction of the total votes controlled. Voting caps (*Höchststimmrechte*) are not taken into account when computing the percentages (Nottmeier and Schäfer 1997: 91).

§ 22 is the most complicated provision of the law; it lays down the rules for 'multi-layer' control of voting shares. It specifies the cases in which indirectly controlled votes are 'attributed' to a shareholder. Becht and Böhmer (1997) show that the current version of §22 is inadequate to provide real transparency concerning those who exercise considerable voting power in German listed companies.

§ 41 is the initial notification rule that provides the starting position from which future 'snapshots' of the ownership structure can be constructed by tracing changes. It states that, unless a notification pursuant to § 21 had already been made before the first general meeting in 1995, shareholders must report holdings above 5%. The provisions of § 22 also apply to initial notifications.

2.4. *Problems*

These articles appear straightforward, but a number of complications do arise. Since the provisions are legally uncharted territory in Germany, the annotations to the WpHG (Schneider 1995) are binding and there are few court rulings to date.[34] Practical issues arising from the day-to-day implementation are discussed in Nottmeier and Schäfer (1997). The authors are responsible for the implementation of the German transposition of the Transparency Directive at the BAWe.[35] The following discussion is based on Becht and Böhmer (1997).

2.4.1. *Banks' proxy votes are not reported.*

The German government, in its annotations to the WpHG, decided that banks do not have to report proxy votes (the controversial *Auftragsstimmrecht* mechanism). This decision is justified by the fact that § 135(5) and § 128(2) AktG oblige banks to consult shareholders, make a voting proposal and, unless the shareholder instructs them otherwise, execute that proposal (*Bundestagsdrucksache* 12/6679. 54). Since the banks must stick with their original proposal, it is argued that the votes should not be attributed to the banks because legally they do not have discretionary power to decide how the shares are voted. Although there are no precise figures on how many bank customers actually take advantage of the possibility of instructing their banks, it is widely assumed that very few do. In practice, there is no difference between 'free to propose and not be challenged' and 'free to vote.' Hence, if the spirit of the Transparency Directive were rigorously applied, a notification should be required and the banks would have to notify the shares for which they have received no explicit voting instructions. Alternatively, they could be required to declare on whose behalf they vote the shares.

2.4.2. *Votes of investment companies are not attributed to anyone.*

While limited reporting requirements apply to *Kapitalanlagegesellschaften* (investment funds), they affect neither their owners nor the holders of investment certificates.[36] One would expect the assets of investment companies to be controlled either by the owners of the investment company or by the unitholders. In practice, however, the voting stock is attributed to neither group. § 10 Ia explicitly exempts the votes held by KAGs from the requirements of § 22 WpHG. Controlling owners of the investment companies do not have to notify, because it is assumed that the managers of the investment fund act in the interest of their clients. Unit holders do not have to notify because they themselves do not exercise control. Hence, in practice *Kapitalanlagegesellschaften* play the role of making controlling ownership anonymous.

2.4.3. *Votes are not always attributed to their de facto owners.*

When the shareholder of the listed company is not an individual but a company, a voting trust, a family pool, or the like, the votes should be attributed to the entity's owners. The interpretation of the relevant clauses, § 21 and § 22, allows for too many exceptions, however, and very often the notification requirement does not extend beyond the shareholder company. For example, Nottmeier and Schäfer (1997: 93) argue that shares held by non-listed firms only have to be attributed to their owner if the owner controls that firm. This judgement is based on § 22(3), where 'control' is clearly defined; Nottmeier and Schäfer argue that other definitions of 'control' found in German or European law are therefore not applicable. This restriction opens up the possibility of hiding controlling stakes by dispersing votes over a number of small intermediate holding companies. For example, shares held by unlisted firms with two 50%–owners are never attributed beyond the level of the unlisted firm, because neither of the owners is deemed to be 'controlling'. Thus, if two individuals control 100% of a listed corporation via two unlisted holding companies, of which each individual owns 50%, they jointly have full control over the listed firm but do not have to notify it.

NOTES

1. We are grateful to the DAX companies, which provided us with copies of their annual reports and statutes. For proxy voting data we also draw on Baums and Fraune (1995) and Gottschalk (1988), who have laboriously collected and analysed the attendance lists of annual meetings of major German corporations.
2. The relationship between ownership, voting power, and stock market liquidity is discussed in Becht (1999).
3. In our analysis of the transparency of the ownership and voting power disclosure procedures (Becht and Böhmer 1997) we investigated selected attendance lists. In the case of Veba AG we found that Allianz AG had notified a 5% voting block, but that its name did not appear on the attendance list of Veba's annual meeting. We concluded that Allianz has its blocks voted through a bank. Other 5% blockholders do appear in the attendance lists. However, since we did not have access to all the lists that were used by Baums and Fraune (1995) or Gottschalk (1988) we had to make a 'worst case' assumption.
4. Under the KonTraG law, effective 1 May 1998, voting caps have to be phased out within a two-year grace period.
5. However, the companies have pledged to the stock exchange to limit the use of this device to 'exceptional circumstances'.
6. According to KonTraG, effective 1 May 1998, multiple voting rights for listed companies to be phased out over a five-year period.
7. There are also advantages as regards disclosure (i.e. non-disclosure). In accordance with the Large Holdings Directive (88/627/EEC), voting blocks in holding companies do not have to be disclosed unless one shareholder has majority control (see Becht and Böhmer, 1997). In fact we have encountered substantial problems in identifying blockholders of (mostly non-listed) holding companies (when this was possible at all).
8. These disclosure issues are discussed in more detail in Becht and Böhmer (1997).
9. The eleven firms we found on KSD are: Amira Verwaltungs AG, Commerzbank AG, Custodia Holding, Garant Schuh AG, IWKA Industrie-Werke Karlsruhe Augsburg AG, Leica Camera, Mannesmann AG, Merck, MLF Holding AG, Quante AG, Westag & Getalit AG; Amira, Custodia, Leica, Merck, Quante, and Westag have substantial blockholdings that were not reported to the BAWe by May 1998.
10. Additional results based on the full sample are reported in Becht and Böhmer (1997).
11. Becht and Böhmer (1997) provide further details on German disclosure requirements.
12. Based on the most recent available versions as of June 1997. Most legal references are made in the tables and, for brevity, are generally not repeated in the body of the chapter.
13. The larger clubs are now considering conversion to listed corporations on the British model.
14. § 139 AktG.
15. § 12 AktG. The KonTraG, effective from 1 May 1998, explicitly outlaws multiple voting rights. Those in being are to be phased out over a five-year period.

16. § 134 I AktG. The KonTraG, effective from 1 May 1998, explicitly outlaws voting caps. Existing caps are to be phased out over a two-year period.

17. §§ 304, 320b. Wenger, Hecker, and Knoesel (1996) analyse such offers to minority shareholders and find that in 39 of 53 cases the offer is below the market value on the day before, and in 32 cases below the market value three months earlier. For the former 39 cases, the market value exceeds the compensation by 74% on average.

18. Even though voting control in excess of 5% must be disclosed to the BAWe, blockholders may use their power to structure their involvement in such a way that true group structures remain undisclosed.

19. §§ 36 II BörsG.

20. § 36 III BörsG.

21. § 44b I BörsG.

22. §§ 2, 9 BörsZulV.

23. § 3 BörsZulV.

24. § 15 I BörsZulV.

25. § 16 BörsZulV.

26. §§ 19 II, 28 II BörsZulV.

27. § 54 I BörsZulV.

28. §§ 71 II BörsG.

29. § 73 I BörsG.

30. § 1 VerkProsG.

31. § 7 VerkProspG and §§ 2, 4, 5, 6, 7, 8, 10 VerkProspVO.

32. § 1 VerkProspG.

33. The complete title of the law is *Gesetz über den Wertpapierhandel und zur Änderung börsenrechtlicher und wertpapierrechtlicher Vorschriften* and is part of the second law to promote the German financial markets (*Zweites Finanzmarktförderungsgesetz*).

34. The *Gesetzesbegründung* was published in the *Bundestagsdrucksache* 12/6679.

35. Although their contribution is not legally binding and the authors stress that it reflects their personal views and not those of the BAWe, it is an account of the de facto interpretation and implementation of the WpHG text, legal guidelines issued by the government with the law, the interaction between the provisions of the WpHG, and other legal texts and legal opinion.

36. § 10 Ia 3 KAGG specifies the limitation to § 21 WpHG that voting control of less than 10% deriving from a fund controlled by the KAG does not have to be reported. This contrasts to the general 5% minimum for other entities.

REFERENCES

Baums, Theodor and Christian Fraune (1995), 'Institutionelle Anleger und Publikums-gesellschaft: Eine Empirische Untersuchung', *Die Aktiengesellschaft*, 3: 97–112.

BAWe (1996), 'Bedeutende Stimmrechtsanteile an amtlich notierten Aktiengesellschaften zum 30 September 1996', Frankfurt a. M.

——(1998), 'Bedeutende Stimmrechtsanteile an amtlich notierten Aktiengesellschaften zum 18 May 1997', Frankfurt a. M.

Becht, Marco and Ekkehart Böhmer (1997), 'Transparency of Ownership and Control in Germany', in *The Separation of Ownership and Control: A Survey of 7 European Countries*,

Preliminary Report to the European Commission, vol. 3. Brussels: European Corporate Governance Network.

Becht, Marco (1999), 'European Corporate Governance: Trading off Liquidity against Control', *European Economic Review Papers and Proceedings*, 43: 1049–56.

Charkham, Jonathan (1994), *Keeping Good Company. A Study of Corporate Governance in Five Countries*, Oxford: Clarendon Press.

Edwards, J. and K. Fischer (1996), *Universal Banking in Germany*, Cambridge: Cambridge University Press.

Franks, J. and C. Mayer (2001), 'Ownership and Control of German Corporations', *Review of Financial Studies*, (forthcoming).

Gottschalk, Arno (1988), 'Der Stimmrechtseinfluss der Banken in den Aktionärsversammlungen von Großunternehmen', *WSI Mitteilungen*, 5: 294–304.

Hoppenstedt Verlag (1997), *Konzernstrukturdatenbank (KSD)*, Darmstadt: Hoppenstedt Verlag.

Nottmeier, H. and H. Schäfer (1997), 'Praktische Fragen im Zusammenhang mit §§ 21, 22 WpHG', *Die Aktiengesellschaft*, 2: 87–96.

Schmidt, H., J. Drukarczyk, and D. Honold (1997), *Corporate Governance in Germany*, Baden-Baden: Nomos Verlag.

Schneider, U. H. (1995), 'Mitteilungs- und Veröffentlichungspflichten bei Veränderungen des Stimmrechtsanteils an börsennotierten Gesellschaften', in H. D. Assmann and U. H. Schneider (eds.), *Wertpapierhandelsgesetz*, Cologne: Verlag Dr. Otto Schmidt.

Wenger, E., R. Hecker, and J. Knoesel (1996), 'Abfindungsregeln und Minderheitenschutz bei börsennotierten Kapitalgesellschaften', Working paper, University of Würzburg.

6

Pyramidal Groups and the Separation Between Ownership and Control in Italy

MARCELLO BIANCHI, MAGDA BIANCO, AND LUCA ENRIQUES

1. INTRODUCTION AND SUMMARY

Like those of most other Continental European countries, the Italian corporate governance system features a high concentration of direct ownership, for both unlisted and listed companies; at first glance this suggests a very limited degree of separation between ownership and control.

The analysis of direct ownership and of the identity of owners reveals that a major role is played by families, coalitions, the State, and above all by other companies. The largest stake in listed and unlisted companies is held by other non-financial or holding companies. Contrary to other European countries, the amount held by financial institutions is limited. In order to evaluate the degree of separation correctly, the shareholdings of non-financial companies have to be taken into account. In fact, more than 50% of all Italian industrial companies belong to pyramidal groups. The main reason for this structure, especially among listed companies, is the possibility of controlling vast resources with a limited amount of capital. That is, it is a means of separating ownership and control. Just how complex the network of links can be is illustrated in Figure 6.1 for the Fiat group.

Taking the pyramidal structure into account one can identify ultimate owners and evaluate the actual degree of separation between ownership and control. Measuring separation as the amount of capital controlled per unit of capital owned, we find that in 1996 the average figure was 2.4 for listed companies; it was higher for private non-banking groups (4.5) and lower for State-controlled groups (1.6); for the ten largest private groups, the ratio was approximately 5.

In Italy, then, pyramidal groups headed by families, coalitions, or the State have supplanted other forms of separation, whereas financial institutions have played a very limited role in fostering separation. The established banking supervisory policy prevented banks from owning shares in industrial companies (with a single important exception, Mediobanca). Nor have other financial institutions such as pension funds or investment funds owned substantial blocks of shares in non-financial companies,

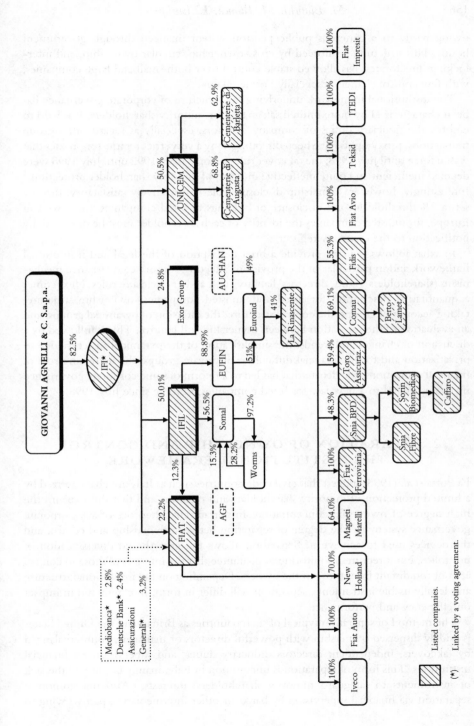

Figure 6.1. *Structure of Agnelli group, 1996.*

owing partly to a generous public pension system financed through government bonds. This structure, reinforced by cross-ownership, circular ownership, and inter-locking directorates, has allowed stable control over both small and large companies, with few control changes, especially hostile takeovers.

The institutional framework underlying this structure of corporate governance has been characterized by quite limited safeguards for minority shareholders. It is hard to enforce the fiduciary duties of company directors, especially as regards intra-group transactions; proxy fights have been discouraged by a very strict regime for proxies that was in force until July 1998; the takeover rules in force from 1992 until July 1998 were deemed inefficient and quite ineffective in terms of minority shareholder protection.[1] Interestingly, however, ownership disclosure rules are relatively satisfactory: the law sets a 2% threshold for the disclosure of holdings in listed companies, the lowest in Europe; for unlisted companies the identity of each shareholder must be disclosed, by notification to the company register.

In what follows we first provide a brief description of the legal and institutional framework and in particular of the provisions affecting corporate governance mechanisms (shareholders' rights, directors' liability etc.), and of disclosure rules. Next comes a quantitative description for listed and unlisted companies: ownership structure, taking account of groups; the control structure; the diffusion of pyramidal groups; and an evaluation of the separation between ownership and control. This is followed by a discussion of changes and trends: the simplification of the pyramidal structure due to privatization and to the financial difficulties of private groups; the increasing role of financial institutions; the debate that has led to a reform of some corporate governance mechanisms and to a new law for listed companies, in force since July 1998.

2. SEPARATION OF OWNERSHIP AND CONTROL: THE INSTITUTIONAL FRAMEWORK

La Porta *et al.* (1998) suggest that civil code countries such as Italy are characterized by a limited protection of minority shareholders and creditors and that this explains the high degree of ownership concentration. Important characteristics of any corporate governance system are the degree of separation between ownership and control and the devices used to achieve it. Separation allows the growth and diversification of portfolios, but it requires monitoring to guarantee that the interests of those in control are not too distant from those of the owners. Depending on the institutional structure and legally usable instruments, separation will differ in form, in extent and in impact on efficiency and performance.

The method of separation typical of such countries as Britain and the United States is widely dispersed ownership with powerful directors or managers, counterbalanced by takeovers, independent directors, fiduciary duties, and supervision by financial institutions. This form of separation is uncommon in Italy, mainly because of the lack of instruments to safeguard minority shareholders' interests.[2] Also uncommon is separation via financial supervision by banks or other intermediaries, partly owing to institutional limitations on their shareholdings in non-financial companies and their voting proxies at shareholders' meetings.

'Legal' sources of separation are deviations from one-share-one-vote. These allow separation at a limited cost, in that law or regulation may directly provide guarantees and compensation for non-controlling shareholders. When such means are not available or are considered too costly by controlling agents, alternatives such as pyramiding, voting pacts, and interlocking directorates may be resorted to. In the absence of strong minority protections, these means could be less efficient than others.

In this section we discuss the characteristics of the institutional framework that are most important for corporate governance in Italy, assessing the extent to which the thesis of La Porta *et al.* (1998) correctly represents the system. We first describe the main legal forms available to companies, as they are the primary instrument of separation. We then discuss the tools available, legal and otherwise, by which separation can be achieved. Finally, we examine how the instruments that allow separation to emerge elsewhere, particularly in the Anglo-Saxon system, work in Italy: e.g. such minority shareholder safeguards as rights in meetings, representation on boards, transparency and market disclosure, or the possibility of monitoring by financial institutions.

In closing it must be observed that in July 1998, in accordance with the consensus view that Italian corporate governance was excessively biased towards certainty of control at the expense of shareholders' protection,[3] a sweeping reform was enacted.[4] These changes will also be dealt with here.

2.1. *Main legal instruments of separation*

2.1.1. *Legal forms available*
In Italy the key legal distinction is between *società di persone*[5] (partnerships), where liability is unlimited for at least some of the owners, and *società di capitali*[6] (limited liability companies), where liability is, normally, limited. For the former the legal regime is quite basic and more room is left to private arrangements between the parties. For the latter, the law also mandates the internal structure of the company.[7] The *società per azioni* is the most important type of limited liability company. This legal form is chosen not only by large, but also by medium-sized firms. In Table 6.1 we present some basic statistics on the number of the various types of company in Italy. Table 6.2 describes the main characteristics of the various legal forms.

The *corporate group*, which we define here as a set of legally distinct companies all subject to the direct or indirect control of a single leadership (an individual, a coalition of individuals, or a government body) is not defined directly by the law; the law instead identifies the concept of control. There are a score of legal definitions of 'control' (see Marchetti 1992). In general, the common element is the concept of 'dominant influence', which is differently specified and exemplified in the various definitions.

2.1.2. *Deviations from 'one-share-one-vote'*
The 'one-share-one-vote' principle is not adopted by Italian law. Shares with limited voting rights (preferred shares, or *azioni privilegiate*) and non-voting shares (savings

Table 6.1. *Total number of active companies and their employees, 1991*

Size class (by no. of employees)	Not-incorporated (imprese individuali)	Incorporated companies (società)	Stock corporations (per azioni)	Limited companies (a responsabilità limitata)	Cooperatives	Other	Total
1–9							
Firms	2,334,999	747,970	7,605	156,962	24,523	24,370	3,107,339
Total employees	3,995,740	2,558,321	29,439	586,862	94,258	70,564	6,624,625
10–49							
Firms	30,176	141,357	13,063	61,758	9,320	1,871	173,404
Total employees	455,532	2,620,277	342,385	1,196,097	184,109	33,709	3,109,518
50–99							
Firms	323	11,271	5,183	4,112	1,024	216	11,810
Total employees	20,670	771,249	364,814	274,504	69,412	15,302	807,221
100–199							
Firms	54	4,960	3,075	1,203	470	154	5,168
Total employees	6,765	677,337	426,308	159,234	64,254	21,385	705,487
200–499							
Firms	9	2,513	1,846	395	220	124	2,646
Total employees	2,296	747,377	550,544	115,211	66,766	39,477	789,150
500–999							
Firms	1	662	491	104	57	66	729
Total employees	755	447,039	332,752	69,150	38,622	45,662	493,456
1000+							
Firms	1	387	320	33	32	67	455
Total employees	1,097	1,292,083	1,124,240	97,388	66,901	779,175	2,072,355
Total							
Firms	2,365,563	909,120	31,583	224,567	35,646	26,868	3,301,551
Total employees	4,482,855	9,113,683	3,170,482	2,498,446	584,322	1,005,274	14,601,812

Source: Istat.

Table 6.2. *Company types*

	Limited liability	Minimum capital (millions lire)	Smallest number of owners	Smallest number of directors	Degree of imperativeness of legal rules
Società semplice[a]	Only for partners not managing the company, if (i) the partnership contract so provides, and (ii) creditors are informed of the existence of such clause	No	2	1	Low
Società in nome collettivo	No	No	2	1	Low
Società in accomandita semplice	Unlimited for 'soci accomandatari'; limited for 'soci accomandanti'[b]	No	2	1	Low
Società per azioni	Yes, unless the company has a single owner	200 approx. Euro105,000	Two at foundation, one thereafter	1	High
Società in accomandita per azioni	Unlimited for 'soci accomandatari' and limited, for 'soci accomandanti'	200	Two at foundation, one thereafter	1	High
Società a responsabilità limitata	Yes	20, approx. Euro10,500	1[c]	1	Medium
Società cooperative	Co-operatives can be founded either as companies with limited liability or as companies with unlimited liability	No	3	1	High

[a]This legal form can be used for agricultural firms only.
[b]Partners are identified as 'accomandanti' or 'accomandatari' in the partnership contract. The liability of accomandanti becomes unlimited if they act as managers of the company.
[c]The 12th Company Law Directive on single-owner companies was transposed with Decreto legislativo 3 March 1993, n. 88.

shares, or *azioni di risparmio*) can be issued by listed companies for a total par value no greater than that of common shares. Unlisted companies can issue shares with limited voting rights (usually only at shareholders' meetings, to decide modifications of the by-laws) but only for par value no higher than the total par value of common shares.

In any case, the technique is not common. At the end of 1997, limited and non-voting shares constituted only 8.4% of the total Milan Stock Exchange capitalization (non-voting shares, 7.1%; shares with limited voting rights, 1.3%).[8]

The cash-flow rights and control rights attaching to such shares, especially after the 1998 corporate law reform, depend on the company's by-laws.[9]

Multiple voting shares have been outlawed since 1942, but voting caps are legal for unlisted as well as for listed companies. They are uncommon among the unlisted companies, given the availability of more effective tools for preventing outsiders from acquiring an influential stake, such as pre-emption agreements and the discretionary power of the board of directors to refuse transfers of shares. Among listed companies, voting caps are imposed by law for cooperative banks and are very common among privatized companies: before the placement of its shares, the government used its powers to introduce voting caps in the by-laws of most of the companies to be privatized, ranging from 3 to 10%. The 1994 law on privatization provided that voting caps could not be repealed by the general meeting for three years after their enactment, but also that they would be automatically annulled if a single person held more than 50% of the full-voting shares following a tender offer.[10]

2.1.3. *Shareholders' agreements*

Another source of separation is shareholders' agreements. Before the corporate law reform, agreements involving listed companies had to be notified within five days to Consob (*Commissione Nazionale per le Società e la Borsa*: the Italian Securities and Exchange Commission) and their essential content published in the press.

The 1998 reform institutes new rules for shareholder agreements involving listed companies and companies that control them. Not only must they be notified to Consob within five days and their content published in the press, but they must also be deposited with the company register (a consortium of chambers of commerce, whose data are available to the public). Shareholder agreements may be for a limited period (no more than three years) or else have no time limit; in this case, however, the parties may withdraw from them at any time. And in any case they may withdraw when a takeover bid for at least 60% of the voting shares has been made.

2.1.4. *Cross shareholdings*

A further source of separation is reciprocal shareholding. For unlisted limited companies, there are no limits to reciprocal holdings, when the two companies are not in a control relationship with one another. If they are, the controlled company may not hold more than 10% of the other's shares.

The rules for listed companies are more restrictive. The ordinary limit on cross-holdings (including shares held indirectly, as by controlled companies) is 2% if both companies are listed. This means that if one listed company holds more than 2% of another's voting shares, the latter may not exercise the voting rights attaching to shares exceeding 2% of the voting shares in the former and must sell such shares within twelve months. If a listed company holds more than 10% of an unlisted company's shares, the latter may not hold more than 2% of the former's shares; conversely, if an unlisted company holds more than 2% of a listed company's shares, the latter may not hold more than 10% of the former's shares.

After the 1998 reform, the limit on cross-holdings between listed companies is raised to 5% on condition that the two general meetings give their consent on the basis of an agreement between the two companies neither already owning more than 2% of the other. The new law also takes connections among groups into account,[11] and specifies that if one company gains control of the other through a takeover bid, it is the votes attaching to the shares held by the acquired company that cannot be exercised.

The separation between ownership and control may also stem from circular holdings, as when company A holds shares in company B, which holds shares in company C, which in turn holds shares in A.[12] These devices are neither prohibited nor limited by the Italian law, and a recent study finds that they are a significant factor of the ownership structure of Italian listed companies.[13]

2.2. *Other means of separation: pyramiding, interlocking directorates*

Another device to separate ownership and control is the pyramidal group. This structure is common among listed companies in Italy (as we shall see). This ownership structure has been recognized by the Italian regulator since the late 1940s but no measures were taken until recently to limit its growth or to attenuate the problems associated with it. On the contrary, pyramidal groups have been favoured by a neutral tax policy (i.e. dividends are taxed only once, no matter how many levels the control chain has) and by the absence of any legal provisions to prevent conflicts of interests between the controlling agent and minority shareholders in the subsidiaries.[14] In the past, the State itself used pyramiding for its own industrial activities. The stock exchange (publicly owned and managed until 1997) accepted the listing of so-called 'scatole cinesi' (Chinese boxes), companies whose sole assets are controlling blocks in other listed companies, and the listing of companies at various levels of the groups (see the Fiat group in Fig. 6.1).

There is no legal restriction on interlocking directorates. Per se, they are not even relevant for antitrust purposes.

2.3. *Minority protection*

2.3.1. *Shareholder meeting*

Shareholders representing at least 20% of the equity issued may convene a shareholder meeting. For listed companies, the 1998 reform lowers the threshold to 10% (or less, if so provided by the by-laws), but specifies that directors may choose not to convene the meeting if they deem that doing so would not be in the interest of the company. The same percentage of equity and the same procedure are required for shareholders' proposals.

2.3.2. *Board of directors and internal auditing*

By law, Italian companies may have either a board of directors or a single director. However, listed companies (in practice) and banks (by regulation) have boards. An internal board of auditors with three or five members (three or more for listed companies) oversees the management of the company. The civil code leaves companies free to determine the election system for directors and auditors; the most common system is 'winner–takes–all'.[15] The 1998 corporate law provides that at least one out of three or two out of the higher number of auditors in listed companies must be named by minority shareholders.

Since July 1998, according to Consob regulations the compensation of each board member and by auditors must be reported in the annual accounts. This is a significant change; previously, no such information was released; now Italian regulations are among the strictest in Europe.

2.3.3. *Derivative suits*

Until July 1998, individual shareholders and minority shareholders were not allowed to sue directors for damages suffered by the company. Only the company, after a resolution by the shareholders' meeting, could do so. Shareholders representing at least 10% of the issued shares[16] could ask a court to order an inspection of the company, alleging serious irregularities; if such irregularities are verified, the court may nominate an officer to direct the company; the latter can take legal action against directors.

The 1998 reform provides that a minority representing 5% of issued equity in a listed company (or a lower percentage, if specified by the by-laws) may start a derivative suit against directors. Although this is a significant innovation, the 5% threshold still seems too high for the major listed companies.

2.4. *Transparency and information*

For unlisted companies—except for partnerships—a 1993 law provides that the identity of each shareholder be disclosed, by way of notification to the company register.[17] Ownership data are collected by the company register but they are made available only at a relatively high cost.[18]

For listed companies there are various statutory requirements concerning ownership information. Since 1974 holdings of more than 2% of listed companies have had to be

Table 6.3. *Accessibility and availability of data*

	Accessibility of data	Availability of data on computer
Company register	Yes	Yes
Market Supervision Authority (Consob)	Yes	Yes
Banking Supervision Authority (Bank of Italy)	No	No
Insurance Industry Supervision Authority (Isvap)	Yes	No
Competition Authorities	Yes	No

reported to Consob. Since 1992, Consob has been obliged to inform the public immediately (in practice, the same day, or the day after). Until December 1998, significant changes had to be reported within thirty days; that is, if the holding percentage went below the 2% threshold or if a variation exceeded 1%.

The 1998 reform confirmed the 2% threshold, leaving Consob to issue a regulation defining significant changes, setting the criteria for the calculation of holdings and the timing for disclosure. The regulation provides that a declaration is due when the holding crosses the thresholds of 5%, 7.5%, and all multiples of 5%; the definition of 'holding' includes all the criteria laid down in Directive 88/627/EEC, also taking account of potential holdings, via options (both call and put), convertible instruments and warrants; if holdings belong to investors linked by a formal agreement that aggregates more than 5% of the voting capital, a specific disclosure rule is provided, even for individual holdings that are less than 2%. The deadline for disclosure is five working days, both for the initial declaration and for the announcement of significant changes.

The law further requires disclosure of listed companies' significant shareholdings (larger than 10%) in unlisted companies. The Milan Stock Exchange does not impose additional ownership data reporting requirements.

2.5. *Monitoring by financial institutions*

We discuss here some of the regulations regarding financial institutions that directly affect their ability and their incentive to conduct incisive monitoring.

2.5.1. *Proxy voting*

Financial institutions' activism in corporate governance is strongly influenced by the possibility and by the cost of proxy voting. From 1974 to 1998, banks were forbidden to act as proxy in shareholders' meetings of both listed and unlisted companies. Only in 1996 were they allowed to offer proxy voting services to customers of their portfolio management departments. In general, no one can act as a proxy agent for more than 50, 100, or 200 shareholders of a listed company (10 for an unlisted company), depending on the par value of its issued shares. The limits do not apply to proxy solicitations in listed companies; the 1998 reform allows any shareholder holding more than 1% to solicit proxies, but under a complex procedure.

2.5.2. *Banks*

From 1936 to 1993, banks accepting demand or short-term deposits were precluded from acquiring significant shareholdings in non-financial companies by the supervisory policy of enforcing separation between banking and industry. The policy did not apply to 'special credit institutions', banks not accepting short-term liabilities, such as IMI and Mediobanca. Mediobanca appears to have been the only credit institution to play a central role in Italian corporate governance in recent decades. Other banks have not adequately supported or advised industrial firms in securing resources or developing strategies for growth.[19] The very strict separation between banks and commercial firms, together with the regulation separating long- and short-term lending, limited the development of long-term relationships and monitoring by banks.

Following EC banking harmonization the limits on equity investments by banks are now less stringent, but it is still too soon to observe more active involvement in corporate governance by Italian banks. In keeping with their primary role as lenders, they seem to have made little use of the new opportunities, except for debt-for-equity swaps in connection with the reorganization of troubled firms.

In fact, the ownership and governance structure of banks is itself an issue. Until recently the banking system was mostly public. In 1990, the government began a privatization programme that is still under way. Many banks that were held directly by government or by IRI (the public holding company founded in the 1930s), have been privatized. Yet a good number are still controlled by banking 'foundations', non-profit institutions having a hybrid nature, neither public nor private. They were created by a 1990 law[20] to facilitate privatization, but they have proved to be most reluctant to divest themselves of their control stakes.

2.5.3. *Insurance companies, pension funds, investment funds*

Insurance companies may use both their technical reserves and their net equity capital, within limits, to buy shares; they have done so only to a limited extent, however.

So far, owing to Italy's very generous public pension system, there have been very few private pension funds, and those few have played no active role in corporate governance. A 1993 law, amended in 1995, regulates private pension plans and seeks to foster them by more generous tax treatment.[21] Pension funds may hold shares (with some limits) in any listed or unlisted company, but never such as to give the fund control of a company.

Open-end investment funds have to abide by some minimal diversification rules laid down by the Bank of Italy. Closed-end funds were first allowed and regulated by a 1993 law imposing very strict and pervasive rules, that in fact discouraged such funds; in September 1997 there were only four active closed-end investment funds in Italy. The 1993 law was repealed by the 1998 corporate law reform, which delegates to the government the regulation of such institutions.[22]

3. THE DATA

Our empirical study is based on two samples (see Table 6.4).

(1) The first includes all listed companies. The source is the administrative data on shareholdings collected by Consob.[23] Within this dataset, groups were identified by the information on control relationships reported to Consob and by means of algorithms based on shareholders' stakes, that detect control relations even when they are not explicitly stated.[24] Data have been analysed with reference mainly to 1996; some evidence is also reported for 1993. The 1993 dataset includes 263 listed companies (including the secondary market).[25] The 1996 data refer to 214 listed companies and their identified shareholders (approximately 1,100 direct and

Table 6.4. *Datasets used*

Size class (by no. of employees)	INVIND[a] (year 1992)		INVIND[a] (year 1996)		Size class (by market capitalization)	Listed Firms[b] (year 1996)	
	No. of firms	%	No. of firms	%		No. of firms	%
50–99	196	20.1	211	20.0	5 percentile	19	8.9
100–199	200	20.6	255	24.2	10 percentile	10	4.7
200–499	291	29.9	307	29.1	25 percentile	31	14.5
500–999	143	14.7	133	12.6	50 percentile	51	23.8
1000+	143	14.7	149	14.1	75 percentile	51	23.8
					90 percentile	31	14.5
					95 percentile	10	4.7
					>95 percentile	11	5.1
Total	973	100.0	1,055	100.0	Total	214	100.0

[a] Yearly survey of the Bank of Italy on manufacturing firms' investments, based on a representative sample of manufacturing firms with more than 50 employees.
[b] All listed firms in June 1996.

800 ultimate shareholders). Values are presented both unweighted and weighted according to market capitalization.[26]

(2) The second is based on a survey of manufacturing companies. A random sample of about a thousand manufacturing companies with more than 50 employees was surveyed both in 1993 and in 1996 as part of the Bank of Italy's survey of firms' investments (called INVIND). The survey includes data on ownership and control structure and control transfers.[27]

4. VOTING POWER

4.1. *Direct stakes*

Given that the Large Holdings Directive (88/627/EEC) does not require the disclosure of ownership data but only of voting power, the former are not available for listed companies. Here we consider first the distribution of direct stakes (i.e. those owned by each independent shareholder), since the Italian transparency law requires the disclosure of these as well as of voting blocks. The next section concentrates on voting blocks, i.e. stakes in a company held directly by different agents but subject to a single controlling entity.

In Italy, direct voting rights are heavily concentrated. Their concentration in manufacturing companies (both unweighted and weighted by the size) for the years 1992 and 1996 is shown in Tables 6.5 and 6.6. In 1992 the top shareholder of manufacturing companies owned on average 67% of a company (the median value being 89%), and the top three owned more than 90%. Concentration increases with firm size: in firms with fewer than 100 employees the largest stake is 60%, on average, while in those with more than 1,000 employees it is 82%. Thus weighting firms according to their size yields even higher values: the average top share, when weighted, is 77%. This depends largely on the fact that the biggest shareholder is often another company with a majority stake, and this is more common for large companies. In 1996, concentration appears to be slightly higher.

The largest shareholder of listed companies in 1993 owned on average 51.4%. For the whole set of companies belonging to listed groups, the largest shareholder owned on average 70.6%, the top three 73.7% (for companies with identified control, the respective values are 86.6 and 89.9%).[28] In 1996 concentration is slightly lower but still very high: the top shareholder averages a 48% stake (with a median of 51; Table 6.7). For smaller firms (the bottom quartile in terms of market capitalization) the largest shareholder has the absolute majority.

Associated with the majority owner there are usually other significant shareholders with average shares of 10% and 4%. On average the top three shareholders own a 62% stake. In 1996, in more than 10% of the companies the top shareholder had a stake larger than 75%, while only in 15% of the cases was ownership fairly dispersed (i.e. the largest shareholder had less than 20%). Figure 6.2 shows that the distribution of the largest stake has a mass point around 50%[29] and that about half the companies have a top stake of over 50%. We do not observe other mass points, even at the 20% or

Table 6.5. *Voting rights concentration of manufacturing companies (1992)*

	Voting rights distribution[a]			
	Largest stake	**2nd**	**3rd**	**4–10th**
Mean				
Size class[b]				
50–99	59.20	20.19	9.90	8.14
100–199	71.95	14.62	6.54	5.46
200–499	78.07	12.99	3.41	3.30
500–999	82.58	10.36	2.62	1.75
1000+	82.48	8.52	1.99	2.12
Total	66.51	17.11	7.69	6.41
Weighted total[b]	76.77	12.11	4.24	3.79
Median	89.00	5.00	0.00	0.00
Std. dev.	102.34	56.21	36.43	43.28
Min.	0.40	0.00	0.00	0.00
Max.	100.00	50.00	33.33	62.50
No. of companies	971	971	971	971

[a]The values are weighted in order to take into account the different coverage of the sample by size, sector, and geographical area.
[b]By employees.

Source: *Indagine sugli investimenti della Banca d'Italia* (1993) on a representative sample of manufacturing companies with more than 50 employees.

33% thresholds, although these used to be the quorums for the extraordinary shareholder meetings. For listed companies alone, as opposed to the sample of manufacturing companies, ownership concentration is not correlated with size. Except for the lowest percentiles (where values may be biased, because we include companies suspended from trading for financial difficulties) and the highest percentile, we observe, as expected, an inverse correlation between concentration and capitalization.[30] The greater a company's market capitalization, the smaller the stake owned by the top shareholder and also by minority shareholders (from the second to the tenth largest) and the larger the share held by the 'market', which we define as the sum of all holdings smaller than 2%.

The difference between listed and unlisted companies reflects the fact that in many cases listed companies are at the top of pyramidal groups (and hence are not owned by other companies), which maximize the resources controlled with the minimum amount of capital allowing control; and the latter decreases as the company increases in size.

For recently listed companies (in 1995 and 1996) concentration is, on average, lower: the top direct shareholder owns 40%, the second 7.3%, the third 4%, and the share of the fourth to tenth shareholders is larger than in listed companies earlier (where it amounts to 8.2%).

Table 6.6. *Voting rights concentration of manufacturing companies (1996)*

	Voting rights distribution[a]		
	Largest stake	**2nd and 3rd**	**Other**
Mean			
Size class[a]			
50–99	63.56	27.81	8.63
100–199	68.44	23.66	7.89
200–499	76.69	16.75	6.55
500–999	80.05	13.76	6.19
1000+	82.55	10.50	6.95
Total	67.69	21.29	8.01
Weighted total[b]	77.78	17.24	6.97
Median	80.00	12.00	0.00
Std. dev.	89.88	68.85	49.40
Min.	9.00	0.00	0.00
Max.	100.00	80.00	82.00
No. of. companies	952	952	952

[a]The values are weighted in order to take into account the different coverage of the sample by size, sector and geographical area.
[b]By employees.

Source: *Indagine sugli investimenti della Banca d'Italia* (1997) on a representative sample of manufacturing companies with more than 50 employees.

4.1.1. *Identity of owners*

The first step in understanding the concentration of ownership and the mechanisms whereby control is exercised is the analysis of who the shareholders are. We classify shareholders into six categories: individuals, holding companies, other non-financial companies (these two cannot be distinguished for listed companies), State-owned companies, foreign companies, and financial companies (for listed companies we can distinguish between banks, insurance companies, mutual funds, and others).

Considering the top ten shareholders in each firm, ownership of the average manufacturing firm is shared almost equally between individuals and companies (48.0% versus 49.7%; Table 6.8). As expected, individuals own a larger share in smaller companies (in those with under 100 employees they have the absolute majority) and a very small one in the largest. In larger firms, the main shareholder tends to be a holding company. But other companies, and in particular holding companies and other private domestic non-financial companies have a role in small and medium-size firms as well. The larger the company, the greater the presence among major shareholders of foreign companies, the State, and holding companies. Even when they are present, financial companies have a minimal share in manufacturing companies.

The main shareholders in listed companies in 1993 were non-financial companies (21.6% on weighted data), the State (19.3%), and individuals (28.7%, measured as the sum of reported shares of individuals and the difference between 100 and all the

Table 6.7. *Voting rights concentration of listed companies (1996)*

	Voting rights distribution[a]				
	Largest stake	**2nd**	**3rd**	**4–10th**	**Market**[b]
Mean					
Size class[c]					
5 percentile	50.54	14.18	4.19	4.20	26.78
10 percentile	51.40	11.07	6.24	5.86	25.42
25 percentile	53.27	8.90	4.92	10.87	20.89
50 percentile	47.56	11.95	5.17	7.01	27.59
75 percentile	49.11	10.11	3.50	6.32	30.74
90 percentile	42.42	9.36	2.95	3.54	41.65
95 percentile	37.02	7.00	3.17	2.23	50.54
>95 percentile	48.63	2.55	2.03	2.31	49.10
Total	48.02	10.13	4.12	6.13	31.50
Weighted total[c]	50.01	4.62	2.16	2.23	40.88
Median	50.97	7.55	3.01	2.01	
Std. dev.	22.20	9.13	4.54	9.15	
Min.	2.11	0.00	0.00	0.00	
Max.	100.00	43.58	26.43	45.37	
No. of companies	214	214	214	214	

[a]The values of direct stakes refer to those held by the largest relevant shareholders in listed companies. Relevant shareholders are defined as those holding at least 2%.
[b]The 'market' is defined as the sum of all holdings smaller than 2%.
[c]By market capitalization.

Source: Consob. Information is based on all the communications to Consob reporting holdings in listed companies larger than 2% of capital.

reported shares). Financial companies (banks, insurance companies, mutual funds, and others) had approximately 25%.

In 1996, among direct owners of listed companies we observe a very large weight of non-financial companies, including holding companies (on unweighted data they represent nearly 40%), again reflecting the diffusion of pyramidal groups (Table 6.9). Individuals do not own significant shares in any single large company. The weight of the State is similar to that found in 1993, owing to the listing of some large State-owned companies.[31] Banks hold approximately 8% of total market capitalization, mainly in other banks and insurance companies, but also, recently, in non-financial companies. The role of other financial institutions (such as investment funds and pension funds) is still very limited, even though in our figures it is certainly under-estimated, because of the 2% disclosure threshold. Estimates to correct for this bias indicate that at the end of 1996 institutional investors owned about 14% of the total market capitalization. This leads to an estimate of individuals' holdings of 29%.

The weighted share of foreign investors is quite modest: they hold about 2.5% of total capitalization, mainly in small companies (their unweighted share is 10%). Again, however, only blocks larger than 2% are reported, and hence they usually represent a

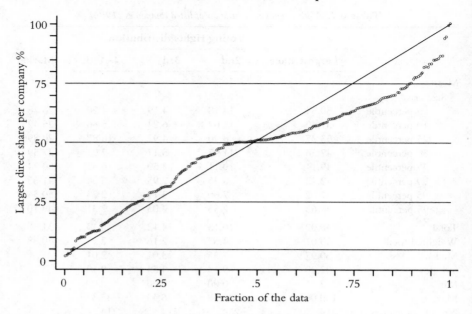

Figure 6.2. *Percentile plot of largest direct stake*

stake in control coalitions. Investment by foreign institutional investors are under-estimated like those of their domestic counterparts.

4.1.2. *Diffusion and role of groups*

The evidence on the identity of owners points to the diffusion of pyramidal groups. The results of the survey for 1992 showed that more than half (56%) of Italian industrial firms belonged to a hierarchical group; by 1996 this value had edged down to 53%. The phenomenon is more common, the larger the companies; virtually all those with 1,000 employees or more adopt this structure. The percentage is also high among small and medium-size companies, however; 40% of companies with more 50–99 employees belonged to a pyramidal group. In short, this is the fundamental form of organization and control in Italian industry.

The main reason for the pyramidal group structure is that it enables one or several individuals to control a wide range of assets and activities with a limited amount of own assets owned (mainly among listed companies). Spreading the voting rights of minority shareholders over a large number of firms and concentrating his own in the company at the top of the pyramid, an entrepreneur can 'obtain control over the greatest possible amount of other people's capital with the smallest possible amount of his own'.[32] This phenomenon is analysed in more detail in the section on separation.[33]

The next step in the analysis of voting rights in listed companies (the only ones for which the necessary information is available) is to evaluate voting blocks, which in Italy are mainly group blocks.

Table 6.8. *Voting rights of manufacturing companies by type of investor (1992)*[a]

	Individual	Foreign company	State-owned company	Holding company	Other non-financial company	Financial company	Total
Mean							
Size class[b]							
50–99	62.86	5.30	1.99	13.65	13.64	0.00	97.43
100–199	37.71	7.69	6.33	28.01	18.64	0.20	98.57
200–499	25.12	14.13	6.84	33.62	17.52	0.53	97.76
500–999	14.37	20.13	15.59	34.04	12.27	0.91	97.32
1000+	6.10	22.98	14.55	42.63	8.16	0.58	94.99
Total	48.03	8.05	4.59	21.57	15.33	0.17	97.72
Weighted total[b]	24.35	15.89	12.23	32.14	11.81	0.47	96.89
Median	0.00	0.00	0.00	0.00	0.00	0.00	
Std. dev.	159.69	85.89	65.43	132.15	115.47	10.01	
Min.	0.00	0.00	0.00	0.00	0.00	0.00	
Max.	100.00	100.00	100.00	100.00	100.00	100.00	

[a]Values are weighted in order to take into account the different coverage of the sample by size, sector, and geographical area.
[b]By employees.

Note: Row sums do not add up to 100 per cent because in the survey only information regarding the 10 largest shareholders was requested.

Source: Indagine sugli investimenti della Banca d'Italia (1993) on a representive sample of companies with more than 50 employees.

Table 6.9. *Voting rights of listed companies by type of investor (1996)*

	Individuals	Foreign	State	Non-financial company	Banks	Insurance	Mutual funds	Other financial	Total
Mean									
Size class[a]									
5 percentile	9.00	17.02	0.00	38.98	6.36	0.07	0.44	1.35	73.22
10 percentile	17.18	13.30	0.00	29.96	10.62	3.52	0.00	0.00	74.58
25 percentile	6.00	11.15	0.00	46.68	12.18	0.47	0.47	2.16	79.11
50 percentile	5.45	9.39	0.60	44.17	8.19	1.13	1.54	1.94	72.41
75 percentile	3.55	10.97	5.87	36.70	8.02	2.88	0.85	0.42	69.26
90 percentile	2.74	4.05	0.70	34.31	10.22	5.61	0.53	0.19	58.35
95 percentile	0.00	1.77	1.38	26.74	17.68	1.05	0.20	0.62	49.44
>95 percentile	0.00	0.43	16.42	17.22	10.40	5.66	0.00	0.77	50.90
Total	4.99	9.25	2.62	37.90	9.53	2.36	0.76	1.09	68.50
Weighted total[a]	0.82	2.52	20.16	23.79	8.42	2.60	0.20	0.66	59.12
Median	0.00	0.00	0.00	44.51	0.00	0.00	0.00	0.00	
Std. dev.	13.47	20.27	13.04	29.95	20.46	10.64	1.76	6.92	
Min.	0.00	0.00	0.00	0.00	0.00	0.00	0.00	0.00	
Max.	74.30	99.39	97.36	100.00	100.00	93.91	8.90	66.86	

[a]By market capitalization.

Note: Data are based on all the communications to Consob reporting holdings in listed companies larger than 2% of capital. This is the reason why row sums do not add up to 100%. The difference between 100 and the row sums is dispersed ownership.

Source: Consob.

4.2. *Voting blocks*

Most voting blocks in Italy are those of groups. Shareholders' pacts account for most of the rest. Interlocking directorates are also briefly discussed, in the next section. Given the data available, only group blocks can be analysed for all listed companies; overall voting block data are restricted to the largest 30 listed companies.

A group block is the total share held by an ultimate owner both directly and through controlled companies.[34] Naturally, the value for group block ownership shows a higher concentration than direct ownership (Table 6.10 and Figure 6.3). The difference between the top direct and group holding is particularly large for listed companies between the 50th and the 90th percentile in size. This suggests that these are the companies for which the group structure is most complex, with the controlling shareholders participating in the listed companies through various channels.

On average the second, third, and other group block stakes are smaller than the corresponding direct stakes, evidence that part of the direct stakes themselves belong to groups through indirect channels. However, they do not disappear: this can be seen as evidence of the presence of shareholders' agreements, very often informal.

The other main source of voting blocks, especially among the largest companies, is shareholders' agreements. In Table 6.11 the voting blocks of the MIB30 companies are broken down by the reason for notification: apart from indirect control (the most common), the only two that are used in practice are explicit voting pacts (3 cases only) and guarantees, used only by some banks.

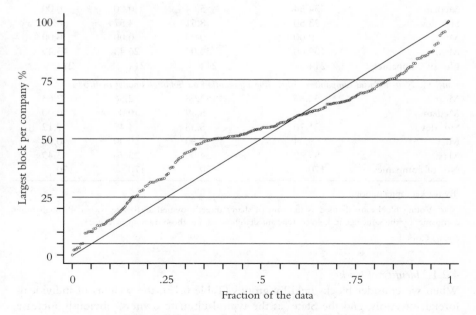

Figure 6.3. *Percentile plot of largest voting block*

Table 6.10. *Voting blocks concentration in listed companies (1996)*

	Ownership distribution			
	Largest stake	**2nd**	**3rd**	**4–10th**
Panel A: Whole sample—All information				
Mean				
Size class[a]				
5 percentile	54.21	12.53	3.45	3.01
10 percentile	51.21	9.29	3.52	8.51
25 percentile	52.25	8.35	4.89	9.82
50 percentile	53.40	8.39	4.12	5.65
75 percentile	55.47	6.48	3.09	4.81
90 percentile	46.06	7.54	2.38	2.27
95 percentile	41.25	4.58	2.62	0.98
>95 percentile	49.36	2.32	1.87	1.89
Total	51.86	7.73	3.46	5.05
Weighted total[a]	52.26	3.45	1.84	1.57
Median	54.53	5.04	2.67	0.00
Std. dev.	23.34	7.93	4.29	9.08
Min.	2.11	0.00	0.00	0.00
Max.	100.00	34.00	26.43	45.40
No. of companies	214	214	214	214
Panel B: Whole sample—Excluding information on holdings smaller than 5%				
Mean	52.26	6.88	2.42	2.15
Median	54.54	5.04	0.00	0.00
Std. dev.	23.50	8.51	4.57	6.44
Min.	0.00	0.00	0.00	0.00
Max.	100.00	34.00	26.43	43.49
No. of companies	214	214	214	214
Panel C: Non-financial companies—Excluding information on holdings smaller than 5%				
Mean	52.85	7.08	2.56	2.63
Median	54.53	5.89	0.00	0.00
Std. dev.	21.70	8.38	4.49	7.12
Min.	9.34	0.00	0.00	0.00
Max.	99.39	34.00	23.76	43.49
No. of companies	170	170	170	170

[a]By market capitalization.

Note: Voting blocks are defined as the sum of shares directly owned and those owned through other companies by the same agent, held by relevant shareholders, i.e. those owning at least 2%.

Source: Consob.

4.2.1. *Identity of blocks*

When we consider blocks held by groups (Table 6.12), the weights of individuals, foreign investors, and the State, as the typical ultimate owners, obviously increase, and that of non-financial companies decreases. A significant portion of group block

Table 6.11. *Disaggregation of voting rights according to the Large Holdings Directive*

Company	Blockholder	Total voting block	Reasons for notification			
			1	2	3	9
Alleanza Assicuruzioni spa	Banca d'Italia	2.02				2.02
Alleanza Assicurazioni spa	Generali spa	65.27		0.01		65.26
Comit	Cartiere Burgo spa	2.03		2.03		0.00
Comit	Compagnie financière	2.96		2.96		0.00
Comit	Generali spa	2.98		1.86		1.12
Comit	Commerzbank	2.99		2.99		0.00
Banca di Roma spa	Banco di Napoli	3.83		3.83		0.00
Banca di Roma spa	IRI	13.77		0.01		13.76
Banca di Roma spa	Cassa Risparmio di Roma	74.29		64.66		9.63
Banca Fideuram spa	IMI	74.90				74.90
Banco Ambrosiano Veneto	Patto Banco Ambroveneto	69.49			69.49	0.00
Benetton group	Ragione	71.28		71.28		0.00
Compart spa	Banco di Napoli	2.46		2.46		0.00
Compart spa	Ministero del Tesoro	2.99		2.99		0.00
Compart spa	Comit	3.25	0.71	0.44		2.10
Compart spa	Monte dei Paschi di Siena	3.38		3.38		0.00
Compart spa	Compagnia di San Paolo	8.43		8.43		0.00
Compart spa	Cassa Risparmio di Roma	10.14		10.14		0.00
Compart spa	Credito Italiano	11.01	2.98	0.89		7.14
Compart spa	Mediobanca spa	15.26				15.26
Credito Italiano	Commercial Union	2.02		2.02		0.00
Credito Italiano	Allianz Holding ag	3.00		3.00		0.00
Credito Italiano	Radici Pesenti Rosalia	3.00		3.00		0.00
Edison spa	Compart spa	61.33		61.33		0.00
ENI spa	Ministero del Tesoro	85.00				85.00
FIAT spa	Patto FIAT	33.38			33.38	0.00
Generali spa	Euralux spa	4.78				4.78
Generali spa	Banca d'Italia	4.88				4.88
Generali spa	Mediobanca spa	12.67	6.66		0.13	5.88
IFIL spa	Pictet % Cie Banchieri	2.10				2.10
IFIL spa	Findim finanziaria	4.78				4.78
IFIL spa	Bankers Trust Int. plc	6.23				6.23
IFIL spa	The public institution	6.90				6.90
IFIL spa	G. Agnelli & C. – SAPA	52.51		52.51		0.00
IMI	Allianz Holding ag	2.51				2.51
IMI	Ministero del Tesoro	8.07		8.07		0.00
IMI	Compagnia di San Paolo	9.91		9.91		0.00

Table 6.11. *(Continued)*

Company	Blockholder	Total voting block	1	2	3	9
IMI	Monte dei Paschi di Siena	9.91		9.91		0.00
IMI	Fondazione Cassa	9.89		9.89		0.00
INA	Banca d'Italia	2.54				2.54
INA	IMI	3.00				3.00
INA	Fondazione Cassa	3.01		3.01		0.00
INA	Compagnia di San Paolo	3.10		3.10		0.00
INA	Ministero del Tesoro	34.38				34.38
Istit. Bancario S. Paolo	IMI	2.21		0.39		1.82
Isitit. Bancario S. Paolo	Ente Banca Nazionale	2.52				2.52
Istit. Bancario S. Paolo	Ferrovie dello Stato	2.90				2.90
Istit. Bancario S. Paolo	Ministero del Tesoro	3.36				3.36
Istit. Bancario S. Paolo	Compagnia di San Paolo	65.04		65.04		0.00
Italcementi spa Fabbriche	Finanza & Futuro	2.28				2.28
Italcementi spa Fabbriche	Radici Pesenti Rosalia	54.51		54.43		0.08
Italgas spa	Banca d'Italia	6.22				6.22
Italgas spa	Ministero del Tesoro	41.93		41.93		0.00
La Fondiaria Assicurazioni	Banca d'Italia	2.32				2.32
La Fondiaria Assicurazioni	Generali	6.56				6.56
La Fondiaria Assicurazioni	Mediobanca spa	13.78				13.78
La Fondiaria Assicurazioni	Compart spa	31.84		0.13		31.71
Mediobanca spa	Patto Mediobanca	50.00			50.00	0.00
Montedison spa	Mediobanca spa	3.77				3.77
Montedison spa	Merrill Lynch & C.	3.88		3.88		0.00
Montedison spa	The Codelouf trust	3.92		3.92		0.00
Montedison spa	Compart spa	32.27		3.36		28.91
Olivetti spa	Mediobanca spa	2.21				2.21
Olivetti spa	Pdfm limited	2.96				2.96
Olivetti spa	Deutscher	4.12				4.12
Olivetti spa	De Benedetti Carlo	14.44		14.44		0.00
Parmalat Finanziaria spa	Janus Capital corporation	2.17				2.17
Parmalat Finanziaria spa	Schroder investiment	3.87				3.87

Table 6.11. *(Continued)*

Company	Blockholder	Total voting block	Reasons for notification			
			1	2	3	9
Parmalat Finanziaria spa	Tanzi Calisto	50.93		50.93		0.00
Pirelli spa	Finanza & Futuro	2.01				2.01
Pirelli spa	Pirelli & C. accomandita	2.57				2.57
Pirelli spa	Societè Internationale	51.21		51.21		0.00
Ras spa – Riunione	Allianz Holding ag	56.13		56.13		0.00
Rolo Banca 1473 spa	Fondazione Cassa	3.96				3.96
Rolo Banca 1473 spa	Allianz Holding ag	4.16		4.16		0.00
Rolo Banca 1473 spa	Credito Italiano	64.83		45.11		19.72
Saipem spa	Ministero del Tesoro	76.10		76.10		0.00
Stet spa'	IRI	63.27				63.27
Telecom Italia Mobile spa	IRI	61.33		61.33		0.00
Telecom Italia spa	IRI	64.59		64.59		0.00

Note: Total voting blocks for the main listed companies are disaggregated according to the reason for the notification as listed in the Large Holdings Directive (88/627/EEC). The reasons, from 1 to 3, correspond to those listed in Article 7 of the Directive. Reasons number 4–8 do not apply in these cases. Stakes listed under the motivation 9 are direct stakes.

holdings (about one-third of declared holdings), however, is held by what we call 'apparent' ultimate shareholders, whose ownership structure does not allow identification of a controlling agent according to Italian law. Some of these are bank foundations, whose ownership and control structures are poorly defined. The others are partnerships or limited liability companies (with 15% of declared holdings) mostly controlled by coalitions, which are considered 'not significant' for the Italian law on transparency.

5. SEPARATION OF OWNERSHIP AND CONTROL

5.1. *Unlisted companies: families, coalitions, groups*

In order to evaluate the degree of separation between ownership and control in this context, where ownership is extremely concentrated, we need to go a step further;

Table 6.12. *Voting blocks in listed companies by type of investor (1996)*

	Individual	Foreign	State	Non-financial firms	Banks	Insurance	Mutual funds	Other financial	Total
Mean									
Size class[a]									
5 percentile	35.81	10.03	0.00	22.39	2.87	0.00	0.63	1.47	73.20
10 percentile	19.88	14.51	0.51	27.11	11.04	0.00	0.44	0.00	73.49
25 percentile	21.90	8.55	7.25	26.47	11.89	0.40	0.55	2.16	79.17
50 percentile	23.48	7.99	4.33	23.34	9.29	0.00	1.41	1.94	71.78
75 percentile	22.13	12.84	8.13	16.80	8.16	0.54	0.85	0.42	69.87
90 percentile	13.76	4.79	6.95	17.82	10.11	3.96	0.53	0.34	58.26
95 percentile	0.50	7.41	5.57	17.15	17.69	0.30	0.20	0.62	49.44
>95 percentile	0.00	5.29	26.91	2.12	10.29	5.44	0.00	0.79	50.84
Total	20.07	9.07	6.79	20.06	9.48	1.07	0.78	1.12	68.44
Weighted total[a]	4.66	4.10	30.81	8.26	8.40	2.01	0.20	0.68	59.12
Median	0.00	0.00	0.00	2.02	0.00	0.00	0.00	0.00	
Std. dev.	28.02	21.75	20.47	28.04	19.95	7.99	1.74	6.94	
Min.	0.00	0.00	0.00	0.00	0.00	0.00	0.00	0.00	
Max.	95.41	99.98	97.36	100.00	95.55	93.91	8.90	66.86	

[a]By market capitalization.

Notes: A voting block is the sum of shares directly owned and those owned through other companies by the same agent. Data are based on all the communications to Consob reporting holdings in listed companies with more than 2% of capital. This is the reason why row sums do not add up to 100%. The difference between 100 and the row sums is dispersed ownership.

Source: Consob.

that is, we need to consider 'ultimate' owners. For listed companies this is done in section 5.2. However, since we do not have sufficient information for the sample of manufacturing companies, we group firms according to 'control models' (Figure 6.4).[35] We define as *absolute control* the case where there is nearly no separation between ownership and control: control is exercised by an individual with a majority of voting rights. In 1992, this model accounted for 9% of total employment (used as a proxy for size) of manufacturing firms with more than 50 employees. As expected, it is more common among small firms and extremely rare among the largest ones. The most frequent corporate governance model is *hierarchical group control*, which accounted for 52% of manufacturing firms total employment and was more frequent among larger firms. However, as noted, for this model we are unable to evaluate the degree of separation. The second most important model is what we call *family control*, where there are family links among the individuals in control or between them and non-controlling shareholders. This can be seen as another device that allows separation between ownership and control. A fourth model is *coalition control*: this model is similar to the family model but slightly more complex. The bond of trust between entre-preneurs and investors is based on common values (being in the same industrial district, belonging to the same political party, etc.) and may be strengthened by formal agreements. Empirically, we proxy this as cases with joint control or individual control without a majority of votes, except when there are family links. It accounts for 9% of manufacturing firms' total employment and is more common among small firms. The *financial supervision* model, in which financial guarantees to non-controlling share-holders are represented by monitoring on the part of financial companies with pri-vileged information (banks, merchant banks, institutional investors, etc.), is proxied by

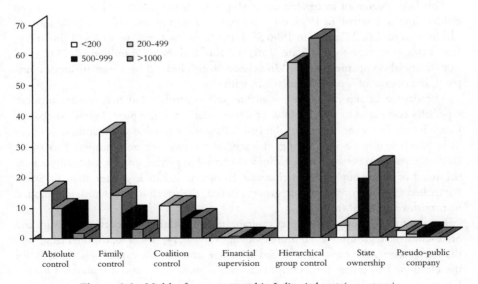

Figure 6.4. *Models of corporate control in Italian industry (percentages)*

cases in which an independent financial company has a significant share (larger than 20%). This model was basically absent among Italian manufacturing firms in 1992. *State ownership* can be interpreted as a model in which the State raises capital directly from savers and finances entrepreneurs by mandating the political authorities to safeguard the interests of investors. This model accounts for approximately 13% of the manufacturing firms total employment and is more frequent among larger companies.

Finally we proxied public companies (i.e. companies with diffuse ownership) as those in which control is exerted without ownership of shares or where ownership is extremely dispersed. A few such firms were identified. In all these cases, however, the market for corporate control was not active and no real takeover threat existed. Hence we have termed this model, which accounts for 1% of manufacturing firms employment, the *pseudo-public company*.

5.2. *Listed companies: the separation between ownership and control*

The final step in measuring the success of pyramidal groups in obtaining separation between ownership and control is the evaluation of 'integrated ownership', i.e. the amount of capital the controlling agent has actually supplied. Integrated ownership is computed for each listed company with an identified controlling agent, moving from the latter's direct shareholding along the control chain. If agent A controls company B with a 50% share and B controls company C with a 50% share, the integrated ownership of A in C is 25%.[36]

In 1996 integrated ownership of controlling agents in the set of all listed companies with an identified controlling agent was 51%. More than half of all such integrated ownership was accounted for by the State.[37]

This high degree of integrated ownership reflects the limited separation between ownership and control. In 1993, on average, ownership of one unit of capital allowed ultimate control of 2.7 units; in 1996 for listed firms the figure was 1.95 (Table 6.13); It was below average for the State (1.6), and above average for individuals (3.62) and non-financial companies (4.48).[38] In private groups headed by a non-financial company, the degree of separation increases with size.

The degree of separation of ownership and control found may appear modest, especially compared to the absolute separation realised in the pure 'public company'. Considering, however, that control is generally not contestable and that there is a very little effective outside monitoring, the separation may not be considered so small. Indeed, separation between ownership and control in private groups, especially where the head of the group is not a financial company, is much greater than in State-controlled groups. For the private groups, in fact, the pyramidal structure is exploited to maximize external finance.

For the top 30 groups by market capitalization, the difference between private and State-controlled groups is even more evident (Table 6.14). In 1996, for the Fiat group, the third-largest, the capital controlled with one unit of own capital was about 9; for the De Benedetti group this control ratio was is about 10^{39}; and it is above 4 for the Compart, Radici Pesenti, Ligresti, Pininfarina, and Falck groups. For State-controlled

Table 6.13. *Separation between ownership and control (1996)*[a]

Size class[b]	Individual	Foreign	State	Non-financial firms	Banks	Insurance	Other financial	Through formal agreements	Total
5 percentile	3.00	1.37	0.00 (0.00)	2.52	0.00	0.00	0.00	1.37	1.97
10 percentile	2.03	2.23	0.00 (0.00)	2.77	3.85	0.00	0.00	0.00	2.52
25 percentile	5.28	1.48	2.23 (2.23)	3.00	1.29	0.00	1.61	2.18	2.53
50 percentile	2.78	1.90	1.95 (1.95)	2.44	1.82	0.00	1.71	1.71	2.22
75 percentile	3.07	1.50	1.40 (1.40)	2.86	1.72	0.00	0.00	1.77	2.05
90 percentile	4.38	1.76	1.71 (1.71)	6.25	1.30	1.06	0.00	1.84	2.42
95 percentile	0.00	1.95	2.81 (2.81)	2.65	2.11	0.00	0.00	2.00	2.30
>95 percentile	0.00	1.78	1.58 (2.51)	9.72	1.54	1.53	0.00	0.00	1.77 (2.55)
Total	3.62	1.74	1.60 (2.33)	4.48	1.67	1.45	1.68	1.86	1.95 (2.40)

[a]Separation is defined as the ratio between the amount of capital under control and the amount of capital owned (integrated ownership).
[b]By market capitalization.

Notes: Only companies with identified controlling agent are considered. Values in parentheses are computed excluding ENI, the largest listed company where the State in 1996 still had 85%. Values are weighted by 'un-integrated' market capitalization, defined as the difference between the company's market capitalization and the market value of the shares held by the company in other listed firms belonging to the same group.

Source: Consob.

M. Bianchi, M. Bianco, L. Enriques

Table 6.14. *Separation between ownership and control in the largest Italian groups (1996)*[a]

Head of the group	Capital under control in proportion to owned
Ministero del Tesoro	1.24
IRI Istituto per la ricostruzione industriale	2.40
Giovanni Agnelli & C. S.a.p.a.	8.86
Compart S.p.a.	4.35
Generali S.p.a.	1.53
Compagnia di San Paolo	1.54
Allianz Holding A.G.	1.78
Benetton	1.46
Cassa di Risparmio di Roma	2.40
Mediobanca S.p.a.[b]	2.00
Credito Italiano S.p.a.	2.35
Pirelli	1.95
IMI Istituto Mobiliare Italiano	1.34
Radici Pesenti Rosalia	4.15
Banco Ambrosiano Veneto[b]	1.55
Tanzi Calisto	1.68
Mediolanum S.p.a.[b]	1.96
Ligresti Salvatore	4.83
Berlusconi Silvio	3.66
Gemina S.p.a. – Generale[b]	2.22
Bulgari S.p.a.[b]	1.80
De Benedetti Carlo	10.33
Fondaz. Cassa di Risp. Genova	1.22
Credit Lyonnais S.a	1.76
Pininfarina Sergio	5.93
INA Istituto Nazionale Assic.	1.06
Banca San Paolo di Brescia[b]	1.98
Bosatelli Domenico	1.39
Falck S.p.a.[b]	4.20
Saes Getters S.p.a.	1.48

[a]Defined as the ratio between the amount of capital under control and the amount of capital owned (integrated ownership). Groups are ordered by market capitalization.
[b]The head of the group is the coalition controlling the company.

Source: Consob. Information based on all the communications to Consob referring to holdings in listed companies with more than 2% of capital.

groups, the value was 1.2 for those controlled by the Treasury ministry, and 2.4 for the IRI group, which were first and second largest groups. For many private groups, moreover, it was impossible to identify the true head of the group, owing to the presence of coalitions controlling the holding company that are not relevant according to the disclosure rules. Were it possible to identify the true head of these groups, the separation would appear to be considerably greater.

6. RECENT DEVELOPMENTS

Some changes are perceptible of late in the Italian corporate governance structure, some of which cannot yet be traced in the data, at least not for 1996.

As far as the group structure is concerned, there is a tendency towards a simplification of pyramidal private groups: this trend seems to be driven primarily by financial difficulties of some groups and it has involved mostly listed companies at the lower levels. In some cases, the simplification reflects a concentration on the group's 'core business' and the consequent sale of non-strategic assets. For example, in the last two years the Agnelli group, whose structure in 1996 is shown in Fig. 6.1, has disposed of companies operating in chemicals (a sub-group headed by SNIA and including four listed companies) and in cement (a sub-group headed by UNICEM and including three listed companies).

The reduction of the role of pyramidal groups is diluting ownership and more generally producing a greater instability of ownership and control structure. Voting block concentration has diminished substantially since 1996, especially for the largest companies. The average top stake, calculated for voting blocks and weighted by market capitalization, has fallen from over 50% to 35% at the end of 1998; the unweighted value has decreased much less (only from 51% to 48%).

In this framework, financial institutions (both banks and institutional investors) are playing a larger role. The growing role of banks is notable most particularly in companies involved in bankruptcy proceedings, while the presence of institutional investors is more widespread, with a leading role of foreign asset management institutions. The number of listed companies in which an institutional investor held more than 2% of the equity rose from 33 at the end of 1996 to 84 at the end of 1998.

Securities market regulations are another factor affecting the ownership structure. The 1998 corporate governance laws reform makes a bid for 100% of the shares mandatory for anyone who acquires more than 30% of the full-voting shares of a listed company. Since this rule came into force, the ownership structure of some listed companies has begun to change, with a trend towards establishing the controlling stake around the 30% threshold. For example, in Pirelli Spa, the controlling stake has come down from about 50% to just over 30%. In other cases, such as Olivetti and SNIA-BPD, which had dispersed ownership, coalitions of shareholders have put together controlling stakes lower than 30%.

The privatization process is increasing stock market capitalization, notably reducing the weight of the State in the ownership of listed companies which has dropped from about 30% in 1996 to under 10% in 1998, although the process is neither linear nor unambiguous. In some instances ownership has been transferred from the state to banks controlled by foundations and can hardly be considered private. In other cases the State still controls companies that have been only partially privatized. In general, the control structure of privatized companies is an intricate puzzle: even when the privatization has been fully realized, a mix of regulatory measures (such as the 'golden share') and by-law provisions (such as voting caps) reduces the role of the market for corporate control.

Thanks in part to fiscal incentives, since 1995, a fair number of medium-sized companies have gone listed, most commonly those with venture capital participation. Most of the new listed companies do not belong to listed groups, as had usually been the case in the past, when very often new listings involved spin-offs of listed companies, to broaden the structure of the group and lengthen the control chain.

7. CONCLUSIONS

In short, the Italian case is peculiar, in that regulation and corporate culture did not favour the development of the kind of relations between banks and companies that emerged in Germany, while the more typically Anglo-Saxon corporate governance devices, acquisitions, fiduciary duties and other financial institutions, also failed to develop. We have not presented data on transfers of control but there is evidence that they are not very common and are rarely hostile in any case. The problem of financing and growth has been solved through the State, families, or coalitions, often organized into pyramidal groups. Banks or other financial institutions have not exercised monitoring or played an active role as advisors or intermediaries in the transfer of control. Takeovers have never worked as a monitoring device. Company and securities laws have not laid down enforceable fiduciary duties, nor have they ever ensured that adequate information was made available to shareholders. A large number of companies are organized into pyramidal groups, notwithstanding the lack of adequate guarantees for minority shareholders. The State has played a central, direct role via ownership and via financial transfers to private companies. There has been widespread reliance on implicit rules, such as family relations and coalitions among owners sharing common interests or values, which has further impeded the exit mechanism from working. The separation between ownership and control has been limited.

NOTES

1. See Brescia Morra, Martiny, and Salleo (1997).
2. Instruments of this kind have been introduced with the recent reform and will be discussed below.
3. See, for example, Barca (1996) and Costi (1995); but, for a different view, see Ciocca (1997).
4. Decreto Legislativo, 24 February 1998, n. 58.
5. *Società semplici, società in nome collettivo, società in accomandita semplice.*
6. *Società per azioni, società in accomandita per azioni* and *società a responsabilità limitata.*
7. Especially for *società per azioni* and *società in accomandita per azioni*. The legal regime for *società cooperative*, i.e. cooperatives, is similar to that of *società di capitali*.
8. Source: Consob. Taking into account only companies which both have ordinary shares listed on the stock exchange and also issue shares with limited votes and/or non-voting shares, non-voting shares account for 13.8% of the total market capitalization of these companies and shares with limited votes account for 1.2%.

9. It should be mentioned here that the takeover law provides that the mandatory bid to be promoted by whoever takes over a listed company does not have to be extended to holders of limited voting or non-voting shares. For cooperatives the deviation from 'one-share-one-vote' takes the form of the 'one-shareholder-one-vote' rule, according to which each shareholder has only one vote, whatever share of capital she holds.

10. See now Section 212 of Decreto Legislativo 58/1998, which modified the 1994 law by providing that voting caps become ineffective if the company is taken over by way of a tender offer on more than 60% of the shares.

11. If a person or entity A holds more than 2% of the shares in a listed company B, B or the person controlling it may not hold more than 2% of the shares in listed companies controlled by A.

12. See Ascarelli (1955).

13. Circular holdings larger than 2% each have been found to connect 20 groups of companies, representing 63% of the total capitalization of non-State-controlled companies and 36% of the Milan Stock Exchange capitalization: 16 groups were connected by 'triangular' holdings and 4 groups were connected by 'square' or 'pentagonal' holdings. See Bianchi, Fabrizio, and Siciliano (1998).

14. See Enriques (1997).

15. Since 1994, the Law on privatization has imposed on privatized companies whose statutes contain voting caps, an election system based on lists of candidates, which should allow minority shareholders to have one-fifth of the board seats and to elect one of the internal auditors.

16. The 1998 reform has lowered this limit to 5% (or the lower percentage specified by the company's statute) for listed companies.

17. The rationale for this Law is not to be found in any business activities: the Law was in fact aimed at preventing money laundering.

18. As a consequence, for our quantitative analysis of such companies we resort to sample information based on surveys. See Table 6.3 for an account on whether and how ownership data are available to the public.

19. See De Cecco and Ferri (1996).

20. In fact, *fondazioni bancarie* used to be banks themselves: with the 1990 Law, their banking assets were spun off in *società per azioni*, which, in the intention of the government, would then be privatised.

21. Decreto legislativo 1993/124.

22. See 'Regolamento recante norme per la determinazione dei criteri generali cui devono essere uniformati i fondi comuni di investimento', adopted by the Ministry of the Treasury with Decree 24 May 1999, n. 228.

23. It has to be noticed that some critical issues in disclosure regulation have an impact on the possibility to identify true shareholders and controlling agents in Italy and hence on the completeness of information in the dataset. The first has to do with *joint control*: in the Large Holdings Directive (see Article 8) and in the Italian Law implementing it, the definition of control covers exclusively those cases in which a single person or entity is in control. Joint control (e.g. 50/50 control) is not taken into account. The second concerns *informal coalitions*: in order to identify a controlling agent in a company, data on control, as defined by the Law on takeovers, had to be used. This law, in force until July 1998, did not take into account informal coalitions and shareholders' agreements concerning issues other than voting rights. A final issue refers to the increasing role of *asset managers*: asset

managers on behalf of their clients often hold major holdings. Formally, shares are in the name of clients, each of them holding a percentage lower than that for which disclosure has to be made. Therefore, no disclosure requirement applies in principle to asset managers.

24. For all the details, see Barca *et al.* (1994) and Bianchi and Casavola (1996).

25. Values referring to this dataset are weighted with an indicator which combines the firm's net worth and the 'consolidated' number of employees. Consolidated employees are the sum of those of the company itself and of all those of companies owned directly or indirectly in proportion to the stake owned by the company.

26. Or with what we define market capitalization 'deintegrated', i.e. the difference between the company market capitalization and the market value of shares held by the company in other listed companies belonging to the same group (integrated ownership and controlled shares).

27. For details, see Bianchi, Bianco, and Enriques (1997).

28. See Barca *et al.* (1994a).

29. It would be interesting to analyse this picture in the future, since it might be expected that the introduction, in 1998, of a mandatory bid rule at the 30% threshold will modify the distribution.

30. The fact that the positive relationship disappears in the highest percentile is partly due to the presence of the oil company ENI, which was in the process of being privatized and has been listed in 1995, thus becoming the largest listed company (15% of total market capitalization). In June 1996 the State still owned 85% of the company and this strongly affects the results.

31. Currently (September 1999) the stake of the State in ENI, the largest company on the stock market, has decreased to 36%; hence the data today would show a larger role for institutional investors (Italian and foreign) and for the market.

32. See Hilferding (1910).

33. Other reasons have been identified for the adoption of the group structure in Italy. See Barca *et al.* (1994b), and Bianco, Gola, and Signorini (1996).

34. i.e. if the agent controls company A and has a share b1 in company B, and company B has a share b2 in B, the group block ownership in B is given by the sum of b1 and b2.

35. See Barca (1996); Barca *et al.* (1994b), and Bianco, Gola, and Signorini (1996).

36. See Brioschi *et al.* (1990), and Barca *et al.* (1994a) for a description of the algorithm that allows us to compute it.

37. If however ENI is excluded, integrated ownership goes down to 42% and the share of the State to about one-third of total value.

38. In many instances it is not possible to move up along the control chain above non financial companies (often partnerships). If ENI is excluded, the value increases to 2.4 for all companies, and is higher also for the State (2.3).

39. Note that since the end of 1995 Olivetti is not controlled any longer by the De Benedetti group.

REFERENCES

Ascarelli, T. (1955), *Saggi di diritto commerciale*, Milano: Giuffrè.

Barca, F. (1996), 'On Corporate Governance in Italy: Issues, Facts and Agenda', Fondazione ENI Enrico Mattei, Working paper no. 10.

Barca, F., Bianchi, M., Brioschi, F., Buzzacchi, L., Casavola, P., Filippa, L., and Pagnini, M. (1994a). *Gruppo, proprietà e controllo nelle imprese italiane medio-grandi*, Bologna: Il Mulino.

——, Bianco, M., Cannari, L., Cesari, R., Gola, C., Manitta, G., Salvo, G., and Signorini, L.F. (1994*b*), *Proprietà, modelli di controllo e riallocazione nelle imprese industriali italiane*, Bologna: Il Mulino.

Bianchi, M. and Casavola, P. (1996), 'Piercing the Corporate Veil: Truth and Appearance in Italian Listed Pyramidal Groups', Fondazione ENI Enrico Mattei, Working paper no. 6.

——, Fabrizio S., and Siciliano, G. (1998), *La proprietà 'circolare' nei gruppi quotati italiani*, in *Rapporto IRS sul mercato azionario 1998*, Milano: Il Sole 24 Ore.

——, Bianco, M., and Enriques, L. (1997), 'Ownership, Pyramidal Groups and the Separation between Ownership and Control in Italy', in *The Separation of Ownership and Control: A Survey of 7 European Countries*, Preliminary report to the European Commission. vol. 3, Brussels: European Corporate Governance Network.

Bianco, M., Gola, C., and Signorini, L. F. (1996), 'Dealing with Separation Between Ownership and Control: State, Family, Coalitions in Italian Corporate Governance', Fondazione ENI Enrico Mattei, Working paper no. 5.

Brescia Morra, C., Martiny, M., and Salleo, C. (1997), 'Il trasferimento del controllo societario: profili di efficienza ed equità', Rome, Banca d'Italia, mimeo.

Brioschi, F., Buzzacchi, L., and Colombo, M. (1990), *Gruppi di imprese e mercato finanziario*, Rome: La Nuova Italia Scientifica.

Ciocca, P. (1997), 'Notes on Firms, Banks, Company Law', *Moneta e Credito* (March).

Costi, R. (1995), 'Privatizzazione e diritto delle società per azioni', *Giurisprudenza Commerciale*, 1.

De Cecco, M. and Ferri, G. (1996), *Le banche d'affari in Italia*, Bologna: Il Mulino.

Enriques, L. (1997), 'Gruppi piramidali, operazioni intragruppo e tutela degli azionisti esterni: appunti per un'analisi economica', *Giurisprudenza Commerciale*, 1.

Ferri, G. and Pesaresi, N. (1996), 'The Missing Link: Banking and Non-Banking Financial Institutions in Italian Corporate Governance', Fondazione ENI Enrico Mattei, Working paper no. 4.

Hilferding, R. (1910), *Das Finanzkapital*, Frankfurt a.M.: Europäische Verlagsansstalt.

La Porta, F., Lopez de Silanes, F., Shleifer, A. and Vishny, R. (1998), 'Law and Finance', *Journal of Political Economy* (December).

Marchetti, P. (1992), 'Nota sulla nozione di controllo nella legislazione speciale', *Rivista delle Società*, 37/1–2.

7

Ownership and Control in the Netherlands

ABE DE JONG, REZAUL KABIR, TEYE MARRA, AND AILSA RÖELL

1. INTRODUCTION

This chapter exhibits some of the available evidence on the ownership and control of listed companies in the Netherlands. We also describe the legal framework of firms in general and ownership disclosure rules in particular, together with some of the specificities of the Dutch legal and institutional framework for corporate governance.

Our work is organized as follows. Section 2 presents important features of major forms of enterprises in the Netherlands. Essentially, this is to set listed firms in context and give an idea of their relative importance. Section 3 describes the framework for reporting and publicizing ownership stakes. Section 4 analyses the ownership and control structure of Dutch listed companies. Section 5 highlights some recent developments. The summary and conclusions are set forth in section 6.

2. LEGAL FORMS OF ENTERPRISES

2.1. *Major legal entities*[1]

A firm is established by a notarial act that records the amount of capital and the number of shares issued, the identity of the founding executives, the statutes including the name, the seat of business (which must be in the Netherlands), corporate purposes, the provisions for replacement of executives and any procedures for blocking the transfer of shares. The approval of the Minister of Justice is needed; it can be denied if people of dubious reputation are involved or if the proposed statutes do not conform to the law. All this information must be reported in the company register (*handelsregister*) kept by the local chamber of commerce. The law specifies the information to be disclosed by individual firms on an ongoing basis (annual accounts, etc.). Such information is publicly available, while extracts and summaries are supplied on request at cost.

The largest and most important firms in the Netherlands are public limited companies (*Naamloze Vennootschap, NV*) and private limited companies (*Besloten Vennootschap, BV*). There are now about 2,000 NVs and more than 150,000 BVs. The NVs are few in number, but they tend to be the largest firms. NV status is usually a requirement for listing on the Amsterdam Exchanges. Some economically less important legal forms are cooperatives, partnerships, associations, foundations, and sole proprietorships. The legal entity of the private limited company, the BV, was only introduced in 1971, when NVs were first obliged by law to publish their annual accounts. Almost 90% of the 50,000 or so NVs existing at that time subsequently converted to BV status. BVs are generally smaller firms and are also sometimes used as a form of professional partnership.

The major differences between the two legal forms concern transferability of shares and constraints on issues and buy-backs. The NV can issue both bearer and registered shares, the BV only registered. The statutes of an NV *can* limit the free transferability of shares; those of a BV *must* do so (allowing only for possible transfers to other existing shareholders, close relatives, and the company itself). Share issue and buy-back rules are stricter for NVs than for BVs. For example, a BV can acquire up to 50% of its own issued equity, while an NV can acquire only 10% without ongoing shareholder approval. In a BV, the statutes can preclude pre-emptive rights for existing shareholders when new capital is issued; in an NV, a resolution by the shareholder meeting is necessary.

All firms that ordinarily employ 100 employees or more must form a works council (*ondernemingsraad*), a consultative body representing the views of employees[2]. The council has the right to obtain relevant information, the right to advise on major decisions (e.g. transfers of ownership, relocation, and important investments); it can delay decisions it disagrees with for one month and appeal to the company chamber of the Amsterdam Court. Its consent is required for changes in labour arrangements (pensions, working hours, wages, safety rules); to proceed against the council's opinion, the employer must obtain a local judge's decision.

Firms with capital and reserves of at least Fl25 million, the legal obligation to set up a works council, and at least 100 persons employed in the Netherlands fall under a special regulation known as the 'structural regime' (*structuurregime*). These firms are then obliged to set up a supervisory board (*raad van commissarissen*), which inherits many powers otherwise held by common shareholders. This board consists of at least three members; new members are appointed by co-optation (unless the shareholders' meeting or the works council objects), and the statutes can provide that one or more members must be government appointees. The supervisory board evaluates important managerial decisions, appoints and dismisses the management board (*raad van bestuur*) and draws up the yearly accounts (which are subject to shareholder approval). In practice, the structural regime gives ordinary shareholders very little say in the appointment or removal of supervisory board members or management.

According to a report published in 1998 by the Monitoring Committee Corporate Governance, 61% of the Dutch listed firms had adopted the structural regime as of 1997. Of these 61% of the firms, 26% adopted the full regime voluntarily, 6% adopted the mitigated regime, and 68% was obliged to adopt the full regime.

In a smaller company (unless it adopts the structural regime) the shareholders' meeting appoints management (*bestuur*) and directors (*commissarissen*) and approves the annual accounts. The management is personally responsible for any misconduct prior to a bankruptcy, for the presentation of misleading accounts, improper payment of taxes, undertaking clearly unmaintainable obligations to third parties, and environmental damage. The shareholders' meeting has residual powers not allocated elsewhere, as well as the right to approve annual accounts, appoint auditors, increase and decrease the firm's capital, hire and fire management, appoint at least two-thirds of directors, and amend the statutes. By law, the statutes cannot require more than a two-thirds majority for most decisions.

2.2. *Listed companies*

Firms that want stock exchange listing must sign a listing agreement (*noteringsovereenkomst*) which sets down trading rules and listing requirements such as the size and composition of the equity issued and the contents of the prospectus. The listing requirements of the Amsterdam Exchanges include the following: a corporate life of at least five years, in at least three of which a profit must have been reported; at least Fl10 million of equity capital; and at least 10% of the equity capital available for trading with a market value of at least Fl10 million. In addition, a listed firm must comply with further requirements specified in the listing agreement, including a code of conduct regarding trading in its own shares by company insiders.

Since the abolition of the Official Parallel Market in October 1993 there has been only a one-tier stock market in Amsterdam. Recently, a second-tier market called the New Market Amsterdam was established; less stringent listing requirements are proposed. The new market is also linked to the second-tier markets in Germany, France, and Belgium under the 'Euro-NM' initiative, an attempt to develop a unified trading forum for small European companies.

As noted, NVs usually qualify for stock exchange listing. At the end of 1997, shares of 248 Dutch companies were listed on the Amsterdam Exchanges. These companies had market capitalization of Fl907 million. Dutch stock market capitalization is equal to more than 50% of GDP (see Moerland (1995) for an international comparison). A unique feature of the Dutch market is the extent of dominance by a handful of large companies. Fifteen companies including Royal Dutch, Unilever, Philips, Elsevier, Ahold, Akzo Nobel, ING, and ABN AMRO represent about 75% of total market capitalization of Amsterdam Exchanges. Royal Dutch alone accounts for 21%.

3. DISCLOSURE OF SHAREHOLDINGS

3.1. *The legal framework*

To our knowledge there is no legal obligation to disclose ownership stakes in unlisted companies (except for single-owner companies, whose owners' identity must be kept in a publicly accessible company register together with a written record of all transactions between the owner and the company). If the company has issued registered shares, as is the case for all BVs and many NVs, its management obviously keeps a register of shareholdings with the names and addresses of all shareholders. But there is no legal obligation to make this information freely and conveniently accessible to the general public.

For listed companies, shareholders are subject to the disclosure requirements of the law transposing the EU Transparency Directive (88/627), namely the Law on Disclosure of Shareholdings (*Wet Melding Zeggenschapsrecht*) which came into effect in February 1992. Shareholders in all listed companies must notify any purchases or sales of share stakes both to the company and to the Securities Board of the Netherlands (*Stichting Toezicht Effectenverkeer*), created in 1988 to supervise stock exchange trading on behalf of the Minister of Finance.

Under the Disclosure Law, a shareholder must report any trade that causes his stake to cross the reporting thresholds of 5, 10, 25, 50, or 66.66%. This obligation to notify applies to both voting rights and ownership or cash-flow rights separately. At the same time, the investor must indicate whether the stake is indirect (*middelijk*), that is, held via a subsidiary company or a third party; and whether it is a potential (*potentieel*) rather than a current stake, as in case of a convertible bond or a warrant.

The listed company is required to transmit this information promptly to the Securities Board, which publishes the announcement in the financial press (in practice, *Het Financieele Dagblad*) in a standardized format, after verifying the information[3]. Before a 1997 amendment the company itself was responsible for making an announcement in a newspaper with nationwide circulation, but it was felt that direct publication by the Board would be more transparent and less subject to error.

A major source of concern with the Board's share stake database is that over time it has become increasingly contaminated. The main problem is that share stakes cross the reporting thresholds whenever the total outstanding share capital of the company changes, as in the cases of employee option plans, stock dividends, or takeovers paid for by issuing shares. A large shareholder who takes no active part in this modification of the denominator, is not required to report the resulting change in his percentage stake, even if as a result of the dilution its stake crosses one of the thresholds. So the quality of the database, which is based on initial notifications of percentage stakes, has gradually deteriorated. The Board has strenuously but unsuccessfully advocated a new law to institute a periodic (say annual) obligation for companies to report their total share capital and the holdings of their known large shareholders, to give a more accurate picture of current blockholdings. The government and a majority in parliament felt that periodic disclosure would be an unnecessary burden for companies and large shareholders. The Board was so concerned by the contamination of its database that it discontinued providing data to third parties (mostly multinationals, institutional investors, analysts, and the press).

The disclosure law is viewed as a means to ensure greater transparency of the ownership structure of listed companies. The Minister of Finance, however, indicated to parliament in 1996 that he felt its role was merely to make market movements visible. Opposition to the tightening of the law was not justified only by administrative cost: since 1995, a pressure group to protect the privacy of large individual shareholders has been working to limit information dissemination by the Securities Board.

In 1996, parliament passed a revised law on the disclosure of blockholdings which became effective in June 1997, remedying shortcomings:

- One important lacuna concerned pre-existing large shareholders of companies listed after the original law went into effect; such shareholders were not obliged to notify their stakes; now all initial shareholders in newly listed companies must disclose any large stakes[4].
- Professional intermediaries (banks, underwriters of new issues) who retain stakes of over 5% 'on the shelf' three months after a new issue or placing, must disclose such stakes, as these will be regarded as part of their investment rather than their trading portfolio.
- Custodians of stocks are now exempt from the obligation to disclose provided that they have no control rights.
- There is now a standard reporting form. The information must include the date on which the notification obligation arose and the details of how the stake is held (e.g. via a subsidiary company).
- The law was reformulated in terms of six percentage 'bands' (0–5, 5–10, 10–25, 25–50, 50–66.66, 66.66 and above); shareholders must report any movement of their stake into a different band. In the past, people did not seem to realize that they also had to report whenever their stake crossed a threshold downwards; this was a significant source of inaccuracy.
- Both open-end and closed-end investment funds now have less restrictive disclosure obligations, with 0–25% treated as one band.
- If a natural person discloses a stake, his or her 'subsidiary' company does not need to do so as well (this was already the case for group companies under the old law). Thus, double notifications are reduced.
- The Securities Board is empowered to correct erroneous data.

Through May 1997, a total of 3,300 disclosures were made. The notifying listed company paid the Board the processing cost, which was running at about Fl2,300 excluding newspaper publication.

3.2. *Public availability of data*

The Securities Board itself does not provide a record of disclosures in electronic form; indeed, in May 1997 it announced that it would no longer provide data to third parties at all because of its concern about the inaccuracy of the database. Starting in 1992, when the Disclosure Law went into effect, the main Dutch financial newspaper *Het Financieele Dagblad* has periodically published a supplement with a complete overview of all disclosed blockholdings, based on the original situation in 1992 updated to account for intervening announcements of changes.

The database has become increasingly inaccurate for a number of reasons. First of all, when shareholders' proportional stakes are changed not by trading but by changes in the number of shares outstanding, they do not need to report such changes. Also, shareholders tend to be forgetful about notifying decreases in their stakes. In some cases large shareholders have attempted to avoid or delay disclosure in order to hide their controlling interest from the public eye[5]. Finally, pre-existing large shareholders in the 70 or so companies newly listed between February 1992 and June 1997 were not obliged to disclose their stakes until July 1997.

The newspaper *Het Financieele Dagblad* has taken some measures to improve the accuracy of the data. When there is a series of filings by the same shareholder in the same company, only the most recent one is kept. Any disclosures of stakes strictly below 5% have been eliminated. Remnants of overlapping stakes (direct and indirect) arising after reporting only one sale have been removed. Some disclosures published in the press but apparently not sent to the Securities Board are included.

For each blockholding, the newspaper gives six categories of data:

a. Total ownership or cash-flow (capital, dividend) rights (includes b and c)
b. Indirect ownership (held by a subsidiary or a firm with which the filing firm has a long-term pact for exercising the voting rights)
c. Potential ownership, as from warrants, convertible bonds, or call options
d. Total voting rights (includes e and f)
e. Indirect voting rights
f. Potential voting rights

Clearly, the data are imperfect; further cleaning up is needed before they can be used in empirical research. For example, indirect holdings need to be clarified. Sometimes an attentive examination of the original notifications may be enough; but sometimes the persons and/or companies involved must be contacted, in hopes that they will be forthcoming. The change in the data over time due to variations in the denominator is hard to deal with unless the law is tightened. Information on share stakes of directors and company insiders is only available when they are reported under the Disclosure Law. This means that insiders can hide the trade as long as their stakes are less than 5%. There is no other trading disclosure requirement for insiders.

For all its deficiencies, the data reported in the financial daily are the only ones currently available; our quantitative analysis is accordingly based on them.

4. OWNERSHIP STRUCTURE AND VOTING RIGHTS

4.1. *The sample*

As noted, the Dutch disclosure requirements only apply to listed firms and share-holdings of 5% or more. The ownership data are taken from the annual overview published in *Het Financieele Dagblad* on 28 May 1996. The data describe the situation on 8 May 1996. The sample consists of 137 Dutch industrial companies listed on the Amsterdam Exchanges.

As there are no groups of listed companies, we do not analyse groups separately. Moreover, we focus on direct holdings only: for indirect holdings, only information on stakes of listed firms in other listed firms is available. Thus, the data for indirect holdings would still be incomplete. In any case, the data for the listed firms only reveal a few minor stakes, no controlling stakes.

We make three adjustments to the data as reported in the newspaper. First, many Dutch firms issue a large proportion of their common shares to an administrative office, which in turn issues depository certificates to other investors after stripping off the voting rights. The ownership stakes reported by these administrative offices are excluded to avoid double counting. In the analysis of voting rights, however, their ownership stakes are included. Second, the potential ownership stakes reported are not taken into account. In general, these potential rights consist of unpaid-up preferred stock placed in a friendly foundation (generally called *stichting preferente aandelen* or *stichting continuiteit*). Third, the indirect ownership stakes reported may lead to double counting, as both the subsidiary and the parent company may have filed information on the same stake. Indeed, if the parent is a natural person and not a company, that was obligatory under the pre-June 1997 law. We try to correct for this by eliminating the subsidiary's stake. Table 7.1 gives an example using data for a company (Wegener) which illustrates our procedure.

For this company we make the following adjustments. The single stake of 99.998% held by an administrative office ('Wegener, St. Adm. Ktr') is not considered in the analysis of ownership rights. The potential stake of 99.99% of preferred stock reported by a foundation ('Wegener, St. Pref. Aand') is also deleted. We investigate the indirect stakes as shown in columns (b) and (e). Although an indirect stake of Amev/VSB is reported, we cannot find the direct shareholder because no stake of the same size is reported. This entry is not deleted. An individual named C. J. Houwert reported an indirect stake of 21.27%. A private company named Van der Loeff Beheer reported a stake of exactly the same percentage. It is very likely that C. J. Houwert controls Van der Loeff Beheer. For this reason this latter entry is deleted. Like that of Amev/VSB, the stake of Telegraaf shows no clear resemblance with the other stakes. We choose to remove double entries as much as possible by eliminating the subsidiaries.

Table 7.1. *Disclosed shareholder stakes of Wegener (percentages)*

Shareholder	(a)	(b)	(c)	(d)	(e)	(f)
Amev/VSB NV	5.15	5.15	0	—	—	—
Britt Holding BV	5	0	0	—	—	—
Heinsbroek, H. Ph. J. E.	5.837	0	0	—	—	—
Houwert, C. J.	21.27	21.27	0	—	—	—
Loeff Beheer, BV van der	21.27	0	0	—	—	—
Scottish Widows Invt.	5.38	0	0	—	—	—
Telegraaf, Holdingsmij NV	15.93	15.93	0	—	—	—
Wegener, St. Adm. Ktr	99.998	0	0	99.998	0	0
Wegener, St. Pref. Aand.	99.99	0	99.99	99.99	0	99.99
Wovang BV	5	0	0	—	—	—

Note: The column headings are defined as follows: (a) total ownership rights (capital and dividend; it includes columns b and c); (b) indirect ownership (held by a subsidiary or a firm with which the filing firm has a voting pact); (c) potential ownership (e.g. warrants, convertible bonds, or call options); (d) voting rights (it includes columns e and f); (e) indirect voting rights; and (f) potential voting rights.

4.2. *Ownership*

Table 7.2 presents summary information on the structure of ownership of cash-flow rights in Dutch listed companies. We find that the mean size of the largest block is 26.94% and the median 18.22%; for the top three blockholders together, the figures are 40.64% and 34.05%: for all large blockholders, 47.74% and 48.4%. There is considerable variation in the ownership stakes. The standard deviation of the top stake is 22%, for the top three 28%. The frequency distribution of share ownership is presented in Table 7.3. We see that a relatively large number of firms have ownership stakes in the 25–50% and 50–75% ranges. Figures 7.1 and 7.2 provide graphical representations of the largest stake.

The results analysing ownership by broad categories of investor are reported in Table 7.4. The average ownership stakes of banks, insurance companies, and other financial institutions are 7.44%, 10.44%, and 14.66%, respectively. There are 78 firms in which a bank is a large blockholder and 44 firms in which an insurance company is another blockholder. Individuals and corporations have average stakes of 10.80% and 2.41% respectively.

4.3. *Voting rights*

Tables 7.5, 7.6, and 7.7 repeat the analysis for voting rights. The average size of the largest voting stake is 42.78%. The cumulative distribution of the largest voting block and the histogram are presented in Figures 7.3 and 7.4. We observe that voting rights in Dutch companies are more concentrated than ownership rights, owing mainly to the blocks controlled by administrative offices, as can be seen from Table 7.7. We find that other categories of owners, such as banks, insurance companies, and pension funds have, on average, very few voting rights.

Table 7.2. *Ownership structure of Dutch companies*

Ownership concentration	Mean	Median	25th percentile	75th percentile	Min.	Max.	Standard deviation
C_1	26.94	18.22	9.42	44.65	0	97.05	21.60
C_3	40.64	34.05	21.78	58.28	0	137.92	26.95
C_5	45.29	44.59	26.96	65.22	0	144.36	27.57
C_{all}	47.74	48.40	27.70	69.69	0	144.36	28.92

Note: The sample consists of 137 Dutch listed companies (investment funds excluded). Ownership data are for 1996. Blockholders owning 5% or more are required to disclose their stakes. The concentration variables C_1, C_3, C_5 and C_{all} represent the percentage of common shares held by the largest blockholder, the three largest blockholders, the five largest blockholders, and all blockholders, respectively. Minimum concentration of 0 represents shareholdings of 5% or less. Maximum concentration of more than 100% is due to multiple disclosures of same shareholdings by different owners (which occurred in case of at least two firms). Ownership stakes of administrative offices are excluded.

Table 7.3. Frequency distribution of ownership concentration

Range (%)	C_1			C_3			C_5			C_{all}		
	Freq.	%	Cum.	Freq.	%	Cum.	Freq.	%	Cum.	Freq.	%	Cum.
0–5	3	2.19	2.19	3	2.19	2.19	3	2.19	2.19	3	2.19	2.19
5–10	35	25.55	27.74	16	11.68	13.87	16	11.68	13.87	16	11.68	13.87
10–25	40	29.20	56.93	25	18.25	32.12	12	8.76	22.63	12	8.76	22.63
25–50	35	25.55	82.84	46	33.58	65.69	50	36.50	59.12	40	29.20	51.82
50–75	21	15.33	97.81	31	22.63	88.32	34	24.82	83.94	39	28.47	80.29
75–90	2	1.46	99.27	9	6.57	94.89	15	10.95	94.89	18	13.14	93.43
90–95	0	0	99.27	3	2.19	97.08	3	2.19	97.08	5	3.65	97.08
95–100	1	0.73	100	2	1.46	98.54	2	1.46	98.54	2	1.46	98.54
100+	0	0	100	2	1.46	100	2	1.46	100	2	1.46	100

Note: See Table 7.2.

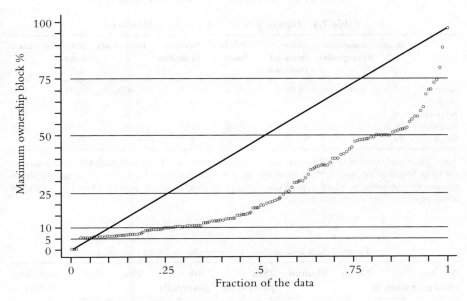

Figure 7.1. *Cumulative distribution of the largest ownership block.*

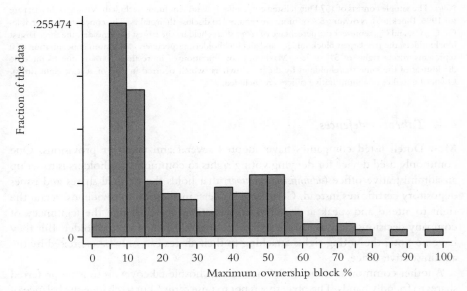

Figure 7.2. *Histogram of the largest ownership block.*

Table 7.4. *Ownership structure by category of blockholder*

	Banks	Insurance companies	Other financial institutions	Pension funds	Venture capitalists	Individuals	Industrial firms	State
Mean	7.44	10.44	14.66	0.60	0.30	10.80	2.41	1.08
Median	5.14	0	8.52	0	0	0	0	0
Minimum	0	0	0	0	0	0	0	0
Maximum	58.28	93.17	85.61	19.06	18.09	97.05	27.01	50.00
Frequency	78	44	87	10	3	48	38	4

Note: The sample consists of 137 Dutch listed companies (investment funds excluded). Ownership data are for 1996. Blockholders owning 5% or more are required to disclose their stakes. The raw 'frequency' shows the number of firms in which a particular category of blockholder is present. Ownership stakes of administrative offices are excluded.

Table 7.5. *Concentration of voting rights in Dutch companies*

Voting concentration	Mean	Median	25th percentile	75th percentile	Min.	Max.	Standard deviation
C_1	42.78	43.46	11.21	60.79	0	99.99	32.10
C_3	58.13	61.08	27.60	92.24	0	148.73	37.13
C_5	61.05	67.51	34.90	92.59	0	148.73	36.73
C_{all}	62.52	69.84	35.81	93.72	0	148.73	36.73

Note: The sample consists of 137 Dutch listed companies (investment funds excluded). Voting rights data are for 1996. Blockholders owning 5% or more are required to disclose their stakes. The concentration variables C_1, C_3, C_5, and C_{all} represent the percentage of *voting* shares held by the largest blockholder, the three largest blockholders, the five largest blockholders, and all blockholders, respectively. Minimum concentration of 0 represents voting rights of 5% or less. Maximum concentration of more than 100% is due to multiple disclosures of the same shareholdings by different owners (which ocurred in case of at least eight firms). Ownership stakes of administrative offices are included.

4.4. *Takeover defences*

Most Dutch listed companies have adopted several anti-takeover provisions. One commonly used device for denying voting rights to common shareholders is to set up an administrative office (*administratiekantoor*) that holds the original shares and issues depository certificates instead. Certificate holders, in addition to dividends, retain the right to attend and speak at shareholders' meetings, to challenge the legitimacy of company decisions, and to call for extra meetings just like any shareholder. But they have no vote; the voting rights attaching to their shares can only be exercised by the administrative office.

Another common method of defence against hostile takeovers is to issue preferred shares to friendly hands. The objective is not to raise capital but to change the balance of power in the shareholders' meeting. Preferred shares with specific control rights are issued to friendly parties. For example, these shareholders may have the right to make a binding

Table 7.6. *Frequency distribution of voting rights concentration*

Range (%)	C_1			C_3			C_5			C_{all}		
	Freq.	%	Cum.	Freq.	%	Cum.	Freq.	%	Cum.	Freq.	%	Cum.
0–5	14	10.22	10.22	14	10.22	10.22	14	10.22	10.22	14	10.22	10.22
5–10	16	11.68	21.90	8	5.84	16.06	8	5.84	16.06	8	5.84	16.06
10–25	19	13.87	35.77	12	8.76	24.82	5	3.65	19.71	5	3.65	19.71
25–50	34	24.82	60.58	24	17.52	42.34	27	19.71	39.42	21	15.33	35.04
50–75	27	19.71	80.29	26	18.98	61.31	23	16.79	56.20	25	18.25	53.28
75–90	9	6.57	86.86	17	12.41	73.72	22	16.06	72.26	23	16.79	70.07
90–95	7	5.11	91.97	8	5.84	79.56	9	6.57	78.83	11	8.03	78.10
95–100	11	8.03	100	18	13.14	92.70	19	13.87	92.70	20	14.60	92.70
100+	0	0	100	10	7.30	100	10	7.30	100	10	7.30	100

Note: The sample consists of 137 Dutch listed companies (investment funds excluded). Ownership data are for 1996. Blockholders owning 5% or more are required to disclose their stakes. The concentration variables C_1, C_3, C_5, and C_{all} represent the percentage of *voting* shares held by the largest blockholder, the three largest blockholders, the five largest blockholders, and all blockholders, respectively. In at least eight companies, there were multiple disclosures of the same shareholdings the sum of which led to apparent ownership of more than 100%. The columns 'freq.', '%', and 'cum.' show the number of firms, the percentage of firms, and the cumulative percentage of firms, respectively. Ownership stakes of administrative offices are included.

Table 7.7. *Voting rights by category of blockholder*

	Banks	Insurance companies	Other financial institutions	Pension funds	Venture capitalists	Individuals	Industrial firms	State	Administrative office
Mean	4.42	8.33	11.10	0.40	0.30	8.86	1.44	1.08	26.89
Median	0	0	0	0	0	0	0	0	0
Minimum	0	0	0	0	0	0	0	0	0
Maximum	39.78	93.04	85.61	19.06	18.90	97.05	27.01	50.00	104.46
Frequency	48	34	61	6	3	36	22	4	54

Note: The sample consists of 137 Dutch listed companies (investment funds excluded). Ownership data are for 1996. Blockholders owning 5% or more are required to disclose their stakes. Maximum voting rights exceeded 100% because of multiple disclosures for the same shareholdings. The raw 'frequency' shows the number of firms with a particular category of blockholder. Ownership stakes of administrative offices are included.

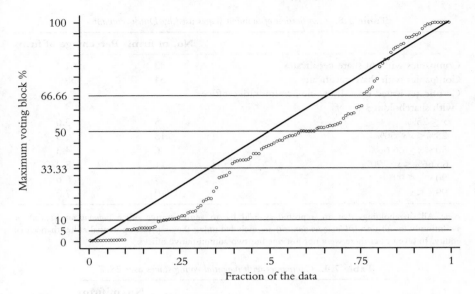

Figure 7.3. *Cumulative distribution of the largest voting block.*

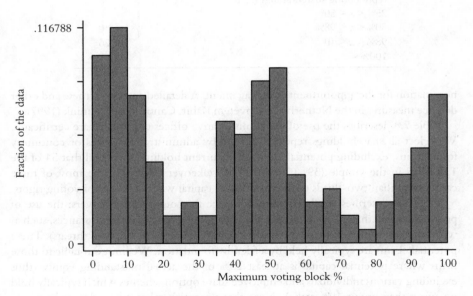

Figure 7.4. *Histogram of the largest voting block.*

Table 7.8. *Certification of common shares used by Dutch companies*

	No. of firms	Percentage of firms
Companies without share certificates	83	61
Companies with share certificates	54	39
Certificates issued by at least one administrative office with shareholdings (x) of:		
$x \leq 25\%$	5	3.6
$25\% < x \leq 50\%$	13	9.5
$50 < x \leq 66.66\%$	6	4.3
$66.66\% < x \leq 90\%$	11	8.0
$90 < x \leq 99\%$	9	6.6
$99\% < x$	10	7.3

Note: All shareholdings that are reported as held by an administrative office (*administratiekantoor*) or a continuity foundation (*stichting continuiteit*) are included unless they represent potential rather than actual equity. In seven cases there were not just one but two administrative offices.

Table 7.9. *Companies with potential voting stakes over 25%*

	No. of firms
No potential capital over 25% reported	101
At least 25% potential capital representing shareholdings (x) of:	
$25\% < x \leq 50\%$	8
$50\% < x \leq 98\%$	0
$98\% < x \leq 100\%$	26
$100\% < x$	2

nomination for the appointment of management. A detailed analysis of these and other defence measures in the Netherlands is given in Kabir, Cantrijn, and Jeunink (1997).

Table 7.8 describes the use of the administrative offices that issue share certificates. We select all shareholdings reported as held by administrative offices or continuity foundations, excluding potential rather than current holdings. We find that 54 of the 137 firms in the sample (39%) used this anti-takeover device. In the most of these cases, more than two-thirds of the firm's share capital was thus shorn of voting rights.

Table 7.9 describes another common device for countering takeovers: the use of potential capital that will only be actually issued under specified circumstances, such as when the continuity of the firm is under threat (i.e. in case of takeover threats). These potential claims are typically held by a friendly foundation. We limit our table to those firms where potential capital is at least 25% of the actual outstanding equity (thus excluding various individuals and employee share option schemes which typically hold no more than about 10% stake). Note that potential stakes can and sometimes do exceed 100%. We find that 36 of the 137 sample firms have substantial amounts of potential capital. For 26 firms, potential capital is 98% or more, suggesting that the purpose is to guarantee a voting majority of at least 50% in case of need.

The various anti-takeover devices may be alternative or complementary. Our results show that the use of non-voting shares and potential shareholdings are not alternative to one another: many firms use both. Eighteen firms, in fact, issue shares to an administrative office and also have outstanding potential equity rights of over 25%.

4.5. *Board supervision*

As we have seen, most listed companies have a supervisory board whose members are appointed by co-optation with no direct shareholder input. The supervisory board in turn names a management board. There is considerable debate at present on whether shareholders and employees of companies should have greater powers to appoint, reappoint, and depose supervisory board members.

As far as we know, no systematic quantitative data have been collected about Dutch supervisory boards. The only information available is the names of individuals acting as members of different boards. According to a report published by the Dutch Committee on Corporate Governance in October 1996, 69 individuals are members of two boards, 39 of three boards, and 20 persons of four or more. We have collected information on the size of the boards of Dutch listed companies; the results are given in Table 7.10. The median size of the management board is 2 while that of the supervisory board is 5. The largest management board has 14 members and the largest supervisory board has 11 members.

Table 7.11 gives information on the percentage of shares held by inside blockholders. The first column lists the 25 firms in which blockholders or their relatives are members of the supervisory or the management board. The second and the third columns report the percentage stakes of members of the management board and the supervisory board, respectively. In the fourth column the percentage of shares owned by people with the same family name as a member of the management and the supervisory board is added. In only 19 firms do members of the management board have shareholdings greater than 5%. For these firms, there is no change in insider block ownership when the supervisory board is added. In 6 firms members of the supervisory board hold stakes but those of the management board do not. The average ownership stakes of the management board members, the supervisory board members, and their relatives in our sample of 137 firms are 4.86%, 1.82%, and 0.49%, respectively.

Table 7.10. *The size of management boards and supervisory boards*

	No. of board members		
	Total	Management board	Supervisory board
Mean	7.7	2.8	4.9
Median	7	2	5
Minimum	3	0	0
Maximum	23	14	11

Table 7.11. *Ownership by inside blockholders in Dutch companies (percentages)*

	Management board	Supervisory board	Relatives
Free Record Shop Holding	88.22	0.00	0.00
Hollandia Kloos Holding	77.10	0.00	0.00
Automobiel Industrie Rotterdam	55.63	0.00	0.00
Randstad Holding	53.06	0.00	0.00
Content Beheer	51.70	0.00	0.00
Burgman Heybroek	49.98	0.00	0.00
Baan	47.60	0.00	0.00
Mulder Boskoop	44.65	0.00	0.00
Kondor Wessels groep	35.35	0.00	5.50
Drie Electronics Beheer	24.40	0.00	24.40
Aalberts Industries	24.00	0.00	7.85
Wegener	21.27	0.00	0.00
Delft Instruments	20.41	0.00	0.00
Rood Testhouse International	19.40	0.00	0.00
Tulip Computers	17.53	0.00	0.00
Dico International	10.58	0.00	0.00
Flexovit International	8.78	0.00	0.00
Nedcon Groep	8.67	0.00	0.00
Grolsch	8.00	7.54	0.00
Naeff	0.00	97.05	0.00
Cindu International	0.00	46.93	0.00
Neways Electronics International	0.00	41.73	0.00
Telegraaf	0.00	29.41	0.00
Gouda Vuurvast Holding	0.00	13.60	18.20
Sligro Beheer	0.00	12.46	11.39
Average (137 firms)	4.86	1.82	0.49

Note: The sample consisits of 137 Dutch listed companies. The data on blocks of inside ownership are for 1996. Relatives are defined as blockholders with the same surname as one or more members of one of the boards.

5. RECENT DEVELOPMENTS

Initially the public debate on corporate governance focused on takeover defences. In its annual report for 1985, the Amsterdam Exchanges pleaded for a discussion in order to reduce the accumulation of takeover defences. As a countervailing power, the association of listed companies (Vereniging Effecten Uitgevende Ondernemingen, VEUO) has been created. Nowadays a much broader view on governance is discussed. As a result of an agreement between the Amsterdam Exchanges and the VEUO, a Corporate Governance Committee was appointed in 1996. The Committee, popularly known as the Peters Committee (following the name of its chairman), consisted of persons that served the interests of both parties and external experts. In 1997 the Committee published the report *Corporate Governance in the Netherlands; The Forty Recommendations*. Generally, the report proposes to increase the control of shareholders through self-regulation by the firms. All listed firms are invited to consider improvements and report their governance situation as compared to the recommendations in their 1997 annual reports. The management of each company is also invited to explain whether they follow, or plan to follow, the recommendations (in case of disagreement a motivation is asked).

The Monitoring Committee on Corporate Governance prepared a report in 1998 on the responses of listed firms in their 1997 annual reports to the Peters Committee's recommendations. Besides, this report provides a detailed overview of the limitations of shareholders' influence. The general conclusions are that most firms did not change their governance structures, while some firms choose to adopt minor changes. In total 14 out of 159 firms included in the study changed their governance structures. Only 13 Dutch firms have no defence measure against shareholder influence (see *Het Financieele Dagblad* of 12 December 1998). In 2000, the Centre for Applied Research at Tilburg University was asked to submit a report to the Dutch Minister of Finance on the impact of the structural regime and takeover defences on financial performance of firms. The report finds some indications that the structural regime and depository certificates negatively influence firm performance. Currently, the debate on corporate governance in the Netherlands mainly focuses on proposed changes in the structural regime.

6. CONCLUSIONS

Our examination of ownership and control of Dutch industrial companies listed on the Amsterdam Exchanges, finds that the average stake of the largest blockholder is 27% and that of the top three blockholders is 41%. We break owners down by categories and observe that banks, insurance companies, and other financial institutions do not, as a rule, have large blockholdings. Analysing the control aspects, we find that administrative offices own major voting blocks. These and some other practices are used widely by Dutch corporations as anti-takeover devices; their prevalence presumably explains the absence of hostile takeovers in the Netherlands.

NOTES

1. Our description is based on Slagter (1996) and Dorresteijn and Verhorst (1994).
2. Firms with 35 employees or more for one-third of normal working hours must also set up a works council, but with limited responsibilities.
3. At the same time, the Amsterdam Exchanges' listing agreement requires the company to report all price-sensitive information promptly so that it can be made public by the exchange on its electronic information system. In practice, most changes in large shareholdings are reasonably considered price-sensitive, so that the information is likely to be made public on the exchange even before the Securities Board publishes it.
4. Large shareholders in the 70 or so companies that were listed between February 1992 and June 1997 were given until 1 July 1997 to disclose their holdings. But by the deadline only 20 notifications had been received, some of them incorrect, whereas the Board had expected about 280, or four notifications per company.

5. *Het Financieele Dagblad*, 7 May 1993. Sanctions range from polite reminders to fines and imprisonment.

REFERENCES

Commissie Corporate Governance (1996), *Corporate Governance in the Netherlands*, Amsterdam: Amsterdam Exchanges.

Dorresteijn, A. and M. Verhorst, 1994, *Inleiding bedrijfsrecht*, 7th edn., Deventer: Kluwer.

Gelauff, G. and C. den Broeder (1996), *Governance of Stakeholder Relationships: The German and Dutch Experience*, Centraal Planbureau, Research memorandum no. 127.

Het Financieele Dagblad, various issues.

Kabir, R., D. Cantrijn, and A. Jeunink (1997), 'Takeover Defences, Ownership Structure and Stock Returns in the Netherlands: An Empirical Analysis', *Strategic Management Journal*, 18: 97–109.

Moerland, P. (1995), 'Corporate Ownership and Control Structures: An International Comparison', *Review of Industrial Organization*, 10: 443–64.

Slagter, W. (1996), *Compendium van het ondernemingsrecht*, 7th edn., Deventer: Kluwer.

8

Ownership and Control of Spanish Listed Firms

RAFEL CRESPÍ-CLADERA AND MIGUEL A. GARCÍA-CESTONA

INTRODUCTION

In terms of the insider–outsider debate on matters of corporate governance, Spain remains in something of an intermediate condition. Market mechanisms do play an increasing role, but at the same time major institutions such as the State, large banks and, more recently, managers of large and, often, recently privatized companies have become controlling shareholders, playing key roles in settling relevant issues in corporate governance.

At the end of 1995, our year of reference, Spanish companies were still engaged in the transition towards a more international, competitive, and open system. The State still held important stakes in several of the largest corporations, although privatization was gathering momentum. We can summarize the Spanish corporate ownership and equity market in the following five points:

(1) The number of listed companies remains still rather small, 606, and accounts for only 0.5% of the public companies in Spain. Nevertheless, in 1995 stock market turnover was equivalent to 10% of GDP. Although still low in respect to UK or USA, this figure compares favourably with the situation in other European countries. Moreover, the depth and importance of the stock market, relative to other financial alternatives, has kept growing year by year and several large Spanish corporations are beginning to be listed on the NYSE and other foreign markets.[1]

(2) Overall, there is a high degree of ownership concentration but it is lower than most European countries. According to our data, the direct shareholding of the largest stake is, on average, 30.27%, rising to 32.13%, for non-financial companies. If we repeat our calculations in terms of voting blocks (i.e. the sum of direct and indirect voting rights in our analysis) the figures increase to a substantial 38.28% and 40.09% respectively. Furthermore, in terms of potential coalitions when the corresponding figures for other large shareholders are added in, the averages go over the majority line quite quickly. Taking the top three largest shareholders (C_3), for instance, we get an accumulated holding of 47.06% for direct shares and a 56.59%

voting block for our sample of 193 non-financial companies. In fact, C_2 measure is enough to achieve a majority in terms of voting blocks; to reach the majority with direct stakes a C_4 must be formed, on average. Alternatively, the degree of ownership concentration measured by the average number of shareholders that report direct stakes of 5% or more reaches 3.5 (3.41 for non-financial companies and 3.66 for the larger sample).

(3) Turning to type of shareholders, we find that industrial (non-financial) firms[2] are the main category, followed by families and non-bank financial firms. We distinguish six types of shareholders: families or individuals, banks, non-bank financial firms, government, foreign firms, and non-financial firms (or industrial firms). From our results, it seems as if Spanish banks, unlike German banks, no longer play an important ownership role. But, when banks do participate in a firm, they take substantial stakes in the case of small and medium-large firms. Foreign firms' participation is also directed to gain control. On the other hand, family or individual ownership is not as prevalent as in other countries. Although individual participation averages 10.93% overall, this figure becomes less than 3% in the largest decile, where the most important companies are.

(4) Although we lack the precise information to address properly the issue of groups, our data on direct and indirect stakes suggest that group voting or voting blocks, as a whole, do not play an important role. Indirect ownership becomes a device used by companies and individuals to exert voting power beyond their direct ownership shares. The indirect ownership contribution via holdings of intermediate companies to these voting blocks is 23%. Nevertheless, the distortion of the relation between voting rights and cash-flow rights is weak, only about 4%. When we compute indirect ownership, the concentration of the largest shareholder averages 8% higher than for direct ownership.

(5) Until recently, state ownership has been very substantial in a number of large Spanish firms, mainly in the historical and natural monopolies (oil, tobacco, energy, and telecommunications). After a strong privatization process, such participation has almost disappeared and the state has been replaced by a large number of Spanish retail investors, some large Spanish institutional investors (banks, for the most part) and some international institutional investors. The State has nevertheless retained a golden share mechanism to be used only under certain quite narrowly defined scenarios. The first time the mechanism was enacted was in 1995 with Repsol, the largest oil Spanish company. Other cases have involved Telefónica, the former telecommunications monopoly, and Endesa, the largest electricity utility. Although the mechanism has been included in the privatization processes as a protection for the public and national interest, the State has not used it to date.

Finally, before 1996 and especially during the last two years, several companies have joined the ranks of the listed companies, either through privatization or through IPOs in the Spanish stock market. This shows the increasing importance of market mechanisms.

OWNERSHIP AND CONTROL: THE LEGAL ASPECTS

The Spanish corporate landscape: the stock corporation (SA)

Table 8.1 summarizes the Spanish corporate landscape according to legal form. Excluding sole proprietorship (without employees), the largest categories are the *Sociedad Anónima*, or SA, and the *Sociedad Limitada*, or SL: that is, the stock corporation and the limited liability partnership. To start up an SL, the minimum capital requirement is Ptas500,000. (approximately, Euro3,000); and Ptas10 million (approximately, Euro60,000) for an SA. The *Sociedad Anónima Laboral* (SAL) is a mixed form, in which workers are the main owners and keep control of the firm. Most were originally stock corporations that went through severe economic problems and that the workers took over in order to keep their jobs.

Cooperatives account for less than 3% of all firms; they are quite small in size and are generally concentrated in specific sectors such as agriculture and distribution. The notable exception is the Mondragon Cooperative Group in the Basque country, which employs more than 34,000 people. This group includes some important industrial cooperatives, a savings bank, several research centres, and other service and agricultural cooperatives. At present, the group is considering raising funds in the stock market through some form of holding companies or intermediate firms. On the whole, however, cooperatives remain quite marginal within the corporate landscape.

Most large Spanish firms are stock corporations. These companies are subject to the Spanish Corporation Act (*Ley de Sociedades Anónimas*), which lays down a number of requirements for information disclosure and corporate governance.

Electronic quotation system

In April 1989, the Spanish stock exchanges began to implement the Electronic or Automated Quotation System, a system of computer-based trading that connects the four exchanges and eliminates the traditional differences among them. In 1997, the Automated Quotation System accounted for 98.7% of total equity volume on the four exchanges. The remaining transactions, involving only the local exchanges, were carried out on the Madrid, Barcelona, Bilbao, and Valencia stock exchanges.

Table 8.1. *Number of companies by legal form, December 1995*

Legal form	Number
Sociedades Anónimas (SA)	116,888
Sociedades Limitadas (SL)	326,644
Sociedades Regular Colectiva (SRC)	604
Sociedades Comanditarias (S. Com.)	85
Cooperativas	16,494
Sociedades Anónimas Laborales (SAL)	5,939
Empresario Individual (Autónomo)	1,086,256

Source: *Anuario El País* 1997.

Table 8.2. *Companies listed on the Spanish stock exchange, equity segment*

	1991	1992	1993	1994	1995
Panel A: Number of companies					
Total	868	801	763	652	615
Electronic Market	122	124	121	127	127
Outcry Market	746	677	642	525	488
Active Companies	715	665	616	608	585
Panel B: Stock exchange activity					
Turnover/GDP at current prices	7.7%	6.3%	8.7%	10.8%	10.9%
Effective Equity trading (Secondary markets, Ptas billions)	4,709.6	4,450.3	6,508.0	9,085.7	7,913.3
Market Capitalization (Equity segment, Ptas billions)	14,902.2	13,961.1	21,253.1	20,895.1	23,629.3

Source: CNMV.

By the end of 1998, 134 of the more than 600 listed firms operate in the electronic market; the rest remain in the outcry market. Not all sectors are equally represented, as Table 8.2 shows; the decrease in the number of listed companies reflects rationalization undertaken by the national stock exchange commission that excluded firms with very low transaction frequencies.

OWNERSHIP DISCLOSURE LEGISLATION

Securities market legislation

The Spanish Securities Markets Act of 1988 (*Ley 24/1988 de 28 de Julio*) reformed the organization and supervision of the securities markets. This legislation and the regulations that followed achieved several goals. We want to emphazise the following: (i) establishing an independent regulatory authority, national stock exchange commission, (*Comision Nacional del Mercado de Valores*, CNMV) to supervise the securities markets; (ii) setting a framework for the regulation of trading practices, tender offers, and insider trading; (iii) requiring listed companies to file annual audited financial statements and to make public quarterly financial information; (iv) establishing the legal framework for the Electronic Quotation System; and (v) providing for transfer of shares by book entry or by delivery of evidence of title.

In particular, Chapter 53 of the Act establishes the obligation to report the acquisition or transfer of significant holdings to the supervisory authorities and to the issuer.

Council Directive 88/627/EEC of 12 December on reporting requirements for significant holdings came after the passage of the Spanish Act. And on 22 March 1989, Royal Decree 276/1989 established the relevant threshold levels and the time considerations for the Spanish markets. Two years later, in order to incorporate the accumulated experience and further implement European legislation, Royal Decree 377/1991 on the Reporting of Significant Holdings and Acquisition of Treasury Stock was enacted.

As to foreign investment, at present non–residents' holdings of Spanish shares must be registered with the Spanish Registry of Foreign Investments.

REPORTING REQUIREMENTS

Any person or group of persons that, directly or indirectly, transfer or acquire shares in the equity of a company listed on a Spanish stock exchange above certain levels must report the transfer. More specifically, when a shareholder's ownership rises above 5% or any multiple of 5%, or decreases below 5% or any multiple of 5% of the equity of a company must, within seven business days, report such transfer to the objective company, to the stock exchange on which such company is listed, and to the CNMV. Furthermore, for the case of a foreign investor, they must report to the *Dirección General de Politica Comercial e Inversiones Exteriores,* the government body in charge of supervising foreign investment. Members of the board of directors must report any transfer or acquisition of the equity of their company, regardless its size.

Under Spanish company law, a person or a group that, directly or indirectly, owns or controls 10% or more of the outstanding shares of a listed company, or that increases the number of shares up to or above 5%, or any multiple, of the outstanding shares, must notify the company of such ownership. Until this requirement is complied with the person or group cannot vote its shares.

Concerning the acquisition by a company of its own equity stock, Royal Decree 377/1991 deals with the reporting of relevant holdings and acquisition of treasury stock. It establishes that any holding equal or above 1% of own equity by the company or by its affiliates, must be reported to the CNMV within seven business days.

INDIRECT OWNERSHIP, INVESTOR GROUPS, AND VOTING PACTS

The Transparency Directive focuses on ensuring public knowledge of large share-holdings, based on voting rights. It is important to distinguish between (i) direct stakes, and (ii) voting blocks, which contain those attributed votes through intermediate companies or persons or other devices mentioned in Article 7 of the Directive (88/627/EEC).

The parent–subsidiary figure, and the intermediate company created as a means to exert substantial voting power are the main instruments used by Spanish listed companies. There are also anti-takeover devices such as voting caps, qualified majority requirements for some decisions, and statutory rules that make access to the board of directors more difficult. We will mention some of them in discussing the case of Telefónica, even though these instruments remain secondary with respect to the ownership structure of Spanish firms.

Spain's transposition of the transparency directive refers to the notification of large shareholdings in terms of ownership rights. It refers to current ownership or voting rights but never to future rights, which could be relevant to holdings of convertible bonds. The law only makes indirect references to voting rights in RD 377/91 for cases where the 'business groups' definition (see next section) is appropriate.

To detach voting rights from cash-flow rights, the Spanish corporation law only allows for the issue of non-voting shares limited to 50% of outstanding equity; and the transposition of the EU transparency directive only considers indirect ownership rights. There is no mention of such other devices introduced in the Directive 88/627 as voting agreements. Of the eight reasons mentioned in Article 7 of the Transparency Directive, only the second ('Voting rights held by an undertaking controlled by that person or entity') is applied in Spain. Thus, the 'group block' concept, under which several direct notifications are assigned to a controlling shareholder who owns stakes in these companies, does not differ in essence from the 'voting block' concept, under which voting attributions different from indirect ownership, such as voting pacts, are also reflected.

BUSINESS GROUPS

Business groups were important in Spain until the mid-1980s, mainly with banks acting as controlling shareholders. Since then large private groups have been largely absent, with a few exceptions, such as the Kuwait Investment Office (K.I.O.), which used an industrial company as head of the group in Spain. Currently, and due in part to the privatization process, some groups of stable shareholders have emerged within the large listed companies. Moreover, they are able, quite often, to exert influence on managers, decisions, and even appointments.

The role of banking groups is substantial in Spain, as in other Continental European countries and the financial system was, and still is, to a certain degree, bank-oriented. Despite significant progress towards incorporation and an increasingly market-oriented system, some major banks continue to exercise key functions.

Even in the cases of banking groups, it is hard to establish which companies belong to a group. The accounting rules determine which companies must submit consolidate reports. According to Spanish Company Law, a firm belongs to a group if one of the following conditions applies: (i) there is a majority of voting rights (direct plus indirect shares); (ii) there is the right to appoint or remove the majority of the board of directors; or (iii) there is a majority of votes through internal contractual arrangements among companies.

For practical purposes the legal definition of 'group' is complex and far from satisfactory for most companies. First, the legal criterion 'having majority of voting rights' is hard to accommodate with the condition 'having the right to appoint or remove the majority of the board of directors'. Second, for a sample of companies, and given our set of voting and ownership data, the definition of 'group' has to establish the percentage of shareholdings considered as 'controlling ownership'. This could be fixed at a simple majority; in this case a company would belong to a group when the parent company or some other group companies, hold more than 50% of shares. To gain the right to appoint or remove board members however, 50% of shares is often not needed. Alternative thresholds, such as 25% of the shares or even less, could be sufficient criterion. Third, the 'existence of a majority of votes through internal contractual arrangements among shareholders' may not be publicly reported; in so far as this is so, this criterion cannot be used in our analysis.

In the end, therefore, given the available data set on large shareholdings, it is quite hard, in practical terms, to determine which firms belong to a business group. The disparities between criteria and their difficult interpretation constitute very stubborn impediments indeed.

VOTING RIGHTS DILUTION AND RESTRICTIONS: THE RIGHTS OF MINORITY SHAREHOLDERS

Direct ownership: we measure direct ownership of a shareholder as the simple voting power of his stake. This is calculated for the top shareholder, the second largest, the third, and so on. To check deviations from the one-share-one-vote rule, we will later compare this notion with the voting-block measure. We also consider other distortions, such as non-voting shares, voting caps, and the golden-share mechanism for newly privatized companies.

Under the current Spanish Company Law (RDL 1564/1989), companies can issue non-voting shares up to 50% of their outstanding equity. To compensate for the lack of voting rights, the law requires that such shares yield a minimum dividend of 5%; above that threshold, non-voting shares have the same dividends as common shares. So far, except for Banco Guipuzcoano, no Spanish company has used this option of raising funds by issuing shares with cash-flow rights but no voting rights.

Some company statutes have been amended to incorporate anti-takeover devices. One such provision limits the voting capabilities of large shareholders with rules like 'no shareholder can exercise more votes than he/she would in case of having 5% of equity'. Large listed corporations have begun to introduce these voting caps, as the example of Telefónica shows below. Other statutory modifications raise the majority required for important decisions such as mergers, business changes, etc. In these cases, the requirement of qualified majorities of 75% or 90% means that some minority shareholders can block key board decisions. A third way to limit voting rights is by altering the rules on the appointment of board members, by requiring some degree of seniority as shareholder or increasing the number of votes required by reducing the size of the board.

ON THE GOLDEN-SHARE MECHANISM

Law 5 of 23 March 1995 regulates sales and certain other transactions involving the Spanish State's interests in those companies providing a public service; such transactions require prior authorization from the Spanish government. The provisions of Law 5/1995 must be applied to each transaction pursuant to a specific Royal Decree. On these lines, the Royal Decree 1525/1995 establishes specific procedures to obtain administrative authorization.

Once the State's ownership of a public firm falls below 15%, for a period of time as long as ten years after the selling date, prior government approval is required for the following scenarios: (i) the direct or indirect acquisition by a group or individual of 5% or more of the capital stock, or any securities that directly or indirectly confer a right to subscribe or acquire 5% or more of the equity; (ii) the direct or indirect acquisition by a group or individual of 10% or more of the equity of any of the relevant companies[3] (and related companies), or any securities that directly or indirectly confer a right to subscribe or acquire 10% or more of the equity of any of the relevant companies; (iii) any resolution to sell, dispose of, or encumber in any way part of the equity of any relevant company of which corporations may be the holder, or any securities held by the corporation that confer a right to subscribe or acquire equity in such relevant company; or (iv) any resolution by the corporation or any of the relevant companies for the voluntary liquidation (*disolución voluntaria*), the split-up (*escisión*), or the merger (*fusión*) of such company with any other company.

If any such transaction or agreement is effected without government approval, such act is null and void, and strict limitations will apply to the voting and other rights attached to any shares or securities subscribed, acquired or transferred pursuant to such unapproved transaction. The Spanish government has not yet made use of this mechanism. Nevertheless, one presumes that such provisions affect the perceptions of potential shareholders and, consequently, the final value of the shares. Interestingly, however, no significant effect seemed to follow the measures, and no debate on their nature and their implications has been opened.[4]

THE CASE OF TELEFÓNICA SA

We briefly present now the case of Telefónica, Spain's largest listed company. Until 1997, the State owned the largest stake in the firm; at the last comprehensive offering the remaining shareholding to be privatized was 21.15%. Non-State shares have been traded for many years, always accounting for an important fraction of daily trading volume on Spanish stock exchanges.

At the time of the privatization, the State was encouraging the active involvement of several large Spanish companies (called core shareholders or *núcleo duro*) in the newly privatized companies. In particular, three financial institutions hold shares larger than 5% in Telefónica: BBV, Argentaria, and La Caixa. The new private company has established that each core shareholder is entitled to name two members of the board of directors. The law also allows for golden shares in former State-owned companies under certain scenarios. Such possibility has been also introduced in the case of Telefónica, although until now the government has never exercised its right of administrative approval. What are the consequences of privatization on the governance of firms? How does this change affect the incentives of managers or the ownership structure of the new firm? These are important questions to be addressed.

By May 1998, after privatization had been completed, the management team of Telefónica succeeded in enacting several measures with a powerful impact on corporate governance:

(a) the approval of a 10% voting cap. That is, independently of his holdings, no shareholder can exercise more than 10 % of the total votes.

At the General Meeting of Shareholders of 24 June 1998, a resolution limited the voting rights attached to shares: shareholders shall have the right to one vote for each share they own or represent, except that no shareholder may exercise more than the number of votes corresponding to 10% of the total voting stock at any given time, even though the number of shares held by such shareholder exceeds 10% of the equity of Telefónica. This limitation also applies to the votes cast by any two shareholding companies that belong to the same group of companies or to any two or more shareholding companies that are controlled by any one shareholder, whether the shares held by such companies are issued jointly or separately. Regardless of the limitations on voting rights, all shares belonging to one holder, to one group of companies, or to one person and his controlled companies, will be included together for the purpose of establishing whether a quorum is present for the carrying on of business at any general meeting of shareholders.

Interestingly, Germany has recently passed legislation prohibiting voting caps. Basically, voting caps and multiple voting rights have to be phased out over the next few years. The reasons invoked include the excessive managerial power that this mechanism may generate.

(b) Requirements for the members of the board of directors: the candidate must have held more than 1,000 shares of Telefónica for at least three years before their nomination, unless 85% of the members of the board agree to waive this condition.

(c) Requirements for chairman or any other position in the executive committee: the candidate must have held a position on the board of directors for at least three years before appointment. Again, this seniority rule can be waived by an 85% majority of the board.

Given the existent dilution of shareholding, these measures provide added power to the managerial team. The case is especially important: as noted this is Spain's largest corporation and could easily be a trendsetter. These measures overturn the one-share-one-vote rule, giving greater discretionary power to managers and seriously affecting the governance of the firm.

DATA COLLECTION

The available ownership and voting data come from the *Comisión Nacional del Mercado de Valores* (CNMV), the Spanish stock exchange regulatory agency. The transposition of the transparency directive in 1989 allows us to collect, and update data up to the present. In Spain, only significant shareholdings (at least 5%) and those of the members of the board must be reported. At 31 December 1995, there were 615 companies listed on the Spanish stock markets (including investment trusts) with a market capitalization of Ptas23.6 trillion (Euro155 billion); trading volume for the year was Ptas7916 trillion (Euro52 billion).

Table 8.3. *Number of companies by sector: Initial data set and sample*

Sector of economic activity	Initial firms	Our sample
Non-financial	342	193
Agriculture and fishing	4	3
Utilities, mining, and electricity production	30	22
Basic metals	21	6
Cement and building materials	18	14
Chemicals	21	9
Metal manufacturing	41	22
Other manufacturing (food, paper, etc.)	77	49
Construction	14	11
Commerce and services	34	15
Transport and communications	20	10
Real estate	62	32
Finance and insurance	379	201
Banking	48	28
Insurance	14	5
Investment trusts	307	164
Investment companies	5	4
Real estate financing	5	
Total	721	394

To make data comparable across countries, we present the tables and the corresponding information evaluated at the end of 1995.[5] There, information covers 721 listed companies, the number available starting on December 1989 (see Table 8.3).

From Table 8.2 we already observe that the number of listed firms is decreasing overtime, whether measured by total number of companies, active companies, or firms listed in the outcry market. But the relative importance of the stock markets and the number of firms in the electronic market, by far the most active, both increased between 1989 an 1995; and the trend has continued since then.

The CNMV data come from the forms that companies and significant shareholders must present to the Commission. Together with the information on ownership positions above 5%, there is also information on important facts that may affect share prices, accounting information, and the shareholdings of individual board members.

The data set of 721 firms has been arranged to produce a sample comparable to other EU countries. The initial sample of companies with information on ownership is biased toward the financial sector due to the inclusion of investment trusts (more than 40% or 307 companies). The sample reduces to 394 firms once we cross ownership data with market values from stock exchanges. The reasons for removing companies are: (i) low trading frequency for some companies, making it difficult to calculate capitalization; (ii) cases where the sum of ownership stakes exceeded 100% due to errors in the shareholders' notifications; (iii) impossibility of obtaining full identification; and (iv) differences in data codification between stock exchanges and the CNMV.

Given our interest in the industrial corporations and the self-imposed requirement of harmonization with other countries, most of the following analysis has been conducted for a sub-sample of 193 non-financial companies; however the results for the larger sample are not qualitatively different. Table 8.3 details sample composition and sectors of activity.

The aggregated market value of the 394 companies included in our large sample is Ptas19.3 billion. This represents 88% of the electronic market capitalization in 1995 and 81.7% of the total capitalization for the four Spanish stock markets. The concentration of capitalization in a small number of companies is a characteristic of the Spanish stock markets. The concentration of trading volume is even more pronounced.

We have calculated voting power and ownership structures using the last notification for every large shareholder and board member before 31 December 1995. The shareholdings reported have been divided into several categories. The first distinction is between Spanish and foreign investors. Spanish shareholders are categorized as individuals (or families) and companies. From the company code, identification as state ownership, non-financial and financial companies follows. The latter are also divided into banks and non-bank companies (investment trusts, investment companies, real estate financing, and insurance companies).

DIRECT OWNERSHIP

The Spanish transposition of the EU transparency directive does not allow us to determine differences between significant shareholdings and voting rights for listed companies. There is no publicly available information on voting agreements or coalitions. However, between the direct share stakes and the ultimate voting blocks, there are frequently indirect shareholdings, which allow some firms or individuals to control listed firms via intermediate companies without the corresponding cash-flow rights. As a consequence, we distinguish between direct stakes and voting blocks. We cannot track the ultimate voting blocks in some companies, so the distinction between direct stakes and group blocks will be identical to the previous one.

First, we present the data for direct stakes of the largest shareholders, by sectors of activity according to the CNMV classification (Table 8.4).

Note that the sum of the largest shares for each type of investor does not coincide with the total figure. This is so by construction: while the second column captures the average proportion of shares owned by the largest investor of any kind, the following columns refer to the average largest share stake for each category (whether or not it is the largest investor in that firm).

It is worth emphasizing that the largest investor holds on average quite a large share. The differences between the average largest stake in the non-financial company sample and in financial companies are not huge (32.13% and 28.49% respectively). We also observe, as Galve and Salas (1993) pointed out, that the predominant largest stake is held by Spanish companies. Chemicals is a good example, with non-financial

Table 8.4. *Direct stakes: Average percentage of direct shareholdings of the largest investor by type of investor, December 1995*

Company activity sector	No.	Total (%)	Banking	Non-bank	Foreign	Non-financial companies	State	Individuals
Agriculture and fishing	3	38.74			6.99	38.74		0.00
Utilities, mining, and electricity	22	40.56	6.65	8.00	5.05	10.84	23.80	0.65
Basic metals	6	26.84	8.81	15.83	4.82	12.15		0.22
Cement and building materials	14	38.29	1.61	2.53	13.96	28.49		2.33
Chemicals	9	21.02	2.26	4.39	2.34	20.90		2.27
Metal manufacturing	22	33.65	1.34	2.60	21.74	11.02	0.70	3.59
Other manufacturing (food, paper, etc.)	49	29.48	1.54	2.19	7.47	13.29	2.17	11.05
Construction	11	25.62	1.99	1.99	4.46	19.86		2.14
Commerce and services	15	32.11	1.32	3.21	11.80	15.94	4.10	4.73
Transport and communications	10	35.42	4.74	4.74	5.41	20.71	14.10	1.84
Real estate	32	31.38	2.83	7.47	5.85	18.64		5.49
Non-financial sample	193	32.13	2.73	4.49	8.75	16.43	4.39	5.07
Banking	28	41.11	29.86	30.17	7.28	2.87	2.51	1.06
Insurance	5	33.28	0.12	0.12	2.68	33.28		1.76
Investment trusts	164	26.54	2.38	5.56	3.43	13.03		13.17
Investment companies	4	14.62	6.11	6.11	2.68	12.67		1.53
Finance and insurance sample	201	28.49	6.20	8.86	3.92	12.05	0.35	11.01
Total	394	30.27	4.50	6.72	6.29	14.19	2.33	8.10

companies holding an average of 20.90% This is a fact that some authors, such as La Porta *et al.* (1999), with a reduced sample for each country, do not detect. They do, however, mention the important influence of State ownership. In Spain, the government role as a main shareholder has been fundamental in certain sectors, such as utilities, transport, and communications (mainly through Telefónica). On average, nevertheless, State participation remains below 5%, even in the industrial sample. It is also important to mention the generally weak influence of banks as top shareholders. Banks emerge as top shareholders only of banks and other financial institutions, showing the parent–subsidiary structure of the banking sector in Spain, with only a relatively small number of independent banks. This would explain the 41.11% largest stake on average in the banking sector.

Foreign firms concentrate their holdings in certain sectors, where they may have the largest stake, such as metal manufacturing and cement and building materials.

Figure 8.1 shows the average and median direct stake of the largest shareholder, the second largest, the third, the fourth, the fifth, and the contribution of the remaining known shareholders for our sub-sample of 193 non-financial companies.

These results follow a pattern similar to that found for the larger sample; there are no significant differences in average direct stakes when we consider only non-financial companies (193 firms) and add up the stakes of other top shareholders.

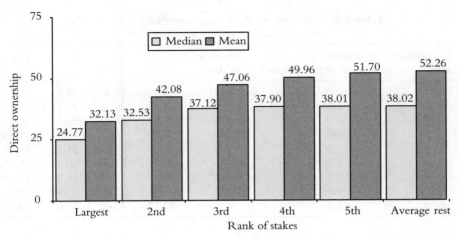

Figure 8.1. *Direct ownership stakes: mean and median of shareholdings. Sample of 193 non-financial companies, December 1995.*

Once the high ownership concentration of Spanish listed companies has been detected, it is also interesting to look at the contribution of other major shareholders and see how quickly majorities can be formed. Thus, the combination of the top three shareholders goes to 47.06%, which seems quite a high figure. The decreasing marginal contribution of the 4th and the 5th largest stakes reinforces the idea of ownership concentration in few hands. The fact that the median values go to zero after the fourth shareholder also denotes high concentration. The top three shareholders are the watershed, in the sense that the marginal contributions of the 4th and the 5th are almost insignificant, with median values close to zero.

DIRECT OWNERSHIP BY SIZE CLASSES

Next, we present our analysis on the 193 industrial companies, crossing direct ownership by company size.

Table 8.5 shows that ownership concentration does not decrease with firm size. Around the median and the third quartile there is a significant number of companies with an average top stake greater than in smaller companies. In fact, for those cases, a coalition of the top three to five direct stakes averages over 50% of the shares.

As the C_1 column shows, the average direct top stake is 32.13%, for the Spanish companies. The figure is even larger for the segment of firms that are relatively large but not the largest, reaching 44.74% in the 75–90% size interval. Such a high figure surely suggests that the largest shareholder enjoys a fair amount of control.

VOTING BLOCKS

Owing to the characteristics of the data available for Spain, 'voting block' becomes identical to the concept 'group block' used in other country reports. The shareholder's

Table 8.5. *Direct ownership by size class: Distribution of the sample of 193 non-financial companies, December 1995*

Percentile size	Capitalization cut-off (Ptas billions)	Fraction of data	C_1	C_3	C_5	C_{all}
<5	Up to 249	0.052	30.88	50.39	59.49	67.22
5–10	249	0.052	31.55	46.25	51.11	59.86
10–25	444	0.145	25.87	45.62	53.46	56.74
25–50	1,561	0.249	23.36	40.77	45.92	49.76
50–75	7,815	0.259	36.41	48.54	51.73	53.28
75–90	41,430	0.150	44.74	57.18	60.82	61.41
90–95	140,007	0.041	38.17	49.77	50.33	50.48
>95	241,100	0.052	30.83	39.78	39.94	39.96
Mean	66,496		32.13	47.06	51.60	54.39

attributed votes are from indirect ownership, through intermediate companies that have voting rights in the listed companies.

We calculate voting blocks counting direct and indirect holdings. To avoid double counting, we correct for indirect holdings greater than 5% (the Spanish reporting threshold) through intermediate companies. In this case, the direct shareholding of the intermediate company is removed as a direct holding and added to the voting block of the parent company. This permits accurate valuation of blocks of votes or ownership when we add up the stakes of several large shareholders.

The average value of the largest voting block for the full sample, that is, including the financial companies, is over 38%, and 40% for the non-financial companies. Overall, non-financial companies are the most important investor category. State ownership is also important, but only in sectors linked to former monopolies, such as utilities, transport, and communication. Comparing these results with direct stakes, foreign and individual investors or families become more powerful in terms of voting blocks, using Spanish companies as intermediary instruments to control corporations.

As in the case of direct stakes, we also give a more detailed analysis of the ownership structure of the 193 firms. Figure 8.2 shows how important the largest shareholder is in controlling companies compared with the direct ownership values. Including indirect shares, the top shareholder averages 40%, and the top two reach absolute majority. That 40% average is far greater than the 10% controlled by the second-largest voting block on average. Again, the low median values from the second block, indicate that the concentration of voting power involves a very few blockholders.

The largest voting block has an average stake of 40%; the three largest go over 56%. Like the previous figure on direct shareholdings, the contribution of the fourth and subsequent shareholders is weak, and only significant for a small number of companies (median close to zero).[6]

Table 8.6. *Voting blocks: Percentage of the largest voting block by type of investors, average*

Sector	No.	Total %	Type of investors					
			Banking	Financial other than banking	Foreign	Non-financial companies	State blocks	Individuals
Agriculture and fishing	3	45.21	0.00	0.00	6.99	38.11		13.97
Utilities, mining and electricity produc.	22	46.03	9.38	10.30	11.59	8.28	28.25	3.88
Basic metals	6	30.82	15.83	7.49	2.73	13.68		0.23
Cement and building materials	14	55.71	3.91	3.91	23.31	28.27		2.11
Chemicals	9	36.02	5.84	5.84	12.99	25.09		6.73
Metal manufacturing	22	36.19	1.40	2.66	22.18	15.34	0.70	5.84
Other manufacturing (food, paper, etc.)	49	36.86	3.05	3.81	9.96	11.78	2.17	17.33
Construction	11	40.82	3.06	3.88	4.71	30.40		7.46
Commerce and services	15	45.56	1.32	3.22	16.45	11.53	4.10	5.17
Transport and communications	10	41.00	16.26	16.26	5.44	15.45	14.10	2.26
Real estate	32	36.12	6.42	8.61	7.46	17.57		13.07
Non-financial sample	193	40.09	5.24	5.98	11.93	16.26	4.90	9.31
Banking	28	51.02	27.59	29.83	9.68	5.61	2.66	1.37
Insurance	5	65.60	2.32	19.50	1.06	59.21		4.81
Investment trusts	164	33.64	4.13	7.13	4.07	14.55		14.78
Investment companies	4	20.71	12.61	12.61	2.68	12.67		7.17
Financial and insurance sample	201	36.55	7.46	10.68	4.73	14.31	0.37	12.54
Total	394	38.28	6.37	8.37	8.26	15.27	2.59	10.96

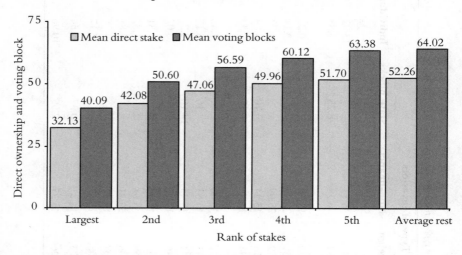

Figure 8.2. *Direct ownership and voting blocks for 193 non-financial companies, December 1995.*

Table 8.7. *Sample of non-financial companies: Voting blocks and size distribution*

Percentile size	Capitalization cut-off (Ptas billion)	Fraction of data	C_1	C_3	C_5	C_{all}
<5	up to 249	0.052	30.99	50.93	62.50	67.96
5–10	249	0.052	38.76	51.79	60.19	65.71
10–25	444	0.145	32.66	53.13	63.13	65.41
25–50	1,561	0.249	33.28	52.68	61.07	63.16
50–75	7,815	0.259	47.43	61.49	67.31	68.30
75–90	41,430	0.150	48.04	61.34	64.59	65.51
90–95	140,007	0.041	39.32	52.75	55.68	55.82
>95	241,100	0.052	45.21	60.40	62.16	62.18
Mean			40.09	56.59	63.38	65.14

VOTING BLOCKS BY SIZE CLASS

It is also useful to present these ownership data for the different sizes of company. Table 8.7 shows that in the medium-size range (25–75%), more than half the companies have a special characteristic, namely, the greatest ownership and voting power concentration. This is, somehow, counterintuitive in that one would expect a decreasing relationship between voting blocks and company size. For a sample of Spanish listed companies in the period 1990–4, Crespí (1998), found an inverse relationship between ownership and size for all categories of shareholders except individuals.

VOTING BLOCKS VS. DIRECT STAKES

Comparing voting blocks with direct ownership provides information on the extent to which large shareholders use intermediate companies to leverage their voting power. The histogram of Figure 8.3 shows us that for direct stakes, a considerable proportion of sample observations is in the low range of ownership. In the 0–5% range, the values are derived from the reports of board members, obliged by law to report their shareholdings in any case. There is a shift to the right starting with the 5% level when accounting for voting blocks, which sum indirect and direct shareholdings. In some cases, the largest shareholder has a small amount of shares via intermediate companies, smaller than 5% taken one by one, but enough to go over the 5% threshold for voting blocks.

From Figure 8.4 we also note some steps around the 25% and the 50% level, which can be interpreted. Spanish takeover legislation determines that in order to acquire 50% of a company's equity, the takeover bid has to be for at least 75% of outstanding shares. This could explain, at least in part, the peaks below the 75% threshold.

For the voting blocks measure, we observe that small shares are now much less prevalent and there still remain some steps around the levels of 25% and 50%, which seem to be sensitive to control. The use of intermediate companies displaces the sample distribution to higher values, when compared with direct ownership stakes.

The insight offered by a comparison of the histograms is confirmed by the percentile plot (Figure 8.4), with its 25% and 50% control thresholds. The contribution of intermediate shareholdings to create voting blocks shifts the curve of direct shareholdings to higher concentration levels of voting power.

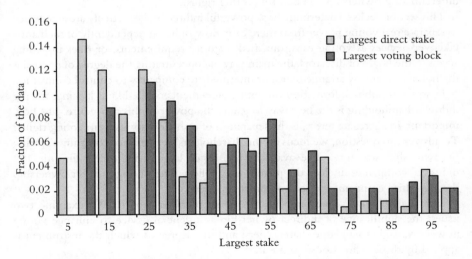

Figure 8.3. *Histogram of the largest direct stake and the largest voting block. Sample of 193 non-financial companies, December 1995.*

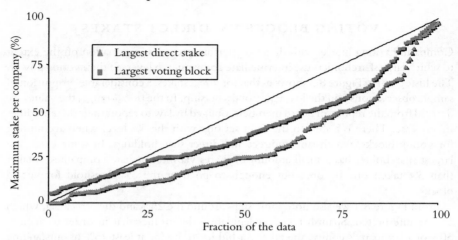

Figure 8.4. *Percentile plot of the largest direct stake and the largest voting block.*

Interestingly, we observe that the 25% threshold contains more companies by both measures, direct holdings, and voting blocks. The provisions of Spanish takeover legislation help us to understand those weak, flat segments.

SEPARATION MEASURES

In the case of Spain, where as a rule the 'one-share-one-vote' principle holds,[7] publicly available information enables us to gauge the importance of voting blocks in differentiating ownership and control (voting rights).

This section seeks to determine how powerful indirect stakes actually are as a device to separate real voting power from mere cash-flow rights. Independently of such anti-takeover devices as voting caps, qualified majority requirements, or rules impeding access to the board of directors, the main way of concentrating the degree of control is the holding company arrangements, or intermediate companies to control companies.

In so far as public information on voting agreements or the like is lacking, tracing indirect shareholding is the best way to gauge the power of this procedure. Just how important, in aggregate terms, is the separation of cash-flow rights from voting rights? To answer this question, we focus on the shareholders' reports, not companies' voting or ownership structure. The available reports of large shareholders for our 193 industrial companies disclose the pattern they follow when using indirect ownership through third companies instead of direct holdings.

The analysis covers two samples of large shareholder reports. We examine two issues: the significance of indirect ownership as a general device to enhance voting power, available to all large shareholders; and the degree to which the instrument is applied by those who choose to use it.

Panel A of Table 8.8 refers to all notifications (direct plus indirect) of holdings of 5% and larger and refers to the importance of indirect shareholdings in building voting

Table 8.8. *Separation measures from direct stakes to voting blocks*

Summary statistics for all blocks (over rows)	Voting power			Cash-flow rights		
	Total voting block	Contribution of component to total block (in %)		Total block	Contribution of component to total block (in %)	
		Direct	Indirect		Direct	Indirect
Panel A (660 observations)						
Mean	20.69	0.77	0.23	19.54	0.78	0.22
Std. dev.	21.40	0.40	0.40	20.35	0.40	0.40
Panel B (211 observations)						
Mean	26.77	0.21	0.79	22.81	0.25	0.75
Std. dev.	24.74	0.36	0.36	22.29	0.39	0.39

blocks. These 660 observations at 31 December 1995, have, on average, 20.69% of voting rights, just 1% above the corresponding cash-flow rights. Direct rights predominate, accounting for 77% compared to 23% for indirect voting rights, without significant deviation from cash-flow rights.

The second question deals with the sub-sample of shareholders' notifications above 5% that declare indirect ownership. When a significant shareholder uses the device of indirect ownership, how important is it compared to direct ownership? When shareholders decide to use it, how important is this separating device for voting from cash-flow rights?

Panel B covers 211 observations (almost 30% of the total): shareholders that declare indirect ownership hold on average 26.7% of voting rights representing 28.1% of cash-flow rights. Even though there is a difference, it is not so pronounced as to imply a powerful separation measure. However, in this group indirect voting rights outweigh direct by 79% to 21%, practically inverting the Panel A data.

CONCLUSIONS

By the end of 1995, Spanish firms show a situation of highly concentrated ownership. Nevertheless, if we compare this data with other European countries, Spanish levels are the lowest with the exception of the UK. Non-financial firms are the most important investors among the different categories. Banks' participation, unlike it used to be the case in the past, is not so important and remains focused in certain sectors and companies. As large shareholders, banks are important mainly in the banking sector, and they also have average values of 16% as larger shareholders in the communication industry, with a voting power similar to the government.

The examination of the direct stakes held by the top shareholder shows that ownership concentration is quite high in Spanish listed companies. Indirect ownership mechanisms do not seem to exert great influence. This view is reinforced by the fact that, on average, the second largest direct stake is also quite big. An important question arises from this: why would Spanish firms need pyramidal schemes? Probably we should discard motives of ownership or control; possible explanations could respond to leverage or tax considerations.

This ownership analysis has recently changed as a result of the privatization process. State participation, that until 1995 was quite relevant in specific sectors and in several large companies, has practically disappeared by mid-1998. To check the consequences of privatization on ownership and other features of corporate governance, such as the incentives of managers, their monitoring and the relation with the new shareholders are important questions that remain to be answered.

NOTES

1. Seven Spanish companies were listed on Wall Street and 13 in Frankfurt 1998.
2. As a simplification, we call this last type 'industrial firms', even though some belong to other sectors. Table 8.2 gives a more detailed description of the sample; most of the 193 firms included do belong to the industrial sector.
3. The notion of 'relevant companies' refers to those firms belonging to a holding being privatized. For example, in the case of Endesa, and for the purposes of the preceding paragraph, this notion includes utilities such as FECSA, ENHER, ERZ, or VIESGO; companies where Endesa has acquired significant shareholdings.
4. A theoretical approach to this problem can be seen in García-Cestona and Salas (1997).
5. Although most of the Tables focus on the 1995 data, we also conduct some comparisons of the ownership structure and its changes from 1991 to 1995.
6. Minimum values equal zero for the second-largest, third-largest shareholder, and so on. This corresponds to companies where there is respectively only one, two, or more shareholders with a stake of direct and indirect ownership stake larger than 5%.
7. There is only one case under the current law, where this deviation is possible. Companies can issue non-voting shares, but to the extent we know, for listed companies only one of them made use of this possibility, Banco Guipuzcoano. Multiple voting shares are not allowed, and except for anti-takeover provisions as voting caps, deviation from 'one-share-one-vote' is done via charter amendments.

REFERENCES

Galve Gorriz, C. and V. Salas Fumas (1993), 'Propiedad y resultados de la gran empresa espa-ñola', *Investigaciones Económicas*, 27/2: 207–38

García-Cestona, A. Miguel, and V. Salas Fumas (1997), 'Efficient Privatization Under Incomplete Contracts', Mimeo, Universitat Autònoma de Barcelona.

Crespí, R. (1998), 'Determinantes de la estructura de propiedad: Una aproximación al caso español con datos de panel', *Moneda y Crédito*, 206.

La Porta, R., F. Lopez de Silanes, and A. Shleifer (1999), 'Corporate Ownership Around the World', *Journal of Finance*, 54/2: 471–517.

LEGAL REFERENCES

Ley 28-7-1988, núm. 24/1988. Mercado de valores.

Royal Decree, 22 March 1989, no. 276/1989, 'Regulación de creación y desarrollo del régimen jurídico de Sociedades y Agencias de Valores'.

Circular, 15 November 1989, no. 6/1989, *Comision Nacional del Mercado de Valores,* 'Comunicación de participaciones significativas en sociedades cuyas acciones estén admitidas a negociación en bolsa'.

Royal Decree, 15 March 1991, no. 377/1991, 'Comunicación de participaciones significativas en sociedades cotizadas y de adquisiciones por éstas de acciones propias'.

Circular, 24 April 1991, no. 2/1991, *Comision Nacional del Mercado de Valores,* 'Modelos de las comunicaciones de participaciones significativas en sociedades cotizadas y de adquisiciones por éstas de acciones propias'.

Council Directive, 88/627/CEE, of 12 December, 'Informaciones que han de publicarse en el momento de la adquisición y de la cesión de una participación importante en una sociedad cotizada en bolsa'.

Royal Decree, 26 July 1991, no. 1197/1991, 'Régimen de las ofertas públicas de adquisición'.

Texto refundido de la Ley de Sociedades Anónimas, aprobado por Real Decreto Legislativo 1564/1989, de 22-12-1989.

9

Ownership and Control in Sweden: Strong Owners, Weak Minorities, and Social Control

JONAS AGNBLAD, ERIK BERGLÖF, PETER HÖGFELDT, AND HELENA SVANCAR

1. INTRODUCTION

The Swedish corporate governance model has been remarkably successful in generating large, internationally competitive companies. It has done so within a financial system combining features of the Continental European and the Anglo-Saxon systems. As in most Continental European countries, large commercial banks have played a pivotal role, serving as house banks for the major Swedish corporations. The two largest banks—SEB and Handelsbanken—have often held large blocks in client firms through their affiliated closed-end investment funds Investor and Industrivärden, respectively. Many firms, even very large ones, are closely held, and a few very large firms dominate the Stockholm Stock Exchange. One ownership sphere—the Wallenberg family—controls companies accounting for half of the market value of the exchange. These arrangements have remained intact for most of the last century.

Yet financial markets are vigorous and are approaching the level of development of their counterparts in the United Kingdom and the United States. Market capitalization and turnover per capita are among the highest in Europe and not far from US levels, and liquidity is relatively high. By European standards, the markets for corporate control, Initial Public Offerings (IPOs) and Seasoned Equity Offerings (SEOs) are active, and the markets for standardized derivatives are sophisticated and very active. Following the abolition of restrictions on foreign ownership in 1993, international institutional investors have bought into the leading companies on a scale surpassed by few European countries. Currently, foreigners own more than one-third of the outstanding equity on the Stockholm Stock Exchange.

Sweden presents a puzzling case for the recent literature on law and finance that attempts to establish a causal relationship from legal origin and level of formal investor protection to ownership concentration, and the development of financial markets (La Porta *et al.* 1997, 1998, and 1999). By the measures used, formal protection of minority investors is weak, and separation of ownership and control strong. Under these conditions, financial markets should be underdeveloped, not flourishing like the Swedish markets, and corporations should be starved of capital. We argue that this literature with its focus on protection of minority investors formal legal texts and misses important elements of the Swedish corporate governance model. This chapter identifies the key features of this model, incorporating both formal control structures and informal mechanisms supporting these arrangements.

We describe the formal control arrangements drawing on the outstanding Swedish data on ownership and control. Control structures are very concentrated and a large fraction of listed firms are privately controlled, most often by a family. The pivotal shareholder is a controlling minority shareholder that contributes less than half of the capital but controls a majority of the votes (cf. Bebchuk *et al.* 1999). Pyramid holding companies (closed-end investment funds) combined with dual-class shares are devices for private (family) control of the very largest firms. Since the pyramids normally only have two layers, dual-class share structures are still the primary control device. In their survey of corporate ownership of 27 developed market economies around the world, La Porta *et al.* (1999) report that Sweden is among the few countries that allow *both* dual-class share systems and pyramidal ownership structures. The normal international pattern is either dual-class share systems or pyramids, but not both, since any of them is a powerful mechanism to separate votes from capital contributions. The combination of these two instruments is so effective that other entrenchment devices seem superfluous, and indeed we find only rare examples of such mechanisms.

While these ownership and control arrangements provide discretion to controlling owners, they are also vulnerable to minority abuse. Yet, investors do not seem to shy away from taking minority positions, and it is difficult to find flagrant examples of violation of minority rights in Swedish corporate governance history. The significant discounts (20–30%) on firms where a private owner controls a large majority of the votes, and on closed-end investment funds, suggest conflicts between controlling owners and minority shareholders. However, discounts are not in themselves indications of poor minority protection; new investors pay a fair price, taking into account the potential for dilution by controlling owners. For incumbent shareholders what matters is the changes in the discounts over time, not the absolute size of the discount.

How then can we explain that controlling owners do not exploit the ample opportunities to expropriate minorities? We argue that these formal governance arrangements are supplemented by informal mechanisms. In particular, concerns over social status discourage controlling owners from minority abuse. While controlling owners do not expropriate minorities as much as predicted, they do enjoy large private benefits, primarily in the form of the social standing associated with control over the large corporations. The size of the discounts gives an indication of the substantial values controlling owners attach to these benefits.

In fact, we believe that the framework focusing on minority protection fails to address the crucial problem in the Swedish corporate governance model. The discounts on privately held firms indicate that these firms would be worth more under another controlling owner or another control structure. The Swedish corporate governance model with its strong separation between ownership and control locks in owners for long periods of time, even from one generation to another. The widespread use of dual-class shares and pyramids can thus have substantial costs in terms of loss of dynamics in ownership and control. Moreover, the costs of raising outside capital may constrain growth options open to corporations. We argue that such lock-in costs are significantly larger and economically more important than costs associated with weak minority protection.

The Swedish model is now facing several challenges that are likely to trigger dramatic changes. The recent large inflow of capital from international institutional investors, and the rapid structural changes in the global economy threaten to undermine its foundation. The transition from very high ownership concentration dominated by private persons to more dispersed ownership with large and rather anonymous institutional investors is occurring very rapidly in Sweden, probably ahead of other European countries. New, institutional owners are less likely to share the implicit basic values and to trust the informal arrangements. They expect the same formal rules and associated sanctions they know from the governance systems in their home countries, primarily the United States and the United Kingdom. In particular, they find it hard to accept the widespread use of dual-class shares to separate votes from capital contributions. Because international investors dislike the arrangement and its high costs of raising funds, ABB and Astra have changed to one-share-one-vote systems after cross-border mergers, and Electrolux and Skandia have eliminated the classes of shares that most drastically differentiated between equity and votes more changes are underway.

To understand the ongoing transition in the Swedish system this chapter covers both recent historical developments and the current trends. It is organized as follows. The next section presents a brief overview of the Swedish financial system, and an in-depth analysis of the ownership and control structure of Swedish listed firms, the mechanisms used to separate votes from capital contributions, and how firms using pyramids and dual-class share structures are valued. The penultimate section interprets the pivotal features of the Swedish corporate governance model and puts it in perspective. The concluding section summarizes the chapter and look at current trends in Swedish corporate governance.

2. OWNERSHIP AND CONTROL

Using data of the highest quality, we present an overview of ownership concentration of listed firms, and type of owners in control following as closely as possible the classifications and presentation form of other chapters in this book. A more detailed look at the specific control mechanisms reveals that dual-class shares and pyramids are the most efficient methods of establishing and maintaining private control of listed firms. But firms that rely heavily on such mechanisms are valued at a discount that gauges agency costs. Moreover, we also illustrate how control considerations affect the markets for corporate control and primary capital.

2.1. *Ownership data*

Ownership and control data is of unusually high quality in Sweden, both in terms of detail provided and timeliness. Accessibility is also remarkable by international standards. The basic source is the *Public Shareholder and Nominee Shareholder Registries* (VPC), which are made public twice a year. The registries track *all* changes in ownership and control. Through the on-line internet commercial services of AMB, a data base administered by *Affärsvärlden*, the leading weekly business magazine, the registry information is aggregated and continuously updated with announcements of disclosures of substantial acquisitions or disposals of shares above certain thresholds from the Stockholm Stock Exchange, and insider trading reported to the Finance Supervisory Board.[1] In principle, the AMB service allows daily updates of control data no older than two weeks at any point in time. AMB includes the 100 largest owners in each company, which gives a very detailed picture of the ownership situation. This service facilitates downloading of ownership data in a format that can be interpreted by a spreadsheet program.

Since the ownership data in AMB is not grouped into interest spheres and families, the definitions of *DN Ägarservice* have been used to group together individual shareholders that can be regarded as representing similar interests. We used two different sources supplied by *DN Ägarservice*. To obtain historical ownership data and definitions of ownership spheres and families we have used the annually published *Owners and Power in Sweden's Listed Companies* by Sundin and Sundqvist, which is regarded as very reliable; the corporations are invited to correct the information before publication. Sundin and Sundqvist also list important deviations from standard corporate charters such as dual-class shares and pre-emptive rights clauses. To verify and supplement this information, we have read and analysed the charters of all 304 firms covered by AMB in October 1998; 251 listed at the Stockholm Stock Exchange, and 53 at the SBI (Stockholms Börsinformation).[2] In addition, we used the on-line Internet service of *DN Ägarservice* to obtain a more recent view of the ownership structure. Thus, our definitions of ownership spheres and families reflect the more recent ownership data that prevails in our ownership database from AMB. See Table 9.1 for definitions of our nine ownership categories based on the identity of the ultimate owner, i.e. the largest owner in terms of votes. The categories are mutually exclusive.

The notion of an ownership sphere is complicated since it lacks a clear definition and relies on subjective evaluations of informed observers. As a result, the sphere concept does not lend itself easily to international comparisons. The spheres nevertheless play a very important role in corporate governance in Sweden and are organized in a holding company framework. Some spheres are family-controlled while others have a financial institution or large corporation at their core. To allow comparisons of type of controlling owners we classify spheres somewhat arbitrarily by type of control. Most importantly, companies belonging to the Wallenberg sphere are classified as family ownership, and those in the SHB (Svenska Handelsbanken) sphere are designated as controlled by a financial institution. This classification probably exaggerates the role of the family in the Wallenberg group, and underestimates the influence of the other corporations in the SHB group.[3]

Table 9.1. *Ownership categories*

Family

All firms controlled by individuals as well as families. The private owner can either be the founder of the firm or an investor who has acquired control. If the company has a long history, it might be that the founder has incorporated her family into the ownership—either as private persons or as a family foundation. Since we look at the ultimate owner some companies that are normally considered institutions are classified as controlled by a family if they themselves are controlled by a dominating family owner; these holding companies are vehicles of power for the family owner.

Sphere

An ownership sphere is defined as a group of shareholders with the same interests. Our definition of spheres is however somewhat different from the widely accepted definition by Sundin and Sundqvist (1998). We have chosen to exclude all companies controlled by shareholders belonging to a family sphere and included them in the category private owners instead. An example is the Wallenberg family. Sundin and Sundqvist (1998) categorize firms controlled by them as sphere-controlled, but we classify them as family-controlled. Consequently, our spheres include groups of shareholders with the same interests but not belonging to a family, for example the Handelsbanken sphere.

Public

Firms controlled by the government or municipalities.

Foreign

Companies belonging to the category foreign owners refer to companies controlled by a foreign owner. This owner can be an institution as well as an individual since it is hard to separate these two groups with certainty.

Insurance company

Insurance company-controlled companies are all firms that have an insurance company as their largest owner. Note however that mutual funds belonging to an insurance company make a separate group of controlling owner.

Mutual fund

As the name indicates, all companies controlled by a mutual fund; a fund can either belong to a bank; an insurance company or the state-owned pension funds.

Bank

Companies that have a controlling owner that is one of the Swedish banks.

Buy-out investor

A buy-out investor is the controlling owner of the companies belonging to this category.

Foundation

This category includes foundations donated by private individuals as well as, for example, various types of profit-sharing funds and pension funds tied to individual companies.

Other

Residual category consisting of all companies not controlled by any of the above-mentioned categories, e.g. firms controlled by a non-listed company/holding company or associations.

2.2. *Ownership types*

Classifying ownership types according to the identity of the investor controlling the largest fraction of votes, Table 9.2 reports the distribution of the nine ownership types for different samples of firms sorted by market capitalization and listing. Figure 9.1 illustrates the distribution of ownership types for the sample of all 304 listed firms. The most common type of largest owner is family or private persons; 62% of all listed firms. An interest or ownership sphere controls 10% of the firms while foreign owners is the third largest group, which controls 9% of the listed firms. Family control is most prevalent in small and medium-sized firms while ownership spheres control the largest and most traded firms. Since both family and ownership spheres are focused on control of firms, the fact that 72% of all listed firms belong to these two categories shows how strongly control-oriented Swedish ownership structures are. Moreover, Ericsson and Astra have the highest market capitalization on the Stockholm Stock Exchange but

Table 9.2. *Ownership types for different samples of firms*

Type of controlling owner	All sample No.	(%)	33 most-traded No.	(%)	20 largest by market cap No.	(%)	O- or SBI list No.	(%)
Family/private	188	61.8	18	54.5	10	50.0	90	60.0
Other interest sphere	31	10.2	9	27.3	6	30.0	8	5.3
Foreign	26	8.6	2	6.1	2	10.0	13	8.7
Insurance	3	1.0	0	0.0	0	0.0	3	2.0
Foundation	1	0.3	0	0.0	0	0.0	0	0.0
Mutual fund	19	6.3	2	6.1	1	5.0	10	6.7
Public	7	2.3	2	6.1	1	5.0	3	2.0
Bank	2	0.7	0	0.0	0	0.0	1	0.7
Buy-out investor	4	1.3	0	0.0	0	0.0	3	2.0
Other	23	7.6	0	0.0	0	0.0	19	12.7
Total	304	100.0	33	100.0	20	100.0	150	100.0

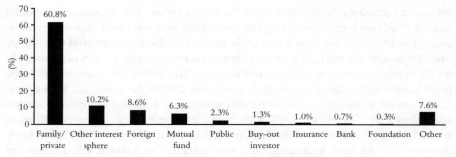

Figure 9.1. *Distribution of ownership types for all listed firms.*

both are controlled by the Wallenberg family through the closed-end investment Investor (control in Ericsson is shared with the institutional sphere around Handelsbanken using the closed-end investment fund Industrivärden).

The dual side of the strong dominance of family and sphere control is that mutual funds, foundations and banks are not frequently the largest owners of firms. Even if more than half of the population regularly saves in pension funds and mutual funds, restrictions limiting their ownership to 5% and 10% of the votes de facto prohibits these funds from directly exercising control. They do, however, exert indirect power and are represented on the boards, but until now they have in most cases remained passive portfolio investors.

The relatively small fraction controlled by foreign investors may be somewhat surprising given the very significant inflow of foreign capital during recent years. But the foreign institutional investors have primarily invested their money in B-shares with lower voting power than A-shares; not infrequently *all* A-shares are controlled by the largest private owner. However, the foreign influence is understated since mergers between a Swedish firm and a foreign firm, as well as foreign acquisitions, are not included. For example, the recent merger between Astra and Zeneca and the acquisition of Volvo's car manufacturing subsidiary by Ford would not be reported, only shown as a delisting.

More generally, since both dual-class shares and pyramids are allowed in Sweden as devices to separate ownership and control, it is no surprise that private control dominates with strong tendencies to become firmly entrenched. However, during the 1990s there is a very noticeable tendency for the fraction of family-controlled firms to be declining as well as the frequency of firms using dual-class share structures. The foreign investors' dislike of dual-class shares, and the growing need to obtain financing, may be the reasons why we observe these trends.

2.3. *Ownership concentration and control*

Looking more carefully at the degree of ownership concentration, it is striking how highly concentrated ownership and control are in Swedish firms, and that the typical firm has a clearly identified controlling owner. Table 9.3A shows the voting stakes of each of the ten largest owners in the 304 companies listed on the Stockholm Stock Exchange (SSE) and on the SBI list in October 1998. The largest shareholder controls on average (median) 37.7% (35.0%) of the voting rights. The second largest voting stake is 11.2% on average, implying that the typical firm has a well-defined owner in control and that the two largest owners have close to absolute control in the average firm. Moreover, the ten largest owners control on average close to 70% of all votes. In 34.1% of the firms the owner in control has more than 50% of the votes. 82.2% of the firms have a well-defined owner with more than 25% of the votes, i.e. with operational control of the firm. The ownership structure is dispersed (no owner controls more than 25% of votes) in 11.9% of the firms, and there are two owners with more than 25% each in only 5.9% of the firms (see Cronqvist and Nilsson 1999). This clearly demonstrates the very high ownership concentration in Sweden when compared internationally.

To capture the difference between votes and capital due to the frequent use of dual-class shares, Figure 9.2 shows the cumulative (average) ownership concentration of the ten largest owners (votes) both in terms of votes and equity. The ratio of votes to equity for the (average) largest owner (V/C ratio) is 1.47, i.e. he controls a fraction of votes that is 47% higher than his proportion of capital contribution. The average ownership of votes (equity) is 41.9% (26.6%) when families and private persons

Table 9.3A. *All companies in sample (%)*

	1st	2nd	3rd	4th	5th	6th	7th	8th	9th	10th
Mean	37.7	11.2	5.6	3.5	2.5	1.9	1.5	1.2	1.0	0.9
Median	35.0	8.7	4.8	3.2	2.1	1.7	1.3	1.0	0.9	0.7
Std. dev.	21.2	8.3	4.3	2.4	1.8	1.3	1.1	0.9	0.8	0.7
Min.	1.6	0.6	0.2	0.1	0.1	0.1	0.1	0.0	0.0	0.0
Max.	93.4	41.2	27.9	15.5	14.5	7.3	5.1	4.2	4.2	3.9

Table 9.3B. *33 most-traded companies (A-list) (%)*

	1st	2nd	3rd	4th	5th	6th	7th	8th	9th	10th
Mean	29.1	11.0	5.0	3.7	2.8	2.1	1.8	1.5	1.3	1.1
Median	30.3	9.1	4.7	3.6	2.7	2.1	1.7	1.3	1.2	1.0
Std. dev.	14.0	8.6	2.2	1.3	1.1	1.0	0.9	0.8	0.7	0.6
Min.	10.5	1.6	1.6	1.3	0.9	0.6	0.1	0.1	0.1	0.1
Max.	58.0	38.8	9.8	5.7	5.3	4.7	4.7	3.6	3.0	2.4

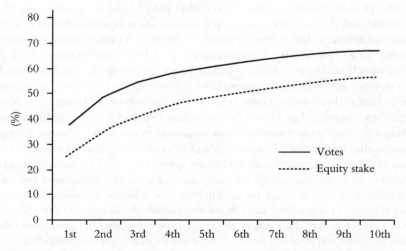

Figure 9.2. *Cumulative (average) ownership concentration of the ten largest owners (votes).*

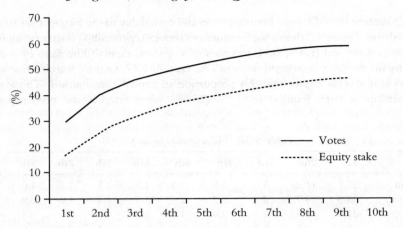

Figure 9.3. *Average and cumulative voting fractions held by the ten largest owners in the 33 most frequently traded firms.*

control firms but only 22.5% (20.5%) if the owners are institutional investors (see Cronqvist and Nilsson 1999). Since the maximum allowed voting differential is 10 (an A-share carries at most 10 votes more than a B-share; both are entitled to the same dividend rights) the owners are not fully exploiting the potential to separate votes from equity in order to establish and maintain control. But there is no legal restriction on the proportion of A-shares being issued.[4] However, as we will soon show, the marginal V/C ratio is higher than the average.

The powerful effects of dual-class shares as a device to separate votes from equity contributions is also evident from Table 9.3B and Figure 9.3 that report the average and cumulative voting fractions, respectively, held by the 10 largest owners in the 33 most frequently traded firms. Interestingly, the concentration of voting power is high; the largest owners control on average (median) 29.1% (30.3%) of the votes also in the largest Swedish firms. The ratio between votes and capital for the largest owner (V/C ratio) for the most traded firms is similar (1.62) to the overall average for the 304 firms. Thus, the extensive use of dual-class shares allows owners even in large firms to increase the capital base without losing control. However, the owners in control are primarily ownership spheres and to a lesser extent families that dominate for all listed firms.

Since we have only measured how dual-class shares cause a strong divergence between the distribution of ownership and of control, we have not considered the effect of pyramids associated with ownership spheres, i.e. we have underestimated the separation of votes and equity. In particular, we have not considered the indirect ownership effects in a tiered ownership structure where the mother firm controls other firms, and a controlling stake therefore amounts also to control of the firms in the lower tiers. However, La Porta *et al.* (1999) have computed the combined effect of dual-class shares and pyramids for the 20 largest firms in 27 countries, including Sweden, using control of at least 20% of the votes as an operational criterion for control. Next to Belgium, Sweden has the highest fraction (53%) of firms with concentrated ownership structures (pyramid or not widely held in their vocabulary). More interestingly, Sweden has the highest V/C ratio (1.58) of all 27 countries in their study compared with a V/C ratio of 1.47 for all Swedish listed firms (as well as the 33 most traded) when we consider *only* the effect of dual-class shares. Thus, dual-class share structures are more important in Sweden than pyramids for the average firm independently of firm and sample size. Unlike countries that only allow pyramids, Swedish pyramids have typically only two tiers since they more efficiently combine the separation effects of both dual-class shares and pyramids.

Turning to firms controlled by families or private persons, Table 9.4 and Figure 9.4 show the average and cumulative fraction of votes for the 10 largest owners. The largest owner controls on average (median) 41.9% (39.0%) of the votes and the average V/C ratio is higher (1.57) than for an average listed firm. The 10 largest owners control on average 57.3% of the capital and 69.8% of the votes, which illustrates how closely held the Swedish family-controlled firms are. For firms where the largest private owners control at least 25% of the votes, the ownership concentration is even

Table 9.4. *Family/privately controlled companies*

	1st	2nd	3rd	4th	5th	6th	7th	8th	9th	10th
Mean	41.9	11.0	5.6	3.3	2.3	1.7	1.3	1.1	0.9	0.8
Median	39.0	8.5	4.4	2.7	1.8	1.3	1.0	0.8	0.7	0.6
Std. dev.	22.4	8.3	4.7	2.5	1.9	1.3	1.0	0.8	0.7	0.7
Min.	1.6	0.6	0.2	0.1	0.1	0.1	0.1	0.0	0.0	0.0
Max.	93.4	36.7	27.9	15.5	14.5	7.0	5.1	4.2	4.2	3.9

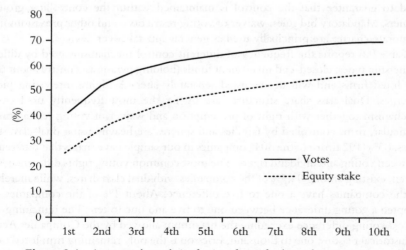

Figure 9.4. *Average and cumulative fraction of votes for the ten largest owners.*

higher (61%) since 89% of the firms have dual-class shares and the average V/C ratio is around 2, i.e. the controlling private owners only contribute a minority of the capital (less than 1/3) but control more than 60% of the votes; close to a 2/3 majority (see Cronqvist and Nilsson 1999). Bebchuk et al. (1999) have coined an appropriate phrase for such ownership structures: 'controlling minority shareholder' (CMS). It is worth emphasizing that the primary device to separate votes and capital in family-controlled firms is dual-class share structures and not pyramid-holding companies, even if the control of the Wallenberg family via Investor, the most important pyramid-holding company in Sweden, is classified as family controlled.

Even if Sweden is portrayed as one of the countries in Europe with the highest ownership concentration in La Porta et al. (1999), their focus on the very largest firms in fact underestimates the average ownership concentration of all listed firms, which is significantly higher, particularly for firms controlled by families and private persons, the most common ownership category in Sweden. Moreover, to establish separation between ownership and control the most frequently used mechanism is dual-class shares, not pyramids, also in this larger universe of firms.

2.4. Control mechanisms

In addition to dual-class share structures and pyramids, we have also identified several other control mechanisms that separate ownership from control or function as entrenchment devices, e.g. cross-holdings, right of pre-emption, mandatory bid rule, agreements between shareholders, waiver of voting restrictions and other provisions in the corporate charter (see Table 9.5 for definitions and presentation of the exact mechanisms). Dual-class structures, pyramids and cross-holdings are the mechanisms used to establish control by separating ownership from control, while right of pre-emption and agreements between shareholders are anti-takeover measures primarily used to guarantee that the control is maintained within the controlling group of owners. Mandatory bid rules, waiver of voting restrictions and other provisions in the corporate charter are principally used as general anti-takeover devices.

Table 9.6 reports the frequency of different control mechanisms used by different ownership types; closed-end investment funds (holding pyramids) control about 6% of the listed firms and will be discussed separately later. A highly interesting picture emerges. Dual-class share structures are by far the most frequently used control mechanism together with right of pre-emption and waiver of voting restrictions. In particular, firms controlled by families and spheres are heavily using dual-class structures. 63% (192 firms) of the 304 companies in our sample have shares that differentiate between voting and dividend rights. The most common voting rights difference is one to ten, existing among 94.5% of the companies with dual class shares, while merely 3% of the companies have a one to five difference. About 1% of the companies have adopted a voting difference between one to five and one to ten. The remaining 1.5% have a voting difference exceeding the maximum allowed by the Companies Act due to historical reasons; one to thousand. Ericsson is the only remaining firm listed on the Stockholm Stock Exchange with a vote differential of one to thousand after ABB,

Table 9.5. *Control mechanisms*

Mechanism	Definition of control mechanism
Dual-class shares	A company that issues more than one type of shares that entitles to different voting rights or a non-voting share type. Strongest anti-takeover provision. A shareholder can gain control without holding the proportional stake of equity.
Pyramidal ownership	A way of assuring ownership concentration among a smaller group of shareholders by investing a majority stake in one company, which in its turn owns large stakes in other companies.
Cross-holdings	A situation where a company indirectly holds shares in itself through its own shareholders. Through indirectly investing in the company using cross-holding arrangements, a controlling owner can strengthen his position *vis-à-vis* other shareholders without bearing the entire cost.
Right of pre-emption	The right to redeem a non-listed share class (A-shares) that have been passed to a new owner. The right of pre-emption is a regulation that restricts the change of control in a company.
Mandatory bid rule	Stipulates that any shareholder that either (i) establishes new control in a firm, or (ii) takes over control by transfer of an old block position also extends an offer for the remaining shares at a fair price. Reason for introducing the MBR is the need for protection of minority rights, which might be compromised in trades of large voting blocks.
Agreements between shareholders	Agreements which do not have to be public. Shareholders can decide how power should be divided between them and upon rules for selling to external actors.
Voting restriction	The main rule in the Companies Act states that no shareholder can represent more than one-fifth of the shares at the general meeting. Can be circumvented through the incorporation of a provision in the company charters, which can either lift the restriction or make it stronger.
Further company charter amendments	Not very frequent and some are even of rather hypothetical character but the law leaves room for them to be used as takeover defence mechanisms.

Electrolux, and SKF recently eliminated such share classes. Investor, the pyramid-holding company of the Wallenberg family, had a very firm control of these three firms but now their ownership is diluted but still significant.[5]

In Ericsson, the SHB (Svenska Handelsbanken) sphere controls 42.5% of the votes but only 3.9% of the capital and the Wallenberg sphere owns 38.8% of the votes but

Table 9.6. *Use of control mechanisms by controlling owner (%)*

Sample (% of total)	Dual-class shares	Right of pre-emption	Voting restriction	Mandatory bid rule	Shareholder agreement
Whole sample (100)	63	13	4	1	5
Bank (1)	50	0	0	0	0
Buy-out investor (1)	0	0	0	0	0
Family (62)	71	16	3	0.5	6
Foreign (8)	46	8	13	4	4
Foundation (0.3)	100	0	0	0	0
Insurance (1)	33	0	0	0	0
Mutual fund (6)	32	5	0	0	0
Other (8)	71	13	0	0	0
Public (2)	29	0	0	0	0
Sphere (10)	61	7	10	7	3

Notes: Frequency of different control mechanisms for 304 firms listed on the Stockholm Stock Exchange and the SBI list in October 1998. The sample is split into sub-samples based on the characteristics of the controlling shareholder and type of mechanism.

Sources: AMB, Sundin and Sundqvist (1998), company charters, and PRV.

only 4.3% of the capital. Thus, with only 8.2% of the capital, the two groups jointly control 81.3% of the votes. A secret shareholder agreement between the two groups from the 1950s regulates the control in Ericsson between them. It is well known that there exists a significant tension between the two controlling owners. The quality of the board and the uneasy relationship between the leading members is widely regarded as the weak part of Ericsson's governance structure and often blamed for its recent problems. US investors provide 35% of the capital in Ericsson; the 25 largest US investors would be among the 50 largest shareholders. The University of California owns more B-shares in Ericsson than the SHB and Wallenberg spheres combined.

The overwhelming majority of the firms in our sample (96%) have actively chosen to waive the non-compulsory rule of the Companies Act that no owner may vote for more than one fifth of the shares represented at the shareholders' meeting. Instead, these companies have allowed for the shareholders to exercise the full voting strength for all shares in their possession. However, 4% (12 companies) have either passively accepted the main rule or actively chosen to implement a more stringent restriction.[6] Moreover, none of the listed firms have adopted a super-majority requirement for specific decisions at the general meeting.

In our sample, 13% (39 firms) of all firms, or 20% of firms using dual-class shares, also include a provision in their charters ensuring the holders of the non-listed share type pre-emptive rights. This is the right to redeem non-listed A-shares that have passed on to a new owner; it is not uncommon that all A-shares are controlled by a family or group and are therefore not listed—around 70% of all firms with dual-class shares and about 90% of family-controlled firms with more than 25% of the votes.

Only three companies listed on the Stockholm Stock Exchange have included a mandatory bid rule in their charters. All companies have defined one threshold of 33.33% of votes and one at 50% of votes. However, from 1 July 1999 a compulsory mandatory bid rule with a threshold of 40% of the votes will be enforced by the Stockholm Stock Exchange even if the legal committee working on the reform of Swedish Company Law did not suggest such a compulsory rule. The committee's argument against were basically that such a rule protects small shareholders in firms with dispersed ownership but may de facto hinder value-increasing takeover activity in closely held firms due to entrenchment of the owners in control (see Bergström *et al.* (1997), and Högfeldt (1999) for formal arguments along these lines). Percy Barnevik, the chairman of Investor, and people associated with the Wallenberg sphere have actively promoted enactment of the rule. It would serve as a takeover defence against international takeovers of Swedish firms.

Cross-holdings were rare during the 1970s but become much more frequent during the 1980s. In the mid-1980s, 39 listed firms were involved in mutual or cross-ownership arrangements (only three-tier relationships) where all owners held at least 2% of the equity or the votes in every link of the ownership chain. In 1988 the number of different companies involved in cross ownership arrangements had diminished to 28. However, currently there is only one cross-holding between firms on the SSE (see Figure 9.5). Earlier cross-holdings were used to build conglomerates and as anti-takeover device. Volvo, Skanska, the SHB sphere, and Sandvik were involved in one of the most elaborate cross-holdings that was dissolved in the aftermath of the failed Volvo/Renault deal. Increasing pressure on creating shareholder value and keeping transparent company structures may have caused the reduction in the number of cross-ownership structures.

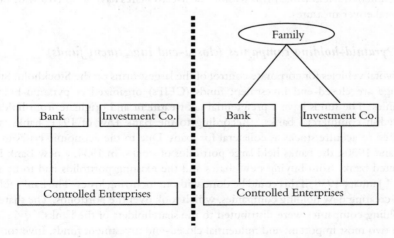

Figure 9.5. *Cross-holdings between firms on the Stockholm Stock Exchange.*

Agreements between shareholders do not have to be stated in the company charters or elsewhere. According to Sundin and Sundqvist (1998), about 5% (14 companies) have such agreements. One company has an agreement stipulating right of first refusal among the holders of A-shares and another has an agreement, which is equivalent to a mandatory bid rule. Out of the 12 not classified, 4 are agreements between certain large shareholders, 5 are agreements between A-shareholders and 3 are owner-specific. Out of the 14 companies with agreements between shareholders 3 have a right of pre-emption clause. Thus, agreements between shareholders are not frequently used.

Which firms apply these control mechanisms? For each separate control mechanism, Table 9.7 provides an answer by testing for qualitative differences between the sub-samples of firms that use and do not use the specific mechanism. Firms with dual-class shares and pre-emptive rights rules have a much more concentrated ownership structure than firms without such provisions. The largest owner controls on average 44% of the votes in firms with such rules, and has more often absolute control than in firms without such rules, and is more often an insider; the differences are statistically significant. Foreign investors own significantly smaller fraction of votes in firms with dual-class shares and pre-emptive rights. Firms that have adopted voting restrictions and mandatory bid rules have a significantly more dispersed ownership structure.

Jointly, these results demonstrate how efficient dual-class share structures supported with pre-emptive rights and no voting restrictions on large blockholders are a means to separate ownership from control and to maintain and protect a very concentrated ownership structure dominated by private persons and families. However, it is important to emphasize the pivotal role of dual-class shares as the most efficient mean to separate ownership from control. Bebchuk *et al.* (1999) provide theoretical arguments for the pre-eminence of dual-class shares as a separating device. Field (1999) shows in an analysis of protective anti-takeover provisions selected by US IPO firms that firms with a dual-class share structure (5% of her sample) tend to have no other entrenchment devices while firms without dual-class shares have adopted a wide range of anti-takeover measures.

2.5. *Pyramid-holding companies (closed-end investment funds)*

The pivotal vehicles for corporate control of the largest firms on the Stockholm Stock exchange are closed-end investment funds (CEIFs) organized as pyramid-holding companies. The funds have a preferential tax treatment and originate from holdings by Swedish commercial banks.[7] According to the Bank Law of 1911, banks were permitted to acquire stocks as collateral for loans. Due to the economic crises in the 1920s and 1930s, the banks held large portfolios of stocks. In 1934, a new Bank Law prohibited banks from buying new shares and the existing portfolios had to be sold before 1 January 1938, if this could be done without incurring losses. The banks solved this by creating new holding companies, which took over the portfolios. The shares of the holding companies were distributed to the shareholders of the banks.

The two most important and influential closed-end investment funds, Investor and Industrivärden, are organized around SE-Banken and Handelsbanken, respectively

Table 9.7. *Comparison of ownership structures and control mechanisms*

	Companies with dual-class shares			Companies with pre-emption clause			Companies with voting restriction			Companies with mandatory bid rule			Companies with shareholder agreement			Total sample
	(1) Sub-sample	(2) Contr. group	(3) Sig.	(1) Sub-sample	(2) Contr. group	(3) Sig.	(1) Sub-sample	(2) Contr. group	(3) Sig.	(1) Sub-sample	(2) Contr. group	(3) Sig.	(1) Sub-sample	(2) Contr. group	(3) Sig.	
Av. voting stake largest shareholder	44.0	26.8	0.000	44.9	36.6	0.028	24.3	38.2	0.033	20.9	37.8	0.169	43.4	37.4	0.302	37.7
Av. foreign ownership	11.6	20.1	0.000	7.7	15.8	0.001	24.4	14.4	0.066	9.9	14.8	0.638	15.6	14.7	0.845	14.7
Av. insider ownership	25.9	10.3	0.000	42.4	16.9	0.000	9.7	20.5	0.186	1.8	20.3	0.232	38.6	19.2	0.007	20.1
Owners with absolute control	36.5	8.0	—	38.5	24.2	—	9.1	26.6	—	—	26.2	—	42.9	25.2	—	26.0
Number of observed companies	192	112	—	39	265	—	11	293	—	3	301	—	14	290	—	304

Notes: Ownership figures refer to % of total votes. Absolute control is defined as representing more than 50% of total votes at the shareholders' meeting. The values in the columns numbered 3 are the *p*-values resulting from two-tailed *t*-tests, i.e. the lowest significance level at which the null hypothesis of equality in the population means of the two groups, as represented by columns marked 1 and 2, can be rejected. An observed *p*-value close to zero thus indicates differences in means among companies with (column 1) and without (column 2) a certain control mechanism, under assumption of equal population variances when the size of the sample of companies are small (i.e. below 30 observations).

Sources: Company charters, PRV, Sundin and Sundqvist (1992–6, 1998).

(see Figure 9.5). Investor is privately controlled by the Wallenberg family through three foundations, while Industrivärden is institutionally controlled since it is a group formed around the management team of the bank that controls the fund. Most investments are in listed Swedish stocks but some firms are wholly owned subsidiaries. The daughters are either loss making firms under restructuring by the fund or cash cows; the funds are cash-constrained due to the significant discount at which their equity trades. Wholly owned subsidiaries allow the funds to cross-subsidize loss-making entities.

The Wallenberg sphere is built around the three foundations. Like other Swedish closed-end investment funds, Investor is a pyramid with only two layers that primarily uses dual-class structures to separate control from ownership in the largest firms on the Stockholm Stock Exchange (SSE): ABB, Atlas Copco, Electrolux, Ericsson, Stora Enso, Scania, and SKF.[8] Table 9.7 reports that in October 1998 the Wallenberg sphere controlled 14 large listed firms with a total market value of SEK 922 billions (42% of the market capitalization at the SSE) with an ownership stake of 19.4% of the capital and 41.3% of the votes in Investor. In particular, since Investor's market share of the total market capitalization is 4.6%, ownership of about 1% of the total market value in Investor by the Wallenberg foundations leads to de facto control of 42% of the market value of the SSE. The Handelsbanken sphere controls 11 listed firms, e.g. SCA and Skanska, with a market capitalization of SEK 259 billions (12% of total market capitalization of the SSE) with an equity share worth SEK 36 billions. Jointly, the two spheres control 54% of the total market value of the SSE using two closed-end funds with a combined market value of 6.2% of the total market capitalization of the SSE, i.e. the funds control equity values about 8 times larger than their own value.[9] It is worth emphasizing that the dramatic leverage effect in separation of ownership and control is the result of the combined use of extensive dual-class structures and the shallow pyramidal structure but that the leverage effect of dual-class shares is the most powerful.

Since dual-class share structures and pyramids exploit values from non-controlling shareholders in closed-end investment funds (see Bebchuk *et al.* 1999, and Wolfenzon 1998), significant separation of ownership and control comes at a price. The price of the shares of closed-end investment funds trade at a significant discount over the funds' Net Asset Value (NAV), i.e. the net portfolio value of its assets significantly surpasses the value of the fund's outstanding equity. The average (median) discount (1984–96) for Swedish CEIFs was 18.22% (19.12%) (see Högfeldt and Synnerstad 1999). The average unweighted discount on the listed SCEIFs was for example 13.2% in December 1996, down from 42% in December 1994; the average discount is volatile but it has not been below 10% during the last 15 years.[10] The substantial discount implies that the financial markets have a negative valuation of the management services of the fund since the portfolio itself has a higher value without these services. Moreover, the funds are financially constrained since it is impossible for them to raise new capital unless the fund itself gives away the discount to the new shareholders. Interestingly, listed firms controlled by closed-end investment funds pay significantly higher dividends than other listed firms.

There are strong indications that the discount is associated with the significant private ownership concentration of the funds since privately controlled funds have a higher discount (23.2%) than institutionally controlled (15%); the corresponding numbers for the US are 14% and 4%, respectively (see Högfeldt and Synnerstad 1999, and Barclay, Holderness, and Pontiff 1992). The discount on funds controlled by a private founder or his/her descendants is on average 15.1% higher than a privately controlled fund without the founder. For example, the current discount of Investor is 34%. If the founding institution still controls the fund, its discount is on average 11.3% higher than if a non-founding private investor controls the fund. In regressions, a dummy indicating if the private founder or his descendants still control the fund explains about 65% of the discount. Hence, 15.1% of a total discount of 23.2% is explained by the presence of a private founder in control. Closed-end investment funds like Custos and Ratos have actively tried to lower the discount by share redemption programmes that redeem shares at the Net Asset Value, i.e. the redeemed shareholders are compensated for the discount. Share repurchases have not been allowed but after a long political indecisiveness, a new law enacted in the spring of 2000 will give firms such an opportunity. The announcement effects of share redemptions have been significantly positive but the effect on discounts is only temporarily lower (see Högfeldt and Synnerstad 1999).

These results show that the large discounts on closed-end investment funds in Sweden reflect agency costs associated with control, in particular private control, that emanates from the combined effect of dual-class shares and pyramids to separate ownership from control. The discount does not reflect small investor sentiments, as perhaps in the USA, since the minority investors are primarily institutions. Discounts on privately controlled closed-end investment funds are perhaps the best measures of the agency costs in a minority-controlling ownership structure when the main conflict is between the private owner in control and minority shareholders.

2.6. *Ownership concentration and firm value*

Not only closed-end investment funds are valued at a discount but also firms with a controlling minority shareholder (CMS), i.e. where an owner controls a majority of the votes but only contributes a minority of the capital. The prime example is family-controlled firms that use dual-class share structures to separate ownership from control. Controlling for among other things industry, size, and capital structure effects, Cronqvist and Nilsson (1999) report the value of family-controlled firms as measured by Tobin's Q peaks when the family controls 25% of the votes. Measured in relation to the peak value, there is a discount that increases in the fraction of votes controlled by the family above 25% of the votes.[11] The discount of a family-controlled CMS is between 11% and 32% depending on how deeply the family is actively involved in firm's business.[12] For example, the average discount is 32% (26%) if the founder is also the CEO (only board member) of the family-controlled firm.[13]

The discounts measure agency costs associated with private control since the controlling minority shareholder maximizes shareholder value *plus* the value of private benefits of control. In particular, the controlling minority shareholders make the pivotal decisions but carry only the capital costs and negative consequences in proportion to their capital contribution. Bebchuk *et al.* (1999) and Wolfenzon (1998) show formally that controlling minority shareholders cause deviations from shareholder value maximization in three principal ways that generate agency costs: (i) by overinvesting in projects with significant private benefits; (ii) by hanging on to loss-making investments segments or subsidiaries too long and by resisting value-increasing takeovers due to entrenchment; and (iii) by more frequently undertaking diversifying investments and takeovers (see Cronqvist *et al.* (2001) for empirical evidence on the last point). Bebchuk *et al.* (1999) also show that the agency costs associated with a controlling minority shareholder increase not linearly but 'rather at a sharply increasing rate' as the size of his/her cash-flow rights decrease. Thus, the smaller in absolute numbers the equity fraction owned by the controlling owner is in relation to his voting fraction, the larger are the agency costs and therefore the discount. The empirical findings on discounts on family-controlled firms above are consistent with this prediction. Moreover, also in line with theoretical predictions, Holmén and Högfeldt (2001) report that the bankruptcy frequency of family-controlled CMS is higher than for a non-CMS firm but that family-controlled firms are significantly less frequently takeover targets.

Jointly, the sizeable discounts associated with private control of both closed-end investment funds and firms with dual-class share structures strongly suggest that there are significant agency costs inherent in ownership structures with a controlling minority owner. Firms with strong separation of ownership from control have well-defined owners but with incentives that are not generally in line with shareholder value maximization. The conflict between the minority shareholder in control and the other shareholders is therefore highly relevant in a European institutional framework. The considerable discounts associated with very concentrated private ownership suggest that there are significant costs associated with dual-class ownership structures and closed-end investment funds.

2.7. *Ownership, market for corporate control, and equity offerings*

The highly concentrated ownership structures also have far-reaching consequences in the markets for corporate control and for new capital. Let us take a brief view of the Swedish takeover market, and the markets for Initial Public Offerings (IPOs), and Seasoned Equity Offerings (SEOs).

2.7.1. *Takeovers*

Since the overwhelming majority of listed firms have a well-defined owner or group of owners that control the majority of the votes or have operational control, change of control is not possible without the consent of the controlling party. This has two implications. First, since owners in control are heavily entrenched, the frequency of takeovers will be relatively smaller than if the firms had a dispersed ownership structure. This implies that most takeovers will be friendly and negotiated between the bidder and the controlling owners of the target (less than 10% of takeover bids over the last 20 years are hostile). However, since a controlling minority shareholder does not bear the full proportional consequences of takeovers, it is more likely that they undertake empire-building acquisitions. This effect tends to increase the takeover frequency among family controlled firms. Second, if the controlling owner decides to sell a control block either through a block transfer or as a part of regular takeover, a takeover is facilitated and more likely to succeed.

Eriksson *et al.* (1998) report empirical results in line with these broad characteristics. Swedish takeover bids are normally negotiated between the main controlling owners of the bidder and the target, and bids are almost universally non-partial and contingent upon 90% of the shareholders accepting the offer.[14] The largest owner in the bidding (target) firms controls on average 41.1% (48.4%) of the votes and are often a private person or family. Cash offers are relatively more frequent and premiums higher when both the target and the bidder are privately controlled firms with dual-class shares. When the controlling owners are institutions, stock-financed acquisitions are relatively more frequent. In particular, the average premiums (29.8%) paid by privately controlled firms in cash offers are significantly higher than premiums (22.3%) offered by institutionally controlled firms in cash offers. It is not uncommon that bidders already own substantial, long-term toeholds, sometimes even de facto controlling the targets. Thus, very few bids fail, and hostile bids as well as competing offers are rare.

Out of 253 takeover bids between 1980 and 1992, when both the bidder and the target are listed on the Stockholm Stock Exchange, 212 (83.7%) were successful. 185 were 'any or all bids' (non-partial), conditional on 90% of the equity accepting the offer and where the remaining 10% of the shares were compulsory acquired (73% of all tender offers). However, 170 (92%) of the 185 non-partial bids that reached the public tender offer stage were successfully completed. 124 (2/3) were full cash bids, while 61 (1/3) involved pure exchanges of different financial instruments (shares, convertible loans, etc) or a mix of cash and financial claims. Of the 185 offers, 49 (26%) concerned single-class target firms, and 136 (74%) dual-class firms. In the latter sub-group, the tender offer price was equal in 81 cases and differentiated between voting and restricted voting shares in 55. Thus, price differentiation between A- and B-shares was not used pervasively even if admissible, possibly because the controlling target shareholder owns a large fraction also of B-shares or does not control all high voting A-shares.

Comparing takeover markets in different countries, a remarkable feature of the Swedish takeover market is that the bidder often has a substantial long-term toehold in the target firm. The average voting position of a bidder is 31%, ranging from 0% to a maximum of 96%.[15] In 58 (31%) cases, the bidder already had control (>50%) prior to the tender offer. The bidder's pre-takeover toehold in the target firm was less than 50% in 66 (36%) cases with an average position of 28%. Finally, the bidder had no toehold in 61 (33%) of the 185 observations.

Thus, the Swedish market for corporate control is dominated by friendly, and uncontested negotiated cash bids either between large private controlling owners of the bidder and the target firms or by offers from a bidder with a sizeable toehold to acquire the remaining shares in the target. The average announcement effect for the bidder is insignificantly positive while significantly positive for the target. The take-over gain is split 20/80 between the bidder and the target, and there is significant long-term underperformance between the relative market index and relative size and market-to-book matched firms after the acquisitions.

2.7.2. IPOs

Initial Public Offerings (IPOs) are particularly interesting from a corporate governance perspective since the ownership structure is endogenously determined. For example, if the original investors would like to exit their investment through the IPO a dispersed ownership structure results, while if they are interested in maintaining control but need to raise capital to finance further investments, the owners in control keep their shares and float new shares to finance the investment. Swedish IPOs are particularly interesting since they are relatively frequent and differ significantly from Anglo-Saxon IPOs as they are much more control-oriented.

Holmén and Högfeldt (2001) report 352 new listings on the Stockholm Stock Exchange between 1979 and 1997; 233 pure IPOs and 119 equity carve-outs and spin-offs. The volume of new listings is substantial since the number of listed firms of the SSE increased from 134 in 1979 to 245 in 1997. Differentiating between IPO firms controlled by families or private individuals (69% of all IPOs) and institutions (non-private; 31%), highly significant differences are reported. The private owners in control usually keep all voting stock (A-shares), do not sell any of their own shares (no secondary issue), and control on average (median) 68.5% (77%) of the votes after the IPO. Thus, the primary issue consists only of B-shares. The motives for going public are (i) to generate new capital for investments, and (ii) to expand by acquisitions of listed firms after the IPO, and paying by issuing new shares. Consistent with Bebchuk's (1999) rent-protection theory, control blocks are never sold piecemeal, only wholesale in block transfer or takeover in order to protect control rents. Control is sold in 27% of the privately controlled firms: 21% in takeovers, and 6% in block transfers. Except for bankruptcy or reorganization, the original owners remain in control also after five years. On average they still control 2/3 of the votes and 44% of the capital. The excessive fraction of controlling votes at the IPO is rational since the controlling owners anticipate future dilution of control when new shares are issued in a directed issue to target shareholders as payment for an acquisition.

Institutional owners divest a significantly larger part of their own holdings at the IPO, especially voting stock, and controlling blocks are eliminated after five years for the median firm. Dual-class shares are less frequently used, and takeovers are more common for IPO firms controlled by institutional owners. This is consistent with an exit motive. Transfer of control does not occur by successively selling shares but through a negotiated takeover of all outstanding shares after the IPO.

Privately controlled firms are significantly more underpriced, in particular if they issue only B-shares. The owner economizes on costs of dilution (no secondary distribution) since the level of underpricing is lower the larger the size of the issue. For institutionally controlled firms, underpricing is lower the larger fraction of equity that is sold, and if secondary shares are sold. The median underpricing costs borne by controlling shareholders as a percentage of their pre-issue holdings are 3.4% for the private controlled firms, and 1.9% for the institutionally controlled. Privately controlled firms where the founder is also the CEO do not have a lower valuation at the IPO as measured by market-to-book than institutionally controlled firms. However, if the privately controlled firm is non-founder controlled, i.e. by the founder's family or by another private individual or group of individuals, it has a significantly lower valuation. The lower valuation of non-founder controlled private firms is a measure of agency costs (lock-in costs) associated with very high private ownership concentration of a listed firm that the owners in control have to pay up front when entering the stock market. The IPO markets value have a positive valuation of the human capital a founder contributes but discounts the effect of other private owners in control since they are not pivotal to the same extent to the success of the firm, and may pursue a different agenda in their own interest. Interestingly, when matched by size and market-to-book, there is no average long-run underperformance in the five-years after the IPO; the worst performers are firms raising new capital after about 18 months using rights offers.

The outstanding features of the Swedish market for IPOs are the relatively high frequency and how control-oriented it is, in particular for family-controlled firms that use dual-class shares to efficiently secure maintained control of the firm even a long time after listing. A very interesting feature is that 60% of the family-controlled firms return to the capital markets after the IPO for stock-financed acquisitions where low voting B-shares are issued to target shareholders.

2.7.3. *Seasoned equity offerings*

The market for seasoned equity offerings (SEOs) is active in Sweden and dominated by rights issues and private placements; public offers are very rare indeed. This is expected since public offers are more expensive but a more efficient way to reach individual shareholders if the ownership structure is dispersed while the reverse is true for rights issues and private placements if firms are closely-held. Hagelin and Retzlaff (1998) report 687 SEOs between 1983 and 1996; about 21% are rights issues and about 79% are private placements. 56% of the private placements are directed issues, i.e. an equity offering to the target shareholders in a stock-financed acquisition, while the reminder are cases of capital infusions to strengthen firms that are not infrequently financially distressed. As a percentage of total issue volume, 13% is earmarked to acquisition of specific assets, usually real estate and ships, 41% is used to improve the capital base while 46% is used to finance takeovers. 63% (48%) of the firms undertaking a SEO have been listed for more than 3 (5) years. Thus, recently listed firms are relatively more frequent in the sample of firms conducting SEOs than as a fraction of all listed firms.

SEO firms have on average significantly higher leverage, higher investment levels, and weaker operating performance than non-SEO firms, and undertake the SEO after a significant stock price run up but underperform comparable firms and stock market indices during a five-year post-issue period (see Hagelin and Retzlaff 1998). The announcement effect of rights issues is on average insignificantly negative while it is significantly positive for private placements. Firms conducting rights issues are significantly overperforming relative to comparable firms and stock indices before the SEO but have the worst average performance in the post-issue period. Firms undertaking rights issues are overwhelmingly privately controlled while the control is more evenly distributed between privately and institutionally controlled firms that do private placements.

The typical rights-issue firm is a recently listed firm with high growth potential, very good stock price performance, and privately (often founder/CEO) controlled but needing more capital to finance growth-related investments. The fact that the firm needs even more capital infusion is interpreted as a negative signal by the market since the growth and value potential is not realized. Since a rights issue is directed towards existing shareholders, the reason behind the choice of a rights issue may be either that outside investors do not want to participate on the offered conditions or because the incumbent owners in control would like to maintain control.

The Swedish market for SEOs is dominated by relatively small, newly listed, and privately controlled firms that raise new capital either to finance investments, to lower leverage or to finance acquisitions of other listed firms. To maintain control after a SEO that dilutes ownership concentration seems to be an overriding objective for privately controlled firms.

In this section, we have shown that the extensive use of dual-class shares to separate control and ownership has resulted in a very concentrated ownership structure where a large fraction of listed firms are privately controlled, most often by a family. The pivotal shareholder is a controlling minority shareholder that contributes less than half of the capital but controls a majority of the votes. Pyramid holding companies (closed-end investment funds) are pivotal devices for private (family) control of the very largest firms. Since the pyramids normally only have two layers, the primary control device is still dual-class share structures. This control device is so pervasive that other instruments seem superfluous; we find only rare instances of other entrenchment devices. However, the stark separation of ownership and control results in a significant discount (20–30%) on the value of privately controlled firms as well as on closed-end investment funds. The discounts suggest agency costs associated with conflict between the owner in control and the other shareholders. The very strong control-oriented nature of Swedish corporate governance is also evident in the markets for corporate control and new capital. The market for corporate control is active, but it is dominated by negotiated bids between controlling owners and by offers from bidders that already have large toeholds or that already control the target. Hostile bids do take place, but they are rare.

3. THE SWEDISH CORPORATE GOVERNANCE MODEL

The design of corporate governance arrangements involves complex trade-offs. The desire to provide sufficient incentives to managers or controlling owners has to be weighed against protecting minority investors. A second important consideration involves a three-way trade-off between liquidity, control, and distortion of incentives. For example, when dual-class shares are issued, control remains concentrated and liquidity is improved in the low-voting shares, but incentives deteriorate since ownership and control are separated. The two trade-offs are interrelated: the effect of incentive distortions is more serious when minority protection is poor, and, vice versa, when incentives are better aligned, controlling owners are less likely to expropriate minorities. These trade-offs are essentially static in nature, but there are also important dynamic considerations, between short-term concerns and long-term interests.

The Swedish corporate governance system has traditionally been built around political consensus between the labour movement and the major capital owners where the emphasis has been on providing incentives to controlling owners. Proponents of the 'Swedish model' often describe this as promoting strong private owners with a long-term investment horizon and a far-reaching social responsibility towards employees and society in general. Corporate law in particular, but also securities law, are quite explicitly favouring firms with strong majority owners and provide a set of rules that enable private owners to establish and maintain control of listed firms. In particular, the prevalent use of dual-class shares and pivotal pyramidal structures has resulted in a very concentrated ownership structure. Protection of minority share-holders and the distortion of incentives stemming from the separation of ownership and control have often been viewed as second order. By the La Porta *et al.* measures (1997, 1998, and 1999), Sweden is a country with lower levels of shareholder pro-tection than the Anglo-Saxon countries and about average by Continental European standards.

With strong separation of ownership and control, and poor minority protection, outside shareholders, in particular individual investors, should be reluctant to invest. Yet financial markets in Sweden are well developed with a high level of market capitalization in relation to GDP, relatively large numbers of firms go public, and individuals invest heavily in stocks, primarily through mutual funds. International investors have a considerable and increasing presence even though many of the largest listed firms are privately controlled and well entrenched using dual-class shares. Expropriation of minorities seems less frequent than suggested by the measures of formal legal protection by La Porta *et al.* (1997) and remarkably absent as an issue in the public debate. In fact, the discussion about minority rights seems most active in countries that already have strong protection by La Porta *et al.* (1997) standards.

How can we explain this enigma? We argue that minority protection, for several reasons, is stronger than suggested by the La Porta *et al.* (1997) measures of formal legal protection. First, these measures have a bias towards Anglo-Saxon practices. For example, in the Swedish case they do not take into account the general clause against expropriation of minority shareholders in the Corporate Law. While there are very few cases taken to court using this clause, it should play a role in preventing minority abuse and could be used if blatant abuses of minority rights become more frequent. Second, strong enforcement and transparency may compensate for potential weak-nesses in the formal law. According to the rule-of-law measures, Sweden ranks at the very top, and standards of legal enforcement and accounting are very high. Ownership and control data are also remarkably detailed and transparent.

Third, and more importantly, minority protection should be understood in a larger context of corporate governance, which in turn comprises a large number of mechanisms affecting how market signals affect corporate decisions. Shareholders are only one of the stakeholders influencing these decisions, and formal legal provisions and enforcement are only some of the governance mechanisms. An important but poorly understood element of the Swedish corporate governance model is the reliance on informal enforcement mechanisms with considerable formal discretion for controlling shareholders. In particular, concerns over reputation and social status limit minority abuse.

Social prestige is an important, even dominant, part of the total benefits associated with control of large corporations in Sweden. Many owner families try to build a legacy around themselves as good citizens and project themselves onto the public arena as important contributors to socially worthy causes like philanthropy, endowments, and research. While violations of minority rights may be very costly in pecuniary terms the next time the firm needs capital, or because they damage sales, such violations may also have important non-pecuniary effects to the extent that they also affect the value of the controlling owners' social capital. We believe that significant control benefits, which are provided and protected by the corporate law, but restrained by informal social constraints has been one of the pivotal elements of the Swedish corporate governance model.

The focus on formal rules of minority protection in the recent literature emanates from the view that controlling shareholders expropriate minority shareholders by de facto stealing corporate resources. But this is a very narrow—and essentially static— perspective that misses more important potential costs when control and ownership are strongly separated. The one-sided focus on minority protection misses what we believe to be the crucial problem with the Swedish corporate governance model—the lock-in effects when ownership and control are strongly separated. The lock-in effect is best interpreted as an entrenchment effect in a wide sense, ranging from blocking of value-increasing takeovers to stale managerial labour markets and to slow reaction to changes. In particular, the resources of the firm are not swiftly and efficiently real-located in response to changing economic conditions. Minority protection is a minor problem because of the disciplining effect of social benefits of control. In this model transfer of control becomes excessively costly and painful. It may even be impossible to find a Swedish, let alone foreign, investor who is willing to pay for the control benefits enjoyed by the incumbent controlling owner. We interpret the significant discounts on privately controlled firms and, in particular, on closed-end investment funds, the primary control vehicles in these arrangements, as representing the markets' evaluation of these inefficiencies, rather than as reflecting minority abuse.

To understand the trade-offs facing controlling owners it is important to look at both benefits and costs of the Swedish model. The lock-in effect makes controlling private owners more likely to pursue long-term interests, build social capital and refrain from myopic investments. This may be particularly beneficial if firms are in traditional and capital-intensive industries where investments have long maturity. But investor patience and a long-term perspective are equally important in the pharma-ceutical and the telecommunication industries, where privately controlled Swedish firms have been very successful internationally.

However, there is a risk that entrenched owners hang on to loss-making investment segments or subsidiaries too long, in particular if it is in prestigious and traditional lines of business, and resist value-increasing takeovers due to loss of control rents. It is also a concern that entrenched owners are less likely to actively look for and respond quickly to new profitable opportunities inside or outside their established line of business.

The separation of ownership and control also distorts incentives of controlling owners. If control rents are large, the controlling shareholder tends to maximize the sum of the value of these rents and his/her fraction of the dividend rights rather than shareholder value in general. This could result in overinvestment in projects with significant private benefits, e.g. by more frequently undertaking diversifying investments and takeovers that enlarge the firm and increase the personal power base.

The discount on the value of privately controlled firms makes it more difficult and more costly, sometimes even prohibitively costly, to raise new capital in the market. In particular, the closed-end investment funds are capital constrained, which limits their freedom of action. This restriction is even more binding since they only raise new capital if their control position is not severely diluted. This capital constraint is perhaps a more efficient disciplining device than potential takeover threats. But the high cost of raising additional capital also fosters growth strategies based on internally generated capital, reliance of borrowed money from closely associated institutions and possibly inefficient cross-subsidization across activities. Such capital constraints are particularly harmful when radical changes are necessary.

Controlling owners in Sweden have obviously understood this commitment problem towards outside investors. Some controlling owners, like the Wallenberg family, have emphasized international competition as a check on excesses by family members and on complacency among managers of the corporations they control. To stay the course and thrive, firms generating more than 80% of their turnover abroad cannot deviate too far from efficiency. The extreme international exposure of the largest and most successful Swedish firms has been a pivotal moderating factor over the last century. By bringing in other owners and listing firms on the public exchanges additional commitment and transparency can be achieved. The liberalization of financial regulation and the resulting vitality of financial markets have given additional strength to these outside mechanisms. Seen over a longer period, the Wallenberg group has been remarkably successful at retaining and increasing its influence over the Swedish industry. Even if their control vehicle Investor in the last few years has underperformed, return on investment over the last two decades has been above the return on the market index. Other families have been less successful. To fully understand what brings about and sustains family control as an ownership form, we need a deeper understanding of the incentives it provides, and the particular internal structures and problems of succession that are inherent in such control. The relationship between the family and the managers of the companies they control is also important. The Wallenberg group has, at least until recently, had a virtual lock on the managerial labour market, recruiting the best talent early and then shifting them across their companies. While such monopsony powers could have adverse incentive effects, the family has given the top executives considerable discretion. For management, as for the controlling owners, pecuniary incentives have traditionally been weak and the role of social benefits important. Ultimately, to evaluate the effects on corporate performance of family control we need to compare it to alternative governance arrangements, e.g., a strong management with large blocks held by institutional investors.

4. THE SWEDISH MODEL UNDER ATTACK

The traditional Swedish corporate governance model is increasingly challenged by the globalization of capital markets and the rapid structural industrial changes fuelled by innovations and increasing international competition. We see three major challenges.

First, the fundamental problem for the Swedish model is how to attract more institutional, particularly foreign, capital while maintaining the closely held, family-dominated governance structure. The ongoing changes in the pension system are creating a number of new institutional owners, and the international diversification of large institutional investors in United States and United Kingdom is putting pressure on existing control structures. The new owners do not enjoy the same type of benefits, at least not in the Swedish context. They demand rules and guidelines resembling those that they know from their home countries. The tendency will be to go from informal agreements and codes of conduct to formal rules and clear sanctions. In particular, the system of using dual-class shares is under attack. Following a number of corporate governance failures, this critque has gained force and has led some international investors to question the level of minority protection provided by Swedish corporate law.[16]

Second, the structural changes generated by increasing international competition pose significant challenges to the old and very large Swedish industrial firms controlled via closed-end investment funds by different power spheres. These firms are large enough to be acquired in a global restructuring involving even larger, truly global firms. The takeover of Volvo's car manufacturing division by Ford and the international mergers in the pharmaceutical industry between Pharmacia and Upjohn and between Astra and Zeneca are just a few examples in an ongoing global restructuring process. One consequence is that Investor has lost control of its most valuable assets and the remaining firms are in mature industrial sectors with rather low growth potential. Ericsson is the only remaining firm with a vote/equity differential of 1/1000. At this point, the question is not whether it will be abolished, only when. The key problem to solve is how to compensate the controlling owners for their control rents. This is most likely to happen as part of a merger or takeover deal involving a large international firm. If this happens, a pivotal part of the Swedish control structure will be removed. Being challenged both by international institutional investors and by industrial competitors with large financial resources, the pivotal pyramidal holding companies will recede and eventually will likely be abolished. This was a very unlikely scenario just a few years ago.

Third, the system is challenged by recent attempts to reactivate the harmonization efforts within the European Union in the area of corporate law. The revised takeover directive currently under discussion contains a more critical stance against dual-class share structures. The growing importance of internationally accepted corporate governance structures in a global economy is evident, in particular after the crises in South-East Asia; see Boone *et al.* (1998) for a thought-provoking analysis of the pivotal role of deficient corporate governance structures in the crises. Efforts by the OECD, and ultimately the US government, to harmonize the global corporate governance structures are well under way. It is likely that within a few years there will be internationally accepted rules for corporate governance that stress the principle of one-share-one-vote and strong formal minority protection. The traditional Swedish model built on strong separation of ownership and control via extensive use of dual-class shares and weak protection of other shareholders will be difficult to uphold. In particular, the governance structure of small and medium-sized firms controlled by families will face tough challenges if the use of dual-class share structures is diminished or eliminated. The larger task in the coming years is to make the transition to the new global standards as smooth and swift as possible, or to fight an uphill battle against the implementation of these addmittedly imprefect standards.

There are clear signs that the old structures are already breaking down in response to these pressures. Cross-holdings have all but disappeared from the Swedish corporate scene. Many large corporations are gradually relinquishing the system of dual-class shares. In particular, the largest firms controlled by the Wallenberg family, such as ABB, Astra, Electrolux, and SKF, have over a very short period, either directly or after an international merger, eliminated dual-share classes that most efficiently differentiated votes from equity ownership. Given the traditional stability of the ownership structures in Sweden over the last 60 years, the recent changes have been dramatic; more has happened during the last few years than over the previous 60 years.

There is also evidence that domestic institutional investors are becoming increasingly active and independent from the traditional players in the market for corporate control. The planned merger between Volvo and Renault was blocked primarily by institutional investors who questioned the economic rationale behind the strategy. The recent hostile sale of Scania shares by a number of institutional investors to Volvo showed increasing independence *vis-à-vis* the Wallenberg family, who controlled Scania, but eventually sold control to Volvo after a public power struggle.

The single most important challenge to the Swedish corporate governance model is to establish structures that promote transfer of capital from the traditional industries controlled by families to growth-oriented sectors with large risks and different incentive structures. There is an apparent risk that the traditional capital will be locked in and the necessary structural changes will not occur at a fast enough pace. In particular, it is less likely that traditional, very risk-avert owners will be the best owners of firms where human capital and therefore appropriate equity-based incentive structures are of pivotal importance. The traditional control spheres were built around banks that financed firms with debt and promoted cautious investments, while the new growth firms represent risky investments primarily financed with equity capital. The recently highly successful Swedish companies in the IT industry have also appeared outside these spheres.

NOTES

1. Any insider trade has to be reported within 14 days to the Finance Supervisory Board.
2. The Swedish Patent and Registration Office (PRV), the agency responsible for registering limited liability companies, was consulted if the company itself did not provide us with their corporate charters.
3. An alternative classification would be to view companies in these two groups as bank-controlled, with one of the banks (SEB) under the control of a family and the other widely held with strong ties between the group bank (SHB) and member companies.
4. However, without an explicit limit, the focal point in the market seems to be 20% A-shares of all outstanding shares. In this case, an investor owning all A-shares contributes 20% of the capital but controls 71.4% (200/280) of the votes with a vote over capital ratio (V/C) of 3.57.
5. After Incentive's ABB shares were distributed to their shareholders and after ABB adopted one-share-one-vote, the voting share of the Wallenberg sphere decreased from 26% to 5.4%. In Electrolux their fraction of votes shrank to 21% from 45%, while it decreased only marginally in SKF from 33.3% to 29.5%.
6. Only 6 firms adopted the suggested legal rule of not allowing anyone to vote for more than 20% of the votes represented at the annual shareholder meeting, while 3 (1) firms adopted the more stringent rule to only allow anybody to vote for only 10% (5%) of the votes represented at the annual meeting.
7. Closed-end investment funds pay annual taxes corresponding to 2% of their book value. Dividends received and financial income are added, and dividends handed out and financial costs are deducted. Hence, by adjusting dividends paid out, a CEIF can avoid taxes; this aspect differs from US rules. If a fund is open-ended it faces no tax consequences for unpaid historical taxes on dividends.
8. Investor used to be the controlling owner of Astra but after the merger with Zeneca, Investor is the single largest owner of the new firm AstraZeneca. It controls about 5% of the shares in the new firm with one-share-one-vote structure.
9. 54% of the market value of the companies where the SCEIFs are the largest, single, shareholder.
10. Högfeldt and Synnerstad (1999) report that the volatility of the return on the fund shares is higher than the volatility of the return on the fund portfolio; i.e. the higher volatility stems from higher volatility of the discount. Moreover, the share price of the fund under-reacts to major events in the portfolio firms.
11. A simple 'back-of-the-envelope' calculation of the value of the private benefits of the controlling minority shareholders and estimates a premium of 80% on their equity value.
12. Discounts may reflect liquidity premiums since firms with large blockholders have less liquid shares (see Bolton and von Thadden 1998). However, using dual-class share structures, control rests with the non-traded A-shares that have more votes, while liquid is provided by the B-shares that are traded in liquid markets.
13. The CEO is almost exclusively the only representative on the board from the management team; the COB is most often not the CEO but an outsider and the board is nominated by outside shareholders.
14. Due to a Compulsory Acquisition Limit (CAL) of 90%, a shareholder controlling a block of at least 10% of the votes can block such a takeover attempt. Because of tax reasons, the offers are de facto for all outstanding shares.

15. Using US takeover data, Bradley, Desai, and Kim (1988) reported an average bidder toe-hold of 9.8%.
16. The best-known case involved Trustor, a closed-end investment fund, where the private owner in control sold the controlling block to Lord Moyne, who acted as the respectable front for a group of Swedish investors who tried to empty the firm using a sophisticated tunnelling scheme.

REFERENCES

Barclay, Michael J., Clifford G. Holderness, and Jeffrey Pontiff (1993), 'Private Benefits from Block Ownership and Discounts on Closed-end Funds', *Journal of Financial Economics*, 33: 263–91.

Bebchuk, Lucian A., Reinier Kraakman, and George Triantis (1999), 'Stock Pyramids, Cross-ownership, and Dual Class Equity: The Creation and Agency Costs of Separating Control from Cash Flow Rights', NBER Working paper no. 6951.

Bergström, Clas, Peter Högfeldt, and Johan Molin (1997), 'The Optimality of the Mandatory Bid Rule', *Journal of Law, Economics, and Organization*, 2: 433–51.

Bolton, Patrick, and Ernst-Ludwig von Thadden (1998), 'Blocks, Liquidity and Corporate Control', *Journal of Finance*, 53: 1–25.

Boone, Peter, Alasdair Breach, Eric Friedman, and Simon Johnson (1998), 'Corporate Governance in the Asian Crisis 1997–98', Working paper no. 137, SITE, Stockholm School of Economics.

Bradley, Michael, Anand Desai, and E. Han Kim (1988), 'Synergistic Gains from Corporate Acquisitions, and their Division Between the Stockholders of Target and Acquiring Firms', *Journal of Financial Economics*, 21: 3–40.

Cronqvist, Henrik, and Mattias Nilsson (1999), 'Agency Costs of Controlling Minority Shareholders', Working paper, Department of Finance, Stockholm School of Economics.

—— Peter Högfeldt, and Mattias Nilsson (2001), 'Why Agency Costs Explain Diversification Discounts', *Real Estate Economics*, 29: 88–126.

Eriksson, Johan, Peter Högfeldt, and Jacob Spens (1998), 'Bidder Share Price Reactions Following Takeover Announcements', Working paper, Department of Finance, Stockholm School of Economics.

Field Casares Laura (1999), 'Control Considerations of Newly Public Firms: The Implementation of Anti-takeover Provisions and Dual-Class Shares Before the IPO', Working paper, Penn State University.

Hagelin, Ann-Christine, and Christel Retzlaff (1998), 'The Long-run Underperformance of Firms Conducting Seasoned Equity Offerings', Master's thesis, Department of Finance, Stockholm School of Economics.

Högfeldt, Peter (1999), 'An Analysis of the Mandatory Bid Rule', Working paper, Department of Finance, Stockholm School of Economics.

—— and Fredrik Synnerstad (1999), 'Discounts on Closed-end Investment Funds', Working paper, Department of Finance, Stockholm School of Economics.

Holmén, Martin, and Peter Högfeldt (2001), 'A Law and Finance Analysis of Initial Public Offerings', Working paper, Department of Finance, Stockholm School of Economics.

La Porta, Rafael, Florencio Lopez-de-Silanes, and Andrei Shleifer (1999), 'Corporate Ownership Around the World', *Journal of Finance*, 54: 471–517.

La Porta, Rafael, Florencio Lopez-de-Silanes, and Robert W. Vishny (1997), 'Legal Determinants of External Finance', *Journal of Finance*, 52: 1131–50.

—— —— —— —— (1998), 'Law and Finance', *Journal of Political Economy*, 106: 1113–55.

Sundqvist, Sven-Ivan, and Ann-Marie Sundin (1990–9), *Owners and Power in Sweden's Listed Companies*, Stockholm: Dagens Nyheters Förlag.

Wolfenzon, Daniel (1998), 'A Theory of Pyramidal Ownership', Working paper, Department of Economics, Harvard University.

10

Strong Managers and Passive Institutional Investors in the UK

MARC GOERGEN AND LUC RENNEBOOG

1. INTRODUCTION

The European 'Council Directive 88/627/EEC on the information to be published when a major holding in a listed company is acquired or disposed of', known more simply as the Transparency Directive, required only limited changes to British law. The UK has traditionally been the Member State with the most extensive investor protection and the strictest rules on the disclosure of equity stakes. The implementation of the Directive was regarded as 'a harmonisation measure, which would "pull up" other systems towards the UK standard' (Dine 1994).

The implementation of EU ownership disclosure rules in Continental countries has highlighted striking differences with respect to the characteristics of ownership and voting rights in the UK. The UK differs from her European partners not only in her higher proportion of listed firms, but also in ownership concentration and the main shareholder classes. Furthermore, the UK is the only European country with an active, hostile market for corporate control (Franks and Mayer 1995).

Whereas a large majority of the listed companies in Continental Europe have a dominant outside shareholder or investment group, most UK firms are controlled by insider shareholders (the management and members of the board of directors). Share ownership could influence managerial behaviour in two ways. Equity stakes may tilt management's incentives towards the pursuit of share-price maximizing strategies, but substantial management ownership could also lead to expropriation of minority shareholders. Managers owning a large percentage of voting rights might derive private benefits from their executive and board positions, which they can insulate from monitoring and disciplinary actions in case of poor performance. Thus, large voting stakes held by insiders may not necessarily lead to performance improvement. For the UK, Franks, Mayer, and Renneboog (2001) show that disciplinary actions against management are undertaken in the wake of poor performance, but directors with large stakes successfully impede overhauls of the board.

Hence, there is a need to reduce discretionary power of the management by regulation. The most recent regulatory codes take the form of self-regulation.[1]

The Cadbury Code (1992), with which the London Stock Exchange has required the compliance of all listed companies from 30 June 1993, lays down standards of corporate governance and emphasizes the responsibilities of the board of directors, and more specifically the monitoring role of non-executive directors. The Code of Best Practice for top executive remuneration, worked out by the Greenbury Committee (1995), was a response to public criticism of what was seen as excessively generous remuneration of directors.

The UK also differs sharply from Continental Europe in the much more important presence of institutional investors. Ownership of UK equities by institutional shareholders soared from around 30% in 1963 to 60% in 1992 (Stapledon 1996). This compares with approximately 20% in Germany (Franks and Mayer 1995). Despite the very high percentage of the total UK market capitalization that they hold, however, these institutional investors are not major players from a principal–agent perspective. First, although their accumulated share stakes are significant, shareholdings in individual companies are small: the largest institutional shareholding averages a mere 5.5%. Hence, the potential benefits from active monitoring can hardly outweigh the costs for institutions; this prompts institutions to free-ride on corporate control (Shleifer and Vishny 1997). Second, some investment and pension funds adhere to low-cost passive index strategies and thus lack the resources for active monitoring of the large number of companies in their portfolios. In order to remain cost-efficient, rather than engage in active monitoring, institutional investors prefer to simply divest from poorly performing firms. A third reason for the low institutional involvement is insider-trading regulations. If companies do not want to immobilize part of their portfolios, they might have to restrict active involvement in corporate strategy. Plender (1997) reports that institutions do not frequently exercise their voting rights: only 28% of pension funds regularly cast their votes, 21% never vote, and 32% vote only on extraordinary items.

This chapter is organized in the following way. Section 2 discusses the different legal forms of incorporation. In section 3 we review the legislation on ownership disclosure and the main features of investor protection. Section 4 reports statistics on the ownership of listed firms in the UK and analyses the importance of various investor categories. Section 5 focuses on the evolution of ownership concentration after the initial public offering (IPO) and contrasts the findings with the German pattern. Section 6 discusses the lack of separation devices in the UK, and section 7 concludes.

2. THE CORPORATE LANDSCAPE

There are three types of company classification in British commercial law:

- registered and unregistered;
- public and private; and
- limited and unlimited.

A registered company is founded by registering certain documents—most importantly the articles of association—with the Registrar of Companies, a public officer. When a registered company is incorporated, it becomes a 'legal person'. Persons who conduct a business or a profession together, but have not chosen to set up an incorporated company, form a 'partnership' (Partnership Act of 1890). Public companies must be registered as such and must be limited-liability (PLCs); the memorandum of association must state that the company is a public company. Currently, their minimum required share capital at creation is £50,000. Public companies must also have at least two members, whereas EU Directive 89/667 permits private companies with only one member ('single member private limited company'). Only public companies can be listed on the London Stock Exchange, which has some 1,900 companies listed. Excluding financial institutions, insurance companies, investment companies, and real estate firms, the number drops to 1,450 industrial and commercial firms.

Registered companies can be of five different types:

- public companies limited by shares,
- private companies limited by shares,
- private companies limited by guarantee,[2]
- private unlimited companies with share capital, and
- private unlimited companies without share capital.

Table 10.1 highlights the main differences between the different types of company.

3. OWNERSHIP LEGISLATION AND INVESTOR PROTECTION

3.1. *History*

The UK has a long tradition of disclosure regulations for shareholdings in companies. The first legislation on disclosure dates to 1945, when the Cohen Committee recommended that the beneficial ownership of shares should be disclosed. Unlike the EU Transparency Directive, British legislation applies to all public companies, not just listed ones. UK Company Law also imposes a threshold of 3%[3] for stakes, not 10% as in the Directive.

Every company has to keep a register of its members. Section 22 of the Companies Act of 1985 (hereafter CA 1985) defines the members of a company as all the persons who have subscribed to the memorandum of association and all other persons who agree to become members. Every member's name and address as well as the date at which he became a member and the date at which he may have ceased to be one must be entered in a register. If the company has share capital, the number of shares each member owns and the amount paid in must be specified.[4]

The register of shareholders may not necessarily reveal the true beneficial holdings as 'nominee' companies may register shares on behalf of a third party. A nominee company may be used either to reduce administrative costs for an institutional investor holding shares on behalf of many individual investors or else to hide true ownership. In the latter case, however, the company secretary of the company in which a substantial stake is held will be aware of the identity of the true owner.

Table 10.1. *Types of company*

Company type	Limited liability	Minimum capital	Minimum no. of members	Register of members	Register of substantial shareholders	Register of directors' interests	Transfer of shares
Public company							
Limited by shares	Yes	£50,000 (only 1/4 needs to be paid-up)	2	Yes	Yes	Yes	No restrictions allowed if listed company)
Private company							
Limited by shares[a]	Yes	No	1	Yes	No	Yes	Articles can impose restrictions
Limited by guarantee	Yes	No, guarantee payable only when company is wound up	1	Yes	No	Yes	n.a.
Unlimited with share capital	No	No	2	Yes	No	Yes	Articles can impose restrictions
Unlimited without share capital	No	No	2	Yes	No	Yes	n.a.
Limited by guarantee with share capital[b]	Yes	No	2	Yes	No	Yes	Articles can impose restrictions

[a]The Companies (Single Member Private Limited Companies) Regulations 1992 reduced the minimum number of members from 2 to 1.
[b]This type of company, also called 'hybrid company', could only be registered until 22 December 1980.

3.2. *Transposition of the EU Transparency Directive in UK company law*

A. *Introduction*

The EU Transparency Directive (88/627/EEC) was transposed into UK law by the Disclosure of Interests in Shares (Amendment) Regulations of 1993 and the Disclosure of Interests in Shares (Amendment) (No. 2) Regulations of 1993.[5] The Regulations apply to interests in shares in the 'relevant share capital' of a public company only. The relevant share capital is defined as the voting capital, i.e. the Regulations only refer to interests in shares that carry 'rights to vote in all circumstances at general meetings of the company'.[6]

B. *Notification procedure: Rules applying to both listed and unlisted companies*

A person[7] acquiring an equity stake of at least 3% in a public company or ceasing to have such an equity stake must notify that company in writing within two days of the change. The notification must specify the share capital acquired and the number of shares, but not whether the interest is beneficial[8] or not. Increases or decreases in the stake require a new notification, if they exceed 1%.[9]

In response to any notification received, the company must record in its share register (also called register of substantial shareholdings) the person's name, the information contained in the notification, and the date of the registration. The change to the register has to be made within a period of three days following the day of receipt of the notification. A person who fails to notify a relevant interest is 'guilty of an offence and liable to imprisonment or a fine, or both'. The competent authority is the Secretary of State or the Director of Public Prosecutions (Section 73).

In the example displayed in Figure 10.1, the Guinness Peat Group acquires 8% of the share capital (and the voting rights) of Bluebird Toys. As the shares are held by different companies of the Group, a 'nominee' company is formed to register the shares in its name and reduce administrative costs.

The members of the board of directors (both executive and non-executive) have to disclose their interests and changes in their stakes regardless of the number of shares.[10] The information on ownership is kept in the register of directors' interests and the register of substantial shareholdings, both of which are kept in the same place by the company secretary. The registers have to be accessible to any member of the company or any other person at no charge.[11] Both members and non-members[12] of the company have access to the register of substantial interests free of charge. Non-members, however, may be charged £ 2.50 per hour (or part) to inspect the register of directors' interests; a fee is also charged for a person who requires copies.[13]

Rules applying to listed companies only. Listed companies must inform the Company Announcements Office (CAO) of the London Stock Exchange immediately of any notifications of major interests received under Sections 198–208 of CA 1985. They have to specify the date of receipt of the notification and (if known) the date of the

---

LETTER TO BLUEBIRD TOYS PLC FROM GUINNESS PEAT GROUP

Disclosure of Interest in Shares Pursuant to Sections 198 to 202 of The Companies Act 1985.

Guinness Peat Group Plc and its subsidiary companies ('the Group') hereby notify Bluebird Toys Plc ('Bluebird') that following the market purchase of 660,000 Ordinary shares on 23 July 1997 at the price of 91p, the Group's interest in the shares of Bluebird amounts to 3,327,000 shares representing 8.00% of the issued share capital.

The additional shares will be presented for registration in the name of Sutherland Nominees Limited.

So far as the Group is aware, no person interested in the shares is party to any agreement or arrangement relating to the exercise of any rights conferred by holding the shares subject to this notification.

From Guinness Peat Group Plc.

Figure 10.1. *Disclosure of an ultimate voting block.*

transaction.[14] Listed companies also have to inform the CAO of any notification received relating to directors' interests, specifying the date of the disclosure, the date and nature of the transaction, the price, amount and class of securities, and the nature and extent of the director's interest in the transaction.

3.3. Disclosure thresholds and notification of family and corporate interests

A person is required to disclose his interests in a public company, as soon as he owns a beneficial stake of 3% of the nominal value of that class of capital or as soon as he controls a stake (whether beneficial or not) of 10% of the voting capital. Beneficial interests are all interests other than those managed on behalf of other persons, those held by market makers in the course of their normal business, and those managed for unit trusts and recognized schemes (Section 199, CA 1985).

By law, a person is held to be interested in the shares that his spouse and minor children or stepchildren hold ('family interest'). He is also interested in shares held by a company of which he controls or exercises at least one-third of the voting rights at the general meeting or of which the directors are in the habit of following his instructions ('corporate interests').

3.4. *Concert parties and voting agreements*

The ownership disclosure notification does not only apply to individuals or companies (including their subsidiaries[15]), but also extends to individuals and companies with voting agreements. Such agreements between two or more persons give rise to the obligation of disclosure, if the target company is a public company and if the combined shareholdings amount to at least 3%.[16] These voting agreements consist in obligations or restrictions between shareholders with respect to the use, retention or disposal of the stakes.

3.5. *Takeover and merger regulation*

The self-regulatory City Code on Takeovers and Mergers, introduced in 1968, provides some protection for the minority shareholders of listed companies that are the object of takeover bids. The Code is issued and administered by the Panel on Takeovers and Mergers, which consists of representatives of the main City institutions such as the Stock Exchange. The chairman and deputy chairman are appointed by the Bank of England. The Code specifies that when a person holds at least 30% of the voting rights of a company, he must make a formal takeover bid, the 'mandatory offer', for all the voting shares. The price of the mandatory offer has to be the highest price that the bidder paid for the target company's shares during the 12 months preceding the date when the stake reached 30%. If the offer is accepted within four months by shareholders owning 90% of the relevant shares, the bidder has the right to acquire the remaining 10%.[17]

In the case of a salvage operation, the Panel can exempt a company from making a mandatory offer (Keenan 1996). Such an exception was granted to Olivetti when it acquired 49.3% of the Acorn Computer Group in 1985. Although Olivetti subsequently increased its holding to 79.8%, Acorn remained listed on the USM, the secondary market.[18]

3.6. *Minority shareholder protection*

The UK is known for its strong protection of minority shareholders (La Porta *et al.* 1997). This protection derives fundamentally from court rulings. *Foss* v. *Harbottle*, 1843, determined that decisions in a company are taken by the majority of the shareholders and that individual shareholders cannot normally appeal such decisions. But, there are exceptions, including a specific 'fraud on the minority' rule that covers what is typically known in agency theory as the expropriation of minority shareholders. The Court of Appeal ruled in *Menier* v. *Hooper's Telegraph Works Ltd*, 1874, that the majority rule from *Foss* v. *Harbottle* may not apply if the majority intend to make a profit at the expense of the minority. A case for a claim can then be brought by a single minority shareholder.[19]

3.7. *Cross-shareholdings and share repurchases*

Companies that intend to reduce their share capital must pass a special resolution (Section 135 of CA 1985),[20] approved by a three-quarters majority of shareholders voting in person or by proxy. Listed companies must also conform to the rules governing share repurchases laid down in Chapter 15 of the Listing Rules. Repurchases have to be notified to the Company Announcements Office as soon as possible and no later than 8.30 on the morning following the calendar day of the transaction. Repurchases within a period of 12 months and covering less than 15% of the equity can be made through the stock market, provided that the price does not exceed the average market price of shares during the 10 business days preceding the transaction by more than 5%. Repurchases covering more than 15% of the equity within a period of 12 months must be made via a tender offer to all shareholders. The tender offer must have a fixed price or a maximum price and must be announced in at least two national newspapers at least seven days before its closing date.

4. VOTING-RIGHT CONCENTRATION IN LISTED AND UNLISTED COMPANIES

4.1. *Sample description*

A sample of 250 companies was randomly selected from all those listed on the London Stock Exchange, excluding financial, real estate, and insurance companies. In order to study the ownership concentration across time and in particular around the decrease in the disclosure threshold from 5% to 3% in 1989, data were collected for a five-year period starting in 1988. In the last three years, about 7% of the companies in the sample were taken over and 2% had their listing suspended, mostly due to receivership. As no reliable public databases covering this period could be found, we collected the data from the annual reports in paper or microfiche format.[21]

The shareholdings are classified into nine categories: (1) banks; (2) insurance companies; (3) investment trusts, unit trusts, and pension funds; (4) executive directors; (5) non-executive directors; (6) industrial and commercial companies; (7) families and individuals (other than directors or their relatives); (8) government; and (9) real-estate companies. Directors' stakes consist of both beneficial and non-beneficial shares. Where stakes were held by nominee companies, we identified the effective investors via information provided by the company secretaries. Shareholdings of nominees were classified under the category of the effective owner.

Shareholders who own shares indirectly through subsidiaries are required to disclose their combined direct and indirect holdings. We consider such stakes as an ultimate voting block. Voting pacts between corporate shareholders are rarely mentioned in the disclosure statements, although individuals (usually family members) sometimes hold a share stake in common.[22] The Companies Act requires large shareholders to disclose their voting rights rather than their ownership percentage. However, as dual-class shares are rare, percentages of ownership (or of cash-flow rights) and voting-right concentration tend to coincide; accordingly, in this section we use concentration of voting rights and of ownership interchangeably.

4.2. *Total ownership concentration*

Panel A of Table 10.2 shows the sum of all ultimate voting blocks held by directors and by all substantial shareholders, the latter being defined as owning total ultimate voting blocks of more than 3% (5% for 1988 and 1989). The companies were divided into two sub-samples: (1) those listed for more than five years, which we designate as 'established firms', and (2) those brought to the exchange during the last five years, called 'recent IPOs' (not shown in Table 10.2).[23] We use three different ratios of concentration: C_{all}, the sum of all the ultimate voting blocks held in the company, C_1, the largest ultimate voting block, and finally a Herfindahl index based upon the five largest blocks.

Table 10.2. *Concentration ratios for ultimate voting blocks*

Year	Sample size	Mean (%)	Min. (%)	Quartile (25%)	Median (%)	Quartile (75%)	Max. (%)	Av. no. of shareholders
Panel A. C_{all}: Sum of all voting blocks								
1988	200	28.2	0.0	5.6	23.6	45.1	90.4	3.1
1989	208	30.2	0.0	9.8	25.7	48.4	86.5	3.4
1990	220	40.6	0.0	21.4	39.1	58.2	96.6	5.7
1991	227	42.9	0.0	24.9	42.3	60.5	99.2	6.3
1992	207	40.8	0.0	26.7	39.0	53.7	98.2	6.2
Panel B. C_1: Largest voting block								
1988	200	14.6	0.0	4.9	10.6	22.8	86.5	
1989	208	15.3	0.0	5.9	11.6	22.9	86.5	
1990	220	16.5	0.0	7.2	12.1	23.7	86.4	
1991	227	15.8	0.0	7.6	11.8	20.4	79.2	
1992	207	15.2	0.0	7.0	10.9	19.6	78.9	
Panel C. Herfindahl index measuring the concentration of the largest 5 ultimate outside voting blocks								
1988	200	10.4	0.0	2.3	6.6	12.3	38.7	
1989	208	10.7	0.0	3.3	7.0	12.5	38.7	
1990	220	11.2	0.0	5.2	7.5	12.5	38.6	
1991	227	10.9	0.0	5.3	7.6	12.0	35.4	
1992	207	10.5	0.0	5.2	7.2	11.2	35.3	

Notes: This table shows the mean, median, and quartiles of the aggregate of all substantial shareholdings of at least 5% (1988–9) or 3% (1990–2). Panel B shows the average and median largest shareholding while panel C reports the Herfindahl index of the top 5 shareholders. The Herfindahl index is defined as the square root of 1/5 of the sum of squares of the top 5 shareholders. Established companies are defined as companies introduced to the London Stock Exchange at least 5 years prior.

Source: Based on annual reports.

Table 10.3. *Concentration ratios for ultimate voting blocks for 1992*
(excluding stakes below 3%)

Measure	Mean	Std. dev.	Min.	Max.
C_1: Top blocks	14.44	12.59	3.40	78.90
C_3: 3 largest blocks	26.84	15.23	3.70	78.90
C_5: 5 largest blocks	32.99	16.35	3.70	84.68
C_{all}: all voting blocks	37.25	18.65	3.70	96.31

C_{all} in established companies was around 30% of the equity for 1988–9 and increased substantially in 1990, averaging over 40% for 1990–3, as a consequence of the lowering of the disclosure threshold from 5% to 3%. Panel A also reports that the average number of shareholders over the threshold was three in 1988–9 and about six, above the 3% mark in 1990–2. In recent IPOs (not shown), ownership concentration is substantially higher: 41.7 versus 28.2% in 1988 and 48.0 versus 40.6% in 1990.

Table 10.3 shows that for 1992 excluding voluntarily disclosed ultimate voting blocks smaller than 3% decreases concentration ratios only marginally. Furthermore, the levels for C_{all}, C_3, and C_5 are very close.

4.3. *The largest ultimate voting block*

The top voting block in established companies varies from 14.6% to 16.5% (panel B of Table 10.2) and is about 5 percentage points higher in recent IPOs. The percentile plot in Figure 10.2 shows the fraction of the sample companies by size of their top voting block for 1992. The fact that the percentiles are substantially below the quadrant intersection shows that the distribution is not normal and that ownership is usually diffuse in most sample companies. Only in about 15% of the companies does the largest block exceed the veto threshold of 25%. This is in sharp contrast with Continental European countries.

Figure 10.3 plots the size distribution of the top shareholder. The median largest block is about 10%. In 41% of the companies the largest shareholder owns a stake of between 5% and 10%. Small peaks at the 25–30% range and the 75–80% range indicate the value of owning a veto minority and a qualified majority. However, in fewer than 15% of the firms does the largest shareholder hold more than 30%, which is the mandatory bid threshold. Given the great dispersion of ownership, stakes of 15–20% may already give a majority of the votes actually represented at the meetings.

Our data show that voting blocks larger than 30% are usually held by families or individuals, who are the founders or their heirs. Of 200 sample companies in 1992, 18 had one shareholder controlling more than 30% of the equity. Eleven of these 18 stakes were held by founding families. In 8 other companies one shareholder held just under 30% (29.8–29.9%); in all eight, this shareholder is another company. These corporate shareholders are obviously intent on holding the largest equity stake possible without transgressing the 30% threshold that would force a takeover bid perhaps beyond their resources.

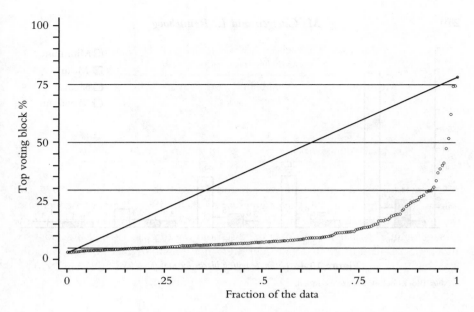

Figure 10.2. *Percentile plot of largest voting blocks in UK listed firms*

Sources: Annual reports for a sample of 250 randomly selected companies.

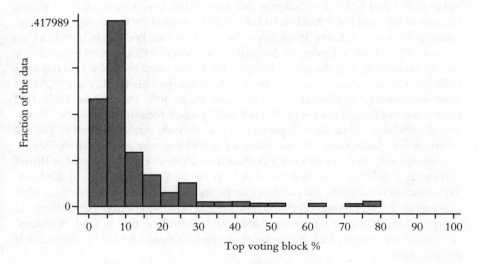

Figure 10.3. *Histogram of largest voting block in UK listed companies.*

Sources: Annual reports for a sample of 250 randomly selected companies.

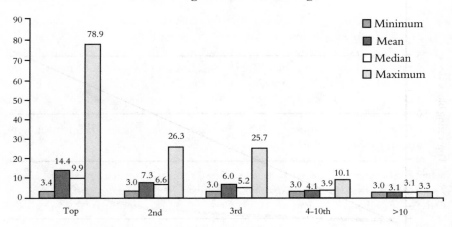

Figure 10.4. *Ultimate voting blocks by rank for 1992*

Note: Blocks below 3% are excluded.

4.4. *Major shareholders*

Figure 10.4[24] shows that the top shareholder owns an average ultimate voting block of 14.4% (with a median of 9.9%); the second and third shareholders have average share stakes of 7.3 and 6.0%. To challenge decisions of the largest shareholder, a voting agreement between the second and third would be needed. In the average company, 7 shareholders own stakes of 3% or more: the fourth and smaller shareholders hold, on average, 4.1%. Thus, whereas the dominant shareholder in Continental companies is usually unchallenged, in the typical British company absolute control would require a coalition. On average, a coalition of the top three shareholders would own 27.7%; all large shareholdings combined would come to about 40%. Panel C of Table 10.2 reports the Herfindahl indices of ultimate voting block concentration across the top five shareholders. Total concentration remains relatively stable over time, and the relatively low values show that the stakes are spread out over several shareholders.

Consequently, the type of agency conflict most likely to be encountered in British companies is different from that found in Continental European firms. In the latter, expropriation of minority shareholders may be the key problem relating to ownership concentration, warranting very stringent safeguards for minority shareholders. In contrast, lack of ownership concentration and control in British (and American) companies necessitates codes that prevent management from acting to the detriment of the shareholders.

4.5. *The nature of ownership*

Panel A of Table 10.4 reports the relative importance of nine categories of block-holders. The category with the largest ultimate voting block is that of institutional investors, i.e. investment and pension funds, which own a combined shareholding of over 21% in the average company[25] and 19% in recent IPOs.

Directors are the second most important category, with an aggregate stake of about 11% in established companies and 22% in recent IPOs. In companies floated recently, the pre-IPO owner, usually a family, keeps about half of the original shares, on average equivalent to about one-third of the post-IPO outstanding share capital. In established companies 65% of the directors' shareholdings are held by executive directors; in recent IPOs, about three-quarters. The category of industrial and commercial companies holds an average block of 6%.

Panel B of Table 10.4 shows the average stake of the largest blockholder by type of owner.[26] The largest blocks are held by industrial companies with an average of 12.5%. Panel C shows that if nil stakes are included (that is if the average is calculated over all the companies in the sample), the power of industrial companies is much less pronounced.

One of the most striking results in Table 10.4 is the relative power of directors. Combining the largest shareholdings of executive and non-executive directors

Table 10.4. *Ultimate voting blocks by blockholder type*

Year	1988	1989	1990	1991	1992
Sample size	200	208	220	227	200
Panel A. Sum of ultimate voting blocks by blockholder type (%)					
Banks	0.1	0.4	1.2	1.8	1.9
Insurance firms	2.8	2.9	5.4	5.8	5.9
Investment/pension funds	6.4	7.3	12.9	14.2	14.2
Total institutions	9.3	10.6	19.5	21.8	22.0
Executive directors	7.3	7.7	7.9	7.4	5.8
Non-executive directors	3.8	3.8	4.5	4.6	4.1
Total directors	11.1	11.5	12.4	12.0	9.9
Industrial companies	5.7	6.0	6.2	5.8	6.1
Families and individuals	1.8	2.0	2.4	3.2	2.5
Government	0.3	0.1	0.1	0.1	0.2
Real estate	0.0	0.0	0.0	0.0	0.1
Sum of blocks	28.2	30.2	40.6	42.9	40.8
Panel B. Average ultimate voting block of the largest blockholder (%)					
Banks	6.0	7.6	4.5	4.5	5.1
Insurance firms	5.3	5.4	3.6	3.8	4.0
Investment/pension funds	8.1	7.4	6.8	7.0	7.0
Executive directors	5.3	5.4	5.8	5.5	4.5
Non-executive directors	6.3	5.9	5.5	5.7	5.0
Industrial companies	14.9	14.5	12.0	10.6	10.6
Families and individuals	5.8	6.3	5.3	4.9	5.2
Government	13.3	6.9	5.5	5.7	6.7
Real estate	0.0	0.0	0.0	0.0	0.1

Table 10.4. *(Continued)*

Year	1988	1989	1990	1991	1992
Sample size	200	208	220	227	200

Panel C. Average ultimate voting block of the largest blockholder (%)

Banks	0.1	0.4	1.0	1.6	1.8
Insurance firms	2.2	2.3	3.6	3.8	4.0
Investment/pension funds	4.6	5.1	6.8	7.0	7.0
Executive directors	5.3	5.4	5.8	5.5	4.1
Non-executive directors	3.1	3.0	3.4	3.4	2.9
Industrial companies	5.0	5.1	5.5	5.1	5.4
Families and individuals	1.3	1.4	1.6	2.0	1.6
Government	0.2	0.1	0.1	0.1	0.2
Real estate	0.0	0.0	0.0	0.0	0.1

Panel D. Number of ultimate voting blocks by blockholder type

Banks	2	11	49	80	71
Insurance firms	83	89	218	259	226
Investment/pension funds	114	144	435	514	474
Executive directors	215	235	249	240	184
Non-executive directors	98	105	137	135	117
Industrial companies	67	73	101	109	102
Families and individuals	45	46	67	92	61
Government	3	3	4	4	6
Real estate	0	0	0	0	1

Notes: This table shows, by category of owner, the aggregate ultimate voting blocks (panel A), the average largest ultimate voting block with as denominator (i) the total number of largest ultimate voting blocks by type of holder (panel B), and (ii) the total of sample companies (panel C), and the number of blockholders (panel D). Blocks below 3% are excluded.

The averages of panel B are calculated with a denominator that excludes companies with no reported shareholdings for each specified shareholder category. The averages of panel C are calculated with a denominator that includes companies with no reported shareholdings for each specified shareholder category.

Source: Based on annual reports.

yields a stake, that ranges from 9.5% to 11.6%, depending on the year (panel B). Directors' shareholdings in a sample of recent IPOs are twice as large. All in all, the entire board, and in particular the executive directors, who hold about 70% of all large directors' stakes, has substantial voting power. In addition, directors can solicit proxy votes from institutional investors. Plender (1997: 140) reports that 21% of the votes of institutional shareholders are proxy votes exercised by the CEO at his discretion.

The second largest blockholder class is that of investment and pension funds, whose largest ultimate block amounts to more than 7% (panel B). Ultimate blocks held by insurance companies and banks are smaller, at 4% and 5.1%, respectively in 1992. Panel C reports that in 40.3% of the sample companies, institutional investors own the largest stakes, but panel B suggests that these shareholdings do not generally exceed 10%.[27] Table 10.5 provides information about the size distribution of the aggregate and largest ultimate voting block by type of blockholder.

Table 10.5. *Size distribution of the aggregate and largest ultimate voting block by type of blockholder (%)*

	Total	[0%, 5%]	[5%, 15%]	[15%, 25%]	[25%, 50%]	[50%, 75%]	[75%, 100%]
Panel A. Aggregate ultimate voting blocks by type of owner 1988–92							
Banks	14.4	8.8	4.3	1.2	0.0	0.0	0.0
Insurance	47.3	10.5	31.7	3.5	1.6	0.0	0.0
Investment funds	58.2	6.4	26.5	12.6	10.1	2.7	0.0
Executive directors	75.1	42.2	14.0	6.8	8.4	3.3	0.4
Non-executive directors	42.0	21.6	9.5	5.1	4.3	1.4	0.0
Industrial firms	28.6	5.1	15.2	4.9	1.6	1.2	0.4
Families and individuals	15.4	2.1	6.8	3.3	3.1	0.0	0.2
Government	1.4	0.2	0.8	0.0	0.2	0.2	0.0
Real estate	0.0	0.0	0.0	0.0	0.0	0.0	0.0
Panel B. Largest ultimate voting block by type of owner 1988–92							
Banks	1.6	0.2	0.8	0.6	0.0	0.0	0.0
Insurance	11.1	1.0	9.7	0.4	0.0	0.0	0.0
Investment funds	27.6	2.3	18.9	3.1	2.7	0.6	0.0
Executive directors	26.1	7.8	5.1	6.4	5.6	1.2	0.0
Non-executive directors	10.9	2.5	3.1	2.5	2.5	0.4	0.0
Industrial firms	14.8	0.4	3.7	5.1	5.1	0.0	0.4
Families and individuals	3.1	0.0	1.4	0.6	1.0	0.0	0.0
Government	0.6	0.0	0.4	0.0	0.2	0.0	0.0
Real estate	0.2	0.0	0.2	0.0	0.0	0.0	0.0
Widely held	3.9	—	—	—	—	—	—

Notes: This table shows the percentage of sample companies with an aggregated shareholding (panel A) and a largest share stake (panel B) by category of owner and size.

Source: Annual reports.

Table 10.6 shows the institutional investors with the greatest number of ultimate voting blocks in a sample of 250 companies in 1992 and each institution's average top block. The five most frequently represented institutions were two insurance companies, Prudential Corporation Group with 70 blocks of at least 3% and Scottish Amicable Life Insurance Society with 50 blocks, and three investment funds, Philips & Drew, Schroder, and M&G with more than 30 relevant stakes in a total of 250 listed companies.

4.6. *Changes in shareholdings*

Table 10.7 reports changes in the concentration of ultimate voting blocks over time and shows whether they are related to total voting block concentration. Year-to-year increases and decreases are recorded for 1990–2 in order to avoid distortion from the lowering of the disclosure threshold in 1989. A distinction is made between increases in

Table 10.6. *Main institutional investors in a random sample of 250 listed companies in 1992*

Institutional investors	Number of ultimate voting blocks	Average ultimate voting block (%)
Prudential Corporation Group	70	5.5
Scottish Amicable Life Insurance Society	50	6.2
Philips & Drew Fund Management	41	4.7
Schroder Investment Management	36	5.7
M&G Investment Management	31	8.6
Barclays Bank	29	4.4
Brittanic Insurance	25	5.6
Guardian Royal Exchange	25	6.0
Norwich Union Life Assurance	24	4.1
Prudential Portfolio Managers	18	4.6
Robert Fleming Holdings	15	5.2
TSB Group	15	4.9
Morgan Grenfell Group	13	4.0
Postel Investment Management	13	4.7
3i Group	12	8.1
Framlington Group	12	5.1
Standard Life Assurance	11	3.8
AMP Asset Management	10	4.3
Sun Alliance	10	4.8
Confederation Life Group	9	5.3
Scottish Widows Fund and Life Assurance	9	3.2
Fidelity Investment	8	5.8
Imperial Group Pension Investments	8	4.7
Pearl Assurance	8	4.3
Royal Insurance	6	3.4
TR Smaller Companies Investment Trust	6	6.5
Edinburgh Fund Managers	5	5.8
Equitable Life Assurance	5	4.0
Abberforth Partners	5	5.6
Henderson Administration Group	5	4.0
Invesco MIM	5	3.2
Provident Mutual Life Assurance	4	7.1

Source: Annual reports.

voting rights held by new blockholders, who did not have a relevant holding in the preceding year, and those of established substantial shareholders. The table shows 925 purchases of blocks, 85% by new shareholders, and 838 sales of at least 3% over the whole sample period.[28] Ninety-eight blocks of at least 10% were acquired and 80 were sold in the group of 250 companies. In conclusion, there is a market for share blocks in the UK, since substantial share stakes of 10% or more were acquired in 12% of the sample.

Table 10.8 reveals that during the period 1990–2, investment funds and insurance companies actively traded substantial share blocks: in 48.7% of the sample companies

Table 10.7. *Number of new large ultimate voting blocks and number of changes in existing ultimate voting blocks by ownership concentration in 1990–1992*

Total ownership concentration	Magnitude of change					
	[3%, 5%]	[5%, 10%]	[10%, 15%]	[15%, 25%]	[25%, 50%]	>50%
Panel A. Number of firms with new shareholdings by magnitude and total ownership concentration						
<15%	67	20	7	1	2	0
[15%, 25%]	63	25	5	3	1	0
[25%, 35%]	106	41	8	3	2	0
[35%, 50%]	143	60	9	4	3	0
>50%	134	75	19	11	4	0
Panel B. Number of firms with increases in existing shareholdings by magnitude and total ownership concentration						
<15%	1	1	0	2	0	0
[15%, 25%]	4	3	1	1	1	0
[25%, 35%]	9	7	1	0	0	0
[35%, 50%]	18	6	5	0	2	0
>50%	26	18	2	1	0	0
Panel C. Number of firms with decreases in existing shareholdings by magnitude and total ownership concentration						
<15%	33	12	1	0	0	0
[15%, 25%]	53	14	2	2	0	0
[25%, 35%]	97	45	6	4	0	0
[35%, 50%]	184	76	12	8	3	0
>50%	151	93	17	16	7	2

Notes: This table reports the number of changes in shareholdings by magnitude of change for different total shareholding concentrations, 1990–2. Panel A reports the number of large new shareholdings by size class; panels B and C reflect the number of increases and decreases in substantial shareholdings by size of holding and ownership concentration. The total sample consists of 250 companies.

Source: Based on data from annual reports.

they sold stakes of between 3% and 25%, and in 50.5% they purchased such stakes. Executive directors acquired major shareholdings in about 10% of the companies and decreased their holdings in 11.4%. Industrial companies traded large share blocks in about 12% of the sample.

4.7. *Ownership concentration in unlisted companies*

A sample of 12,600 unlisted British companies was drawn from Jordan's database (Amadeus CD-Rom supplied by Bureau Van Dijk, Brussels) for 1996. In about 78%, the entire share capital is held by a single shareholder. In the rest, one shareholder holds a majority stake of at least 50% (Figure 10.5).

Table 10.8. *Number of changes of ownership by blockholder type*

	No.	[3%, 5%]	No.	[5%, 25%]	No.	[25%, 50%]	No.	>50%
Panel A. Number and percentage of sample firms with sales of ultimate voting blocks								
Banks	60	8.0	21	2.8	0	0.0	0	0.0
Insurance firms	152	20.3	45	6.0	0	0.0	0	0.0
Investment funds	213	28.4	123	16.4	1	0.1	0	0.0
Executive directors	25	3.3	31	4.1	4	0.5	0	0.0
Non-exec. directors	12	1.6	18	2.4	2	0.3	0	0.0
Industrial firms	32	4.3	48	6.4	3	0.4	2	0.3
Families and individuals	24	3.2	22	2.9	0	0.0	0	0.0
Panel B. Number and percentage of sample firms with purchases of ultimate voting blocks								
Banks	55	7.3	23	3.1	0	0.0	0	0.0
Insurance firms	148	19.7	43	5.7	0	0.0	0	0.0
Investment funds	231	30.8	178	23.7	1	0.1	0	0.0
Executive directors	32	4.3	15	2.0	1	0.1	0	0.0
Non-exec. directors	16	2.1	11	1.5	2	0.3	0	0.0
Industrial firms	46	6.1	45	6.0	9	1.2	0	0.0
Families and individuals	43	5.7	24	3.2	2	0.3	0	0.0

Notes: This table shows the number of sample companies with sales and purchases of substantial shareholdings over the period 1990–2 (after the disclosure threshold was lowered). The sample consists of 250 listed companies. The numbers of sample companies are cumulative over 3 years. The columns with percentages indicate the percentage of sample companies with a change in share stake owned by a particular class. Panel A shows decreases in share stakes; panel B increases.

Source: Annual reports.

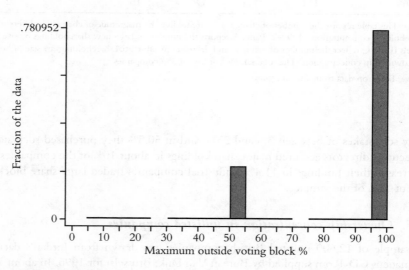

Figure 10.5. *Histogram of largest ultimate voting block in unlisted companies in 1996.*

Sources: Jordan's Database on Share Ownership 1996.

5. EVOLUTION OF OWNERSHIP

We have seen that virtually all unlisted companies have a high ownership concentration while listed companies tend to have a dispersed ownership structure. This raises the question of how long it takes for a new firm to reach a diffuse shareholding structure and the separation of ownership and control as defined by Berle and Means (1932). Brennan and Franks (1997), Goergen (1998, 1999), and Goergen and Renneboog (2001) address this question and analyse the evolution of ownership and control in UK firms from the time they go public. Brennan and Franks find that in a sample of 69 IPOs, two-thirds of the equity, on average, is owned by new shareholders after seven years.

Goergen (Table 10.9) finds that British firms reach low ownership concentration faster than their German counterparts. German IPOs floated by individuals between

Table 10.9. *Average proportion of voting rights held by the old and new shareholders in 55 German and British IPOs matched by market capitalization*

Time after IPO	Country	Old shareholders	New shareholders	Dispersed holdings
Immediate	Germany	76.4%★	1.5%★★★	22.2%★
	UK	62.8%	0.1%	37.2%
		(55, 3.292, 55)	(55, 1.874, 55)	(55, −3.797, 55)
1 year	Germany	73.7%★	2.4%	24.0%★
	UK	51.4%	5.5%	43.1%
		(55, 4.666, 54)	(55, −1.452, 54)	(55, −4.615, 54)
2 years	Germany	69.6%★	5.4%★★	25.0%★
	UK	47.3%	13.3%	39.5%
		(54, 4.288, 53)	(54, −2.513, 53)	(54, −3.435, 53)
3 years	Germany	64.9%★	9.8%★	25.3%★★
	UK	37.7%	26.4%	36.0%
		(49, 4.490, 48)	(49, −2.825, 48)	(49, −2.267, 48)
4 years	Germany	59.4%★	15.5%★★	25.0%★★
	UK	33.6%	28.8%	37.6%
		(42, 3.919, 41)	(42, −2.019, 41)	(42, −2.508, 41)
5 years	Germany	50.7%★	23.1%	26.3%★★
	UK	31.4%	32.1%	36.5%
		(37, 2.705, 36)	(37, −1.176, 36)	(37, −2.001, 36)
6 years	Germany	45.0%★★	30.2%	24.8%★
	UK	30.0%	29.2%	40.8%
		(33, 2.009, 32)	(33, 0.125, 32)	(33, −2.813, 32)

★Indicates that the difference in means is significantly different from zero at the 1% level for the two-tailed test.
★★Indicates that the difference in means is significantly different from zero at the 5% level for the two-tailed test.
★★★Indicates that the difference in means is significantly different from zero at the 10% level for the two-tailed test.

Notes: German sample size, t-statistic for the difference in means, and UK sample size in parentheses. The samples are balanced samples, i.e. if one firm drops out of one sample, the matching firm from the other country is withdrawn.

Source: Goergen 1998.

1981 and 1988 were matched with British IPOs of similar size or industry, also floated by individuals. Within six years of going public a third of the British companies are taken over, a third become widely held, and a third remain controlled by the family share-holder.[29] Five years after the IPO, the old shareholders of a German corporation still own a majority of the voting rights, while old shareholders in UK companies own less than a third. This study also reports that at the time of the IPO firms have an average life of 14 years, whereas German firms only go public about 50 years after their creation.

6. LACK OF SEPARATION DEVICES

Although some devices to separate ownership and control—such as non-voting shares—are legal in the UK, firms tend to avoid them for two reasons. For one thing, such devices have been discouraged by institutional shareholders as well as by the Stock Exchange. Second, the high degree of dispersion of corporate ownership does not spur creation of such devices. In this section, we first discuss the legal separation devices that are available and the reasons why these devices are not normally used by companies. Second, we examine how the substantial power of company directors is further increased by the characteristics of the British system of corporate governance.

6.1. *Non-voting shares and restrictions on share transfer*

Although UK companies are legally entitled to issue non-voting shares, they are rare, especially for listed firms.[30] Brennan and Franks (1997) state that 'investing institutions and the London Stock Exchange have discouraged the issuance of non-voting shares and other devices for discriminating against different shareholders.' Also, most of the few companies that still had non-voting shares—such as Boots, Great Universal Stores, and Whitbread—cancelled them at the beginning of the 1990s. As the LSE allows no restriction on the transfer of shares, only unlisted companies have them, especially private companies (Keenan 1996).

6.2. *Proxy voting*

The board of directors often sends proxy forms to shareholders. The Listing Rules require that proxy forms 'provide for two-way voting on all resolutions intended to be proposed . . .', i.e. shareholders must always be offered the choice to vote for or against any resolution. However, shareholders are free to appoint their own proxy,[31] and are not required to use the proxy form provided by the board of directors. If a shareholder does not specify how the proxy should vote on an issue, the proxy is free to vote as he pleases.

Proxy voting in the UK differs from proxy voting in Germany, where proxy votes are normally exercised by the bank with which the shareholder deposits his shares. If the shareholder does not express his voting intentions, the bank is free to vote as it pleases. In the UK, by contrast, proxy votes are normally exercised by company directors and thus confer additional power on the latter. Davies and Prentice

(1997: 580) argue that the provision for two-way voting does little to prevent this:

It cannot be said, however, that these provisions have done much to curtail the tactical advantages possessed by the directors. They still strike the first blow and their solicitation of proxy votes is likely to meet with a substantial response before the opposition is able to get under way. Even if their proxies are in the 'two-way' form, many members will complete and lodge them after hearing but one side of the case, and only the most intelligent or obstinate are likely to withstand the impact of the, as yet, uncontradicted assertions of the directors. It is, of course, true that once opposition is aroused members may be persuaded to cancel their proxies, for these are merely appointments of agents and the agents' authority can be withdrawn either expressly or by personal attendance and voting. But in practice this rarely happens.

6.3. *Voting at shareholders' meetings*

The way voting is conducted may further enhance the directors' power. Unless a resolution is controversial, voting is normally by show of hands only. Consequently, each shareholder has only one vote, however large his stake, and proxy votes are excluded. Unless the articles of association state otherwise, the chairman has complete discretion to decide whether an item on the agenda is controversial or not. If an item is controversial, a poll can be taken, even before a vote by hand has been held. In a poll, shareholders will have as many votes as their shares confer and proxy voting is allowed.

The voting procedure at meetings, i.e. the show of hands, is probably a weak point in the British system of corporate governance. Minority shareholders typically do not attend, and proxy voting is only allowed in a poll. As British company directors normally hold shares, they will be voting by show of hands along with the other shareholders attending and can thus decide corporate issues in their own interest.

6.4. *One-tier board structure*

Unlike German public companies (*Aktiengesellschaften*), British companies do not have a two-tier board structure. Both executive and non-executive directors sit on the same board, and the chairman may be an executive director.[32] One of the main recommendations of the Cadbury (1992) report is to increase the independence of non-executive *vis-à-vis* executive directors, calling for an increase in the proportion of non-executive directors and the separation of the roles of the chairman and the chief executive. Stapledon (1996) shows that the portion of non-executive directors in listed industrial companies rose from 30% in 1979 to 44% in 1993. Franks, Mayer, and Renneboog (2001) confirm that executive directors still outnumber non-executive directors in listed industrial companies (60% versus 40%). The proportion of listed firms with separate chairmen and chief executives also increased substantially, but 23% still do not separate the two roles. They are potentially liable to serious failures of monitoring of the board. Franks, Mayer, and Renneboog (2001) report that corporate restructuring triggered by poor performance usually enhances the independence of the non-executive directors from management.

The Hampel Committee—headed by Sir Ronald Hampel, the chairman of ICI—was set up at the end of 1995 as the successor to the Cadbury Committee. It has raised the issue of whether the United Kingdom should move towards a two-tier board structure. It is also considering whether institutional investors should be forced to vote at shareholders' meetings as in the United States. However, the Committee seems inclined towards a non-interventionist approach, not compulsory rules.

6.5. *The market for corporate control*

Theoreticians argue that managers who perform poorly will eventually be disciplined by the market for corporate control (see e.g. Manne 1965). If a company does badly, then it should be profitable for an investor to take control and increase shareholder value by replacing the management. Along with the USA, the UK is one of the few countries with an active market for corporate control. Franks, Mayer, and Renneboog (2001) report that on average every year 4% of listed companies are taken over. Franks and Mayer (1996) point out that there were 80 hostile takeover bids in 1985–6, as against just three hostile takeovers in Germany since World War II.

However, two recent empirical studies—Franks and Mayer (1996) on the UK and Schwert (2000) on the USA—question the disciplining role of takeovers. They concur that the performance of targets of hostile bids is not significantly different from that of targets of friendly bids or non-targets. This suggests that the main device for disciplining poor managers does not work efficiently and that managers are in general free to do whatever they choose.

7. CONCLUSION

The ownership structure of British listed companies differs radically from that found on the Continent. Above all British ownership is diffuse: a coalition of at least eight shareholders is required to reach an absolute majority of voting rights in the average company. Though dispersed ownership is the rule, in about 10% of firms the founder or his heirs still hold more than 30%. The structure is also shaped by regulation; the mandatory takeover threshold of 30%, for example, has an important impact. In about 4% of our sample companies, corporate shareholders hold stakes of just under 30%. Second, institutional investors are the most important category of shareholders. However, they tend to be passive and often fail to exercise their voting rights. Third, the passive stance adopted by institutions works to increase the already significant power of directors, who are the second most important category of shareholders. Franks, Mayer, and Renneboog (2001) show that when directors own substantial holdings they use their voting power to entrench, and can impede monitoring by other shareholders with a view to changing the board, even corporate performance is poor. Fourth, there is an important market for significant stakes. Fifth, some of the features of the British system of corporate governance, such as proxy voting and the one-tier board, further strengthen the discretionary power of directors. In short, given the diffuse ownership structure, the main agency conflict is the potential expropriation of shareholders by management.

Corporate governance mechanisms such as hostile takeovers (Franks and Mayer 1996) and the market for controlling stakes (Franks, Mayer, and Renneboog 2001) do not seem to work very well in the UK. Consequently, more independent non-executive directors or a separate supervisory board would appear to be needed to curb the potential agency conflicts between management and shareholders. Executive compensation linked directly to performance would also produce a better alignment of managerial and shareholder goals. A stricter legal definition of the fiduciary duty of directors would allow courts to rule more effectively on directors' responsibilities. The Cadbury Committee (1992), the Greenbury Committee (1995), and now the Hampel Committee have proposed codes of corporate governance and executive compensation. The establishment of an independent regulatory body to advise on pay-for-performance issues, control board composition, and safeguard minority interests would limit the potential agency conflicts.

NOTES

1. One of the distinctive features of the UK capital market is its self-regulatory character. Both the City and the London Stock Exchange are subject to auto-regulation (see Franks *et al.* 1997).
2. The difference between liability limited by share capital and by guarantee is that at least part of the former has to be paid up before winding up the company. The guarantee is only due at liquidation if the liquidation value is lower than the guaranteed capital. Since 1980, only private companies can be created by guarantee.
3. The threshold was 5% from 1985 until 1989.
4. Although not all shareholders are necessarily members of the company, in practice owning a shareholding is generally tantamount to membership. In the remainder of the chapter, we use the term 'shareholder' instead of 'member'.
5. The Regulations were published in No. 1993/1819 and No. 1993/2689, respectively, of Statutory Instruments. They were made on 20 July 1993 and went into force on 18 September 1993. The Regulations are an amendment to Part VI—the part on the Disclosure of Interests in Shares—of the Companies Act of 1985 (as well as to Section 210A, which was added to the Act by Section 134 of the Companies Act 1989).
6. The relevant share capital also includes voting shares whose voting rights have been temporarily suspended.
7. In the following sections of this chapter, we will be using the term 'person' as it is used in UK Company Law. This term as well as the pronouns 'he' and 'him' do not refer only to 'individuals', but also to 'bodies corporate' (companies). See Mayson, French, and Ryan (1996), section 0.1.9 'A note on terminology' for more detail. Legal texts use the term 'individual', if corporations are to be excluded.
8. Company Law uses the term 'material' rather than 'beneficial'. Beneficial refers to the fact that the person enjoys all the proprietary rights. In the case of listed bearer shares with voting rights, the main rights are: voting at the general assembly, receiving dividends, and the right to dispose of the shares. Non-beneficial shares are held by a trustee, usually for a family, charity, or corporation that will receive dividends.
9. When a person's stake drops below the 3% threshold, he must notify the company. Subsequent decreases do not require a notification.

10. See Section 324 of CA 1985. If a director also has an interest in his company that exceeds the thresholds laid down in Section 199 for substantial shareholdings, he must make two distinct notifications.

11. According to Section 234 of CA 1985, the directors of a company are required to prepare for each financial year a directors' report specifying changes in their and others' interests and any purchases of own shares by the company. The directors' report is released along with the company accounts to: 'every member of the company, every holder of the company's debentures, and every person who is entitled to receive notice of general meetings' (Section 238).

12. Shareholders and non-shareholders, if the company has issued shares.

13. If a person requests copies, the company must send them within ten days, subject to an administrative charge. If a company fails to satisfy the request within the deadline, it and any of its officers are liable to a fine on a daily basis. If the company refuses to satisfy a request, 'the court may by order compel an immediate inspection of it; and in the case of failure to send a copy required . . . , the court may by order direct that the copy required shall be sent to the person requiring it.' The fee payable for copies of the register of interests in shares and the register of directors' interests is specified in the Companies (Inspection and Copying of Registers, Indices and Documents) Regulations 1991 and is: £ 2.50 for the first 100 entries (or part of them), £ 20.00 for the following 1,000 entries (or part) and £ 15.00 for each additional 1,000 entries (or part).

14. Under Section 212, a public company can request a person (individual or company) it knows or suspects to be interested in its voting share capital to declare whether or not this is the case. The company may also be asked by members representing at least 10% of the paid-up voting capital (on the date of the request) to make such a request under Section 212. If the company does not do so, it and any of its officers who are in default will be liable to a fine.

15. The Companies Act of 1989 (hereafter CA 1989) defines parent company, wholly-owned subsidiary, holding company, and subsidiary. A wholly-owned subsidiary is a company that does not have any members apart from the parent company, the parent company's wholly-owned subsidiaries or persons acting on behalf of the parent company or any of its wholly-owned subsidiaries. A company is a subsidiary of another company, the holding company, if the latter holds the majority of the voting rights, is a member of it and appoints a majority of the directors, or is a member of it and controls the majority of the votes in accordance with an agreement with the other members or shareholders. Parent companies are required to publish consolidated accounts.

16. See Section 204 of CA 1985. Birds *et al.* (1995) argue that 'Section 204 is the statutory equivalent of the City Code rules in respect of "concert parties" in the context of a takeover bid.' The City Code will be discussed in detail in section 3.5.

17. See Part XIIIA of CA 1985.

18. The USM (Unlisted Securities Market) required companies to have at least 10% of their listed class of shares widely held. The proportion is 25% for the Official List.

19. Keenan (1996) provides a good discussion of the principles governing minority protection.

20. Additional details on creditor protection, reduction of share capital below the authorized minimum, etc. can be found in Part V, Chapter IV of the CA 1985.

21. The London Stock Exchange (LSE) covers the changes in an on-line Regulatory News Service but does not store data. The LSE data are collected and stored by Extel Financial, which cannot make data accessible electronically but publishes a Weekly Official Intelligence Report. Copies of the hardcopy notifications have been available since 1992, but at

substantial cost—£ 15,000. Jordan's database on ownership gives a one-year snapshot, as old data are overwritten. Back-up copies of historical data are not available. For current ownership we used Jordan's database, which covers 1,580 listed companies, but analysis did not give results compatible with the more detailed analysis of the random sample. Closer scrutiny revealed that this database may have misclassified a good number of companies, so we did not consider it to be suitable for our study. All in all, there is no reliable database providing a good overview of shareholdings or historical database for our sample period. Newspaper coverage (e.g. the *Financial Times*) of substantial shareholdings or directors' holdings is far from comprehensive and cannot be used for research purposes.

22. Data on voting pacts are not available in annual reports over the sample period, and newspaper coverage of such pacts is sporadic at best.

23. For instance, for the year 1990, the recent IPO sample consisted of 30 companies listed after 1985. The sample of recent IPOs shrinks year by year: companies that went public in 1983 remain in the IPO sub-sample until 1988 but are counted as 'established companies' from 1989 onwards. In addition, some companies were taken over, went into receivership, or had missing data.

24. For all companies, all holdings of 3% or more are collected, except those of directors, for whom all shareholdings were obtained. This figure takes only blocks of at least 3% into account, however.

25. The substantial change from 10.6% in 1989 to 19.5% in 1990 reflects the fact that on average two additional institutional investors had to disclose their stakes when the threshold was reduced to 3%.

26. For each category of owner, the largest share stake was recorded (if available). The number of largest shareholdings by category is used as denominator.

27. In panel C of Table 10.3, the average of largest voting blocks by class of owner is divided, not by the total number of relevant top shareholdings by class, as in panel B, but by the number of sample companies. As pension funds own share stakes in almost all the companies of our sample, the average largest shareholding does not differ much from panel B (7%). Both executive directors and industrial companies have top shareholdings with an average of more than 5%.

28. This underestimates the true changes in blocks, as blocks purchased after the beginning of the year but sold before the end of the year are not included.

29. A company is considered to be controlled by its family shareholder, if he owns the largest stake and this is at least 25%.

30. The Listing Rules (Chapter 13) do not prohibit the issue of non-voting or restricted-voting shares, but they must be clearly marked.

31. Section 372 of CA 1985.

32. Stapledon (1996: 144–5) distinguishes three cases: (1) the chairman and the chief executive officer are the same; (2) the chairman is an executive and there is a different chief executive officer; (3) the chairman is a former executive director.

REFERENCES

Berle, A. and G. Means (1932), *The Modern Corporation and Private Property*, New York: Macmillan.

Birds, J., A. J. Boyle, E. Ferran, and C. Villiers (1995), *Boyle and Birds' Company Law*, Bristol: Jordan Publishing Limited, 3rd edn.

Brennan, M. and J. Franks (1997), 'Underpricing, Ownership and Control in Initial Public Offerings of Equity Securities in the UK', *Journal of Financial Economics*, 45: 391–413.

Cadbury, A. (1992), *Report of the Committee on the Financial Aspects of Corporate Governance*, London: Gee & Co. Ltd.

Davies, P. and D. Prentice (1997), *Gower's Principles of Modern Company Law*, London: Sweet & Maxwell, 6th edn.

Dine, J. (1994). *Company Law*, Basingstoke: Macmillan Press Ltd, 2nd edn.

Franks, J. and C. Mayer (1995), 'Ownership and Control', in H. Siebert (ed.), *Trends in Business Organization: Do Participation and Cooperation Increase Competitiveness?*, Tübingen: Mohr, repr. in A. Soppe, J. Spronk, E. Vermeulen and A. Vorst (eds.), 'Financiering en Belegging', Rotterdam: Erasmus University.

—— —— (1996), 'Hostile Takeovers and the Correction of Managerial Failure', *Journal of Financial Economics*, 400: 163–81.

—— —— and L. Renneboog (2001), 'Who Disciplines Management in Poorly Performing Companies', *Journal of Financial Intermediation*, in press.

—— S. Schaefer, and M. Staunton (1997), 'The Direct and Compliance Costs of Financial Regulation', *Journal of Banking and Finance*, 21: 1547–72.

Goergen, M. (1998), *Corporate Governance and Financial Performance: A Study of German and UK Initial Public Offerings*, Cheltenham: Edward Elgar.

Goergen, M. (1999). 'Insider Retention and Long-Run Performance in German and UK IPOs', School of Management, UMIST, mimeo.

—— and L. Renneboog (2001), 'Prediction of Control Concentration in German and UK Initial Public Offerings', in J. McCahery, P. Moerland, T. Raaijmakers and L. Renneboog, *Convergence and Diversity in Corporate Governance Regimes and Capital Markets*, Oxford: Oxford University Press.

Griffin, S. (1996), *Company Law. Fundamental Principles*, London: Pitman, 2nd edn.

Keenan, D. (1996), *Smith & Keenan's Company Law for Students*, London: Pitman, 10th edn.

La Porta, R., F. Lopez-De-Silanes, A. Shleifer, and R. Vishny (1997), 'Legal Determinants of External Finance', *Journal of Finance*, 52 (July): 1131–50.

Manne, H. (1965), 'Mergers and the Market for Corporate Control', *Journal of Political Economy*, 73: 110–20.

Mayson, S., D. French, and C. Ryan (1996), *Mayson, French & Ryan on Company Law*, London: Blackstone Press, 13th edn.

Plender, J. (1997), *A Stake in the Future: The Stakeholding Solution*, London: Nicholas Brealey.

Renneboog, L. (1997), 'Shareholding Concentration and Pyramidal Ownership Structures in Belgium', in M. Balling, E. Hennessy, and R. O'Brien (eds.), *Corporate Governance, Financial Markets and Global Convergence*, Amsterdam: Kluwer Academic.

Schwert, W. (2000), 'Hostility in Takeovers: In the Eyes of the Beholder?', *Journal of Finance*, 55: 2599–640.

Shleifer, Andrei and Robert W. Vishny (1997), 'A Survey of Corporate Governance', *Journal of Finance*, 52/2: 737–83.

Stapledon, G. (1996), *Institutional Shareholders and Corporate Governance*, Oxford: Oxford University Press.

Study Group on Directors' Remuneration ('Greenbury Committee') (1995), *Code of Best Practice*, London: Gee Publishing.

Wamsley, K. (1997), *Butterworths Company Law Handbook*, London: Butterworths, 11th edn.

11

Beneficial Ownership in the United States

MARCO BECHT

INTRODUCTION

In the United States the focus of the corporate governance debate has been on the power of executives and directors and the weakness of the large public corporations' dispersed owners. This chapter takes a 'European view' and analyses the distribution of voting power that is exerted by 5%+ blockholders ('beneficial owners') of listed companies in the United States. The main purpose of the chapter is to report statistics that are comparable to European voting power data that is disclosed on the basis of the Large Holdings Directive (88/627/EEC).[1]

The definition of voting blocks in the European Union's Large Holdings Directive (88/627/EEC) and the definition of beneficial ownership in Rule 13D-3 of the 'General Rules and Regulations promulgated under the Securities Exchange Act of 1934' are very similar.[2] However, the general disclosure provisions under US securities regulation are more detailed than in Europe. Most statistics on voting control in the United States use the most detailed information available, for example, total holdings by directors and officers, which makes them unsuitable for cross-country comparisons.[3] The statistics reported here focus on the comparable portions of the US data.

The exploratory analysis confirms that blocks and blockholders do not play a prominent role in the governance of most US issuers. Almost half of the non-financial, US incorporated companies that are listed on NASDAQ or the New York Stock Exchange do not have a single 5%+ blockholder and less than half have a non-board member blockholder. For 92.2% of NYSE companies, no block is larger than 25% (82.3% for NASDAQ). As the other chapters in this book show, less than half of the non-financial listed companies incorporated in Continental European have no blockholder controlling less than 50% of the total voting rights.

The full text of the acts, rules and forms referred to in this chapter can be obtained from the *Securities Lawyer's Deskbook* published for The Center for Corporate Law at the University of Cincinnati College of Law by the Center for Electronic Text in the Law (http://www.law.uc.edu/CCL/intro.html). The texts referred to here were consulted on 3 March 1999 and they were believed to be accurate at the time.

Most of the institutions that hold a large number of blocks are not explicitly concerned with corporate governance. FMR Corp. (Fidelity) holds the largest number of blocks in NYSE companies (at least 94),[4] but does not usually take explicit corporate governance action and explicitly rejects board representation (Roe 1994: 120). The fund with the second largest number of blocks (Dimensional Fund Advisors, at least 79 blocks) is a passive investor because it 'believes that markets are efficient'.[5] Despite these limitations there is evidence that, when they exist, blockholders can have a substantial impact on the governance and performance of US corporations (Holderness 2001).

There is evidence that the influence of shareholders over boards and management through other devices is limited. Hostile takeovers are no longer a substitute for monitoring by blockholders. A number of studies show that US corporations are very well protected against hostile takeovers and some of the most potent anti-takeover devices can be put in place without a shareholder vote (Danielson and Karpoff 1998). The shareholder activism literature suggests that even the most activist shareholders have a relatively small impact (see Black 1997, Karpoff 1997, Gillan and Starks 1998, and Romano 2000 for recent surveys).

The remainder of this chapter is organized as follows. Section 1 provides a more detailed discussion of the European versus the US disclosure system and SEC rules that generate the data that is analysed in the remainder of the chapter. Section 2 summarizes the main results. An Appendix contains tables and figures with the descriptive statistics (that should be comparable to similar tables and figures for the EU). The full text of Rule 13d-3, that defines 'beneficial ownership', is reproduced in an Appendix. The text of the relevant Sections of the 34 Act, the relevant SEC Rules, Forms and actual filings can be found on the Internet (see References).

DISCLOSURE RULES

Companies that satisfy the conditions of Section 12 of the Securities and Exchange Act of 1934 have to register with the Securities and Exchange Commission, even when their stock is not listed on a stock exchange. In the European Union, all companies are registered through company law, but the Large Holdings Directive (88/627/EEC) only applies to companies listed on an official market.

Although the purpose is the same—to ensure investor protection through transparency—the practical implementation on both sides of the Atlantic differs substantially. In the case of the European Union, the Large Holdings Directive sets explicit minimum standards that are transposed into law by national parliaments. In most cases, these laws are very detailed and contain specific implementation rules that must be respected by the competent authority. In the United States, the 1934 Act sets out the general principles, but usually gives the Securities and Exchange Commission the freedom and authority to devise rules and regulations 'as necessary or appropriate for the proper protection of investors' (Section 13, 'Periodical and Other Reporting').[6] The result is a uniform set of forms and filing instructions that are revised periodically by the Commission. Changes to forms do not require new laws to be passed by parliaments.

Under US Securities Regulation, there are several rules on the disclosure of ownership and voting power:

(1) Companies have to disclose information relating to management and directors, and compile statements from filings by third parties, for example in annual reports (filed on Form 10-K) or proxy statements (filed on Schedule 14D).

(2) Declarations by 5%+ 'beneficial owners', pursuant to Regulation 13D. This requirement was originally motivated by takeover regulation. The emphasis is on the control aspects of voting power and cash-flow rights (beneficial ownership is defined through 'voting power' or 'investment power').

(3) Insider filings pursuant to Section 16 of the 34 Act (on Forms 3, 4, 5 and 144). To determine whether someone is a beneficial owner the definition of Section 13D applies. However, the disclosed beneficial ownership is calculated using a different definition. 'The term beneficial owner shall mean any person who, directly or indirectly, through any contract, arrangement, understanding, relationship or otherwise, has or shares a direct or indirect pecuniary interest in the equity securities.'[7]

(4) Portfolio disclosure by institutional investors:

    4.1. General institutional holdings filed on Form 13F (going back to 1978 when this measure was introduced);

    4.2. Mutual fund holdings;

    4.3. Insurance company holdings;

    4.4. Pension fund holdings.

This chapter relies on 13D and 13G filings by 5%+ 'Section 13 blockholders' that are reported in proxy statements (14A). Section 13 of the 34 Act, Regulation 13D and the associated forms provide for a definition of 'voting block' that is very similar to the provisions of the EU's Large Holdings Directive (88/627/EEC). Hence, at least in terms of their definition, the voting blocks I observe for the United States can be compared to the European voting blocks observed elsewhere in this book.[8]

DATA SOURCE

The data used in this chapter is taken from the Global Researcher Database assembled by Disclosure Inc. and produced by Bureau van Dijk. In addition, some comparisons with filings on the SEC's Edgar database were performed.[9]

The Disclosure disk contains four types of ownership and voting power data from three different sources:

1. Director, officers, and 5%+ voting block data collected by Disclosure proper and taken from Schedule 14A (the proxy statement);
2. Insider filings of directors, officers, and 10%+ beneficial owners collected by CDA Technologies from Forms 3, 4 and 5;[10]
3. '5% Owner information' on 5%+ voting blocks collected by, again, CDA from Forms 13D, 13G and 14D;
4. Ownership stakes of institutional investors collected by Everson and taken (presumably) from Form 13G.

Table 11.1. *Sources of voting block information*

Source (Form)	No. of 5%+ blocks	%	Cum. %
10-K	216	1.4	1.4
8-K	38	0.2	1.6
14A	10,058	63.4	65.0
n.a.	5,554	35.0	100.0
Total	15,866	100.0	

Notes: Form 10-K is an annual report. Form 8-K contains more recent information that would normally be included in an annual report. Schedule 14A is the proxy statement. Schedule 14A is incorporated in Form 10-K by reference. An overview of the SEC universe of Forms is provided at http://www.sec.gov/edaux/forms.htm.

Source: Global Researcher and own calculations.

Since this chapter aims to compile statistics that are comparable to European data, the Disclosure data from the proxy statements or the CDA data from 13D filings might have been appropriate. Becht (1997) analysed the CDA data compiled from 13D and 13G filings. Unfortunately, this source is inaccurate. Hence, this chapter relies on the Disclosure data and 14A filings.[11]

The data that is reported in this chapter was taken from the May 1997 edition of the Global Researcher Database. The database contains a unique Disclosure identification number for 11,600 US registered companies. Of these, 9,982 companies are marked active. There are 15,870 blocks and four of these blocks are smaller than 5%. These were eliminated, giving a total of 15,866 blocks distributed over 5,417 companies.

Table 11.1 shows that the 63.4% of the information on a 5%+ block was obtained from proxy statements. For over one-third of the sample, no information on the source is available.

To distinguish between board and non-board member blocks, the surnames of board members were matched with blockholder names. Random checks confirmed that this procedure is relatively accurate. Mismatches occur when a blockholder and a board member have the same surname, but they are not related (i.e. John Smith and Adam Smith from different Smith tribes). For the overall results, these cases should be negligible.

RESULTS

The distribution of blocks

The results confirm that the number and size of 5%+ blocks held in NYSE and NASDAQ companies is limited. Slightly less than half of the NYSE and NASDAQ companies sample have no 5%+ blockholder. The total number of blocks is relatively large and companies with at least one block have, on average, 2.7 blockholders (3.1 for NASDAQ). For NYSE companies, board members hold about 20% of all blocks but 40% for NASDAQ (Table 11.2).

Table 11.2. *Voting blocks by rank*

Exchange	Total No. >5%	Largest voting block					2nd Largest voting block					3rd Largest voting block					4–10th largest voting block					>10th voting block				
		>5%	Min.	Med.	Mean	Max.	>5%	Min.	Med.	Mean	Max.	>5%	Min.	Med.	Mean	Max.	>5%	Min.	Med.	Mean	Max.	>5%	Min.	Med.	Mean	Max.
NYSE																										
All	1,824	668	0.0	5.4	8.5	92.9	504	0.0	0.0	3.7	40.1	321	0.0	0.0	1.8	25	331	0.0	0.0	0.9	15.9	—	0.0	0.0	0.0	0.0
Board	363	225	0.0	0.0	3.0	92.9	91	0.0	0.0	0.7	35.5	30	0.0	0.0	0.2	19.7	17	0.0	0.0	0.1	13.7	—	0.0	0.0	0.0	0.0
Non-board	1,461	618	0.0	6.8	6.8	83.6	425	0.0	0.0	2.8	30.9	228	0.0	0.0	1.2	15.6	190	0.0	0.0	0.6	12.1	—	0.0	0.0	0.0	0.0
NASDAQ																										
All	5,165	1,643	0.0	8.6	13.0	99.5	1,348	0.0	0.0	5.7	48.8	969	0.0	0.0	3.0	24.1	1,204	0.0	0.0	1.6	22.1	1	0.0	0.0	0.0	6.2
Board	2,147	1,196	0.0	0.0	8.6	99.5	608	0.0	0.0	2.5	41.6	235	0.0	0.0	0.7	22.7	108	0.0	0.0	0.2	20.8	—	0.0	0.0	0.0	0.0
Non-board	3,018	1,290	0.0	0.0	7.7	98.2	839	0.0	0.0	2.7	46.3	479	0.0	0.0	1.2	23.1	412	0.0	0.0	0.6	13.0	—	0.0	0.0	0.0	0.0

Notes: The total number of companies in the sample is 1,309 for the NYSE and 2,831 for NASDAQ. The total number of blocks 1,824 for NYSE companies and 5,165 for NASDAQ. When no 5%+ voting block was observed a zero was assigned (641 cases for NYSE and 1,188 for NASDAQ. For each company the blocks were sorted by size and a serial number was assigned. Ties were not taken into account; i.e. when there were two blocks of 20% the first became the largest and the second the second largest. The procedure was repeated for all blocks held by board members and again for non-board members.

Table 11.3. *Board and non-board member blocks for NYSE companies*

At least one 5%+ block is held by a director and/or officer	At least one 5%+ block is held by a non-board member		
	No	Yes	Total
No	641	443	1,084
Yes	50	175	225
Total	691	618	1,309

Notes: For each company, two indicator variables were created; they show whether at least one block is held by a non-board or a board member respectively. The two variables are tabulated against each other. The frequencies are reported in the table.

Table 11.4. *Board and non-board member blocks for NASDAQ companies*

At least one 5%+ block is held by a director and/or officer	At least one 5%+ block is held by a non-board member		
	No	Yes	Total
No	1,188	447	1,635
Yes	353	843	1,196
Total	1,541	1,290	2,831

Note: See Table 11.3.

At NYSE companies, non-board member blocks dominate (Table 11.3). Non-board member blocks often coincide with non-board member blocks at NASDAQ companies (Table 11.4).

The distribution of blocks is highly skewed. Few of the largest blocks are larger than 20% (Tables 11.5 and 11.6; Figures 11.1–11.6). The importance of the 10% and 20% threshold is most visible in the percentile plot of the largest non-board member blocks (Figures 11.2 and especially 11.5). The thresholds are perfectly consistent with regulatory explanations of blockholding patterns that have been advanced by Black (1990), Roe (1994), and others.

For example, the staff of the SEC is said to hold the view that a 10% block creates 'a rebuttable presumption of control, especially if such holdings are combined ... with membership of the board' (cited in Coffee (1991: 1348)). A 20% voting block is so large that the SEC shares the 'widely held belief that ownership of 20% ... voting power in a widely held company in most instances constitutes control' (cited in Coffee (1991: 1348, fn. 23)).

Having control, as defined by the SEC, can have undesirable effects for institutional investors. Coffee (1991: 1348) argues that 'an investor or investor group that possesses "control" faces two problems: (1) it cannot sell its shares, absent registration or an exemption, and (2) a "controlling" shareholder is prima facie liable for federal securities law violations committed by the "controlled" corporation, unless an affirmative

Table 11.5. *Distribution of 5%+ voting blocks for NYSE companies*

Range (%)	All 5%+ blocks			Non-board members			Directors and officers		
	Freq.	%	Cum. %	Freq.	%	Cum. %	Freq.	%	Cum. %
0–5	641	49.0	49.0	691	52.8	52.8	1,084	82.8	82.8
5–10	243	18.6	67.5	276	21.1	73.9	82	6.3	89.1
10–25	323	24.7	92.2	274	20.9	94.8	102	7.8	96.9
25–50	69	5.3	97.5	46	3.5	98.3	30	2.3	99.2
50–75	26	2.0	99.5	19	1.5	99.8	7	0.5	99.7
75–90	6	0.5	99.9	3	0.2	100.0	3	0.2	99.9
90–95	1	0.1	100.0				1	0.1	100.0
95–100									
Total	1,309	100		1,309	100		1,309	100	

Notes: The ranges exclude the top values, i.e. 0–5% includes 0% but is smaller than 5%. The range 5–10% is larger equal 5% but less than 10%, etc.

Table 11.6. *Distribution of 5%+ voting blocks for NASDAQ companies*

Range (%)	All 5%+ blocks			Non-board members			Directors and officers		
	Freq.	%	Cum. %	Freq.	%	Cum. %	Freq.	%	Cum. %
0–5	1,188	42.0	42.0	1,541	54.4	54.4	1,635	57.8	57.8
5–10	345	12.2	54.2	493	17.4	71.9	338	11.9	69.7
10–25	796	28.1	82.3	583	20.6	92.4	535	18.9	88.6
25–50	371	13.1	95.4	156	5.5	98.0	250	8.8	97.4
50–75	104	3.7	99.1	41	1.5	99.4	63	2.2	99.7
75–90	22	0.8	99.8	15	0.5	99.9	7	0.3	99.9
90–95	2	0.1	99.9				2	0.1	100.0
95–100	3	0.1	100.0	2	0.07	100	1	0.0	100.0
Total	2,831	100		2,831	100		2,831	100	

Notes: See Table 11.5.

defence of non-negligence can be established.' The clustering around the 10% and 20% thresholds is consistent with this explanation.[12]

Another view has been put forward by Bebchuk (1999). He argues that minority shareholders in the United States are well protected, that the ability of blockholders to extract rents is limited and that hence investors do not want to hold control blocks. Control is defined as the ability of 20%+ blockholders to extract rents (control), which is not very valuable because of good investor protection. Although this explanation is not inconsistent with the data, it is less convincing than the regulatory explanations. Why do investors choose to sell their blocks to fall just below the SEC defined lines of control (20% and 10%)? Does the SEC's regulatory definition coincide with the rent-seeking (economic) definition of control?

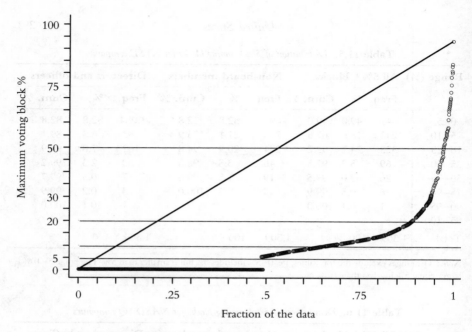

Figure 11.1. *Largest voting block for NYSE companies.*

Note: For each of the 1,309 NYSE companies the largest block was identified, and when no 5%+ block was found, the 'blocksize' was set to zero. The resulting 1,309 blocks were sorted by size along the horizontal axis and their value plotted on the vertical axis.

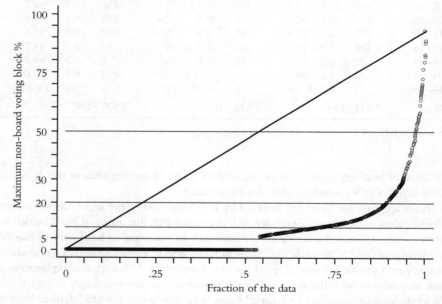

Figure 11.2. *Largest non-board member voting block for NYSE companies.*

Note: As Figure 11.1, but only for blocks held by non-board members.

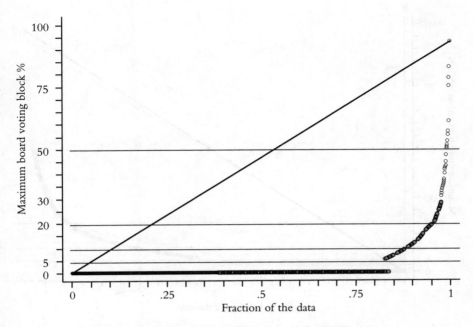

Figure 11.3. *Board-member voting blocks by rank for NYSE companies.*

Note: As Figure 11.1, but only for blocks held by board members.

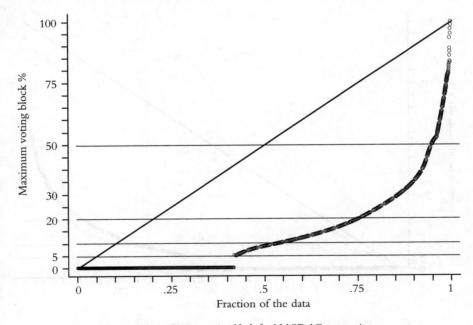

Figure 11.4. *Largest voting block for NASDAQ companies.*

Note: As Figure 11.1, but for the largest blocks in the 2,831 NASDAQ companies.

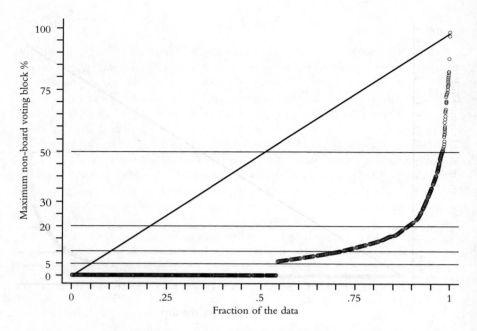

Figure 11.5. *Largest non-board-member voting block for NASDAQ companies.*

Note: See Figure 11.3.

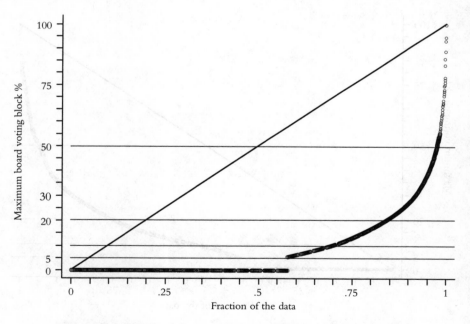

Figure 11.6. *Board-member voting blocks by rank for NASDAQ companies.*

Note: See Figure 11.3.

Although the distribution of blocks in the United States looks similar to the distribution for the United Kingdom (see Goergen and Renneboog in this volume), there is an important difference. One, the regulatory explanations are not the same. In the United Kingdom the distribution is shaped by the mandatory bid-rule and the listing requirement that boards must be independent of 30%+ blockholders. In the United States the distribution seems to be shaped by the SEC's definition of 'control'. In the United Kingdom it is possible to 'bulldozer' the threshold by making a fully-fledged bid. In the United States there is no provision of this type.

Two, in the United Kingdom, companies with dispersed voting power are poorly protected against unsolicited or unfriendly takeover bids. In the United States, the absence of permanently concentrated voting power does not imply that corporate control is generally contestable. Institutional Shareholder Services (ISS) estimate that in a sample of S&P 500 or Fortune 500 companies more than 50% have 'bullet-proof' anti-takeover defences, either in the form of dual-class stock with unequal voting rights or through a combination of a poison pill and a charter-based classified board.[13] While the former should be visible in the blockholding data, the latter is not.[14] The Institutional Research Responsibility Center (IRRC) reports that 38% of the companies they research have installed a poison pill/classified board defence.[15]

Blockholders have names

Who holds the largest blocks? For the New York Stock Exchange sample, no institution holds more than three 20%+ blocks. Citicorp Venture Capital Inc. and Gabelli Funds hold 3 blocks (35–48% and 23–27% respectively). Texas Industries Inc., a listed company, holds the largest block in the sample (in Chaparral Steel Inc., 83.6%), an example of a US 'mini-pyramid'.

Who holds the largest number of blocks? For the New York Stock Exchange sample, FMR Corp. (Fidelity) and its investment funds hold the largest number of blocks (94). Dimensional Fund Advisors Inc. (79), Wellington Management Co. (36), the State of Wisconsin Investment Board (30), and Heartland Advisors (29) follow.[16]

For NASDAQ the ranking of the blockholders, by number of blocks held, follows the pattern found for the NYSE. Again, FMR Corp. (Fidelity) holds the largest number of 5%+ blocks (115), followed by Dimensional Fund Advisors (84). Wellington Management (59), Heartland Advisors (39) and the State of Wisconsin Investment Board (33) follow. The Capital Group Companies play a less important role (23) for NASDAQ companies.

Judging from their published investment strategies, these funds do not take an active stance in corporate governance. Fidelity's 'approach to money management is simple: work harder, work smarter, and work longer'.[17] As a smart and hard working active investor, Fidelity should have divested before corporate governance problems arise. The Capital Group Companies also believes in research. They 'scrutinize companies up-close'.[18] Dimensional Fund Advisors pursue the opposite strategy. They are passive because they believe that markets are efficient; including the market for corporate control.[19]

Heartland Advisors pick stocks according to 10 published criteria. These are supposed to help them identify 'undervalued' companies.[20] They prefer companies with high insider ownership because 'Executives who invest in their own stock have their interests aligned with those of other shareholders.' Hence, instead of challenging insiders, the fund invests in companies where insiders have voting power. Indeed, it is not clear whether insider ownership is supposed to provide for a faster recovery from 'being undervalued' or that it is the cause of 'being undervalued'.

CONCLUSION

The descriptive results of this chapter confirm that corporate governance in the United States is not driven by 5%+ blockholders. The institutions with the largest number of blocks either 'vote with their feet', they are passive, or they have stock-picking strategies that make them invest in companies with strong insiders. The focused initiatives of active investors that build on the threat of temporary concentrations of voting power are not observable in the block data. Finally, due to the existence of statutory defences, corporate control in the United States is less contestable than the raw voting power numbers might suggest.

NOTES

1. The European chapters in this book report block statistics for the main primary market in each country and do not distinguish between blocks held by board and non-board members. In this chapter I report separate statistics for NYSE and NASDAQ companies and board and non-board member blockholders. I deliberately avoid the use of the word 'insider' because its meaning can be ambiguous. Often, only directors and officers are referred to as insiders. However, according to the insider trading regulation of the United States, 10%+ beneficial owners are also insiders.
2. Like in Europe, the disclosure of blocks in the United States is dynamic, yet international voting power comparisons rely on cross-sections. This renders statistics on block trades, which are compiled from Rule 13D filings, unsuitable. Cross-sections that commercial data providers compile from Rule 13D filings are often unreliable (Anderson and Lee 1997). The present chapter overcomes this problem by using cross-section data that is taken from proxy statements (Schedule 14A, Item 6, 'Voting Securities and Principal Holders Thereof'. In turn, Item 6 draws on Item 403 of Regulation S-K, 'Ownership of Certain Beneficial Owners and Management', which draws on the definition of beneficial ownership in Rule 13d-3). Although the data in proxy statements is compiled on the basis of 13D filings as well, companies must compile—to the best of their abilities—accurate cross-sections.

3. Officers and directors have to disclose their total ownership and voting power, a requirement in some European countries, but not all. When an officer or director commands 5%+ voting power, the proxy statement will report his or her name and the amount of shares beneficially owned. The same is true for disclosure under the EU's Large Holdings Directive, so this provision does not pose a problem. A problem of interpretation arises because blocks held by directors play a larger and different role in the United States than in Europe. To distinguish between board member and non-board member blocks, the name of the blockholder was matched with the surname of the officers and/or director. A second problem arose because directors and officers have to report even when they command less than 5% of voting power. Eliminating all voting blocks smaller than 5% solved this problem.

4. Since FMR Corp. does not appear with a single name in the list of blockholders it is possible that some of its 5% + blocks were not attributed to FMR.

5. See http://www.yeske.com/dfa.htm.

6. See http://www.law.uc.edu/CCL/34Act/sec13.html.

7. The provisions of Rule 16a-1 are somewhat confusing. To determine whether an individual or institution qualifies as a beneficial owner, 'Section 13(d) of the Act and the rules thereunder' applies (Rule 16a-1, note to paragraph (a)). However, the beneficial ownership that is actually disclosed (on Forms 3, 4, and 5) is calculated according to the 'pecuniary interest' definition in Rule 16a-1(a)(2). See http://www.law.uc.edu/CCL/34ActRls/rule16a-1.html.

8. The full text of Form 13D and the full text of Rule 13d-3 ('Determination of Beneficial Ownership') are reported in an appendix. They are clearly written and I shall not discuss them further here. The interested reader is referred to the *Securities Lawyer's Deskbook* published for The Center for Corporate Law at the University of Cincinnati College of Law by the Center for Electronic Text in the Law (http://www.law.uc.edu/CCL/intro.html). It contains the full text of the 34 Act, all the Rules and Regulations and most of the Forms that are mentioned in this chapter.

9. See http://www.disclosure.com, http://www.bvdep.com and http://www.sec.gov respectively.

10. See http://www.cda.com.

11. I am grateful to Roberta Romano for alerting me to this deficiency. The data on the Global Researcher Disk is also contained on a disk produced by Disclosure and distributed under the name 'Compact Disclosure'. This database has been analysed by Anderson and Lee (1997) who compared it to original proxy statements. They find that the CDA 5% ownership information suffers from a 'stale data' problem. The database is not updated completely at all times. Hence, the most recent information for the most active companies is mixed with stale information. Anderson and Lee (1997) also find that the Disclosure data is not always inaccurate. The largest discrepancies occur when companies have issued dual-class stock. Disclosure reports the voting power, whereas Anderson and Lee (1997) wanted to measure insider ownership. This is not a problem for the current study, because it focuses on voting power. I confirmed the results of Anderson and Lee (1997) for a smaller sample of companies.

12. Roe (1994) provides another regulatory argument that is consistent with the observed thresholds. He argues that prudential and other regulation bars important institutional investor from holding blocks that are larger than 10% or 20%.

13. The numbers were taken from a personal communication of David Dando of Institutional Shareholder Services (ISS), London.

14. As was pointed out earlier, voting power data from CDA, but to some extent also from Disclosure, underestimates voting power concentration for companies with dual-class stock and unequal voting rights.

15. 'IRRC's universe of 1914 companies contains 243 companies that have dual class common stock. It shows 729 companies that have both a classified board and a poison pill. The database does not make the distinction between a classified board in the charter and one residing only in the bylaws.' Personal communication from Ginny Rosenbaum of IRRC received on 28 March 2000.
16. See http://www.fidelity.com, http://www.yeske.com/dfa.htm, and http://www. capgroup.com/ respectively.
17. See http://personal141.fidelity.com/products/funds/.
18. See http://www.capgroup.com/gig/philos.html.
19. Former students of Eugene Fama who, together with Kenneth French, devises many of the trading strategies run the fund. 'Dimensional's approach is firmly rooted in the belief that markets are "efficient", and that investors' returns are determined principally by asset allocation decisions, not market timing or stock picking. All portfolios employ a passive strategy designed to capture the return behavior of an entire asset class.'
20. Heartland Advisors call this 'value investing'; see http://www.heartlandfunds.com/individuals/passionforvalue/evaluate/equity.html.

REFERENCES

Anderson, R. C. and D. S. Lee (1997), 'Ownership Studies: The Data Source Matters', *Journal of Financial and Quantitative Analysis*, 32 (Sept.).

Bebchuk, L. (1999), 'A Rent-Protection Theory of Corporate Ownership and Control', Cambridge, Mass.: NBER Working paper 7203.

Becht, M. (1997), 'Beneficial Ownership of Listed Companies in the United States', in *The Separation of Ownership and Control: A Survey of 7 European Countries*, Preliminary report to the European Commission, vol. 4, Brussels: European Corporate Governance Network.

Black, B. S. (1990), 'Shareholder Passivity Reexamined', *Michigan Law Review*, 89: 520–608.

—— (1997), 'Shareholder Activism and Corporate Governance in the United States', in Peter Newman (ed.), *The New Palgrave Dictionary of Economics and the Law* (forthcoming).

Coffee, J. C. (1991), 'Liquidity versus Control: The Institutional Investor as Corporate Monitor', *Columbia Law Review*, 91: 1277–1366.

Danielson, M. G. and J. M. Karpoff (1998), 'On the Use of Takeover Provisions', *Journal of Corporate Finance: Contracting, Governance and Organization*, 4/4: 347–71.

Disclosure Inc. (1997), *Global Researcher*, CD-ROM, Special edn. (May), Brussels: Bureau van Dijk.

Gillan, S. L. and Laura T. Starks (1998), 'A Survey of Shareholder Activism: Motivation and Empirical Evidence', *Contemporary Finance Digest*, 2/2: 10–34.

Holderness, C. (2001), 'A Survey of Blockholders and Corporate Control', *Economic Policy Review* (forthcoming).

Karpoff, J. (1997), 'The Impact of Shareholder Activism on Target Companies: A Survey of Empirical Findings', University of Washington School of Business, Seattle, mimeo.

Larner, R. J. (1966), 'Ownership and Control in the 200 Largest Non-Financial Corporations, 1929–1963', *American Economic Review*, 16/4: 781–2.

Roe, M. J. (1994), 'Strong Managers, Weak Owners', in *The Political Roots of American Corporate Finance*, Princeton, Princeton University Press.

Romano, R. (2000), 'Less Is More: Making Shareholder Activism A Valued Mechanism Of Corporate Governance', Yale Law & Economics Research paper no. 241, and Yale ICF Working paper no. 00–10.

Securities and Exchange Act of 1934, Center for Electronic Text in the Law, University of Cincinnati College of Law (http://www.law.uc.edu.CCL/Act34/).

Appendix I. The Large Holdings Directive

COUNCIL DIRECTIVE

of 12 December 1988

on the information to be published when a major holding in a
listed company is acquired or disposed of

88/627/EEC

THE COUNCIL OF THE EUROPEAN COMMUNITIES,

Having regard to the Treaty establishing the European Economic Community, and in particular Article 54 thereof.

Having regard to the proposal from the Commission,[1]

In cooperation with the European Parliament,[2]

Having regard to the opinion of the Economic and Social Committee,[3]

Whereas a policy of adequate information of investors in the field of transferable securities is likely to improve investor protection, to increase investors' confidence in securities markets and thus to ensure that securities markets function correctly;

Whereas, by making such protection more equivalent, coordination of that policy at Community level is likely to make for greater inter-penetration of the Member States' transferable securities markets and therefore help to establish a true European capital market;

Whereas to that end investors should be informed of major holdings and of changes in those holdings in Community companies the shares of which are officially listed on stock exchanges situated or operating within the Community;

Whereas coordinated rules should be laid down concerning the detailed content and the procedure for applying that requirement;

Whereas companies, the shares of which are officially listed on a Community stock exchange can inform the public of changes in major holdings only if they have been informed of such changes by the holders of those holdings;

Whereas most Member States do not subject holders to such a requirement and where such a requirement exists there are appreciable differences in the procedures for applying it; whereas coordinated rules should therefore be adopted at Community level in this field,

Council Directive has been reproduced with permission from the *Official Journal of the European Communities*.

[1] OJ No. C 351, 31.12.1985, p. 35, and OJ No. C 255, 25.9.1985, p. 6.
[2] OJ No. C 125, 11.5.1986, p. 144, and OJ No. C 309, 5.12.1988.
[3] OJ No. C 263, 20.10.1986, p. 1.

HAS ADOPTED THIS DIRECTIVE:

Article 1

(1) Member States shall make subject to this Directive natural persons and legal entities in public or private law who acquire or dispose of, directly or through intermediaries, holdings meeting the criteria laid down in Article 4(1) which involve changes in the holdings of voting rights in companies incorporated under their law the shares of which are officially listed on a stock exchange or exchanges situated or operating within one or more Member States.

(2) Where the acquisition or disposal of a major holding such as referred to in paragraph 1 is effected by means of certificates representing shares, this Directive shall apply to the bearers of those certificates, and not to the issuer.

(3) This Directive shall not apply to the acquisition or disposal of major holdings in collective investment undertakings.

(4) Paragraph 5(c) of Schedule C of the Annex to Council Directive 79/279/EEC of 5 March 1979 coordinating the conditions for the admission of securities to official stock exchange listing,[4] as last amended by Directive 82/148/EEC,[5] is hereby replaced by the following:

(a) The company must inform the public of any changes in the structure (shareholders and breakdowns of holdings) of the major holdings in its capital as compared with information previously published on that subject as soon as such changes come to its notice.

In particular, a company which is not subject to Council Directive 88/627/EEC of 12 December 1988 on the information to be published when a major holding in a listed company is acquired or disposed of* must inform the public within nine calendar days whenever it comes to its notice that a person or entity has acquired or disposed of a number of shares such that his or its holding exceeds or falls below one of the thresholds laid down in Article 4 of that Directive.

Article 2

For the purposes of Directive, 'acquiring a holding' shall mean not only purchasing a holding, but also acquisition by any other means whatsoever, including acquisition in one of the situations referred to in Article 7.

Article 3

Member States may subject the natural persons, legal entities and companies referred to in Article 1(1) to requirements stricter than those provided for in this Directive or to additional requirements, provided that such requirements apply generally to all those acquiring or disposing of holdings and all companies or to all those falling within a particular category acquiring or disposing of holdings or of companies.

---

* OJ No. L 348, 17.12.1988, p. 62.　　　[4] OJ No. L 66, 16.3.1979, p. 21

[5] OJ No. L 62, 5.3.1982, p. 22.

Article 4

(1) Where a natural person or legal entity referred to in Article 1(1) acquires or disposes of a holding in a company referred to in Article 1(1) and where, following that acquisition or disposal, the proportion of voting rights held by that person or legal entity reaches, exceeds or falls below one of the thresholds of 10%, 20%, 1/10, 50% and 2/10 he shall notify the company and at the same time the competent authority or authorities referred to in Article 13 within seven calendar days of the proportion of voting rights he holds following that acquisition or disposal. Member States need not apply:

- the thresholds or 20% and 1/1 where they apply a single threshold of 25%.
- the threshold of 2/1 where they apply the thresholds of 75%.

The period of seven calendar days shall start from the time when the owner of the major holding learns of the acquisition or disposal, or from the time when, in view of the circumstances, he should have learnt of it.

Member States may further provide that a company must also be informed in respect of the proportion of capital held by a natural person or legal entity.

(2) Member States shall, if necessary, establish in their national law, and determine in accordance with it, the manner in which the voting rights to be taken into account for the purposes of applying paragraph 1 are to be brought to the notice of the natural persons and legal entities referred to in Article 1(1).

Article 5

Member States shall provide that at the first annual general meeting of a company referred to in Article 1(1) to take place more than three months after this Directive has been transposed into national law, any natural person or legal entity as referred to in Article 1(1) must notify the company concerned and at the same time the competent authority or authorities where he holds 10% or more of its voting rights, specifying the proportion of voting rights actually held unless that person or entity has already made a declaration in accordance with Article 4.

Within one month of that general meeting, the public shall be informed of all holdings of 10% or more in accordance with Article 10.

Article 6

If the person or entity acquiring or disposing of a major holdings as defined in Article 4 is a member of a group of undertakings required under Directive 83/249/EEC[6] to draw up consolidated accounts, that person or entity shall be exempt from the obligation to make the declaration provided for in Article 4(1) and in Article 5 if it is made by the parent undertaking or, where the parent undertaking is itself a subsidiary undertaking, by its own parent undertaking.

Article 7

For the purposes of determining whether a natural person or legal entity as referred to in Article 1(1) is required to make a declaration as provided for in Article 4(1) and in Article 5, the

---

[6] OJ No 1, 193, 18.3.1983, p. 1.

following shall be regarded as voting rights held by that person or entity:

- voting rights held by other persons or entities in their own names but on behalf of that person or entity,
- voting rights held by an undertaking controlled by that person or entity;
- voting rights held by a third party with whom that person or entity has concluded a written agreement which obliges them to adopt, by concerted exercise of the voting rights they hold, a lasting common policy towards the management of the company in question,
- voting rights held by a third party under a written agreement concluded with that person or entity or with an undertaking controlled by that person or entity providing for the temporary transfer for consideration of the voting rights in question,
- voting rights attaching to shares owned by that person or entity which are lodged as security, except where the person or entity holding the security controls the voting rights and declares his intention of exercising them, in which case they shall be regarded as the latter's voting rights,
- voting rights attaching to shares of which that person or entity has the life interest,
- voting rights which that person or entity or one of the other persons or entities mentioned in the above indents is entitled to acquire, on his own initiative alone, under a formal agreement; in such cases, the notification prescribed in Article 4(1) shall be effected on the date of the agreement,
- voting rights attaching to shares deposited with that person or entity which that person or entity can exercise at its discretion in the absence of specific instructions from the holders.

By way of derogation from Article 4(1), where a person or entity may exercise voting rights referred to in the last indent of the preceding subparagraph in a company and where the totality of these voting rights together with the other voting rights held by that person or entity in that company reaches or exceeds one of the thresholds provided for in Article 4(1), Member States may lay down that the said person or entity is only obliged to inform the company concerned 21 calendar days before the general meeting of that company.

Article 8

(1) For the purposes of this Directive, 'controlled undertaking' shall mean any undertaking in which a natural person or legal entity:

(a) has a majority of the shareholders' or members' voting rights; or

(b) has the rights to appoint or remove a majority of the members of the administrative, management or supervisory body and is at the same time a shareholder in, or member of, the undertaking in question; or

(c) is a shareholder or member and alone controls a majority of the shareholders' or members' voting rights pursuant to an agreement entered into with other shareholders or members of the undertaking.

(2) For the purposes of paragraph 1, a parent undertaking's rights as regards voting, appointment and removal shall include the rights of any other controlled undertaking and those of any person or entity acting in his own name but on behalf of the parent undertaking or of any other controlled undertaking.

Article 9

(1) The competent authorities may exempt from the declaration provided for in Article 4(1) the acquisition or disposal of a major holding, as defined in Article 4, by a professional dealer in securities, in so far as that acquisition or disposal is effected in his capacity as a professional dealer in securities and in so far as the acquisition is not used by the dealer to intervene in the management of the company concerned.

(2) The competent authorities shall require professional dealers in securities referred to in paragraph 1 to be members of a stock exchange situated or operating within a Member State or to be approved or supervised by a competent authority such as referred to in Article 12.

Article 10

(1) A company which has received a declaration referred to in the first subparagraph of Article 4(1) must in turn disclose it to the public in each of the Member States in which its shares are officially listed on a stock exchange as soon as possible but not more than nine calender days after the receipt of that declaration.

A Member State may provide for the disclosure to the public, referred to in the first subparagraph, to be made not by the company concerned but by the competent authority, possibly in cooperation with that company.

(2) The disclosure referred to in paragraph 1 must be made by publication in one or more newspapers distributed throughout or widely in the Member State or States concerned or be made available to the public either in writing in places indicated by announcements to be published in one or more newspapers distributed throughout or widely in the Member State or States concerned or by other equivalent means approved by the competent authorities.

The said disclosure must be made by publication in the official language or languages, or in one of the official languages or in another language, provided that in the Member State in question the official language or languages or such other language is or are customary in the sphere of finance and accepted by the competent authorities.

Article 11

The competent authorities may, exceptionally, exempt the companies referred to in Article 1(1) from the obligation to notify the public set out in Article 10 where those authorities consider that the disclosure of such information would be contrary to the public interest or seriously detrimental to the companies concerned provides that, in the latter case, such omission would not be likely to mislead the public with regard to the facts and circumstances knowledge of which is essential for the assessment of the transferable securities in question.

Article 12

(1) Member States shall designate the competent authority or authorities for the purposes of this Directive and shall inform the Commission accordingly, specifying where appropriate, and division of duties between those authorities.

(2) Member States shall ensure that the competent authorities have such powers as may be necessary for the performance of their duties.

(3) The competent authorities in the Member States shall cooperate wherever necessary for the purpose of performing their duties and shall exchange any information useful for that purpose.

Article 13

For the purpose of this Directive, the competent authorities shall be those of the Member State the laws which governs the companies referred to in Article 1(1).

Article 14

(1) Member States shall provide that every person who carries on or has carried on an activity in the employment of a competent authority shall be bound by professional secrecy. This means that no confidential information received in the course of their duties may be divulged to any person or authority except by virtue of provisions laid down by law.

(2) Paragraph 1 shall not, however, preclude the competent authorities of the various Member States from exchanging information as provided for in this Directive. Information thus exchanged shall be covered by the obligation of professional secrecy to which persons employed or previously employed by the competent authorities receiving the information are subject.

(3) A competent authority which receives confidential information pursuant to paragraph 2 may use it solely for the performance of its duties.

Article 15

Member States shall provide for appropriate sanctions in cases where the natural persons or legal entities and the companies referred to in Article 1(1) do not comply with the provisions of this Directive.

Article 16

(1) The Contact Committee set up by Article 20 of Directive 79/279/EEC shall also have as its function:

(a) to permit regular consultations on any practical problems which arise from the application of the Directive and on which exchanges of view are deemed useful;

(b) to facilitate consultations between the Member States on the stricter or additional requirements which they may lay down in accordance with Article 3, so that the requirements imposed in all the Member States may be brought into line, in accordance with Article 54(3)(g) of the Treaty;

(c) to advise the Commission, if necessary, on any additions or amendments to be made to this Directive.

Article 17

(1) Member States shall take the measures necessary for them to comply with this Directive before 1 January 1991. They shall forthwith inform the Commission thereof.

(2) Member States shall communicate to the Commission the provisions of national law which they adopt in the field governed by this Directive.

Article 18

This Directive is addressed to the Member States.

Done at Brussels, 12 December 1988.

For the Council
The President
P. ROUMELIOTIS

Appendix II. Proposal for a Council Directive

COMMISSION OF THE EUROPEAN COMMUNITIES

COM(85) 791 final

Brussels, 23 December 1985

Proposal for a
COUNCIL DIRECTIVE

on information to be published when major holdings in the capital
of a listed company are acquired or disposed of

———

(submitted to the Council by the Commission)

COM(85) 791 final

Explanatory memorandum

I. Introduction

(1) The Community's work on securities markets is aimed at two main objectives: firstly, ensuring that securities markets function properly and, secondly, encouraging increasingly greater inter-penetration of those markets at Community level. In order to achieve those two objectives, it is necessary, inter alia, to strengthen public confidence in securities dealt in on those markets. Since such confidence largely depends on the quantity and quality of the information made available to the public, a sound information policy on securities and the issuers of securities is essential in the Community if the two objectives referred to above are to be achieved. The Council has already adopted three Directives on stock markets, essentially with those aims in mind. They are Directive 79/279/EEC coordinating the conditions for the admission of securities to official stock exchange listing;[1] Directive 80/390/EEC on the listing particulars to be published for the admission of securities to official stock exchange listing;[2] and Directive 82/121/EEC on information to be published on a regular basis by companies whose shares have been admitted to official stock exchange listing.[3]

(2) This proposal for a Directive, which provides for the disclosure of acquisition or disposals of major holdings in the capital of listed companies, is aimed at reinforcing at Community level the information policy already adopted by the Council. Such disclosure will provide investors with information on persons liable to influence a company's management, sometimes to a considerable extent, and thus enable them to follow developments in its ownership and gain a clearer idea of what is happening internally. This is important information which may affect investors' assessment of securities issued by the company and may consequently play a crucial role in their investment or disinvestment decisions.

Since this information is important, it should be made available to the public, not only because it is of use to investors but also in order to prevent uncontrollable rumours and stop misuse of price-sensitive information. There is a real risk of such misuse occurring when information is not made public but is confined to a restricted circle of people.

(3) It should be noted that the first two stock market Directives adopted by the Council already lay down a requirement, albeit partial, to disclose acquisition of major holdings. Schedule A, point 3.2.7, of Directive 80/390/EEC on the listing particulars to be published for the admission of securities to official stock exchange listing stipulates that the particulars must contain, 'in so far as they are known to the issuer, indication of the shareholders who, directly or indirectly, hold a proportion of the issuer's capital which the Member States may not fix at more than 20%'.

In addition, Schedule C, point 5(c), of Directive 79/279/EEC on the conditions for the admission of securities to official stock exchange listing lays down that 'the company must inform the public of any changes in the structure (shareholders and breakdown of holdings) of the major holdings in its capital as compared with information previously published on that subject as soon as such changes come to its notice'. It is clear from the above that this proposal for a Directive does not impose any new requirements on listed companies. The object is merely to clarify the content of the obligation laid down in Directive 79/279/EEC and to facilitate

---

[1] OJ No. L 66, 16.3.1979.   [2] OJ No. L 100, 17.4.1980.   [3] OJ No. L 48, 20.2.1982.

implementation of that obligation by requiring persons acquiring or disposing of major holdings in a listed company to inform that company accordingly. It is a matter, therefore, not of subjecting listed companies to a new rule but rather of clarifying and coordinating the content of an existing rule.

(4) Three Member States – France, the United Kingdom and Italy – already apply specific rules and regulations that require the company and/or the public to be notified of major changes in the structure of a company's capital. Other Member States either have more fragmentary rules in this area or none at all.

(5) The foregoing shows that some very marked discrepancies exist between Member States' rules and regulations in the area concerned. This means that the information made available to investors in the different Member States varies widely and, therefore, that the safeguards afforded to investors by the various stock markets of the Community are not equivalent. If effective inter-penetration of the stock markets within the Community is to be achieved, however, it is essential that those markets should provide comparable safeguards. That is a further argument in favour of coordinating at Community level the rules and regulations governing the disclosure of acquisitions and disposals of major holdings in listed companies.

II. Comments

1. Scope

(1) The Directive is relatively wide in scope in that it applies to any legal or natural person who acquires or disposes of a major holding in a listed company. It therefore covers not only companies (including those which do not have legal personality) and States or their regional and local authorities, but also individuals. Although it is relatively rare nowadays for a natural person to acquire a major holding in a listed company, such an event is no less relevant to investors when it does occur. The public should therefore be notified in the same way as for major holdings acquired by a company or other legal person. A last point to make is that the Directive applies not only to nationals of a Member State, but also to persons domiciled in a non-member country.

(2) It was thought advisable that this Directive should cover the acquisition of holdings only in *listed companies governed by the law of one of the Member States of the Community*, and not in listed companies from non-member countries. Companies from non-member countries would experience serious difficulties in complying with the Directive where no equivalent provisions required major shareholders in those companies to inform them of such holdings. Where comparable provisions exist in their country of origin, companies from non-members countries will have to declare major holdings in their capital also in the member countries in which they are officially listed, pursuant to the provisions on equivalence of information contained in Directive 79/279/EEC on the conditions for admission to stock exchange listing. Schedule C, point 6, of that Directive lays down that companies whose shares are listed on the stock exchanges of both a Member State and a non-Member State must make available to the stock market of the Member State information which is equivalent to that published in the non-Member State.

(3) It should be noted that the Directive applies to major holdings only in companies whose shares are listed on a Community stock exchange, excluding those whose shares are not listed on such an exchange. The reasons for this limitation are that it is shares in listed companies which are dealt in regularly and the general public tends to invest primarily in those shares. It is only

natural, therefore, that those companies should be subject to more extensive information requirements than unlisted companies. The same approach was adopted as regards Directive 82/121/EEC on information to be published on a regular basis, which likewise applies to listed companies only.

(4) It is not only important to inform the public of acquisitions in a company; it is also of interest to the public to learn when a person pulls out of a company or reduces his holding. Consequently, this Directive applies *not merely to acquisitions but also to disposals* of major holdings in the subscribed capital of a listed company.

2. Content of the information

What matters to the investor is to know what influence a major shareholder can have on a listed company. This influence is exercised mainly through the shareholder's voting rights. For investors to be well informed, therefore, it would be necessary to disclose the percentage of voting rights held by persons acquiring or disposing of major holdings. Article 3, however, lays down that such persons need only notify the company of the percentage of subscribed capital held by them. This approach was chosen because it may be very difficult in certain cases for persons acquiring or disposing of holdings to know what percentage of the voting rights they hold. This difficulty arises mainly for the following reasons:

- in certain countries, certain shares carry dual voting rights on either a temporary or a permanent basis;
- in certain countries or for certain companies, ceilings are placed on the voting rights which may be held by any one person; those ceilings may even vary according to the subject of the vote;
- where convertible bonds have been issued, it is difficult to establish the total voting rights as this total depends on the number of bonds converted into shares.

It is clear from the above that person acquiring or disposing of shares cannot always know the total number of existing voting rights and cannot, therefore, determine what percentage of the voting rights they themselves hold.

In order to ensure that investors are nevertheless properly informed, Article 8(2) provides that companies must notify the public not only of the percentage of subscribed capital held by persons acquiring or disposing of major holdings, but also of the percentage of voting rights held by such persons where those two percentages differ. Supplying such information does not cause companies any difficulty as they know at all times the total voting rights and any ceilings on those voting rights.

3. Thresholds

It must be acknowledged that the choice of thresholds which trigger compulsory notification are necessarily somewhat arbitrary.

It should be noted, however, that the thresholds in the proposal for a Directive are based on work previously carried out at Community level. They correspond to percentages already laid down in the company law Directives. The various threshold were adopted for the following reasons:

(1) *10%*: Articles 7 and 8 of the Seventh Directive on company law[4] result in a 10% holding in an undertaking being significant in connection with an exemption from

---

[4] Seventh Council Directive of 13 June 1983 concerning consolidated accounts (83/349/EEC) (OJ No. L 193, 18.7.1983).

sub-consolidation. It seemed advisable, therefore, that this 10% threshold should also be adopted here.

(2) *20%*: For the purposes of Article 17 of the Fourth Directive on company law,[5] the holding of more than 20% of a company's capital is presumed to constitute a participating interest creating a durable link with that company. On the basis of this principle, Article 33(1) of the Seventh Directive on company law also specifies that: 'An undertaking shall be presumed to exercise a significant influence over another undertaking where it has 20% or more of the shareholders' or members' voting rights in that undertaking'. 20% is therefore another important threshold which should be notified if exceeded.

(3) *One third and two thirds*: Article 40(1) of the Second Directive on company law[6] provides that several important decisions (increase, reduction, redemption, etc. of capital) must be taken by a majority of not less than two thirds of the general meeting of shareholders.[7] The same majority is required by Article 7 of the Third Directive on company law,[8] for a merger decision and by Article 5 of the Sixth Directive on company law[9] for a decision on a division. A holding of one third would make it possible for these decisions to be opposed. It thus seemed appropriate to adopt those thresholds of one third and two thirds of a company's capital, which are particularly significant from this point of view.

(4) *50%*: Since 50% signifies absolute control, it is essential that the public be informed whenever that threshold is exceeded.

(5) *90%*: Under Articles 27 and 28 of the Third Directive on company law,[8] provision is made for certain derogations from the rules on acquisitions or mergers in cases where one party holds 90% or more of the shares. Under some countries' legislation this threshold permits the compulsory purchase of the outstanding shares. It was therefore included in the proposal.

(6) The Directive lays down that the percentage of capital actually held by a person must be disclosed when that percentage reaches or exceeds the above mentioned thresholds following an acquisition or goes below those thresholds following a disposal. It is not, therefore, the percentage acquired or disposed of in such a transaction which is to be disclosed, but the percentage of capital actually held since that is the figure which matters.

(7) The Directive contains minimum rules. Pursuant to Article 2, Member States may apply stricter provisions than those laid down by the Directive, or additional provisions. Member States may therefore also make provision for thresholds other than those specified in the Directive.

---

[5] Fourth Council Directive of 25 July 1978 on the annual accounts of certain types of companies (78/660/EEC) (OJ No. L 222, 14.8.1978).

[6] Second Council Directive of 13 December 1976 on coordination of safeguards which, for the protection of the interests of members and others, are required by Member States of companies within the meaning of the second paragraph of Article 58 of the Treaty, in respect of the formation of public limited liability companies and the maintenance and alteration of their capital, with a view to making such safeguards equivalent (77/91/EEC) (OJ No. L 26, 31.1.1977).

[7] See Articles 29(4), 29(5), 30, 31, 35 and 38 of the same Second Directive.

[8] Third Council Directive of 9 October 1978 concerning mergers of public limited liability companies (78/855/EEC) (OJ No. L 295, 20.10.1978).

[9] Sixth Council Directive of 17 December 1982 concerning divisions of public limited liability companies (82/89/EEC) (OJ No. L 378, 31.12.1982).

4. *Methods of holding shares*

(1) It is important for investors to know the total number of shares really held by a person acquiring or disposing of a holding so that they may assess just what influence that person may exert on the company. To this end, the person acquiring or disposing of a holding must disclose not only the number of shares which he holds directly, but also the number held by other persons in their own name on his behalf (e.g. nominee holdings). By the same token, a company must declare not only shares which it holds itself but also those held by its subsidiaries. It should be noted that the definition of 'subsidiary' given in Article 5 is strictly based on that in the Seventh Directive on company law (83/349/EEC of 13 June 1983 on consolidated accounts).

(2) Article 6 lays down that, where two or more persons act in concert, the holdings of each one of those persons must be added together in order to determine whether one of the thresholds in Article 6 has been crossed. If that has happened, each of the persons acting in concert must make a declaration, indicating the percentage of subscribed capital held by him and the percentages of such capital held by each of the other persons with whom he is acting in concert. That procedure was adopted in order to make each of the persons acting in concert responsible for the declaration provide for in Article 3. Concerted action was defined on the basis of an existing definition in Directive 80/390/EEC of 17 March 1980 on the listing particulars to be published for admission to stock exchange listing.

5. *Time limits*

In order to ensure that the market is informed promptly, persons acquiring or disposing of holdings must notify the company within seven calendar days; the company itself has seven calendar days in which to notify the public. Those relatively brief periods should make it possible to prevent, or at least restrict, misuse of such information, particularly through insider dealing.

6. *Declaration*

The arrangements for informing the public were specified within the framework of Directive 79/279/EEC on the conditions for admission to stock exchange listing. Those arrangements also apply in the present context. Article 17 of the Directive on the conditions for admission to stock exchange listing lays down that the information to be made available to the public must be published in one or more newspapers distributed throughout the Member State or distributed widely therein or must be made available to the public either in writing in places indicated by announcements to be published in one or more newspapers distributed throughout the Member State or widely distributed therein or by other equivalent means approved by the competent authorities.

7. *Derogations*

In two specific cases, it was considered expedient to allow the competent authorities to derogate from the rules. The purpose of the derogations is to take account of the interests of the parties concerned. Article 7 thus makes it possible for Member States to exempt acquisitions or disposals of major holdings made by market makers in the performance or their activity from the notification requirement. Similarly, Article 9 provides that the disclosure of information which would be against the public interest or would seriously harm either persons acquiring or disposing of holdings or the company in which the holding is being acquired, may be waived by the competent authorities.

Proposal for a
COUNCIL DIRECTIVE

on information to be published when major holdings in the capital
of a listed company are acquired or disposed of

THE COUNCIL OF THE EUROPEAN COMMUNITIES,

Having regard to the Treaty establishing the European Economic Community, and in particular Article 54(3)(g) thereof,

Having regard to the proposal from the Commission,

Having regard to the opinion of the European Parliament,

Having regard to the opinion of the Economic and Social Committee,

Whereas a policy in the securities field aimed at keeping investors properly informed is likely to enhance investor protection, to increase investor confidence in securities markets and thus to ensure that securities markets function correctly;

Whereas coordination of that policy at Community level, by making such protection more equivalent, is likely to make for greater inter-penetration of Member States' securities markets and therefore help to establish a true European capital market;

Whereas to that end investors should be informed of changes in major holdings in the capital of Community companies whose shares are officially listed on a stock exchange situated or operating within the Community;

Whereas it is to achieve that objective that Schedule C, point 5(c) of Council Directive 79/279/EEC of 5 March 1979 coordinating the conditions for the admission of securities to official stock exchange listing[10] stipulates that a company whose shares are officially listed on a Community stock exchange must inform the public of any changes in the structure (shareholders and breakdown of holdings) of the major holdings in its capital as compared with information previously published on that subject as soon as such changes come to its notice;

Whereas if that requirement is to be applied in an effective manner coordinated rules should be laid down concerning its detailed content and the procedure for its application;

Whereas companies whose shares are officially listed on a Community stock exchange can inform the public of changes in the structure of the major holdings in their capital only if they have been informed of such changes;

Whereas most Member States do not require investors to inform companies of acquisitions or disposals made by them of major holdings in the capital of such companies; whereas there are appreciable differences between the Member States in which there is such a requirement;

Whereas coordinated rules should therefore be adopted at Community level in this field,

[10] OJ No L 66, 16.3.1979, p. 21.

HAS ADOPTED THIS DIRECTIVE:

Article 1

(1) This Directive shall apply to persons who acquire or dispose of major holdings, as defined in Article 3, in the subscribed capital of a company which is incorporated in a Member State and whose shares are officially listed on a stock exchange situated or operating within a Member State.

(2) Where the acquisition or disposal of major holdings is carried out by means of certificated representing shares, this Directive shall apply to the bearers of those certificates, and not to the issuer.

Article 2

Member States may subject the persons and companies respectively referred to in Articles 1 and 8 to stricter requirements than those provided for by this Directive, or to additional require-ments, provided that they are generally applicable.

Article 3

Where a person acquires or dispose of shares in a company as referred to in Article 1 and where, following that acquisition or disposal, the percentage of subscribed capital held by that person in that company reaches or exceeds the thresholds of 10%, 20%, 1/3, 50%, 2/3 or 90% of the subscribed capital or goes below those thresholds, he shall notify the company within seven calendar days of the percentage of subscribed capital he holds following that acquisition or disposal.

Article 4

(1) In order to assess whether a person acquiring or disposing of holdings is required to make the declaration provided for in Article 3, account shall be taken of shares held by other persons in their own name but on behalf of the person acquiring or disposing of the holdings.

(2) Where the person acquiring or disposing of holdings is an undertaking, shares held by a subsidiary or shares held by other persons in their own name but on behalf of a subsidiary shall also be deemed to belong to the person acquiring or disposing of the holdings.

Article 5

(1) For the purposes of this Directive, 'subsidiary' means any undertaking in which another undertaking:

    (a) has a majority of the shareholders' or members' voting rights;
        or
    (b) has the right to appoint or remove a majority of the members of the administrative, management or supervisory body and is at the same time a shareholder or member;
        or
    (c) is a shareholder or member and controls alone a majority of the shareholders' or member' voting rights pursuant to an agreement entered into with other shareholders or members of undertaking (subsidiary).

(2) For the purposes of paragraph 1, the parent undertaking's rights as regards voting, appointment and removal shall have added to them the rights of any other subsidiary and those of persons acting in their own name but on behalf of the parent undertaking or any other subsidiary.

Article 6

(1) For the purposes of Article 3, where persons act in concert, the holdings of each one of such persons shall be added together. In this case, the obligation to make the declaration provided for in Article 3 shall fall upon each one of them. This declaration shall indicate the percentage of subscribed capital held by the person making the declaration and the percentages of such capital held by the persons with whom he is acting in concert.

(2) 'Persons acting in concert' means persons who have concluded an agreement which may lead to their adopting a common policy in respect of a company.

Article 7

Member States may exempt acquisitions or disposals of major holdings made by a market maker in the pursuit of his activity from the declaration provided for in Article 3.

Article 8

(1) A company which has received the declaration referred to in Article 3 shall in turn notify it to the public in each of the Member States in which its shares are officially listed on a stock exchange not later than seven calendar days following receipt of that information.

(2) Should the percentage of subscribed capital held by the person making the declaration provided for in Article 3 differ from the percentage of voting rights actually held by that person, the company which has received the declaration shall notify the public of both percentages.

(3) The information shall be made available to the public in accordance with the rules of Article 17 of Directive 79/279/EEC.

Article 9

The competent authorities referred to in Article 10 may exempt the persons and companies respectively referred to in Articles 1 and 8 from the requirement to notify, as defined in Articles 3 and 8 respectively, where those authorities consider that the disclosure of such information would be against the public interest or would seriously harm those persons or companies, provided that the absence of such notification would not mislead the public in its assessment of the shares concerned.

Article 10

(1) Member States shall designate the competent authority or authorities and shall inform the Commission accordingly, specifying any division of duties between those authorities. They shall, moreover, ensure that this Directive is applied.

(2) Member States shall ensure that the competent authorities have such powers as may be necessary for the exercise of their duties.

(3) The competent authorities in the Member States shall cooperate wherever necessary for the purpose of carrying out their duties and shall exchange any information required for that purpose.

Article 11

The Contact Committee set up by Article 20 of Directive 79/279/EEC shall also have as its function:

(a) to permit regular consultations on any practical problems which arise from the application of this Directive and on which exchanges of view are deemed useful;
(b) to facilitate consultations between Member States on the stricter or additional requirements which they may lay down in accordance with Article 2, so that the requirements imposed in all the Member States may finally be brought into line, in accordance with Article 54(3)(g) of the Treaty;
(c) to advise the Commission, if necessary, on any additions or amendments to be made to this Directive.

Article 12

(1) Member States shall take the measures necessary to comply with this Directive not later than 1 January 1991. They shall forthwith inform the Commission thereof.

(2) Member States shall communicate to the Commission the provisions of national law which they adopt in the field governed by this Directive.

Article 13

This Directive is addressed to the Member States.

Done at Brussels,

For the Council

Appendix III. Comparative Tables

Table AIII.1. *Voting blocks by rank*

Country	No. of companies	Largest voting block				2nd largest voting block				3rd largest voting block				4–10th largest voting block				10th voting block			
		Min.	Med.	Mean	Max.	Min.	Med.	Mean	Max.	Min.	Med.	Mean	Max.	Min.	Med.	Mean	Max.	Min.	Med.	Mean	Max.
Austria[1]	50	10.0	52.0	54.1	100	0.0	2.5	7.8	34.0	0.0	0.0	2.6	21.0	0.0	0.0	1.1	11.2	0.0	0.5	0.0	7.9
Belgium[2]	140	8.4	56.0	55.9	99.8	0.0	6.3	10.3	44.3	0.0	4.7	4.5	18.3	0.0	4.7	4.7	18.3	0.1	3.8	3.9	7.8
Germany[3]	372	0.0	57.0	49.6	100	0.0	0.0	2.9	45.2	0.0	0.0	0.6	32.0	0.0	0.0	0.5	24.0	0.0	0.0	0.0	0.0
Spain[4]	193	5.0	34.5	40.1	98.0	0.0	8.9	10.5	36.1	0.0	1.8	3.5	24.3	0.0	0.36	3.3	22.7	0.0	0.0	0.6	7.0
France[5] CAC40		0.0	20.0	29.4	72.7	0.0	5.9	6.4	19.7	0.0	3.4	3.0	8.5	0.0	0.0	0.5	7.1	0.0	0.0	0.1	2.0
Italy[6]	214	2.1	54.5	52.3	100	0.0	5.0	7.7	34.0	0.0	2.7	3.5	26.4	0.0	0.0	5.1	45.4	0.0	0.0	0.2	10.9
Netherlands[7]	137	0.0	43.5	42.8	99.9	0.0	7.7	11.4	58.5	0.0	0.0	4.0	44.9	0.0	0.0	4.4	43.7	0.0	0.0	0.0	0.0
Sweden[8]	304	1.6	34.9	37.6	93.4	0.6	8.7	11.2	41.2	0.2	4.8	5.6	27.9	0.0	1.3	1.8	15.5				
UK[9]	207	3.4	9.9	14.4	78.9	3.0	6.6	7.3	26.3	3.0	5.2	6.0	25.7	3.0	3.9	4.1	10.1	3.0	3.1	3.1	3.3
United States[10]																					
NYSE	1,309	0.0	5.4	8.5	92.9	0.0	0.0	3.7	40.1	0.0	0.0	1.8	25.0	0.0	0.0	0.9	15.6	0.0	0.0	0.0	0.0
NASDAQ	2,831	0.0	8.6	13.0	99.5	0.0	0.0	5.7	48.8	0.0	0.0	3.0	24.1	0.0	0.0	1.6	22.1	0.0	0.0	0.0	6.2

Sources: This volume; [1]Gugler, Kalss, Stomper, and Zechner, Fig. 2.1, data for 1996; [2]Computed by Becht, data for 1995; [3]Becht and Böhmer, Fig. 5.2, data for 1996; [4]Crespí-Cladera and García-Cestona; [5]Bloch and Kremp; [6]Bianchi, Bianco, Enriques, Table 6.6, data for 1996; [7]de Jong, Kabir, Marra and Röell, Table 7.5, data for 1996; [8]Agnblad, Berglöf, Högfeldt, Svancar, Table 9.3A, data for 1998; [9]Goergen and Renneboog, data for 1992; excludes blocks held by directors; [10]Becht, includes blocks held by directors and officers; data for 1996.

Table AIII.2. *Percentiles for voting power concentrations*

Range	Austria[1] C_1 %	Cum.	Austria[1] C_{all} %	Cum.	Belgium[2] C_1 %	Cum.	Belgium[2] C_{all} %	Cum.	Germany[3] C_1 %	Cum.	Germany[3] C_{all} %	Cum.	Spain[4] C_1 %	Cum.	Spain[4] C_{all} %	Cum.	Italy[5] C_1 %	Cum.	Italy[5] C_{all} %	Cum.
0–5%	0.0	0.0	0.0	0.0	0.0	0.0	0.0	0.0	1.1	1.1	1.1	1.1	1.0	1.0	1.0	1.0	2.3	2.3	0.9	0.9
5–10%	0.0	0.0	0.0	0.0	0.7	0.7	0.0	0.0	1.9	3.0	1.6	2.7	6.7	7.8	1.6	2.6	2.8	5.1	0.5	1.4
10–25%	14.0	14.0	4.0	4.0	5.7	6.4	3.6	3.6	14.5	17.5	4.8	7.5	26.4	34.2	4.1	6.7	14.5	19.6	2.3	3.7
25–50%	18.0	32.0	6.0	10.0	27.9	34.3	20.0	23.6	18.3	35.8	14.0	21.5	33.2	67.4	20.7	27.5	24.3	43.9	9.3	13.1
50–75%	54.0	86.0	64.0	74.0	47.9	82.1	47.1	70.7	25.5	61.3	21.8	43.3	20.7	88.1	36.3	63.7	45.3	89.3	44.4	57.5
75–90%	8.0	94.0	20.0	94.0	14.3	96.4	21.4	92.1	17.5	78.8	28.2	71.5	6.7	94.8	15.5	79.3	8.9	98.1	32.7	90.2
90–95%	6.0	100	6.0	100	2.1	98.6	4.3	96.4	5.7	84.4	7.3	78.8	3.1	97.9	10.4	89.6	0.9	99.1	2.8	93.0
95–100%					1.4	100	3.6	100	15.6	100	21.2	100	2.1	100	10.4	100	0.9	100	7.0	100

Range	Sweden[6] C_1 %	Cum.	Sweden[6] C_{all} %	Cum.	The Netherlands[7] C_1 %	Cum.	The Netherlands[7] C_{all} %	Cum.	United Kingdom[8] C_1 %	Cum.	United Kingdom[8] C_{all} %	Cum.	USA (NYSE)[9] C_1 %	Cum.	USA (NYSE)[9] C_{all} %	Cum.	USA (NASDAQ)[10] C_1 %	Cum.	USA (NASDAQ)[10] C_{all} %	Cum.
0–5%	1.3	1.3	0.0	0.0	10.2	10.2	10.2	10.2	10.6	10.6	2.4	2.4	52.8	52.8	52.8	52.8	54.4	54.4	54.4	54.4
5–10%	3.9	5.3	0.0	0.0	11.7	21.9	5.8	16.1	36.2	46.8	2.9	5.3	21.1	73.9	8.6	61.3	17.4	71.9	8.1	62.5
10–25%	27.6	32.9	0.3	0.3	13.9	35.8	3.7	19.7	37.2	84.1	17.4	22.7	20.9	94.8	20.2	81.5	20.6	92.4	17.2	79.8
25–50%	40.8	73.7	5.9	6.3	24.8	60.6	15.3	35.0	13.5	97.6	44.5	67.1	3.5	98.3	14.5	96.0	5.5	98.0	14.0	93.8
50–75%	19.7	93.4	30.9	37.2	19.7	80.3	18.3	53.3	1.4	99.0	26.6	93.7	1.5	99.8	3.1	99.1	1.5	99.4	4.9	98.7
75–90%	5.9	99.3	41.4	78.6	6.6	86.9	16.8	70.1	1.0	100	3.4	97.1	0.2	100	0.9	100	0.5	99.9	0.9	99.5
90–95%	0.7	100	14.1	92.8	5.1	92.0	8.0	78.1	0.0	100	1.9	99.0	0.0	100	0.0	100	0.0	99.9	0.3	99.8
95–100%	0.0	100	7.2	100	8.0	100	14.6	93.0	0.0	100	1.0	100	0.0	100	0.0	100	0.1	100	0.3	100

Sources: This volume: [1]Gugler, Kalss, Stomper, and Zechner, Table 2.4, data for 1996; [2]Computed by Becht; data for 1995; [3]Becht and Böhmer, Table 5.5, data for 1996; [4]Crespí-Cladera; and García-Cestona; [5]Bianchi, Bianco, Enriques, data for 1996; [6]Agnblad, Berglöf, Högfeldt, Svancar, data for 1998; [7]de Jong, Kabir, Marra and Röell, Table 7.6, data for May 1996; [9,10]Becht; data for 1996.

Table AIII.3. *Voting blocks by blockholder type*

Range	Austria[1]					Germany[2]					Spain[3]				
	No.	Min.	Mean	Med.	Max.	No.	Min.	Mean	Med.	Max.	No.	Min.	Mean	Med.	Max.
Families/individuals	45	5.0	26.0	12.3	100	205	5.0	26.9	18.2	100	163	5.0	16.0	9.5	87.5
Government	9	24.0	53.1	51.0	81.6	18	8.2	45.3	40.7	99.0	37	5.7	46.8	49.0	95.2
Banks	11	6.4	42.0	41.9	100	77	5.1	23.8	15.0	99.0	48	5.0	21.2	13.6	91.5
Insurance						34	5.0	11.9	20.1	96.7	56	5.0	20.8	14.6	91.5
Domestic firms	10	6.6	39.4	51.5	64.3	180	5.0	61.6	70.6	100	203	5.0	24.1	16.7	98.0
Foreign firms	26	5.7	31.6	18.7	87.0						125	5.0	20.7	9.1	97.2
Assoc./pools						21	5.9	45.2	49.1	100					
Holding						53	6.9	52.9	50.3	100					
Investment firm						36	5.5	25.1	40.0	99.0					
Bank rel.inv.firm						5	10.2	18.1	11.0	41.4					
Foundation						16	8.0	50.1	51.6	98.1					
Other						3	13.0	18.9	20.2	23.6					
All blocks	101	5.0	33.1	22.7	100	648					632	5.0	20.7	12.3	98.0

Range	Italy[4]					The Netherlands[5]					United Kingdom[6]				
	No.	Min.	Mean	Med.	Max.	No.	Min.	Mean	Med.	Max.	No.	Min.	Mean	Med.	Max.
Families/individuals	234	0	20.1	0	95.4	36	0.0	8.9	0.0	97.1	61		5.2		
Government	34	0	6.8	0	97.4						6		6.7		
Banks	156	0	9.5	0	95.6	48	0.0	4.4	0.0	39.8	71		5.1		
Insurance	13	0	1.1	0	93.9	34	0.0	8.3	0.0	93.0	226		4.0		
Domestic firms	160	0	20.3	2.0	100	22	0.0	1.4	0.0	27.0	102		10.6		
Foreign firms	116	0	9.1	0	99.9										
Invest./pen. fund	57	0	0.8	0	8.9	6	0.0	0.4	0.0	19.0	474		7.0		
Exec. directors											117		4.5		
Non-exec. directors											184		5.0		
Real estate											1		0.1		
Other financal institutions	18	0	1.1	0	66.9	61	0.0	11.1	0.0	85.6					
State						4	0.0	1.1	0.0	50.0					
Admin. office						54	0.0	26.9	0.0	100					
Other															
Total	788	0	68.4	71.5							200				

Sources This volume: [1]Gugler, Kalss, Stomper, and Zechner, Table 2.8, data for 1996; [2]Becht and Böhmer, Table 5.5, data for 1996; [3]Crespí-Cladera and García-Cestona; [4]Bianchi, Bianco, Enriques, data for 1996; [5]de Jong, Kabir, Marra and Röell, Table 7.6, data for May 1996; [6]Goergen and Renneboog.

Index